La Seule France

France in the New Europe

Changing Yet Steadfast

RONALD TIERSKY
Amherst College

Wadsworth Publishing Company
Belmont, California
A Division of Wadsworth, Inc.

Political Science Editor: Brian Gore
Editorial Assistant: Jennifer Dunning
Designer: Andrew H. Ogus
Print Buyer: Barbara Britton
Editing, Illustration, Production & Composition: Summerlight Creative, Eugene, OR
Cover Designer: Andrew H. Ogus
Cover Photo: ©, 1994, Comstock, Inc.
Printer: Malloy Lithographing

Credits and permissions:
Figure 5.2 from *Financial Times*, March 20, 1993. Reprinted by permission.
Figure 7.1 from *L'Express Magazine*, January 2, 1992. Reprinted by permission of The New York Times News Service.
Figures 7.2, 8.1, 8.2, 8.3 from *The Economist*. ©1991/1993 The Economist Newspaper Group, Inc. Reprinted with permission. Further reproduction prohibited.

 This book is printed on acid-free recycled paper.

I(T)P ™

International Thomson Publishing
The trademark ITP is used under license.

Printed in the United States of America

1 2 3 4 5 6 7 8 9 10—98 97 96 95 94

Library of Congress Cataloging-in-Publication Data

Tiersky, Ronald, 1944–
    France in the new Europe: changing yet steadfast / by Ronald
  Tiersky.
        p.   cm.
    Includes bibliographical references and index.
    ISBN 0-534-18924-5
    1. France—Politics and government—1981– 2. European Economic
Community—France. 3. Europe 1992.   I. Title.
JN2594.2.T54 1993
944.083'8—dc20
                                                        93-41085
                                                          CIP

In memory of Raymond Aron.

◆

Contents

✦

Acronyms and Abbreviations   xiii

Preface   xv

CHAPTER 1

Introduction: The End of French Exceptionalism   1

France: Changing Yet Steadfast   1

France and Europe   3

France as a Power   7

Economic and Social Problems in France Today   8

France as It Really Is   11

Endnotes   11

CHAPTER 2
··············
Political Culture and Public Attitudes 13

Four Images of France on Which to Meditate 13

French "Exceptionalism": History and Genealogy 14

The Fading of French Exceptionalism: Decline or Renewal? 19

The Legitimate Republic: One Thousand Years in the Making 21

Watershed: The Eclipse of Marxism in French Political Culture 25

The Muting of Class and Class Conflict 26

French Youth and the Political Culture 30

Religion and the Political Culture 31

Immigrants, the Problem of Racism and the Question of French National Identity 33

The Changing Political Culture of French Protest 38

After Exceptionalism, What? 40

Endnotes 41

CHAPTER 3
··············
The Logic of French Institutions 46

The Fifth Republic's Institutions 50

The President and the Others 50

President and Prime Minister: Ambiguity and the Threat of Dyarchy 51

The Nature and Future of "Cohabitation"   56

The Condition of Parliament in the Fifth
Republic   61

The Senate   62

The National Assembly   63

The European Parliament and French
Parliamentary Life   70

Judicial Review: France Changes, but Slowly   71

Decentralization: A Socialist or a French
Success?   74

Mitterrand's Constitutional Reforms   76

On Using the Referendum Well or Badly   80

Maastricht and French Institutions   82

Conclusion   83

Endnotes   83

CHAPTER 4
....

Political Parties: The Centering of Right and Left   89

Consensus or Impotence?   89

French Parties Today   96

The Presidential Parties: PS, RPR and UDF   96

The Nonpresidential Parties   107

Conclusion   117

Endnotes   117

CHAPTER 5
....

Elections and Electoral Strategies   120

Ambiguous Majorities: The Gaming of Presidential and Parliamentary Elections   122

The Logic of French Elections   123

As the Partisan Wheel Turns   124

Rising Abstentions: A Normal Aspect of Recenteredness?   128

The European Parliament and French Parties   132

Elections, Centrism and Consensus   133

The 1993 Parliamentary Elections and Cohabitation II   139

Conclusion   141

Endnotes   142

CHAPTER 6
....

Interests and Groups   143

The French "Partenaires Sociaux" and the Single European Market   144

French Business Today and the German Model   147

Workers and the Decline of Labor Unions   153

French Farmers, the CAP and the GATT   158

SOS–Racism: Human Rights Activism in the Post-Marxian Age   162

Conclusion   166

Endnotes   167

CHAPTER 7
....
**Public Policy: Some Key
Issues 169**

"Ordinary" Public Policy 169

Economic Issues 172

Unemployment 172

Nationalizations: The "Neither–Nor" Solution 179

Immigration, Racism and "Foreigners" 185

Women and Politics in France 197

AIDS as a Public Policy Issue in France 201

Endnotes 204

CHAPTER 8
....
Political Economy 208

The Fading of French Economic
Particularity 209

Broad Characteristics of the French
Economy 216

French External Accounts 217

Unemployment and Tax Burdens 221

France's Economy and the EC's Single
Integrated Market 226

The French Franc and the European Monetary
System 228

France and the Goal of Full European Monetary
Union 231

Conclusion 235

Endnotes 235

CHAPTER 9

Geopolitics and Foreign Policy   238

Introduction   239

France and the European Revolution, 1989–91   240

France and German Unification   240

France and the New Germany   243

France's European Strategy   246

European Citizenship and National Identity   253

After the Cold War   256

Conclusion   257

Endnotes   257

CHAPTER 10

Conclusion   260

French Nationalism: Martyr or Forerunner?   260

France and the Future of the State   262

National Sovereignty and Pooled Sovereignty   262

Sovereignty and "Qualified Majority" Voting   263

France and the Future of the Nation   264

Endnotes   266

SUGGESTED READINGS   267

INDEX   275

Acronyms and Abbreviations

✦

CDS	Social Democratic Center
CFDT	French Democratic Confederation of Labor
CFSP	Common Foreign and Security Policy (Maastricht Treaty)
CFTC	French Confederation of Catholic Workers
CGT	General Confederation of Labor
CNPF	National Council of French Industrialists
CSCE	Conference on Security and Cooperation in Europe
Euratom	European Atomic Energy Authority
EC	European Community (EEC, ECSC, Euratom)
ECSC	European Coal and Steel Community (1951)
ECU	European Currency Unit (for future European currency)
EEC	European Economic Community
EFTA	European Free Trade Association
EMS	European Monetary System
EMU	European Monetary Union (Maastricht Treaty)
EP	European Parliament (for EC)
EPU	European Political Union (Maastricht Treaty)
EU	European Union (created by Maastricht Treaty to include the EC, EMU, and EPU)
FEN	Federation of National Education
FN	National Front
FNSEA	National Federation of Farmers' Unions
FO	Workers' Force union
GATT	General Agreement on Tariffs and Trade
MRG	Movement of Left-Wing Radicals
PCF	French Communist party
PR	Republican party
PS	Socialist party
RI	Independent Republicans
RPF	Rally of the French People (Gaullists, 1947)
RPR	Rally for the Republic (neo-Gaullists today)
SEA	Single European Act (1987; creates EC single market)
SFIO	Socialist party (1905–1971)
UDF	Union for French Democracy
UDR	Union of Democrats for the Fifth Republic (Gaullists, 1962–74)
UNR	Union for the New Republic (Gaullists, 1958–62)
WEU	Western European Union (European security cooperation separate from NATO)

Preface

✦

This book is a frank *mélange de genres*. It is an essay disguised as a textbook. I hope that it features some of the virtues of its defects as well as, more certainly, the defects of such an undertaking. I hope that *France in the New Europe* will prove to be an attractive introduction for students while yet being of some genuine intellectual interest to advanced readers and even to my specialist colleagues.

Basic texts often err doubly by providing more details than readers want to know, without saying enough about why things are important. Essays naturally do the opposite. If *France in the New Europe* errs on one side, it tries to put substance and content before coverage, the essay before the textbook. For this I make no apologies, except to Howard Wiarda, who was good enough to ask me to write this book for the new Wadsworth Comparative Politics series of textbooks.

France in the New Europe aims to be a reliable yet intellectually engaged overview of the contemporary French political scene at a time of significant domestic political changes, grand debates over European integration and frankly worsening social problems. The book's chapters are thematic, and the essay overall makes a definite, strong argument about the course of French political development. In some places *France in the New Europe* is a personal account, not only because an author's own experience matters but also to make amends (at least to myself) for another book I had in mind a decade ago. What is truly useful, I think, is never lost.

Several colleagues—American, English, French—have produced other sorts of basic texts, certainly much better than I could have done. Writing this essay has vastly increased my respect for their work, and chapter endnotes will only partially convey my debts.

My intent is to provide an accessible, vivid study of France in the 1990s, between past and future, domestically between an "exceptionalist" political history and the "recentered" politics of today, in foreign affairs between nationalist digging in and European integration. The subtitle—*Changing Yet Steadfast*—pays homage to my teacher Raymond Aron's 1959 book, which analyzed France during the shock of transition from the Fourth to the Fifth Republic, during the strife of decolonization and the deepening French war in Algeria. Aron's *France Steadfast and Changing* (the French title was *Immuable et changeante. De la IVe à la Ve république*) emphasized the longstanding French resistance to change and the consequent French political tendency to crisis rather than reform. Maurice Duverger had written the epigram for French political development to that point: "In France," he said, "reform is impossible, only revolution is possible."

Thirty-five years on, the dispassionate observer—Raymond Aron's self-characterization—can and must reverse Aron's emphasis. Today what impresses one most in French public life is the scope and rapidity of change over the last two decades, nevertheless carried out within a cultural steadfastness that is the natural conservatism of any people, being its own justification.

Especially in an essay designed for students and others thinking about France for the first time, we should emphasize right away how recently—a mere few decades ago—France was considered one of Europe's political and economic "sick men." Only against knowledge of France's tumultuous past, which Charles de Gaulle scorned as "living permanently on the edge of the abyss," can one measure how broad-scale and multifaceted French development has been. France is certainly no longer the nation that, to quote de Gaulle once again, demonstrated a "vocation of being perpetually in danger."

As this manuscript is finished, the March 1993 elections have just produced a new "cohabitation" situation, with a conservative government facing a Socialist president. This will test French institutions, and it cannot be guaranteed that the analysis in Chapter 3 has foreseen everything. The mixture of presidential and parliamentary constitutional elements, especially when the rules of the real constitutional game are only partly written down, means that what has come to appear as a stable institutional consensus may in fact not be so. Stability is obviously easier to maintain in good times than in crisis; worsened social and economic conflicts could suddenly create an institutional crisis about the division of powers in the regime. It is not likely, but it cannot be ruled out.

Indeed, as the conservative Balladur government headed into its second week in early April 1993, social problems flared up in the form of police killings and beating of immigrants. Would the change of government from left to right have more brutal implications than had been apparent before the elections? Or would the second experiment in French cohabitation prove to be a new soft landing for hard problems?

The answers will have roots reaching far back into French history and also, because of continuing European integration, increasingly into the histories of other countries—France's neighbors, erstwhile adversaries, today's partners.

✦ ✦ ✦

Any errors of fact or interpretation in the following pages are naturally the author's own responsibility. Sincere thanks go to many colleagues, including several Wadsworth reviewers—Mark J. Miller, University of Delaware; Roy Ginsberg, Skidmore College; Bernard Brown, City University of New York; Howard Wiarda, the University of Massachusetts and the National Defense University; and George Ross, Brandeis University and the Harvard Center for European Studies—for comments, corrections and other help on the manuscript.

In particular I would like to thank Pierre Hassner, whose large knowledge and complex ways of putting problems have always influenced my thinking about France and about European international relations. In terms of the American community of French politics scholars, let me pay homage to Stanley Hoffmann's great influence on all of us, and express thanks for his stimulating hospitality as chairman of Harvard's Minda de Gunzberg Center for European Studies. I thank Stanley, George Ross and Laura Levine Frader, coeditors, for allowing me to be a regular contributor to *French Politics and Society*, a capacious journal that published first versions of some of the analyses developed in this book. Nicholas Wahl has for many years held down another end of the American French politics tent as director of New York University's Institute of French Studies. The NYU–IFS–sponsored "Inter-University Consortium for Social Research on France" has hosted annual meetings that colleagues in the various fields of French studies have found stimulating and congenial. Knowledge and teaching have benefited greatly from these enterprises.

Mr. Ilya Somin has been a remarkable undergraduate research assistant. He has my sincere thanks for his diligence and excellent help.

Howard Wiarda has my gratitude for asking me to write this volume in the new Wadsworth Comparative Politics series. For financial support I want to thank the Amherst Dean of the Faculty, Ronald Rosbottom, the Amherst College Faculty Research Fund, and the Centre d'Etudes des Relations Internationales (CERI), part of the French CNRS. CERI's Director, Professor Jean-Luc Domenach, and its Secretary-General, Mme. Hélène Arnaud, were instrumental in arranging a CNRS fellowship. More than just a source of financial support, the CERI, and many colleagues, have been institutional home and intellectual family to me in Paris for many years.

In dedicating this book to Raymond Aron's continued presence in my intellectual life, I also send a fraternal greeting to the members of Aron's famous faculty seminar, from whom I learned so much. Those three years, 1970–1973, were a constant intellectual thrill, finely mixed with awe and a bit of terror. I wouldn't have missed it.

RONALD TIERSKY

1
✦
Introduction: The End of French Exceptionalism

> **A**lthough the old regime is still so near to us in time— every day we meet persons born under its auspices—it already seems buried in the night of ages.
>
> —Tocqueville, *The Old Regime and the Revolution* (1865, Part 2, Chapter 1, p. 26)

> What gives French politics an aspect of scorched earth is less the change in the landscape to which we were accustomed, than the brutality of the change, done in so little time. The old France is still close, and the majority of the French, except the youngest, have it in their political memories, all the more so in that [the old order] survived its disappearance for a moment precisely in politics. . . . What French politics shows as specifically French has to do with the suddenness of this slippage of the terrain, which recalls, even with the differences, the ruptures of the 19th century.
>
> —François Furet (1987, in Furet et al., *La République du centre* [The centrist republic], p. 65)

France: Changing Yet Steadfast

France has always fascinated foreigners. French culture was admired, French history seemed to contain lessons for the whole world, and French politics, perpetually dramatic and full of possibilities, seemed a mixture of the admirable and the reckless. Naturally, at the same time the French as people infuriated foreigners, because they seemed self-important and arrogant. After World War II, Gaullist France infuriated others with pretensions of grandeur and world rank beyond French means.

Yet even in decline, France for a long time continued to loom larger than life. From Benjamin Franklin to post–World War II expatriates, Americans and other foreigners believed that every cosmopolitan person, mind and body, had two homes—one's own and Paris, which remained a beacon to the world. French theorizing, including neo-Marxism, post-structuralism and deconstruction, was widely taken up, especially in American universities. To be in Paris was to be in the center, not necessarily of world history or power, but of world culture and intellectualism. French elites indeed thought, and sometimes spoke of themselves as "the party of intelligence" among the nations. French "exceptionalism" had a quite plausible history and pedigree.

In closing *The Old Regime and the Revolution*, Alexis de Tocqueville observed that

> the [French] nation itself [has been] far more remarkable than any of the events in its long history. It hardly seems possible that there can ever have existed any other people so full of contrasts and so extreme in all their doings, so much guided by their emotions and so little by fixed principles, always behaving better, or worse, than one expected of them.[1]

Today, however, France, Paris and the French all must seem less, not more, remarkable than their history, less exceptional compared to other peoples and other countries. Whereas French political life was once an example and aspiration for others, France at the end of the twentieth century tries ardently to resist merely being pulled along by international trends beyond its control and by cosmopolitan, transnational impulses over which the French themselves have only modest influence.

But this is exactly what makes contemporary France such a significant case both in comparative political understanding and in parsing the contradictory elements in the process of European integration. France used to be a bellwether of nationalism's irreconciliability to cosmopolitanism, of national interest's rejection of interdependence. General Charles de Gaulle, the savior of France in 1940 and president of the republic from 1944 to 1946 and 1958 to 1969, embodied this French resoluteness. "Gaullism," a vague yet vital patriotic and nationalist reflex, seemed to be French policy par excellence.

Today we see that this is not so, or rather no longer so. Without necessarily being less national-minded, the French today, from President François Mitterrand to the man in the street, have had to accustom themselves to a banalization of their country, to a "normalization" of French politics and an internationalization of French culture, as well as to a decline of what the economists call French economic "specificity." In just a short time an observable evaporation of French "exceptionalism" has occurred. And in the decade just past, as these changes matured, French intellectuals and politicians not surprisingly debated the origin and the future of "French identity."[2] Unfortunately this sort of reasonable and intellectually stimulating inquiry into the national identity became involved in sometimes racist debates, widespread in Europe because of immigration, over a supposedly imperiled French national identity.

In France the focus of prejudice has been the country's large, sometimes second- and third-generation North African, Arab and Muslim population—mostly Algerians, Moroccans and Tunisians. Popular worries about French identity (as well as limited jobs, social services, etc.) have been a natural theme of nationalist extremists. This obviously means the right-wing *Front National* (FN) but also, paradoxically, the hidebound French Communist party. The PCF, like the international communist movement overall, was always, in spite of praiseworthy internationalist and egalitarian ideas, in reality in many ways a hothouse of chauvinist, racist and anti-Semitic attitudes.

Of course no such "crisis of French identity" is the case. This overpoliticized, overintellectualized complaint is really the frustrated French reaction to having constantly to reinsure one's place in a permanently changing and competitive world. The old French world was stable, socially and culturally very conservative underneath a surface political instability. Nevertheless the current perception of a "crisis of identity," even if a minority view, can and does have significant political effects.

France and Europe

The most logical of France's contemporary dilemmas as a nation-state is European integration.

Both cause and consequence of becoming "more like the others," French policy during the Mitterrand presidency, contrary to Gaullism's confederal preference, embraced European integration and adopted the goal, long-term at least, of a federal Europe. In practice, the French commitment to the Maastricht Treaty's goals of monetary and political union has nevertheless been tempered by persistent, sometimes fierce displays of national interest.

The European integration game is at bottom a complex attempt to reach national goals that increasingly require, rather than resist, internationalized means. French national sovereignty has already been diminished in certain areas, for example, in the effective domination of European monetary policy, especially interest rates, by German Bundesbank decisions. In this situation a strategy of "pooled" or Europeanized sovereignty, as in the Maastricht Treaty's goals of a single currency and a European Central Bank, could regain for the French at least a portion of already lost sovereignty.

With Germany, France has been at the center of European integration, both to maximize its own political–diplomatic influence and to try to contain the effects of Germany's economic strength. The so-called Franco–German couple has always been the motor force of European integration projects, from the European Coal and Steel Community in the early 1950s to the Maastricht Treaty of December 1991, launching the idea of an expanded European Union that will add monetary and political union to the single integrated market fixed in the "1992 project."

Such integration plans have raised the question of the future of nation-states in the European Community (EC). While national identities may not be in danger, the issue of the future of national sovereignty, once thought an impossible nut to crack, is on the table. In 1966 Stanley Hoffmann wrote that "the critical issue for every student of world order is the fate of the nation-state." Considering the nuclear danger and the advance of economic interdependence, Hoffmann argued the nation-state had become "dangerous for peace and illogical for welfare."[3] It was surely natural that Hoffmann focused these concerns in an essay emphasizing Gaullist France. Starting with the middle years of de Gaulle's presidency—from the first veto of British membership in 1963 to the "empty chair" assertion of French sovereignty in 1966—Gaullist European Economic Community (EEC) policy epitomized nationalist resistance to international and supranational integration.

However, de Gaulle himself had already shown that he knew how to make a virtue out of concession to necessity. He had been invited back to power in the crisis of May 1958, when the French generals fighting the Algerian war in Algiers rebelled against the vacillating civilian parliamentary leadership in Paris. He was naturally thought an intransigent colonialist who would fight to keep Algeria part of France. Probably this was so at the beginning. But after a short time in office, and taking account of the inevitability of national liberation—Algeria was but one instance of a worldwide trend—General de Gaulle decided to change policies and cut French losses. He authorized Algeria's independence, made peace with the Algerian rebels in the 1962 Evian Accords, and began to pose as the champion of complete decolonization and "Third World" concerns in the councils of the great power nations. De Gaulle thereby achieved for himself, and for France, a durable reputation as the underdeveloped world's most sympathetic advocate among the world's big powers.

A major theme of this study is that French policy since de Gaulle has learned his lesson of decisiveness, and has given up the self-defeating policy of refusing to choose. Like the decision to accept national liberation of the colonies, France has similarly tried to make a virtue of the necessity of European integration and even, bittersweet as it must be, the decline of French "exceptionalism." Accept what you cannot change. More powerful than national interests and policy goals are, said de Gaulle, "circumstances." The French have had to accept what they could not prevent: the transformation of France into an "ordinary" nation and the inevitability of pursuing European integration in some form, meaning above all the necessity of forming a "couple" with Germany. Successive French governments have tried to wax enthusiastic about European integration (President Mitterrand really has been). French policy has attempted to get the benefits—currency stability, low inflation and competitive exports, plus the political gain of creating a European diplomatic power—while minimizing the disadvantages—reduction of national sovereignty, plus the discomforts of international competition and unceasing political negotiations with partners in analogous situations of ambivalence.

Nevertheless, France despite all the changes is still France, and the French are still the French. The recent minor panic among intellectuals and populist extremists about a loss of "French identity" is, as already stated above, an ideological exaggeration of some real issues. French society has changed and is continuing to change dramatically. But there is also a rock-solid steadfastness, all those ways in which the French are still distinctively themselves and ineradicably different from their neighbors and partners, all those characteristics grown up over millennia, from language to political culture to customs to institutions, which indicate to the tourist or the scholar, the friend or the detractor, that one is in France.

This combination of change and constancy in France today is the overarching theme of this book. France is still such a fascinating and useful case in comparative politics precisely because it is that European country which has had the most intense, most vivid sense of its distinctiveness, its undeniable exceptionalism. Gaullist France was, in Stanley Hoffmann's apt term, the strongest "resister" to Europeanism. Today France is—without at all abandoning its national interest and in spite of the lukewarm 51 percent "yes" vote when the country voted on the Maastricht Treaty in September 1992—one of the strongest advocates of European Union.

How can this be? France has changed, but so has the way in which the question of nationalism versus integration is posed. The "fate of the nation-state" no longer must seem, as it did in the 1960s, a zero-sum affair. European integration is demonstrating that national sovereignty is not a single "thing" as it used to be conceived. It is rather a *bundle* of state powers—trade sovereignty, monetary sovereignty, foreign policy sovereignty, and so on—that can be unpacked, split up or pooled. Years ago it was clear in any case to Europe's political leaders that total resistance to integration was self-defeating, particularly in the face of increasing world trade interdependence and increasing integration of vast monetary markets (see Chapter 7) outside the purview of states. The neo-Gaullist leaders of the "no" vote on September 20, 1992, Philippe Séguin and Charles Pasqua, said that they were not against European integration as such, but rather the overly federal plan designed in the Maastricht Treaty. Whether neo-Gaullists actually have accepted "Europe" is less important than that they are forced by circumstances to act as if they have.

Thus France in the new Europe, France in the 1990s, is a vastly changed and modernized country. It is much different from an older France still shot through with revolutionary sentiments and secular contradictions between tradition and modernity, which I first encountered as an American graduate student in the late 1960s. In 1974 Stanley Hoffmann published a collection of remarkable essays on "France since the 1930s" with the title *Decline or Renewal?* (a phrase taken from General de Gaulle's *War Memoirs*). The answer to this question has proven to be, for the most part, renewal and change, not decline. Hoffmann's teacher had been Raymond Aron. Aron's 1959 book, to which I owe my general theme, saw France at that difficult moment—the Fourth Republic had just collapsed, the Fifth Republic was being launched—as a country in travail, "steadfast and changing."

Today another observer, lucky enough to have been a student of Aron's a generation later, must change the emphasis: France in the new Europe is "changing yet steadfast," strikingly symbolized by Socialist President Mitterrand's patronage of a glass and steel pyramid, designed by I. M. Pei, placed controversially in the courtyard of the Louvre museum. Even the magnificent old Louvre can adapt in order to be more than a mere monument.

The old France used to inhibit change too much; the new France worries that things are changing too quickly. The old France was old and sure wine in new and fragile bottles; the new France is new and sometimes uncertain wine in often old bottles.

France as a Power

France is generally rated as the second power in Europe. And this, despite all French feelings of inferiority and foreign mockery, is not nothing. France, for example, is by some measures the world's fourth largest exporting economy (after Germany, Japan, and the United States), as well as the world's third military power (after the United States and Russia). Until the sudden demise of divided, "Yalta" Europe and the unexpected advent of German unification, France had been generally regarded as the European Community's leading political and diplomatic power. The former West Germany, yet bound by memories of World War II, was still "an economic giant but a political dwarf," of which former Chancellor Helmut Schmidt (1974–82) used to say that "its economic policy *is* its foreign policy." Today, France together with unified Germany continues to be the motor of the European Community, one half of the Franco–German tandem whose joint policies have long been the core of European integration plans. In short, even if condemned by geography to a perpetual struggle with its German neighbor's economic and geopolitical advantages, France, while second rank in some areas, does not lack for points of pride and even optimism about the French future in the European equation. Remarkably, with Germany in an economic recession caused by the problems of unification, at the end of 1992 the French economy—overseen for a decade by Socialists—appeared as the healthiest in Europe.

Nevertheless, a persistent worry about German power is a permanent characteristic of the traditional French political and foreign policy class, meaning government ministry officials, the party leaders and many political commentators in the media. French thinking often still stresses the sovereign and nationalistic power concepts of the old geopolitical Europe, the result of which is a constant French tendency to presuppose France's inferiority or even submission to Germany and German policy decisions. Much of what the traditionalists say and write, in other words, bemoans France's loss of power. Only a few commentators and political leaders encourage the French frankly to embrace the uncertainties of international competition and to look optimistically to the future. President Mitterrand has been one of these: "If Germany grows, France will too. . . . Why should France think a priori that it won't be capable of keeping pace? . . . France has every chance, and thus the development of Germany is an incentive to do better. . . . The greatness of one of the two countries must be accompanied by the greatness of the other. They must proceed together."[4] Mitterrand's view of the Franco–German balance, though intentionally upbeat, cannot be dismissed so simply. On the one hand, French historical dynamism, as I have already argued, is renewable. On the other, unified Germany, with all its new problems and also the accumulated (dis)advantages of its acquired postwar interests, may falter or become bloated with its own successes. Franco–German partnership may be as much the future trend as Franco–German rivalry. In any case, in the early 1990s, we do not have the evidence to say for certain which way things will go.

An old German proverb defines the good life as "being happy as God in France." History, of course, has shown more than amply that the French were right to fear the covetousness of this compliment. In terms of sheer quality of life the French, though they greatly admired postwar American cultural energy and economic innovativeness,[5] need not envy any other people in Europe or elsewhere. The French intellectual concept of France as a "hexagon"—a perfect form that is roughly matched by the actual geographical shape of the country—contains space, completeness and equilibrium. The hexagon is taught to French school children and becomes a renewable resource of pride in the *patrie* if not in the *régime*. Hexagonal France is big for a European country. It is "finished," manicured and maintained (de Gaulle used the metaphor of a garden; he was, of course, the gardener). It is a refined equilibrium of tendencies and types, not the same as a mere balance, a wonderfully variegated territory simultaneously of the North Sea and the Mediterranean, of mountains and lowlands, of world-class urbanity and rural opulence, of history and modernity. In this France there is a proper human relation between work and leisure, in innumerable natural settings of great beauty and attractiveness. And there is the unique beauty of Paris, an exceptionalism of its own, approached by only a few other cities. France, in this sense, is also a "power," or if not a power, then a "pole of attraction" whose magnetism still has incomparable pull in Europe and beyond.

Economic and Social Problems in France Today

But the much-admired and imitated French quality of life, which remains a formidable aspect of French international influence, coexists with severe domestic social problems. Some of these—the emblematic French problem of alcoholism, for example—have diminished in recent years. Average per capita consumption of alcoholic beverages has declined sharply, while the number of alcoholics is also down, but less so. Other problems, especially problems of race and ethnic prejudice and a new problem of urban homelessness, have gotten much worse.

In France today, as in the United States and all the wealthy industrial nations, the advantages of the comfortable are built to some extent on the very inequalities that produce classes of unjustifiably disadvantaged people. Some of these deficiencies are old, some are new, and none are specifically French even if France has its particular profile of misery. What it has in common with all other societies is that large numbers of people suffer, but probably fewer in France relatively speaking.

In twentieth-century France revolutionary and reactionary political schemes persisted well beyond their decline in neighboring societies. The French believed that society was perfectible and therefore that its problems were unacceptable, because "unnecessary." Today the French are largely disabused of their long-held millenarian political enthusiasms. Even the French now realize there is no way of turning society inside out like a glove to remake it—whether a right-wing reactionary nostalgia for *la France profonde*, the "genuine" France of traditional values, or a left-wing Communist or *autogestion* dream of "socialism." Disabused as they are, the French have become "normalized" in the realization that in reading the scales of misery only comparative judgments of real situations matter. The French today judge themselves, and others, less ideologically than before.

One particularly French social and political problem is a devastating emptying of the countryside. Rural France is in the last stages of economic "modernization." The increased efficiency of France's farm production is, no doubt, an excellent result of modernization. On the other hand, the winnowing and wasting away of rural France has in the short space of three decades changed the face and character of French society by eliminating much of the human resource and rich local culture of what the French call with affection and respect *la France rurale, le pays réel.**

French history over centuries had created a spectacularly endowed rural life. The greatest flowering of this rural culture was surely the Second Empire (1852–70) and the golden period of the Third Republic (1870–1914), which saw the Impressionist painters, a remarkable literature written or set in the countryside, and an opulence of daily life that gave a new meaning to the term *la vie simple.***

Still 30 percent rural at the end of World War II, in French society today only 3 to 4 percent of the population are farmers and their families. The near disappearance of competitive small farms today substantially changes, and in certain ways literally threatens the economic, social, cultural and ecological equilibrium of the French quality of life. Hundreds of thousands of (mainly small) farms have become economically unsustainable, and few successors can be found to take up the work of an older generation of farmers who began as "peasants" in a different eco-

---

* rural France, the true country
** the simple life

nomic era. In consequence, numbers of once vibrant villages have become ghost towns. And entire areas of the countryside—not Provence and not the Mediterranean coast, but not less worthwhile—have lost that human cultivation which created the extraordinary rural culture of Third Republic France, which survived until devastated as an unintended consequence of the French economic miracle of the so-called *Trente Glorieuses*[*] (1945–73) and of international competition.

The worry is felt even in foreign policy. French obstinacy in the Uruguay Round of the General Agreement on Tariffs and Trade (GATT) talks over reducing farm subsidies in the EEC's Common Agricultural Policy seemed to foreigners merely French special pleading or the electoral interest of the incumbent government. There is a larger dimension. Of the approximately 1 million farmers remaining today in a population of 57 million, half will disappear by the turn of the century because of economic factors. The French will thus have finally solved the problem of "modernizing the peasantry" and of creating a small group of large economically and internationally competitive farms. But in the same movement, millions of peoples' lives will have been disrupted and harmed, and a vital aspect of traditional France, one of its desirable and unique aspects, will have been put in the way of extinction.

On the other hand, what about the urban "class struggle" in France today? France, as Marx and Engels wrote, was a key example of the economic class struggle and in particular its political aspect. In France, Engels wrote, one saw at their clearest the political conflicts raised by class differences.[6]

Unemployment and poverty among workers and their families were traditional French political flashpoints, not surprising in a strongly class-conscious political culture, largely Marxist on the left and dominated by a powerful Communist party and Communist-led trade-union movement. Given this it may seem surprising that the rising unemployment of the past decade, nearing 12 percent of the work force in 1993 (and striking the *cadre* upper and lower managerial strata hard as well as workers) has been roughly tolerated politically and coped with socially. One explanation is certainly the decline of trade union power: The power of the union and the strike was greater when times were better economically. Another factor is the international one: Nearly all comparable countries have similar unemployment, thus it is unconvincing to argue that French authorities are to blame.

In any case the 1980s have produced a new class of economic casualties in France. French writers are calling them the "new poor" to distin-

---

[*]thirty glorious years

guish them from the "old poor," the traditional unemployed working-class victims of capitalist economics. This class of "new poor" people is, of course, an international phenomenon, larger in the United States than in France and other European countries. The new poor are a largely urban, racially mixed and often homeless "underclass," quite different from the old working-class poor of industrial society. Other destructive problems are often part of the constitution of this underclass—racism, illegal immigration, drugs, battered women, youth violence, AIDS, and so on. Any adequate political analysis of France today must deal with the political causes and consequences of these phenomena, which are new, at least in their intensity, for the French. We may find that French political society has undergone a more consequential social mutation than commentators generally seem aware.

France as It Really Is

Let us conclude in this introduction that the condition of the country today is paradoxical and thus worthy of deeper study. France is in many ways a lot healthier and more dynamic politically and socially than over-zealous critics are willing to say. Yet France simultaneously is beset with worsening domestic problems, and internationally it is locked into a permanent close embrace with its immovable, stronger German neighbor. Moreover, the Franco–German relationship has just been made more difficult, again paradoxically, precisely by the end of the Cold War and the end of divided Europe (and divided Germany) that French foreign policy had demanded for four decades.

If the standard by which to measure French success is de Gaulle's thesis that France "is not really herself except in the first rank," then unavoidably *la France seule* will never regain her past glory. And even if the French of the future need not be disappointed at not equalling, say, an American geopolitical or a Japanese economic and financial standard, there will always be—because of geography, industry and history—the looming German neighbor. Because of this, if for no other reason, France's commitment to European integration should not be doubted. That is why this essay on contemporary France must be called "France in the New Europe."

Endnotes

1. Alexis de Tocqueville, *The Old Regime and the Revolution* (New York: Doubleday Anchor, 1955), p. 210 (originally published 1865).

2. See Fernand Braudel, *L'identité française* (Paris: Flammarion, 1986) 2 vols.; Hervé le Bras and Emmanuel Todd, *L'invention de la France: Atlas anthropologique et politique* (The invention of France: Anthropological and political atlas) (Paris: Librairie Générale Française, 1981); and Pierre Chaunu, *La France: Histoire de la sensibilité des Français à la France* (France: History of the French people's sensibility) (Paris: Editions Robert Laffont, 1982).

3. Stanley Hoffmann, "Obstinate or Obsolete: The Fate of the Nation-State and the Case of Western Europe," *Daedelus* (Summer 1966); published in revised form as "Obstinate or Obsolete? France, European Integration, and the Fate of the Nation-State" in *Decline or Renewal? France since the 1930s* (New York: Viking, 1974); quotation from p. 363.

4. From a speech to the European Forum; in *European Affairs* (Winter 1990), p. 37.

5. The best-selling example was Jean-Jacques Servan-Schreiber's *Le défi Américain* (Paris: Editions Denoël, 1967). Published in English as *The American Challenge* (New York: Atheneum, 1968).

6. For example, Marx's famous polemical essays "The 18th Brumaire of Louis Bonaparte" and "The Class Struggles in France: 1848 to 1850" and Marx and Engels, *The German Ideology*.

2

✦

Political Culture and Public Attitudes

Enlisting in the Recentered Republic

Four Images of France on Which to Meditate

Of late, the Social-Democratic philistine has once more been filled with wholesome terror at the words: Dictatorship of the Proletariat. Well and good, gentlemen, do you want to know what this dictatorship looks like? Look at the Paris Commune. That was the Dictatorship of the Proletariat.

—Friedrich Engels, "Introduction" to Marx, *The Civil War in France* (1891)

It would be worthwhile examining whether these French books which have so much popularity and authority in Europe truly represent France, or whether they have not exhibited certain exceptional and very unfavorable aspects of character. And these pictures, where people seldom see anything but our vices and our defects, have they not done our country an immense disservice among foreign nations? . . . France has this against herself: she shows herself naked to the nations. In one way or another all the others remain clothed and dressed. Germany, and even England with all her parliamentary commissions and all her publicity, are little known by comparison. They cannot see themselves for lack of centralization.

—Jules Michelet, from "Preface: To Edgar Quinet," *The People* (January 24, 1846)

All my life I have thought of France in a certain way . . . like the princess in the fairy tales or the Madonna in the frescoes, as dedicated to an exalted and exceptional destiny.

—Charles de Gaulle, *War Memoirs* (Volume 1, Chapter 1, 1954)

French drivers are conceding defeat in a matter of color prejudice which has left them isolated in the eyes of the world. From January 1, 1993, the yellow headlights that make them the only people to behave as if they were in a perpetual fog will no longer be compulsory. Bright white will take over from mellow yellow, in the name of European integration. . . . Most [French people] have forgotten that yellow lights were introduced in 1936 to distinguish French vehicles from German.

—*The European* newspaper (December 9, 1991, p. 4)

French "Exceptionalism": History and Genealogy

As epigram to *France: Steadfast and Changing*, Raymond Aron put an astonishing passage from *The Old Regime and the Revolution*, the assertion by Tocqueville that the people's basic characteristics

> are so constant that we can recognize the [French nation] in portraits made of it two or three thousand years ago, and yet so changeful are its moods, so variable its tastes that the nation itself is often quite as much startled as any foreigner at the things it did only a few years before.[1]

Could this possibly have been literally true? Can contemporary scholarship, inoculated against the abuses of "national character" analysis, credit such an assertion, even from the pen of a master of social theory, the premier student of French society? And Tocqueville continues, extending his point: "It hardly seems possible that there can ever have existed any other people so full of contrasts and so extreme in all their doings, so much guided by their emotions and so little by fixed principles, always behaving better, or worse, than one expected of them." The French, he concluded, were "at once the most brilliant and the most dangerous of all European nations, and the best qualified to become, in the eyes of other peoples, an object of admiration, of hatred, of compassion, or alarm—never of indifference."

But in 1856, when *The Old Regime* was published, French centrality in European geopolitics was already past, having been punctured by Napoleon's defeats in Russia and at Waterloo. France's long-suffering German neighbors had been provoked, as much as anything by French imperialism, to coalesce the small and weak German states. In Prussia's wars of 1866–70 against Austria and France, a unified German Reich replaced France as the most worrisome, most fearsome European nation. Indeed, in the Franco–Prussian War of 1870 Wilhelm I and Bismarck's army easily defeated the French forces, capturing the Emperor himself at Sedan, but 14 short years after *The Old Regime* made its anachronistic claims. It is in any case not necessary to decide whether Tocqueville meant to be literal or just literary in the famous passage above. The point here is to emphasize how often and how easily France's eighteenth- and nineteenth-century political commentators did connect the French with their putative Gallic ancestors, in order to explain or to criticize French geopolitical aggression and, above all, internecine divisiveness.[2] The French seemed to be a nation of "enemy brothers."

In France's often painful modern history, several times when the country was threatened or actually invaded, definable groups in society preferred saving their own privileges to standing for the nation's interest, choosing their class over their country. The most important example was the so-called Vichy state (1940–42) set up in southern France in cooperation with Hitler under the aegis of Marshal Philippe Pétain. Vichy was not just a Nazi puppet regime, but, as tenacious scholarly investigation by Robert Paxton and others has shown, it became to some extent a home-grown Fascist state with its own Vichyite racial practices often ahead of German orders. Horribly, the Vichy government used the occasion of national defeat in 1940 to wreak a policy of conservative–Fascist revenge on republicans, Jews, gypsies, Freemasons, Socialists, Communists and all other "left-wing anti-national" elements.[3] The Resistance—a mixture of Gaullists, Communists and those in between—proved that the Vichyites were wrong about what kind of French people embodied national patriotism and even about whether Vichy represented the entire former French right.

After the liberation of France, Charles de Gaulle wrote, more in anger than in sadness, of the continued "ferments of dispersal" intrinsic to French attitudes, which were blocking France's necessary postwar renewal. De Gaulle's "certain idea of France," imbued with (besides Tocqueville) the classic texts of Charles Maurras, Michelet, Chateaubriand, and others, foresaw inevitable recurring French national crises. These were surmountable through a combination of three factors: (1) a suddenly revealed heroic leader (Joan of Arc, Bonaparte, General de Gaulle himself); (2) underlying popular awe of the state (the French people normally a nation of sheep, nevertheless capable of being called to right action by a national leader); and (3) historical mindfulness of France's vocation to be an example to the world.

The megahistorical hypothesis of a natural French tendency to domestic uproar persists quite clearly to today. President François Mitterrand, in his annual Bastille Day interview in 1992, downplayed a paralyzing countrywide French truckers' blockade of the roads and farmers' occupation of town squares by saying it was basically "the old Gallic disease, well recognized," he said, "since Vercingéntorix." Yet the same Mitterrand often justified his foreign policy actions—especially when it was a matter of resisting so-called American diktats—as France's duty to make its "unique contribution" to international relations. And the current prime minister, Edouard Balladur, talks of domestic reforms as a chance to show "a French example" to France's EC partners.

There are other conceptions and aspects of the idea of French exceptionalism. Raymond Aron, for example, began *Steadfast and Changing* with the droll observation that "If the Soviet Union didn't exist, France [in 1959] would have the doubtful glory of being the most commented country in the world."[4] France was simply attractive. Foreigners were drawn, by admiration usually but sometimes also by pity, to think about French politics, French culture and French food. The rest of the world found France fascinating and puzzled over Montesquieu's famous question, "How," he asked, "is it possible to be French?"

Indeed, what did it mean to be French? The four epigrams to this chapter give us various places to begin.

In nineteenth-century Socialist analysis, France was, as Marx and Engels declared from the point of view of dialectical materialist thinking, the very epitome of class struggle. France was that country in which the class struggle between bourgeoisie and proletariat appeared in its most pristine, violent clarity. Twentieth-century French Socialist and Communist theorists of France's development saw, not surprisingly, exactly what their sages had predicted—a desperate division of society into bourgeoisie and proletariat that augured *le grand soir**—that is to say, the barricades, a workers' revolution and socialist transformation. The fact that Marxist socialism was always a pseudoscience doesn't mean that class and class conflict were illusions. Class divisions and class conflict were, in fact, a large part of the social basis of French politics in the era of the two world wars.[5] Class antagonism was so unavoidable a political theme that de Gaulle himself sometimes spoke of *la lutte des classes,*** generally to

---

* the triumphal night
** class struggle

chastise the irresponsibility of the upper classes and to appeal to their self-interest in implementing, for example, his 1960s scheme for "an association of capital and labor."

However this may be, Marxism always accorded France, as a country and a "case," an exceptional place in Socialist thinking. To the Socialists, the nineteenth-century class wars in France—1830, 1848, 1871—were heroic models for class struggles in other countries. The Paris Commune of 1871 was even baptized by Marx and Engels as the first "dictatorship of the proletariat." They knew it was nothing of the kind (despite its revolutionary aspects, it was neither proletarian nor Socialist, but nationalist). But the dictatorship of the proletariat slogan reverberated around the world for a century. Most importantly, the Paris Commune and French thinking were important references for Lenin, Trotsky and the Bolsheviks in 1917.

By contrast, various kinds of French liberal views, politically moderate or social democratic and intellectually eclectic by comparison with Marxism, conceived of France from Tocquevillean premises. This meant that to emphasize social classes and even class struggle was possible without drawing pseudoscientific conclusions about the laws of social development, and without denying full weight to other factors.

Liberals tended to emphasize the unique French political culture, as opposed to bourgeois economy or social structure. French political culture, the product of centuries of French political development, was a seriously flawed set of values and ideas, whose democratic inconsistencies and sociopolitical volatility produced France's exceptional political history. From this point of view, French political history was, as Tocqueville conceived it, a titanic struggle between a growing culture of centralized power and a weakly resistant civil society. In the decades after Tocqueville's death, however, came successful struggles to limit and balance centralized power: (1) the Third Republic's secular public school system and official separation of church and state; (2) the Third and Fourth Republic institutions of Parliament's political supremacy over the executive power; and (3) in the Fifth Republic the partially fulfilled promises of strengthening civil society and reducing the state's control in the economy.

Altogether France has been fortunate in her historians and commentators. Scholarship on France has been extraordinarily vivid, and writers both French and foreign have felt the country as an intellectual passion rather than a mere object of study.

In the postwar decades the most enlightening accounts of French politics—picturesque yet scholarly studies, disengaged yet striking portraits, small literary masterpieces in their genre—combined the sociological idea of a "stalemate society" with the political conception of a

paralyzed "republican synthesis." The Third and Fourth Republic regimes were thus based on a least common denominator, a *faute de mieux**
consensus that, in Stanley Hoffmann's memorable phrase, "had plenty of
brakes and not much of a motor."[6] The French sociologist Michel Crozier and the political scientist Hoffmann were the preeminent writers of
this school, responsible for a particularly rich analysis of the exceptionalism of French political culture. These Tocquevillean and Aronien liberals, faced in the 1950s and 1960s with the continued ideological
predominance of Marxist themes, conceived a very different explanation
of *le mal français*, the French pathology or "French disease." The root of
the French problem was located not in sociology—that is, in the class
struggle—but in the political culture and structures. A rear-guard, status-
fixated political culture hostile to easy and effective cooperation—Crozier called this "a French horror of face-to-face relations"—plus excessive
bureaucratization ("the bureaucratic phenomenon") and also a fear of the
social costs and losses of economic and technical modernization were all
combining to block French development. In 1976 Alain Peyrefitte, a
former Gaullist minister known for semischolarly best-selling books,
published a conservative yet still intellectually liberal popularization of
this view, called *The Trouble with France*.[7]

In contrast to various kinds of Marxist analysis, Stanley Hoffmann
found in the Third and Fourth Republics a political class that was relatively autonomous from society, as opposed to being directly driven by
social and economic class interests. Society in Third and even Fourth
Republic France remained considerably "a nation of peasants and shopkeepers," with only a truncated, socially unintegrated industrial working
class available for Socialist and Communist mobilization.

The French bourgeoisie was the key to the "stalemate society-republican synthesis system," and its own internal divisions precluded the formation of any hegemonic social class or clearly class-based state. As
Hoffmann put it succinctly (p. 14), "the political history of France since
the Revolution is largely the history of the political divisions of the
bourgeoisie." The republican synthesis described by Hoffmann combined
a paradoxical centralization of power and a limitation of the state's role in
society compared to earlier regimes. It was an agreement that the parliamentary government do little—an agreement on stalemate—since to pose
the fundamental problems of society would have broken the political
system apart. So the Third and Fourth Republics featured a parliament
supreme but immobile, and political parties more like interest groups
than aggregators of interests. The paradox of this immobilist regime was

---

* for lack of a better alternative

precisely that it fit the "stalemate society" so well: Peoples tend, after all, to get the governments that suit them.

The "stalemate society-republican synthesis" conception was a brilliant vocabulary and intellectual framework for understanding French society and the pattern of French exceptionalism 1875–1958. In the past few decades, however, and especially following the bizarrely abortive "revolution" of May–June 1968, it has become harder and harder to avoid the conclusion that the idea of French exceptionalism had lost touch with reality, had become an anachronism. And in the past ten or fifteen years the theorists of French exceptionalism, not to mention the French people themselves, have gradually and often wistfully agreed that France had become normalized and internationalized, altogether a more ordinary country.

The Fading of French Exceptionalism: Decline or Renewal?

The epigrams at the top of this chapter suggest some parallel between the 1980s and the Great Revolution, but it is of course a gross exaggeration to imply that changes in French life in the 1980s were somehow equivalent to the grand bouleversement of the Revolution of 1789, which, in Tocqueville's apt term, literally "exploded" the French society of the Old Regime.

Nevertheless, basic developments and discontinuities matured in France in the 1980s, and for this reason it requires an effort of historical imagination to understand France today. To comprehend the depth of the changes in French politics and society that came to fruition in the 1980s one must be sympathetic to the task of imagining France on the verge of that change. It is necessary to picture in one's mind a polity that, nearly two centuries after the Revolution of 1789, was still divided into "two Frances," a people politically torn for so long and in such permanently recognizable ways that the roots of these "two Frances"— red and white, red and black—stretched back, often literally, through generations of actual people, families and groups, to the Revolution's destruction of the Old Regime.[8] This effort of imagination must "hear" French historian François Furet's self-evident yet controversial call of 1988: "The French Revolution is now ended," the power of its divisiveness finally exhausted after two centuries.[9]

The prolonged, secular consequences of the French Revolution thus are essentially played out, and not in the clear victory of one side over the other, but usually in the form of compromises creating a realm of consensus on the parameters of what is acceptable public policy. It takes a real

effort of imagination today to realize that the events of May–June 1968—
a massive uprising of society against the state, of *la Nation* against *le
Pouvoir* (the State)—happened only 25 years ago—in historical terms,
only the day before yesterday.

May '68, a quintessentially French reprise, was probably the final
episode of the exceptionalist, post–French Revolution political culture of
revolution and reaction. What other West European people, so politically privileged and economically prosperous, could, in the face of all its
comparative advantages not to mention the specter of Soviet-dominated
Eastern Europe, have mounted such a political–social "psychodrama" in
which literally half the work force (9–10 million people) staged a general
strike shutting down the economy and threatening the overthrow of the
regime? And what kind of people will troop off to the polls a month later,
in a showdown parliamentary election, to hand the ruling party, the
Gaullists, a massive absolute majority, the first in the Fifth Republic's
history? The answer is—or was—the exceptionalist French, about whom
it still seemed to make sense in 1968 to ask Montesquieu's question, how
is it possible to be French?[10]

The upshot is clear. To understand France today one must imagine a
radical discontinuity. French politics and political culture changed,
abruptly in historical terms, in the 1970s and 1980s. France today is not
the old France a few years further along.

Important political developments matured in the 1980s, and these can
be summarized as four kinds of legitimation and consensus: (1) legitimation of the Fifth Republic's institutions, and especially of the powerful
Gaullist presidential office as the keystone of the regime; (2) legitimation
of the French Socialists, and thus of the French left, as a government
alternative; (3) legitimation of the capitalist market economy, with a
corresponding delegitimation of formerly powerful Socialist statist economic ideas; and (4) acceptance by the French left of Gaullist nationalism
and specifically of the so-called Gaullist defense policy consensus.

The extent of the change in French life can be easily missed, above all
by those with little consciousness of how recently things were very different. When Raymond Aron published *Steadfast and Changing* in 1959, he
wanted to emphasize positive changes amidst the characteristic French
"steadfastness" of governmental instability, political weakness and refusal
of economic and social modernization.

In France today, whether the French like it or not, change has become
normal, ordinary. The French have adapted to, if not fully accepted, the
ordinary, competitive and disruptive conditions of international economic and political life. The French as a nation and as a political culture
are no longer so exceptional, so extravagant, if for only the negative
reason that the environment no longer indulges such particularities. In

sum, French exceptionalism, along with the secular consequences of the French Revolution, historically exhausted themselves in the last 25 years. The protean general strike and political psychodrama of May '68 mark a paradoxical French turn toward an ordinary, normalized country, though this in no way means that in May 1968 the French somehow "learned their lesson."

But in addition to deep-going change, France and the French simultaneously remain steadfast, as we shall see, in countless ways. The balance between living by modern technological and international standards or by historical habits may have changed radically, yet the French still demonstrate that a people is more than just a language, a nation more than just a government.

The Legitimate Republic: One Thousand Years in the Making

France as a recognizable polity became 1,000 years old in 1987 on the *millénnaire* of the first Capetian king's election. Chosen by an assembly of the French nobility, Hugues Capet was the first of the "forty kings who built France." Remarkably, most of them lie entombed in a single cathedral, at Saint-Denis, ironically now a working-class suburb and longtime Communist party fiefdom in the suburban "red belt" surrounding Paris proper. This astonishing collection of royal tombs—even Louis XIV, the "Sun King," is there—constitutes a physical reminder of the exceptional duration of royal legitimacy in France suddenly snapped by the Revolution. This long rule epitomizes, as much as anything else, the Old Regime political culture: centralized, absolutist and finally unsustainable.[11]

"Qui t'a fait duc?" demanda Hugues Capet. "Qui t'a fait roi?" lui repondit Adalbert de Périgord.

This well-known (if apocryphal) dialog between Hugues Capet and one of his electors shows how conflicts over legitimacy nevertheless existed from the very beginning of modern French political history. Who is to govern is the question, and by what right? "Who made you Duke?" asked Hugues Capet, demanding that a siege be raised. "Who made you king?" replied Adalbert of Périgord. In a way this was the question raised again in the French Revolution, in all the revolutions, rebellions, treasons and renewals of the nineteenth and twentieth centuries.

The problem of legitimacy at the top of the state characteristically has been crucial to understanding the political history of France, even of contemporary France. Much of Charles de Gaulle's political writings as well as the institutional history of the Fifth Republic, for example, cannot be rightly comprehended without realizing to what degree Gaullism poses the problems of political life in terms of a certain idea of legitimacy. From de Gaulle's hard-won "historical legitimacy" in launching the Resistance in 1940 to his argument that "only states" can legitimately speak for peoples and nations, otherwise the fundamental units in world politics, Gaullist thinking is rooted in an organic, historicist conception of legitimate authority.

One can pose the problem even of French communism's significance in terms of the issue of legitimacy.[12] The Communists, like the Gaullists, had rejected the Fourth Republic, albeit for different reasons. The Gaullists opposed the parliamentary republic because it was a weak government, the Communists because it was capitalist. Yet both were in their different ways "antisystem" parties, one result being that in the chaotic elections of 1951, Gaullists and Communists nearly constituted a theoretical antisystem majority in Parliament, the consequences of which, in the midst of the Cold War, could have been grave.

After de Gaulle's return to power, during the Fifth Republic's first decades a few leftist politicians such as Pierre Mendès-France and François Mitterrand continued to reject the excessive presidential "personal power" of the Gaullist institutions, but only the French Communist party (*Parti Communiste Français*, or PCF) stuck to fundamental opposition to the new regime. Gradually the PCF made half-gestures toward the growing consensus on institutions, but it always brandished the idea that capitalism and the established political system ultimately had to go.

Today the decimated PCF has, with the demise of international communism, not so much accepted the Fifth Republic as become irrelevant. Nevertheless, for a half-century Communists and sympathizer voters found in the PCF the most effective, fear-inspiring way to protest *le Pouvoir* and to register their rejection of bourgeois capitalist democracy's legitimacy.

The last "moment" of legitimacy was, as stated above, the social upheaval of May–June 1968, more massive a contestation of the state than any in Europe since World War II excepting the Polish Solidarity movement in 1980–81. Roused by student university protests and televised police beatings of student strikers (some their own children), the nation's *forces vives* rose up, engulfing the student protests in a genuine general strike and occupation of workplaces.

The protest of police violence quickly became a repudiation of Gaullism's "personal power," paternalism and general aloofness—that is, of the Gaullist regime as a whole. But workers and unions quickly added traditional wage and benefit demands to the popular protest of Gaullism and the psychodrama. The 1968 strikes were finally settled in the tripartite Grenelle Accords signed by the government, the association of business and the trade unions. According to Grenelle, salaries and benefits of workers went up; socialism and "the imagination in power" got lost.

How could it have happened that the student strike became so widespread and so resolute? How could it have happened that half the nation's work force joined a mass sympathy strike with the students? Why did the trade unions make traditional, if steep bread-and-butter demands of their own, taking advantage of the student strike? Why did the Communist party—at that time still the strongest political party also controlling the most powerful, most feared labor union, the General Confederation of Labor (*Confédération Générale des Travailleurs*, or CGT)—not try to seize power? Then, how could such a widespread, intense movement have collapsed so quickly? How could the conservative Gaullist party (*Union pour la Nouvelle République*, or UNR), so repudiated in May, win a huge absolute parliamentary majority only one month later, following de Gaulle's desperate dissolution of Parliament?

Such questions echo Tocqueville, Aron, Crozier and Hoffmann: What, indeed, does it mean to be French? No other people, at least Europeans living in a democratic society, would seem capable of arising in such a sudden, unpredictable bout of collective fury. How could an entire people act as the French did in May 1968?

But times change and, because even culture changes over time, even the French can change. In the twenty-five years since May '68 the dispute over French institutions and the structure of society seems finally to have reached a flexible equilibrium. Now as then, 1968 seems a watershed in French history, but in a different way. Tocqueville's French seem no longer to inhabit the country. Or, as implied in the wistful title of French actress and leftist Simone Signoret's recent memoir, *Nostalgia Isn't What It Used to Be.*[13]

In France, right and left, secular and clerical, presidential and parliamentary views of how political life should be run have entered a broad consensus, effective enough even if vague in spots. The left has been legitimized as a governing party, and the Fifth Republic's institutions have gained near-universal legitimacy with the left's acceptance, after Mitterrand's victory in 1981, of the strong presidency. A few major constitutional corrections need to be made, including the nature of the Constitutional Council and the extent of judicial review, Parliament's inordinately weak role, political party financing, and residual questions about secularism in education and of state support of religion—for example, state subsidies for religious schools and government support and protection of mosques. But the solution of none of these requires a Sixth Republic (see Chapter 3).

The recent achievement of the legitimate republic in France came fortunately in the nick of time for France to play a major role in European political union (see Chapter 8). Italy, for example, was able to muddle on in its institutional inadequacies because it has been a follower rather than a leader in European integration. France on the other hand has been, with Germany, the EC's political driving force. This would not have been possible if the French were still divided among themselves over their own institutions.

French domestic policy disagreements also are mitigated today because they must be increasingly weighed in the context of the larger process of European integration. French political parties simply can no longer claim they want to change society from top to bottom; revolutionizing France would amount to waging war on European integration. Raymond Aron would surely have said that this is not so much a positive national unity in the face of foreign dangers as it is one of the many "disillusions of progress."[14]

On the other hand, the institutional consensus is positive, not negative, in addition to being nearly universal. By contrast, Stanley Hoffmann's "republican synthesis" explanation of the Third Republic pointed to an essentially negative consensus, "the regime which divides us least" as Adolphe Thiers said, institutions quite appropriate to the "stalemate society." The legitimized Fifth Republic is basically approved by the French nation, as party behavior and opinion polls repeatedly show in all sorts of ways. In sum, the secular French radical mentality seems to have been boxed in by history or at least by modernity. This means that, as any watcher of CNN World News, the International Channel or SCOLA learns, French media today rehearse the same sorts of policy problems discussed in the other EC and other "G-7" countries, with greater or lesser local emphasis, with more or less Frenchness. But France's problems today can in any case rarely be considered unique, even by the French.

The Dreyfus Affair (1894–1906) was in its time an exemplary instance of French exceptionalism, of the Western world (and more) being caught up in French affairs. It was still certainly a time when France, or Paris, was one of the most commented countries in the world. Equivalent to the Dreyfus story today might be the French AIDS scandal in which contaminated blood was knowingly distributed by official blood banks to hundreds of hemophiliacs during several months in 1985, with fatal results. The legal and moral responsibility of government agencies and cabinet-level officials is clear, and even one former prime minister was nearly indicted with others in 1992. Yet when the motives and justifications are laid out, there seems little that is particularly French about this tragedy. A similar horrible case might produce its contemporary Zola and a contemporary *J'Accuse* in any of dozens of languages. This banalization of even French scandals is rooted in reality.[15]

Nevertheless, France is still France and Paris, as Oscar Wilde said, is still the place where good foreigners go when they die. Contemporary France, even after the epoch of French exceptionalism, remains a mixture of fascinating tendencies and contradictions. Moreover, France has a new vocation, that of making Europe. France is one of the key countries in building the European union; and European integration, by moving beyond the nation-state, is a leading edge of world political development (see Chapters 9 and 10).

France today is still fascinating; steadfast and changing, changing yet steadfast. The comparativist observer's task remains, as Raymond Aron sketched it out, to investigate a changing equilibrium of achievements and failures, of successes and mediocrity.

Watershed: The Eclipse of Marxism in French Political Culture

Political culture in France was more deeply affected than any other Western European society by communism's decline. This was because Marxist attitudes had suffused post–World War II political culture in France more extensively than in either West Germany or Britain, while in Italy the strong Italian Communist party (PCI) had been a communist revisionist already for three decades prior to Gorbachev's arrival in power, struggling to replace Leninist doctrines of "proletarian dictatorship" with softer, homegrown Gramscian conceptions of political and ideological "hegemony." Commentators on France during these postwar and Cold War years observed that whereas the right had the power of government, Marxism dominated the French intellectual environment.[16] The French Communist party during these years wielded a power of ideological intimidation in the country hard to imagine today. It was an intellectual and moral hegemony built partly on the Communist party's reputation for courage and sacrifice in the French Resistance and partly on a widespread infatuation in France with the Soviet Union's claims to be a new type of society. The PCF was able to maintain a sort of veto power over what the French left—that is, the so-called non-Communist left—could say or do. The result was that the French left remained internally paralyzed by the unbridgeable split between the Socialists and the Communists, and unelectable because voters worried the French Communists would try to make a "revolution from within," to stage a "Prague coup" in Paris.

The tumultuous Communist crises of the 1950s and 1960s shook the French left, but did not break Marxism's hold on a large swath of French political culture or the persisting fascination with the idea that the Soviet

Union was a socialist proletarian workers' state. Khrushchev's "secret speech" denouncing Stalin plus the smashing of the Hungarian counter-revolution, both in 1956, set off a first wave of exits from the French Communist party. The Warsaw Pact's crushing of the "Prague Spring" attempt at "socialism with a human face" in August 1968 (just after the French "events of May") caused a second moment of intellectual and moral crisis in the Communist and Socialist left. But even after all this, Marxism in France and the French Communist party at the beginning of the 1970s still seemed to be rising forces.

Three further turning points finally forced French acceptance of the truth about Stalinism and communism, deflecting French left-wing intellectuals as a group into the anti-Stalinist, anti-Soviet camp. The first was what Pierre Hassner called "the Solzhenitzyn effect." French intellectuals, living in a free country and thus so to speak condemned to read Alexander Solzhenitzyn's books, finally accepted the facts about the Soviet Union, as irrefutably contained in the 1974 French translation of *The Gulag Archipelago*. Second, as a consequence of Mitterrand's presidential victory in 1981, diehard idealistic hopes of remaking society were chastened by the "union of the left's" run-in with reality and rapid turn toward less unrealistic policy. Finally, the vaunted French Communist party, assailed by Soviet communism's tailspin and by its own failures to dominate the French left, collapsed electorally, politically, socially and morally. Political revolution in the U.S.S.R. destroyed the PCF's seventy-year-old founding myth and point of reference. French communism has become a hollow shell today, a structure that has lost its function and even the reason for which it had originally been created.

The upshot was rapid change not only in how immediate problems were perceived in the French policy process, but also in the political culture as a whole. In the last half of the 1980s, the real, practical problems of unemployment, immigration and racism replaced ideological anticapitalism and socialism as the main issues debated on the French left as well as in French society (see Chapters 7 and 8). Historians will mark the waning of class struggle ideology in the 1970s and 1980s as a watershed in French political history and in the history of political ideas in France.

The Muting of Class and Class Conflict

Even if Marxism was always a false theory of history, certain aspects of Marxist analysis were—and still are—extremely pertinent. Social class and its political implications have, in particular, been fundamental to the analysis of European societies. Karl Marx used the concept of class in two ways: class *an sich* and class *fuer sich*, or class "in itself" and class "for itself." A class "in" itself is a group of people defined by objective criteria, such as position in relations of production (e.g., industrial workers) or income levels. Marx's own simple distinction of "workers" and "capitalists" was inadequate to the analytical task, as technological development added all sorts of intermediary and other categories (especially the distinction between owners and managers) that obscured his basic distinction. (Marx's own empirical books in fact showed the problem of his theory.) Nevertheless, one could still designate *working, middle* and *upper classes* by objective criteria: for example, blue collar versus white collar, workers "by hand" and "by brain," or classes organized according to income levels or sources (salaries, dividends) of income. The problem is to know whether the objective criteria adequately encompass the various social and political meanings of "class."

In a general sense, all societies divide themselves sociologically, or can be divided by analytical categories, into classes. In *political* terms the main issue, on the other hand, is not to know whether there are classes but whether people *perceive* themselves as belonging to classes, and, most important, whether this perception, right or wrong, has political consequences. Analysis of the role of class in political culture is, in other words, an analysis of Marx's class "for itself," of people perceiving themselves in a like objective situation in relation to (or against) other classes or to the government.

Historically, the French were probably as highly class-conscious a people as any in the world. In France, once the Revolution brought the idea of class hatreds to the fore, class differences were automatically conceived as the basis of a natural struggle to dominate society, sometimes for survival itself. Birth into the lower classes was a perfectly reasonable basis for feelings of resentment and hostility toward the possessing classes. "Historically, the social system of France (was) much like that of any other Western European country that experienced feudalism and inherited a society divided into classes of nobles, clergy, townsmen (bourgeoisie) and peasants."[17] William Safran is correct, except that, as the Revolution and subsequent developments showed, the French situation was worse. As Tocqueville said, the French Revolution ended up not merely a political but also a social revolution against all forms of privilege and inequality. The Great Revolution was a genuine class revolution, a smashing of society in order to recast it totally, not just the political institutions or the position of religion and the church.

But this did not fit Marx's neat scheme of a "bourgeois" revolution either. At first a revolution of all classes against the nobility and the aristocracy, the French Revolution dissolved after a few years into a kind of class-against-class anarchy, and soon ended in a reign of terror of the revolutionary state against the people and against a collection of random enemies, including many of its own makers such as Robespierre. Against all this, France today, at the end of two centuries of a political history drenched with class ideology, exhibits a rather clear muting of class antagonisms and class conflict rightly understood. Not that social conflict is disappearing—far from that. The point is that clashes of social and economic interests are less and less perceived as class conflicts in a traditional French or Marxist sense.

The evolution of French political culture over the past twenty years is what could be divined from the general thesis of this essay: a decline of French exceptionalism. Specifically the strong class identity traditional in French political culture has faded since the 1970s. This indicates—though historians would need to investigate the problem—that class belief, class "for itself," was always more a function of political education than of objective situation. Yet following Marx's distinction we should remember that a lack of class antagonism doesn't necessary mean that objective class inequalities and injustices are insignificant.

In prerevolutionary France, class resentments and fears moved center stage politically as the Ancien Régime tottered toward its collapse. Then, as a consequence of the Great Revolution's incompleteness, class identities and animosities continued to be stimulated, even overdetermined, by a pattern of political development in which no class, certainly not the internally divided French bourgeoisie, permanently gained the upper hand.[18] This lack of a hegemonic class was the French particularity, as contrasted for example with the British or German situations where, in the first case a self-confident bourgeoisie, and in the second a self-confident landed aristocracy, the Junkers, dominated the socioeconomic and political arenas. In the long view the political history of France 1789–1939 was as much a history of class and class conflict as of the conflicts between religion and secularism, or between the French state and civil society. But Marxism was not so much an explanation of this class conflict as a stimulus of it.

The crucial class in Marxist sociology was of course *la classe ouvriere—les ouvriers*. This was the class whose putative political interest, "communism," the Communist Manifesto's first sentence had described as "a specter haunting Europe." If, on the other hand, the working class was not bent on revolution, then the European and French bourgeoisie could continue to sleep soundly at night.

Against the background of Marxism's long hold in French political culture, it is significant that since the 1970s the muting of class identity is particularly strong among workers. Surveys show a decline from about 75 to 50 percent in blue-collar workers' consciousness of a class identity. Since people who identify with a political party tend to rate higher on class identity, the significant decline in working-class identification must be due in great measure to the transformation of the French left, to the decline of the French Communist party and the decline of ideology in the Socialist party (*Parti Socialiste*, or PS). During the decades when the PCF controlled a quarter of the electorate and influenced "fellow travelers" and other sympathizers, it was a running joke that every politically engaged French person "either is, was, or will be" a member of the Communist party. Once commonplace, to be a member of the Communist party now seems increasingly odd and little understood, some sort of nostalgia or a certain kind of stubbornness. Recent surveys, according to one standard text, show that "French blue-collar workers identified themselves as belonging to a class less frequently than any other major salaried group."[19] This is a particularly striking finding, given the demographic and political decline of the industrial working class contrasted with the demographic explosion of the middle classes and professions.

In addition the significance of the act of embracing a class identification has certainly changed. Thirty years ago to feel oneself part of the working class had a clear political meaning; it wasn't a form of self-pity. It meant one was on the left and part of a revolutionary, rising social force, part of the future. The Communist party in the 1970s probably never had more than several hundred thousand members, but the trade union confederation it dominated, the CGT, had 1.5 million to 2 million members, and the CGT controlled or strongly influenced millions more in factories and homes.

Today, union membership in France has declined to a historic low, perhaps under 10 percent, lower—remarkably—than any other large industrial country.[20] And the once-fearsome Communist-dominated CGT is in many ways not stronger than the independent Workers' Force union (*Force Ouvriere*, or FO), born originally as a U.S.-sponsored liberal splinter from the CGT when Communists took over the big union's leadership at the outbreak of the Cold War in 1947.

To take another situation, thirty years ago to admit to a "bourgeois" or managerial class identity was to suspect that one was on a certain side—the exploiting side—in the class struggle. Today, to the contrary, managers and businesspeople place themselves in the class structure more often and easily than industrial workers, and with less angst about the pejorative connotations. High class standing, for better or worse, has become in France as in the United States a measure more of success than of social or political positioning. The "class struggles in France," as Karl Marx titled his famous pamphlet on the revolution of 1848, have been muted, at least for the foreseeable future.

French Youth and the Political Culture

Young people in France, like industrial workers and nostalgia, are also not what they used to be politically and culturally. Whereas a French student of the 1950s or '60s could be found or at least easily imagined arguing politics and philosophy in a cafe, today students at a *fac* (a public university), a *lycée* or a *collège* (a lower secondary school) want to be tied into international fads more than existentialists and trendsetters of political engagement.

Urban, upwardly mobile French youth are no longer even sure to know the difference between political "right" and "left," or, worse still, to think that it matters much. And this is quite understandable and mundane. How could French youth born between 1970 and 1975 and after, for example, be certain whether privatization of industry was a policy of the left or the right? The French Socialists under Mitterrand in the 1980s first nationalized massively in 1981–82, then changed their minds and began a privatization program that was expanded by the conservative "cohabitation" government led by Jacques Chirac in 1986–88. Then President Mitterrand, in campaigning for reelection in 1988, made a famous "neither–nor" promise: There would be no more nationalizations or privatizations. And then at the end of 1991 Mitterrand relaxed that promise—but not with more "left-wing" nationalizations, rather with more privatizations!

And with Pierre Bérégovoy pursuing a strong franc and low inflation, at the cost of very high unemployment, could a French teenager be certain whether he was finance minister of the left or the right?[21] With the Socialists having joined the French consensus on institutions, defense and Europe, what was the real difference between major parties? In sum, depoliticization, self-absorption and political apathy increasingly characterize French young people, who on the contrary used to be much esteemed, or at least romanticized for their political and philosophical aspirations.

French young people today, the first generation networked so extensively beyond French borders for their cultural and intellectual cues, have become very much part of the international teenage commercial culture that sets political attitudes and social behavior in addition to tastes in music, films and videos. Many French teenagers and college students embraced get-rich "yuppie" attitudes in the 1980s as intensely as they once had embraced politics, and in the 1990s there is a considerable fad for American-inspired "hip-hop" music and behavior. Both reach the French, as in all European countries, through a combination of American and local versions of MTV-type shows broadcast on the expanded and increasingly internationalized cable television networks. Their mental world seems today as much a product of American and international "rap" images as of specifically French culture. In this way too French life, for better or worse, has become less exceptionalist, more tied to international developments; and the pace of cultural change may even be accelerating.

Religion and the Political Culture

Catholic France, because of its loyalty, was once known as "the eldest daughter of the Church." Today France is, according to the Vatican's official criteria of practice and observance, a "de-Christianized" country.

But while church and state were officially separated in 1905 and while religious observance is low, it would be wrong to think that Catholicism is without political influence and effect, though these have more to do with Catholicism as a culture than as a religious belief and practice per se.

Historically, France is a Catholic country and the French remain, on the whole, a Catholic people. Statistically, more than 90 percent of French society today is of Roman Catholic background, with the rest being longstanding Protestant and Jewish minorities, the new Muslim immigrant minority, and small congeries of nonaffiliated people. In current opinion polls about 80 percent of the respondents describe themselves as Catholic. But only 10 to 15 percent are regular churchgoers, and fully half of the 80 percent never go to church.[22] Young people are the least practicing segment of the population. However as in other countries there is a tentative renewal of churchgoing today, even or especially among young people. A search for renewed meaning might be expected in a society whose culture and politics have rapidly evolved.

In addition, Catholicism's hold on the people's loyalties and affections may be considerably stronger than that of the Church itself. Catholicism in France, even for the de-Christianized, remains a broad cultural background—for many people it is simply part of being French, which of course can create problems of social and political integration, especially for the Muslim minority (see Chapter 7).

The strength of this persistent, latent public feeling for Catholicism as a culture and way of life was verified when the Socialist government in 1984 wrote a bill limiting already restricted state financing for parochial schools. The goal was to finish the Socialists' idea of a secularized state by phasing out state subsidy of parochial—mainly Catholic—grade schools and high schools. The largest popular protest since 1968, about half a million people, rallied with conservative parties in a street demonstration in Versailles to protest this bill. Sensing that public opinion didn't see the necessity of a fully secularized state in the Socialist mode,

President Mitterrand, in an exercise of Gaullist presidential fiat, abruptly withdrew the bill from under the noses of his prime minister and education minister. (It is necessary to add that many French parents look·upon private religious schools primarily as a permanent "second chance" for students who do poorly in the state-run public schools, thus their endorsement has less to do with religious content than with educational opportunity.)

Religion was, in republican France as in Europe generally, the persistently most reliable predictor of voting behavior.[23] Religious people voted conservative, seculars voted on the left. Does religion still affect party allegiances and the vote so strongly?

Recent data suggest a narrowing of the cultural gap between the religious and antireligious traditions in France, but also that religion nevertheless is still the most important indicator of voting preference, more important in any case than class position.[24] On policy problems that don't involve religious beliefs directly—for example, economic and social policy, questions about the institutions, foreign policy and so on—surveys show the emergence of a rough consensus, that "the current thinking of the faithful and of agnostics," as Ehrmann and Schain put it, "now coincides rather than diverges."[25]

Yet voting behavior still is skewed along religious lines, but a divide between observant and nonobservant Catholics. Even as late as the mid-1980s, only about 10 percent of practicing Catholics placed themselves on the left, and, from election to election, about three-quarters continued to vote consistently with the right. In the 1970s, Michelat and Simon had found that less than 10 percent of workers who were practicing Catholics voted for the left, while nonpracticing Catholic workers voted nearly 75 percent for the left. What this indicates is that *nonpracticing* Catholics in the past two decades have found it increasingly acceptable and attractive to vote for the left, meaning the Socialists, not the Communist party. And this is a finding confirmed by data showing that support for the left increased to over 50 percent on the part of the nonpracticing middle-class Catholics.

There is a tacit compromise in French life today between the Catholic Church, with its needs, and a state that, Church leaders must assume, will often be in the hands of seculars. Except for the one unresolved issue of government subsidies to parochial schools, it is hard to see what interest the Catholic Church could or would serve by becoming once again a focus of political controversy.

Full French Catholic acceptance of diversity, of "multiculturalism," is a different matter however. Paris's Cardinal Jean-Marie Lustiger, born a Polish Jew, has had a remarkable personal destiny. Yet French society is unable to rid itself of a residual anti-Semitism, not to mention a similar, though less intense, Catholic prejudice against France's Huguenot Protestant minority. (The 700,000 French Jews, the largest European Jewish population outside the former Soviet Union, are a little over 1 percent of the population; the approximately 1.5 million Protestants make up about 2 percent of the population.) But today's classic religious and cultural prejudices in France's Catholic society pale when compared to contemporary discrimination in France against Muslim Arabs—Algerians, Tunisians and Moroccans. This 1990s dilemma involves a particular conjunction of French problems with religious, ethnic and racial differences.

The presence and demographic growth of large numbers of North African Muslims as permanent residents and citizens has, over four decades since national liberation, created a distinctly contemporary and international need to deal with multiculturalism. The issue is sometimes minimized by pointing to the prejudice, beatings and occasional murders of Polish and Italian immigrants in France before World War II, or of Yugoslav and Portuguese immigrants in the 1950s and 1960s. But today's problem, because it involves people of non-European origin, of the Muslim religion and of brown skin, is more intense and intractable than the problems faced by earlier generations of immigrants.

This is really a clash of cultures, larger than the religious rivalry of church and mosque. Yet the religious difference certainly is a specific part of the multicultural clash. To be French for many French citizens means to be Catholic; or rather the reverse is true: Not to be Catholic means not to be fully French. This Catholic bias cuts against French Jews more than French Protestants, who are naturally perceived as closer to Catholics because they are, "after all," Christian. But religious prejudice surely affects Muslims most intensely of all, and it is intensified by racial, ethnic and cultural resentments.

Immigrants, the Problem of Racism and the Question of French National Identity

All this raises the so-called crisis of French national identity. In France as in so many countries, the combination of religious differences with ethnic and racial tensions and economic fears is an explosive, permanently threatening mixture.

The centrality of Catholicism in France has been used by race baiters such as the National Front to argue that Muslims can never assimilate, can never be fully integrated into French society, in part because French identity cannot (or should not) evolve to become more accommodating to sharply increased social differences in society. Similarly at the European

Community level, applications from countries such as Turkey and Tunisia receive the controversial, unspoken response that Europe is culturally Judeo-Christian and that European identity would be diluted and the EC's internal coherence weakened by admitting Muslim countries to membership. This cumulates, of course, with the objective fact of underdevelopment, the fact that Muslim countries could meet very few EC economic, financial and political standards.

In the French outlook, in addition, the truly gravest ethnic troubles in Europe are elsewhere, far from French borders. To be sure, political intellectuals such as André Glucksman have raged over French and European complacency about the civil war in former Yugoslavia, which is, Glucksman observed, "one and one-half hours from Paris by plane." The fact is that the suffering in former Yugoslavia doesn't directly threaten France, as the government's foreign policy has demonstrated (see Chapter 9).

Yet ethnic tensions have of course become a serious issue at home for the French. Prejudice against the Arab Muslim population, especially visible in Paris, Marseille and a few other big cities, creates conspiratorial talk about how foreigners are responsible for "French" unemployment, about alleged exploitation by foreigners of social services, and about the threat to the French national identity. Through the false image of a continuing "invasion" of immigrants into France this "French" fear even becomes a vague premonition about the national security. It has affected recent EC efforts to eliminate borders inside the Community and has increased cooperation among national police forces to patrol illegal immigration.

Although the average French person tends to assume that France has always had a homogenous population, this is just wrong. France today has one of the largest immigrant populations (in numbers and percent) of any EC country, and it was historically a country of considerable immigration whose sparsely inhabited spaces (in Western European terms) needed to be filled if French geopolitical goals, over several centuries and regimes, were to be attained. By the mid-nineteenth century, industrialization was a new factor. It required a sharply larger urban work force, while French demography to the contrary had begun its century-long decline, culminating in the interwar period's absolute population drop. In the 1950s and 1960s France "welcomed" foreign workers to fill out requirements for a booming postwar economy. But then in the 1970s and 1980s came recessions and slowdowns, with the consequence, as in other EC countries, that foreign workers, only some of whom had become citizens, were no longer so welcome.

Unemployment no less than *tripled* in fifteen short years, and in the second half of the 1980s France had, in electoral terms anyway, the largest antiimmigrant, racialist party in Europe, the National Front. In the 1990s unemployment and hatred (racial, ethnic and religious) have become the twin scourges of Community Europe. Is France—historically the country of the Rights of Man—a racist country today? Are the French people a racist people? The answer is complex.

Viewed from abroad, the National Front and its demagogic leader Jean-Marie Le Pen often appear to be the sum and substance of racist politics in France. But the end of a divided Europe has ushered in a period when contact between peoples rather than division is the source of grief. The civil wars in former Yugoslavia are only the worst of these cases. In France as elsewhere, European integration, whatever its benefits, has stimulated domestic worries about "foreigners."

Within the EC the Schengen Agreement foresees eliminating all intercountry border controls on people. As of December 1992 it had been signed by ten of the twelve EC countries, but its full implementation, originally scheduled to coincide with inauguration of the single integrated market on January 1, 1993, has been put off at least into 1994. Managing the Schengen consequences is the subject of continuing discussions in the so-called Trevi Conference, the most important, even if informal, international EC police grouping, which discusses methods of internal security cooperation. On October 31, 1991, for example, a meeting of twenty-six East and West European governments agreed on a new list of measures—including a crackdown on gangs smuggling refugees for money, mobile forces to patrol remote frontier areas, and harsh penalties for airlines that don't adequately verify passports and travel documents at the point of departure—to check a surge in illegal East–West migration. Unified Germany was naturally the main advocate at the meeting, because it is the frontier with several former Eastern-bloc countries, the main source of economic migrants. But given that Schengen allows anyone in Germany access to all other "Schengenland" territory, it was obvious how the other countries, France among them, are also involved.[26] Here is another practical instance of how the contradictions of European integration raise new problems even as they benefit national interests.

The human problems crystallized in the National Front's demagogy— immigration and foreign workers, unemployment, the right to acquire nationality and citizenship—have no simple solutions and few palliatives. As elsewhere in Community Europe, in France every other political party has to deal with the passions of race feelings and the fears for homeland and identity, but without the simplistic attitudes of the National Front.

Yet neither are prejudiced attitudes a monopoly of the right or the FN. In the putatively fraternal French Communist party, for example, chauvinism and racism (such as that toward the Communist parties in French colonies such as Algeria) always were, as in the Communist International at large, an ugly reality behind the facade of "proletarian internationalist" brotherhood—just as bourgeois, sexist attitudes about women were the reality undergirding the facade of Potemkin village females in the Central Committee secretariat and Politburo. And a complicated anti-Semitism, as is well known, was the paradoxical reality of communism despite all the prominent Jewish Communist leaders and the hundreds of thousands of dedicated Jewish party members. Communism devalued all of these "secondary" aspects of peoples' identities in order to maximize obeisance to workerist doctrines (some of the strongest negative attitudes about Jewish identity were held by Jewish Communists) and the sacred totem of proletarian supremacy.

But discussion of racism must not be limited only to the extreme right and extreme left parties, for if racist attitudes and behaviors are widespread in a society they will surely be found throughout the political spectrum and to some extent among all types of people. However, this is not to say that all political and social groups are racist or that "everyone is to some extent racist." But clearly the question of *les étrangers* concerns the mainstream as well as the extreme right and left in French politics.

Inflammatory antiimmigrant rhetoric is a natural temptation for leaders of the two major conservative parties, the neo-Gaullist Rally for the Republic (*Rassemblement pour la République*, or RPR) and the center–right Union for French Democracy (*Union pour la Démocratie Française*, or UDF), who compete for those votes that otherwise go to the National Front. For example in the summer of 1991 Jacques Chirac, the neo-Gaullist leader, mayor of Paris and permanent presidential candidate, created a scandal by saying in a newspaper interview that he "understood very well" why the French resent large immigrant families "surviving on welfare" and can't abide the "smell" of living next to them. Though widely criticized for his harsh words, Chirac also gained 5 points in the next political popularity polls. A few months later, in September 1991, former president Valéry Giscard d'Estaing—who is trying like Chirac to remain a contender for the next presidential election—wrote in *Le Figaro Magazine*, a leading conservative newspaper, that France's immigration problem was equivalent to an "invasion." Giscard d'Estaing cited an opinion poll in which 22 percent of the respondents said Jean-Marie Le Pen was the "politician most likely to solve the immigration problem satisfactorily." Other polls have from time to time shown one third of respondents in general agreement with the National Front's ideas on immigration. Such statistics probably exaggerate the extent of hardline racism in French society, while probably understating the extent of mild prejudices that have small or at least hidden consequences.

French nationality law still provides that any infant born on French soil is automatically French, no matter the nationality of the parents. (France, unlike many other countries, permits dual nationality.) But a controversial addendum, which seemed inimical to "foreign" children, was passed by the conservative Chirac government in 1986. It requires a legal declaration by children of foreigners, at the eighteenth birthday, in order to keep French nationality.[27]

The contradiction is that French public policy still encourages a larger population, and for better reasons now. French and EC population growth rates for several years have been substantially below replacement levels. Moreover France, a big country in Europe, is among its least densely populated areas: 266 persons per square mile versus 635 in the former West Germany and 943 in the Netherlands. Only Spain, Greece and Ireland have lower population densities. "If France had the same population density as other major European powers," notes one text, "there would be more than 125 million inhabitants."[28] (Relations with Germany would change, and General de Gaulle would certainly be smiling in his grave!)

Yet France's geopolitical thought about a larger population is no longer such a simple matter. If there were to be 100 or 125 million French people today, unavoidably tens of millions of them would be brown, black, yellow and mixed. Geopolitical thinking thus intersects now with intense contemporary feelings about race and religion, including the delicate question of birthrate differences among the races.

Altogether it is as difficult for the French to give up old geopolitical dreams as to tolerate the prospect of a multicultural society. Would France still be "France" without, as de Gaulle said, "greatness"? Would it be France if the population were a rainbow of skin colors and a patchwork of religions and ethnicities?

Former president Giscard d'Estaing, in the controversial article cited above, argued that "France must preserve and cultivate its own identity." This he translated into policy terms by suggesting that state subsidies and tax relief be restricted to ethnic French mothers only, invoking the German-style principle of *jus sanguinis*. This was attacked as a racist idea by conservative former European Parliament president and concentration camp survivor Simone Weil (now the French social affairs minister) and even by Giscard's younger rival in the Republican party, François Leotard. One Socialist government voice was particularly sharp in criticizing the former president. Kofi Yamgnane, the secretary of state for integration, a black man who came to France as a child with his parents from Togo, said that "Giscard d'Estaing prefers the blacks who

Jean-Bédel Bokassa of the Central African Republic and to a scandal that helped defeat Giscard in 1981—"to those who sweep the streets of Paris."[29] In spite of the outcry against him, Giscard d'Estaing showed up 7 points higher in the next poll rating public support for various leaders.

The temptation to shore up support by pandering to popular racial prejudices extends especially to those in government, for they have the responsibility, and pay the price, of making policy. A telling example was Edith Cresson, appointed Socialist prime minister in summer 1991. In a misconceived gesture to reassure voters that, despite her left-wing beliefs, including her appointment of Kofi Yamgnane, she would be tough on the illegal immigration question, Cresson said that "charter flights" might be used to return illegal immigrants to their home countries—as if, in spite of her left-wing instincts, she expected to start shipping them off in great masses! In October 1991 her government passed a law further tightening the policing of illegal clandestine jobs and of foreigners found without residence permits. The new controls were justified as a way to "protect legal employment," which was clearly understood as a veiled way of saying to fight unemployment of the "French." So the Socialists in office, obliged by circumstances and tempted by public opinion, at times acted like the conservative parties. Consensus of a sort, it is also an uncomfortable truth.

The Changing Political Culture of French Protest

Modern France has been a natural laboratory for the scholarly study of popular protest. And scholars themselves, because France so invited a personal engagement, have rarely been nonpartisan. The shelves of books on this subject—from Marx and Engels to Jules Michelet, Albert Soboul, Charles Tilly and many more—constitute in themselves a history of intellectuals' intense political engagements with the meanings and lessons of France's exceptional political development.[30]

France between 1789 and 1968 was a nearly permanent theater of political revolutions, counterrevolutions and revolts. France was, par excellence, the country of irreconcilable oppositions where in politics "everything" seemed to be permanently at stake, including liberty and survival itself.[31]

Born from the Great Revolution's very success, or rather from the excesses of revolutionary success, which after running their course provoked counterrevolution, French political culture was filled with contradictory symbols, supporting the political dreams and fears of "two Frances." The taking of the Bastille, the regicide, the Reign of Terror, became the political symbols and myths of "Revolutionary France," while the Thermidorean Reaction, the counterrevolution in the Vendée and in Britanny *(les chouans)* became sacred undertakings of royalist, reactionary France.

On the left and above all in Paris, taking to the streets became the tradition of populist politics, with throwing up of barricades and defiant occupation of territory becoming the standard repertory of political struggle. The barricades of 1830 and 1848, romanticized in Victor Hugo's *Les Misérables* (and in its current international musical version), were conscious reenactments by succeeding generations of the historical barricades of 1789.

The Commune of 1871, another unpredictable yet typical action, was a nationalistic rising against the invading Prussians in the Franco–Prussian War. But it was also a popular rising of the Parisians, *le peuple de Paris*, against their own "treasonous" upper-class government at Versailles. This remnant of Napoleon III's regime was scheming to sign an agreement with the invaders to save the lives and property of the upper classes by making huge concessions, which the people would pay for, to the Germans. Seventy years later the Vichy state seemed to reprise this upper-class "antinational" policy of treating with the enemy at the expense of the nation, and the Communist Louis Aragon could plausibly define the French Resistance as a new revolutionary movement of *le peuple*.

Thus French populism, as in countries that took it as an example, was built on a tradition of protest in the streets, not on elections. When left-wing political parties were formed, toward the end of the nineteenth century, and when trade unions finally developed (the originally anarcho-syndicalist CGT was created in the fifteen years before World War I), these workers' organizations were more at home marching in the streets in protest than they were lobbying the government or running for office. In this populist-worker part of Third Republic civil society, the political powder keg of the "stalemate society," collective bargaining was the exception, not the rule.

As a result of World War II's alliances between liberals and Communists, a sudden massive expansion of Communist influence in French politics and especially in the trade-union movement exacerbated and fixed the mutual hostility of capitalists and workers in the 1920s and 1930s. The French simply had not developed legalized, routinized good-faith collective bargaining between management and labor. A large part of the reason was that on one side French business was in practical terms largely reactionary; on the other side, the Communists (and Socialists) were counting on overthrowing the system. But another part of the reason was that French political culture for 150 years had conditioned all sides to count on the worst—even though an ebullient French proverb has it that "The worst is never certain"!

In postwar and Cold War France the street demonstration as a mode of collective action was a specialty of the left, though the Gaullists as well as extremist neo-Fascist groups were also proficient. And on the left the Communists were much more potent organizationally than the Socialist party, then still called the SFIO. The PCF—with its huge membership and mass of sympathizers, its CGT trade-union protectorate and its "Moscow gold"—could reliably put hundreds of thousands of people into the street on any issue. This fearsome Communist mass-mobilization capacity was one of the essential political facts of Cold War French politics. The PCF could not hope to govern the country but could paralyze it.

The street demonstration was an extension of the strike, and both were premised on the unlikelihood of fair treatment by "capitalists," *le Patronat*, or by the state, which was the boss of the many state-owned industries. Communist and Socialist factory strikes used to be, therefore, not merely a demand for negotiations about salaries and working conditions, but also an implicit rejection of the government, the "bourgeois" republic and capitalism. So long as the Communists held sway on the left, Socialists and others were intimidated into unrelenting anticapitalist, antiliberal thinking.

The street demonstration was, one could say, a natural mode of protest and political action by trade unions and by antigovernment political parties. Its widespread use revealed, on the one hand, the missing link—regular consensual collective bargaining—in the French system of industrial relations and, on the other, that important political parties on the left *and* the right were against not only the government but also the system. In the permanent tension of Cold War Europe, the various "third force" governing groups were reassured that France was a NATO country. And it was solace for almost everyone that the Federal Republic of Germany served as a geopolitical buffer for France to the east.

After Exceptionalism, What?

The classic French culture of revolutionary protest has evolved quickly into a seemingly reconciled pluralism of participation and legitimacy in which even occasional spectacular demonstrations by farmers, truckers or hospital personnel no longer mean the regime is in danger. Television news programs have been disrupted by striking groups, but not to take over the station, only to protest inadequate coverage by journalists. Wildcat actions today are an attempt to influence the media and public opinion for public policy ends, not to challenge the Fifth Republic's legitimacy.

In sum, May '68 was presumptively the last act—*caveat emptor!*—of modern France's history of great rebellions and revolutions. "There is another way to say the same thing," François Furet writes. "France has closed its political theater of the exceptional, and it has entered into the common law of democracies."[32]

Endnotes

1. Alexis de Tocqueville, *The Old Regime and the Revolution* (New York: Doubleday Anchor, 1955), Part 3, Chapter 8, p. 210.

2. Tocqueville had in mind Roman historians, Tacitus and Julius Caesar's *Gallic Wars*. They reported that the Gauls were "said to be such fierce warriors that they would be impossible to defeat were they not so divided among themselves." Tocqueville (*The Old Regime*, p. 2) also quoted Edmund Burke's *Reflections on the Revolution in France*, saying that the Revolution would weaken France almost to the point of extinction. "We may assume that for a long time to come France need no longer be reckoned with as a military power. Indeed, she may be destroyed, as such, forever, and men of the next generation may repeat those ancient words: *Gallos quoque in bellis floruisee audivimus* (We have heard tell that the Gauls, too, once excelled in warfare)."

3. The best book remains Robert O. Paxton, *Vichy France: Old Guard and New Order, 1940–1944* (New York: Columbia University Press, 1972). Paxton's compelling archival evidence broke a long French silence on this question, launching a French controversy. See also Michael Marrus and Robert O. Paxton, *Vichy France and the Jews* (New York: Shocken, 1983).

4. See page 29 of Raymond Aron, *Immuable et changeante. De la IVe à la Ve république* (Paris: Calmann-Levy, 1959). Published in English as *France Steadfast and Changing: The Fourth to the Fifth Republic* (Cambridge: Harvard University Press, 1960).

5. An impressive new study in this vein is Herrick Chapman, *State Capitalism and Working-Class Radicalism in the French Aircraft Industry* (Berkeley: University of California Press, 1991).

6. See Crozier, *The Bureaucratic Phenomenon* (Chicago: University of Chicago Press, 1964), and Hoffmann, "Paradoxes of The French Political Community," in Hoffmann et al., *In Search of France* (New York: Harper Torchbooks, 1965) (quote from p. 17). Other

books in this group would be Nathan Leites, *House without Windows: France Elects a President* (Evanston, Ill.: Row, Peterson, 1958); Leites, *On the Game of Politics in France* (Stanford, Calif.: Stanford University Press, 1959); and one by Swiss journalist Herbert Luethy, *France against Herself* (New York: Praeger, 1955). The very striking, pioneering anthropological work of Laurence Wylie, especially *Village in the Vaucluse* (Cambridge: Harvard University Press, 1957), should also be included. Wylie's studies showed how political anthropology at the village level could say much about French political culture as a whole, thus joining with the macrolevel viewpoints of Hoffmann, Crozier, and others.

7. *Le Mal français* (Paris: Plon, 1976). Published in English as *The Trouble with France* (New York: Alfred A. Knopf, 1981). See also the early book by a former editor-in-chief of the newspaper *Le Monde*, Jacques Fauvet, *The Cockpit of France* (London: Harvill Press, 1960), which conveys with journalistic verve and immediacy the political culture of the Fourth Republic.

8. Good overviews are to be found in Henry Ehrmann and Martin Schain, *Politics in France*, 5th ed. (New York: HarperCollins, 1992), Chapter 1; and David Thomson, *Democracy in France since 1870* (New York: Oxford University Press, 1964), Chapter 1.

9. The interested reader should see Furet's *La Revolution, de Turgot à Jules Ferry, 1770–1880* (Paris: Hachette, 1988), and also François Furet and Mona Ozouf, *Dictionnaire critique de la révolution française* (Critical dictionary of the French Revolution) (Paris: Flammarion, 1988). Significantly, in the 1980s, Furet, a political and intellectual liberal, succeeded several decades of Marxist and Communist "deans" of French historiography of the Revolution in the Sorbonne University's chair of the history of the French Revolution.

10. Raymond Aron's analysis of the political "psychodrama" of 1968 is translated as *The Elusive Revolution* (New York: Praeger, 1969). Enthusiasts of the uprising of course believed Aron's psychodrama interpretation to be wrong and dismissive. For a skillful overview analysis of the strikes as well as an insightful inventory of interpretations of May '68, see Bernard E. Brown, *Protest in Paris: Anatomy of a Revolt* (Morristown, N.J.: General Learning Press, 1974).

11. There exists at least one fair equivalent to a French "Roots" story, the rich, readable novel by Jean d'Ormesson, *Au plaisir de Dieu* (At God's pleasure) (Paris: Gallimard, 1974), which chronicles the centuries of a noble and aristocratic family whose roots reach back to the Crusades. It became a resounding six-part television series.

12. See my study, *French Communism, 1920–1972* (New York: Columbia University Press, 1974).

13. *Nostalgia Isn't What It Used to Be* (New York, 1978). Simone Signoret and her husband, entertainer Yves Montand, were among the many French celebrities and intellectuals persistently and naively sympathetic to the PCF and the Soviet Union during the Cold War years. Both changed their views in the 1970s, and Yves Montand became a controversial celebrity anti-Communist spokesman. He was even vaguely considered a possible presidential candidate for a few years in the 1980s, a tangential yet revelatory sign of changes in French politics.

14. *Progress and Disillusion: The Dialectics of Modern Society* (New York: Mentor Books, 1969).

15. See, for example, Ezra N. Suleiman, "The Politics of Corruption and the Corruption of Politics," *French Politics and Society*, vol. 9, no. 1 (Winter 1991), pp. 57–69.

16. The best and most tenacious study is now Tony Judt's *Past Imperfect: French Intellectuals, 1944–1956* (Berkeley: University of California Press, 1992). Raymond Aron's classic study of French intellectuals' infatuation with revolution still bears attentive re-reading: *The Opium of the Intellectuals* (New York: W. W. Norton, 1957).

17. William Safran, *The French Polity*, 2nd ed. (White Plains, N.Y., 1985), p. 32.

18. See Stanley Hoffmann's classic discussion of this in "Paradoxes," op. cit.

19. Ehrmann and Schain, p. 88ff.

20. Pierre Rosanvallon, *La question syndicale* (The union question) (Paris: Calmann-Levy, 1988).

21. Antoine Pinay, the popular "hard franc" hero of French finance ministers, celebrated his 100th birthday in December 1991. Interviewed on television, he praised the conservative former finance minister Eduard Balladur, but also praised Bérégovoy, saying the Socialist minister's policy was "exactly what he would do today." Bérégovoy, he said, had told him with pride that people were calling him "the Pinay of the left."

    "Béré," as he was nicknamed, was promoted to prime minister in 1992, replacing the controversial Edith Cresson, serving until the Socialists' big electoral defeat in March 1993. Pierre Bérégovoy's suicide a few weeks later shocked French public life profoundly; President Mitterrand bitterly criticized the French media,

give away diamonds"—a reference to the notorious former Emperor
which had been reporting personal and political allegations against
Bérégovoy.

22. Ehrmann and Schain, pp. 76–77.

23. See Gordon Smith, *Politics in Western Europe*, 5th ed. (New York: Holmes & Meier, 1989), Chapter 2.

24. See Ehrmann and Schain, op. cit., pp. 81ff; also, for massive data on an earlier period, now out of date, see Guy Michelat and Michel Simon, *Classe, religion et comportement politique* (Paris: PFNSP, 1977), as well as their article in English, "Class, Religion and Politics," *Comparative Politics*, vol. 10, no. 1 (October 1977).

25. Ehrmann and Schain, op. cit., pp. 74–86.

26. The Schengen–Trevi links were discussed at a conference of the Centre d'Etudes des Relations Internationales (CERI) (Center for the Study of International Relations), Paris, October 25, 1991. On the October 30, 1991, agreement, see John Tagliabue, "Europe Agrees to Help Germans Control Immigrants," *International Herald Tribune*, November 1, 1991, p. 1. These measures were endorsed by interior ministers from all twelve EC states, plus Switzerland, Austria, and thirteen Eastern European governments including Albania, the newly independent Baltic republics and the Ukraine. The Trevi decisions have provoked criticism that EC security measures will create a post-Communist *economic* division of Europe, succeeding so-called Yalta political Europe.

27. Generosity with nationality reflects historical French geopolitical concerns to have a large, powerful population. Even today, and contrary to worries elsewhere about overpopulation, French social policy encourages natality (e.g., a generous family subsidy beginning with the second child). French foreign policy officials, including President Mitterrand himself, have stressed that one aspect of Germany's economic edge over France is the sheer population difference. (This recalls Anatole France's classic quip, that the "German problem" was quite easy to explain: "There are twenty million too many of them!")

French policy contrasts sharply with the German neighbor's policy. Of approximately 40,000 children born to Turkish parents on German soil, because of the German doctrine of *jus sanguinis,* meaning citizenship restricted to blood ties, only about 1,000 become Germans. The French *jus soli* law gives nationality to all those born on French soil. Of about 30,000 babies born on French soil to foreign parents, over 28,000 become French, on the jus soli principle. See Dominique Schnapper, *La France de l'intégration: Sociologie de la nation en 1990* (France and integration: The nation's sociology in 1990) (Paris: Gallimard, 1991), pp. 54 and 58. See Chapter 7 of this volume for a more complete discussion of immigration and "foreigners."

28. Ehrmann and Schain, op. cit., p. 27.

29. See *The European* newspaper, September 27–29, 1991, p. 8. Yamgnane came to France at the age of 10, and now resides in a Breton village. He once told an interviewer, "To have chosen me [as a government minister] created a huge factor of hope among immigrants. In a way, I am a movement for integration all by myself." *Le Quotidien*, December 20, 1991, p. 3.

30. A vivid essay on the classic French way is Stanley Hoffmann, "The Ruled: Protest as a Way of Life," pp. 111–144 in *Decline or Renewal? France since the 1930s*. Charles Tilly's studies, some classics, set an even larger context; for example, *The Contentious French: Four Centuries of Popular Struggle* (Cambridge: Harvard University Press, 1986).

31. The well-written, introductory history of France's political crises by Michel Winock, *La fièvre hexagonale. Les grandes crises politiques, 1871–1968* (Hexagonal fever: The great political crises, 1871–1968) (Paris: Calmann-Levy, 1986) is a large fresco. A good historical overview focused on the left is Georges Lefranc, *Les gauches en France, 1789–1972* (The left in France, 1789–1972) (Paris: Payot, 1973).

32. *La République du centre*, p. 54. A recent scholarly collection of essays on the political culture of French protest is Pierre Favre (ed.), *La manifestation* (The demonstration) (Paris: PFNSP, 1990). Favre concludes that the use of the demonstration in France has been "routinized," and that, since they are used by various sides, they often tend to cancel out each other's political influence. Sidney Tarrow's densely argued studies comparing protest in Italy and France are a broader view of the issue (see the suggested readings).

I have not founded a new republic. I merely gave the republic foundations which it never had before. . . . What I have tried to do is to achieve a synthesis between the monarchy and the republic.

—Charles de Gaulle

Fourteen years is too long.

—François Mitterrand[1]

3
✦
The Logic of French Institutions

De Gaulle Was Right, but Reforms Are Needed

Political institutions are one variable in national development. Institutions are more or less independent from the economy and from social structure, in some countries more so, in others less. Autonomy also varies over time. In any case, there is no absolute rule of thumb about the independence or subordination of politics to economics and sociology. Each country is its own story.

Scholars agree that in Britain, society created the state, and the evolution of British political institutions should be seen in the context of a long historical development of British society. In France, on the other hand, the French state has historically molded the parameters of French society, and the nature of the state was unusually autonomous from the nature of society. Only during the Third and Fourth Republics, and to some extent again during the Fifth, has desire for a strengthened civil society risen. The Gaullist Fifth Republic has been, for the most part, another *étatiste*, or statist French regime, relatively autonomous from society's groups and from public opinion, and with a tutelary attitude toward economic and social activities. Three factors were decisive at the Fifth Republic's creation in 1958–62. The first was the Fourth Republic parliamentary regime's weakness, resoundingly clear in Parliament's desperate appeal to General de Gaulle, in his rural village home, to return to take power in Paris. De Gaulle, France's heroic savior, had determinedly bided his time for years, and now a chastened parliamentary class abjectly implored him, in May 1958, to lead the nation once again away from "the abyss" of national disaster.

The second factor was de Gaulle's successful demand to be allowed to write a new constitution, in effect to reform the French republic by creating a new one. And third, the new regime, a "Gaullist Republic" in which the general governed as a kind of republican monarch president, was soon altered decisively by the Gaullist constitutional referendum of 1962, instituting direct election of the president of the republic. In this "extra" reform, the strong executive regime was guaranteed and legitimized.

Based on the imperious Gaullist presidency, the Fifth Republic's parliamentary characteristics, even after de Gaulle's departure in 1969, have remained subordinate to a de facto presidential—some commentators prefer to say "semipresidential"—system.[2] The exception is parliamentary–presidential "cohabitation," which first occurred in 1986–88 and again in 1993, imposed because parliamentary elections result in an Assembly majority opposed to the sitting president. Because the Assembly majority has, as always, the parliamentary power to overthrow a government and to reject laws, the president no longer can dominate. The prime minister then becomes the effective head of government. The president, demoted by "cohabitation" in most respects to the parliamentary-type head of state written de jure into the 1958 constitution, maintains his de facto Gaullian political authority only in defense and security policy and a few other matters, mainly diplomatic rather than policy making.

But cohabitation is still the exception, though it may not always be, in the still very Gaullist Fifth Republic. The presumption must persist that the strong president and de facto imbalance in favor of Gaullist presidential power will continue to be the norm, though this essay is being completed in spring 1993 just as the second try began at cohabitation. Edouard Balladur has taken office as prime minister saying that his government will last "two years at most," and on all sides eyes are already fixed on the presidential election of 1995 when the focus of French government is expected to return to the presidency.

Therefore in its usual functioning, the Fifth Republic combines a uniquely powerful president with a partially empowered prime minister and a largely suffocated parliament. In the judicial branch there are two high courts. First is a strong, historically well-anchored Council of State, which is an administrative and advisory court but not a constitutional or supreme court. The 1958 Constitution established the Constitutional Council, supposed to be purely an advisory body and precisely not a supreme court with judicial review power. The Constitutional Council has, however, in the past twenty years begun to be invested by the executive and parliamentary branches with limited genuine judicial review powers, in a political culture whose doctrine of Parliament's sovereignty long held back the idea of a true supreme court. If the essence of French Fifth Republic government had to be compressed into a sentence, one would have to stress that the French presidency normally is preeminent to an extent much beyond executive power in any other democratic regime.

Why then has France not been considered a dictatorship? And, if de Gaulle was supposedly so powerful in office, how to explain the paradox that succeeding presidents have wielded *even more* power than he did? What is the "logic" of the Fifth Republic's strange, hybrid institutions? And why have they achieved legitimacy? Why has such presidential power not destroyed representative government?

The writing of a constitution is usually the result of a process of development rather than a single, isolated event. It can even be thought of as a kind of peace treaty, ending, or at least punctuating, a condition of civil war. In few countries has this been more literally true than in France, where the fantastic post-1789 parade of fourteen regimes and sixteen constitutions gave rise to national instability and a literature of self-mocking jokes. A famous one is the story of the Paris bookseller, during the Fourth Republic, who was unable to sell a visiting constitutional law professor a copy of the current French Constitution because, he explained, he "didn't deal in periodical literature"!

Nevertheless, to point out the deficiencies of institutions is not to discredit them. All regimes, even democracies, are imperfect, and institution-building choices do not seek perfection, only choose which flaws and biases to prefer over others. Government is in its nature imperfect, and the least bad solution is, in a sense, always the best solution. Moreover, the reform of one imperfection may engender another that may be worse. And, because political regimes are historical developments, part of the natural history of a nation, there is no single best democratic solution to a given constitutional problem. A democratic constitution will always be like a loose-fitting garment, to be altered and tailored to the people who will wear it, a suit of clothes that will assume its particular comfort and discomfort only with use. Democracy, in any given nation, is the result of particular historical conflicts and particular political and cultural characteristics created in them. In short, in democracy there is almost always more than one plausible way to achieve a given result, be it representation, governmental accountability or effectiveness, or compliance with the law.

As opposed to the American choices of presidentialism and a strong supreme court to conduct judicial review, the democratization of European political systems historically took parliamentary forms. Gordon Smith, in an excellent textbook, observes that the logic of European political regimes is therefore found first of all in the relations between the executive and the legislative branches of government:

> At the heart of the liberal democratic order is the relationship which has evolved between assemblies and their executives; historically, it has been the struggle between these two which in the end provided the essential constitutional structure, around which the other institutions are grouped in a supportive manner.[3]

In a parliamentary system, the key to this relation is the life-or-death power each of the two branches holds over the other. Parliament can vote a motion of no confidence, ousting a government; a prime minister can dissolve Parliament, forcing deputies and their parties into new elections. However, in either case, the "killer" may not survive intact. This makes the fear of inadvertent self-destruction a potent stabilizing factor in parliamentary government's reciprocal executive–legislative vulnerability. Other things being equal, the weapons of politicide—censure and dissolution—will not be used lightly in the parliamentary system.[4]

This said, the logic of French institutions defies simple description because of two intertwined practices unique among advanced democracies: (1) the highest powers normally are not found where the constitution appears to put them; and (2) in a saving democratic grace, the bulk of political power shifts dramatically, from the presidency to the prime minister and the parliamentary majority, if elections—that is, the people's will—so obliges. General de Gaulle, in April 1961, gave the simple explanation, "Our constitution is simultaneously parliamentary and presidential." While clear, this is not very helpful, for as André Passeron commented at the time, "by itself [this explanation] does not say what the nature of the Fifth Republic is."[5] In successive editions of Henry Ehrmann's excellent textbook on France, the author quoted de Gaulle's slightly more helpful comment that he had not founded a new republic, but had rather made a synthesis of the monarchy and the republic.

Is such institutional flux not dangerous? Should the Fifth Republic's Gaullist constitutional "synthesis" be praised for suppleness and adaptability? Or should it be condemned for de facto presidential dominance in violation of the constitution, and for de jure constitutional ambiguity and opaqueness?

Experience argues that de Gaulle was right about what sort of regime—a strong executive government—would be good for France, but that significant institutional reforms still need to be made. President Mitterrand, once a virulent critic of Gaullist "personal power," finally, after a Gaullist decade in office, put constitutional reforms on the government agenda in late 1992. At this writing it is not certain—because it is not clear whether the conservatives or the left would profit most—whether constitutional changes are to be an important part of the Balladur government's business in "Cohabitation II."

The Fifth Republic's Institutions

The President and the Others

De Gaulle's own views of the presidency and the Constitution were decisively influenced by the fall of France in 1940. Third Republic President Albert Lebrun had no other power in the face of the French military defeat than to designate a new premier. He did have the responsibility of trying to guarantee the Republic's institutions. Lebrun once told de Gaulle, "If I had been [constitutionally] responsible, I'd have gone to Algiers." De Gaulle replied that if Lebrun had gone to Algiers, "taking with him the legitimacy, the Republic," then he, de Gaulle, would not have played his historic role, which he took on because no one senior to him would organize resistance to the armistice.[6]

From this origin in two national disasters—1940 and 1958—one can understand the unusual language and conception in which the Gaullist president's role was cast. The president of the Republic, according to Article 5, "shall see that the Constitution is respected. He shall ensure, by his arbitration, the regular functioning of the governmental authorities, as well as the continuity of the State. He shall be the guarantor of national independence, of the integrity of the territory, and of respect for Community agreements and treaties." In addition, the president is given, in Article 16, the right to emergency powers. This can sound frightening (and reminiscent of Weimar Germany) to anyone not familiar with the origin of the clause, the seeming French calling, as de Gaulle once wrote, "to be perpetually in danger." Thus, Article 16:

> When the institutions of the Republic, the independence of the nation, the integrity of its territory, or the fulfillment of its international commitments are threatened in a grave and immediate manner and when the regular functioning of the constitutional public authorities is interrupted, the

President of the Republic shall take the measures required by these circumstances, after official consultation with the Prime Minister, the Presidents of the Assemblies, and the Constitutional Council. He shall inform the nation of these measures by a (public) statement.

In 1990s Community Europe, Article 16 seems anachronistic. But in the emergency context of drafting the new constitution in 1958, providing for a president–protector seemed a requirement of the times. In 1992 President Mitterrand suggested eliminating Article 16, but found little public support, even within the constitutional commission he had appointed to make recommendations on several proposed reforms.

Altogether, it was a foregone conclusion that the Fifth Republic would be a strong executive system of government under de Gaulle. What is to be explained is why under Pompidou, Giscard d'Estaing, and even the Socialist François Mitterrand the "elective monarchy" persisted.

The simplest answer is that the Gaullist system worked. But what does it mean to "work"? Let us say that to work means both to render adequate effectiveness and to satisfy those in a position to change it.

President and Prime Minister: Ambiguity and the Threat of Dyarchy

What are the president's and the prime minister's powers? What are the ambiguities, hence the dangers therein?

Leaving "cohabitation" aside, there have still been differing degrees of presidential power under the several presidents, supported by various parliamentary majorities.

In the old French parliamentary republics, as in contemporary Germany or Italy, the president of the republic was given a modicum of basically honorific powers. Included were the ceremonial domestic and diplomatic functions usual to the head of state; formal naming of the premier, subject to the real authority of Parliament's vote of confidence; formally presiding at the council of ministers and designating high civil servants, bound by the premier's choices; countersigning ordinances and decrees of the council of ministers; official promulgation of laws; the right to have a message read in Parliament; formal convocation of extraordinary sessions of Parliament; the right of clemency; and the responsibility of overseeing judicial independence.

The real political decision making behind the president's formal powers occurred in the interparty parliamentary negotiations and in decisions by the premier and the cabinet. The parliamentary regime president, appropriate to the function's limited role, was indirectly elected by a college of parliamentary, local and other officials. And the long seven-year term had the purpose of freeing the elected president from partisan concerns. When the Fifth Republic was created, the seven-year term adopted for the presidency was another sign that the deputies as a whole, and even Gaullists like Michel Debré, thought they were establishing a lot of continuity. De Gaulle's ambiguous explanations before the Parliament of what he had in mind institutionally did not disabuse them.

First of all, the prime minister and the government, not the president, are supposed to make policy. Article 20 explicitly states, "The Government shall determine and direct the policy of the nation." Article 21 says, "The Prime Minister . . . shall be responsible for national defense [and] shall ensure the execution of the laws." Nothing could be clearer. Indeed François Mitterrand, until he became president himself, repeatedly cited those articles in criticizing "government by personal power," whether of de Gaulle, or Pompidou or Giscard d'Estaing.

In the 1958 Constitution, the parliamentary priority was clear. The president would be basically an "arbiter," a referee and a guardian of the Constitution. The arbiter's function was to "ensure the regular functioning of the public authorities" (Article 5), mainly by appealing, in a situation of deadlock, to another power—to the National Assembly, to the Constitutional Council, or, by using the right to dissolve Parliament, ultimately to the people.[7] De Gaulle in 1966 told a historian that he had always felt "the president of the Republic must govern, but no one had wanted that [in 1958]. I could not say so. Afterwards, gradually, we got there, with precautions, with detours, but, in the end, without much difficulty." This sounds very much like de Gaulle. If he didn't actually say it, he should have.

Nevertheless, under three succeeding presidents there have been significant differences in the practical extent of presidential prerogative. Contrary to what the average French person thinks, among the four Fifth Republic presidents, General de Gaulle allowed his prime ministers (Michel Debré, Pompidou and Couve de Murville) the *greatest* autonomy in domestic affairs. Why should this be so? For one thing de Gaulle was interested mainly in "high politics" and the strategic and tactical game of international relations. For another, his conception of the institutions did accord this separate realm in domestic affairs to the prime minister and the government, with de Gaulle of course having a *droit de regard*, a right of general oversight. In any case, de Gaulle did *not* want an American-style presidential system, with structural separation of powers and a president responsible for the work of the entire government.

Georges Pompidou was a much more interventionist president than de Gaulle in domestic affairs. His expansion of the president's role grew out of his particular interests and talents. For one thing, having been de Gaulle's prime minister in 1962–68 gave him a wide knowledge of issues, of the levers of power and of peculiarly French political dangers (the "events of May" revolt). So he was, practically speaking, probably better qualified in domestic policy than his own prime ministers, Jacques Chaban-Delmas and Pierre Messmer. Furthermore, as a former banker with Banque Rothschild, Pompidou was expert in financial and economic policy, where de Gaulle had relied on others. And President de Gaulle's own international financial ideas were often geopolitical rather than financial strategies: One can cite in point his decision to redeem American "Eurodollars" held by the Bank of France for "Fort Knox" gold as a way to squeeze the U.S. dollar's freedom of action in the Bretton Woods international financial system.

But Valéry Giscard d'Estaing was, thus far, the president most extensively involved in domestic policy as well as foreign policy. His obsession with making all the decisions went far beyond Pompidou's management, and was even thought a bit maniacal by some commentators.[8] François Mitterrand, in 1979, said of Giscard with sardonic irony:

> [The] president of the republic can do anything, the president of the republic does everything, the president of the republic substitutes for the government, the government for the parliament, thus the president of the republic substitutes himself for parliament. The president of the republic takes care of everything, even the gardens along the Seine.[9]

But has François Mitterrand himself acted differently in domestic policy and local affairs?

After his election in 1981, Mitterrand's long, well-advertised attacks on "government by personal power" augured a sharp turn, to make practice agree with the written text of the Constitution. In 1964 he had viciously interrogated Georges Pompidou, then de Gaulle's prime minister, in a memorable Assembly debate, demanding that he explain

> how and why you give up the essential of your prerogatives, by the continuous transfer of your powers to the president of the republic, who is himself not responsible to the parliament; and how and why you authorize yourself, in doing this, to progressively take away from Parliament its fundamental right of control and political decision, outside of which this parliamentary regime would be nothing but an alibi for government by personal power?[10]

Nothing could have been clearer. Yet when president himself, François Mitterrand used and accepted the institutions he had so severely criticized. As early as a few weeks after taking office, Mitterrand put it bluntly in an often-quoted remark: "The institutions had not been made with me in mind, but they are well-suited to me."[11] At no moment in his presidency, not even in the constitutional reforms proposed in 1993, has he advocated a full return to parliamentary government or even an end to semipresidentialism. His proposals (see below) at most give Parliament greater autonomy in legislation and more powers to keep the executive branch accountable.

During the crucial first years of his presidency, the "union of the left" experiment 1981–84, Mitterrand was inevitably omnipresent, involved willy-nilly in all policy sectors. The Socialists were in power for the first time in twenty-five years, the Communists in thirty-five years, and this government of "enemy brothers," trying to win over each other's supporters, was supposed to be simultaneously bringing about socialism! A powerful "arbiter," as the Constitution calls the president, was vitally necessary. During the succeeding cabinet of Laurent Fabius 1984–86, President Mitterrand started to distance himself from domestic decisions. He let the prime minister oversee policy making in the various ministries, intervening and sometimes proving his latent absolute authority only on major issues or in crisis situations.[12] Mitterrand continued in this manner (after the 1986–88 cohabitation when he was excluded from domestic policy) during the Socialist minority governments of Rocard, Cresson and Bérégovoy.

To sum up: The Fifth Republic president in practice normally has final authority in all policy areas—whenever he so chooses and despite the Constitution's clear assignment of parliamentary supremacy in government. The exception to presidential supremacy is cohabitation, an electorally obliged power sharing in which the Parliament's constitutional power to oust a government means the president must accept oppositional control of the majority and thus of policy, or else provoke a constitutional crisis opposing the president's normal de facto powers and Parliament's de jure supremacy. The president surely would lose such a contest.

A related French institutional particularity is the unusual presidential "reserved domain" in foreign policy, defense and national security policy. Its wartime origin is its explanation if not necessarily an adequate justification.

The Fifth Republic's Constitution was drafted in the midst of the Algerian crisis, with France's earlier military disasters, those of 1940 and even 1914, still painful in the national consciousness. It was, so to speak, a "security constitution." In language that appears strange unless one can imagine the context, the Fifth Republic president is said to "be the guarantor of national independence, of the integrity of the territory," and also of the very "continuance of the State."

De Gaulle, of course, was supreme in matters of foreign policy, plus defense and security policy. During the Pompidou presidency, following de Gaulle's resignation in 1969, Prime Minister Jacques Chaban-Delmas conceptualized de Gaulle's de facto supremacy into a so-called reserved domain of presidential powers. In this handily hijacked domain, to which de Gaulle added institutional questions (the Constitution does say that presidential "arbitration" is to "ensure . . . the regular functioning of the governmental authorities"), the personal authority of the president is decisive.

For two decades the reserved domain was widely but wrongly assumed to be a constitutional fact. But it has no foundation in the Constitution's words. As it happened, in 1969 Prime Minister Chaban-Delmas, with his "new society" domestic program, gave this hostage to President Pompidou because he wanted to be completely in charge of domestic policy. But rivalry ensued between the president and the prime minister and Chaban-Delmas, after only two years, was asked by the president to leave. Yet the new concept of a presidential reserved domain in foreign and security affairs endured because it served a purpose, justifying what people wanted even though it was nowhere in the Constitution.

However, today the concept is increasingly challenged, for two sorts of reasons. First, in a cohabitation situation, the prime minister and the government, according to Article 20 of the Constitution, can legitimately claim all powers, including the reserved domain. Jacques Chirac rued having bowed to Mitterrand's use of the reserve domain in 1986–88 (Chirac in 1993 said he "had not been determined enough" with Mitterrand in the first cohabitation government). In the 1993 Cohabitation II, Prime Minister Balladur early on let it be known that President Mitterrand's role in these policy areas depended on his agreement with him, implicitly disputing the presumption of a reserved domain. Second, the presidential reserved domain powers are under attack because no contemporary government can neatly separate domestic policy and foreign policy. From agriculture to currency and exchange-rate problems, to trade protectionism and subsidies, foreign policy and domestic policy are increasingly linked. He who is empowered in domestic policy is necessarily also empowered in foreign affairs.

Military and geopolitical questions might be totally reserved for the president in theory, but in fact the Mitterrand–Balladur relationship in foreign and security policy sketched out in the first weeks of Cohabitation II seems an effective solution: Take no decisions in foreign policy where there is not presidential and prime ministerial agreement. This shows a degree of consensus and openness to left–right compromise unthinkable in the old France, but which in the "recentered Republic" is more and more evident.

As president, Georges Pompidou in a March 1972 press conference gave two requirements for a proper prime minister: His policies must correspond as closely as possible to those of the president and he must accept the institutions of the Fifth Republic, meaning the president's primacy in general policy and in important decisions. Beyond this, the reality of the "normal" presidential–prime ministerial tandem is all in the relationship between two leaders behind closed doors.[13]

The Nature and Future of "Cohabitation"

From one day to the next in the March 1986 parliamentary elections, the uniqueness of French institutions was made visible: The locus of power in the regime shifted away from the president, via the new parliamentary majority, to the conservative prime minister, Jacques Chirac, whom the Socialist president felt duty-bound to appoint.[14]

The powerful change was immediately felt as Chirac, rather than the president, chose his own government ministers. Chirac allowed Mitterrand only a limited veto regarding appointments to a few key ministries, for example in the suddenly questionable reserved presidential domain in foreign affairs and defense, where the president had a claim to continued control. This reversed the "normal" Fifth Republic tradition, in which the president managed cabinet appointments and the prime minister had only a limited bargaining power in favor of his own choices.

During the two-year cohabitation the "new" constitution was a parliamentary regime, almost completely so in domestic affairs and in most of the ongoing aspects of foreign affairs.[15] The major decisions in foreign, military and defense policy, in European integration negotiations, and in France's international political and economic relations, were either presidential decisions or became awkwardly reached Mitterrand–Chirac bargains.

Chirac had taken over the government budget, of course, but not for long enough to erode the president's reserved domain (which he respected in principle) from below through the power of the purse. For example, Chirac gave in to Mitterrand's decision to maintain French land missiles on the Albion Plateau even though this contradicted his own plan for mobile launchers.[16] And on several high policy matters, especially military decisions, the two leaders agreed or saw no alternatives. In 1986 there were three of these: the military withdrawal from Lebanon, as a consequence of the terrorist bombing of French and American troop barracks; the dispatch of a small military force to police a threatened coup in Togo; and, on the first day of cohabitation, the refusal of American overflight of French territory in the Reagan Administration's bombing raid on Libya to punish Muammar Qadaffi's terrorist activities. Mitterrand's surely was the key voice in all three decisions, even though, especially regarding the U.S. denial, Chirac was supposedly the neo-Gaullist. The refusal of overflight was extremely controversial, remembered bitterly by the Americans and by most NATO governments. But in foreign policy beyond these matters Prime Minister Chirac took control, as Article 20 of the Constitution seems to warrant. The presidential Elysée Palace, for example, was very thinly outfitted technically, and its small staff (including the president) had always relied on the prime minister's technical support operations at Matignon. To enforce the prime minister's new primacy, Chirac, at the beginning of cohabitation, simply cut the Elysée off from diplomatic cables, the basic information flow in foreign policy! Later on, Matignon shared information with the Elysée staff, but the president's vulnerability to a "technical coup d'état" by a cohabitation prime minister had been impressively demonstrated. (Soon Mitterrand had the Elysée Palace equipped to guarantee the president's information.) Furthermore Chirac, because he commanded the quai d'Orsay foreign ministry and thus the foreign policy bureaucracy in addition to Matignon, efficiently took over France's relations with other governments, except in a few areas of high policy or continuing negotiations in which he was obliged to deal with Mitterrand.

Some facets of cohabitation added a lighter note to this new and stressful constitutional situation. In particular, there were suddenly one too few "French" chairs at international tables, which created puzzling, sometimes comical protocol dilemmas. At a meeting of heads of government, would Mitterrand or Chirac represent France? When heads of government and foreign ministers met, would Chirac sit with his foreign minister, Jean-Bernard Raimond, or would Mitterrand? At the first G-7 meeting to face the French cohabitation regime, an additional chair was found. But another time Chirac gave way to the president, and yet another time the foreign minister, Raimond, was made to give up his place to the prime minister, so that Chirac could sit at the table alongside Mitterrand. Throughout these humiliating shenanigans, Mitterrand and Chirac both repeated solemnly and unconvincingly to the international press that "France speaks with a single voice." The initial G-7 meeting, held in Japan, was marked by especially hilarious episodes, with separate presidential and prime ministerial jets racing through the sky, desperate either to arrive, to take off or to arrive back in Paris before the other! Cohabitation thus embarrassed the French diplomatically, and this self-inflicted damage to France's international "prestige" had to amuse France's partners, who often paid the price of Gallic protocol.

However this may be, François Mitterrand deftly preserved or constructed a range of other presidential powers in those two years. For one thing, he was able to transform heretofore purely formal presidential prerogatives into real, if limited powers. The principal instance was an inventive use of the presidential countersignature, by which Mitterrand disrupted Chirac's plan for a quick, neoconservative, anti-Socialist legislative package. Chirac's legislative program—a justified anti-Socialist crusade or a policy of political revenge, depending on how one looked at it—had three main points: (1) privatization, to reverse the left's nationali- zations; (2) changing the electoral law back to majority voting, to reverse Mitterrand's proportional representation law for the just-held 1986 elec- tions; and (3) deregulation of working hours restrictions and enlarged legal conditions for laying off workers, to reverse parts of the Socialist "Auroux laws," which had expanded workers' guarantees and rights.

Chirac's hope was to impress French public opinion rapidly, to be seen as rolling back Mitterrand's socialism and turning France instead toward Reaganite and Thatcherite policies, which, because of temporarily boom- ing stock markets and growth rates, were in their halcyon period.

In spite of a strong majority, Chirac believed that if he went to Parlia- ment with his program the Socialists would load up on amendments or filibuster, thus weakening the political shock effect. So he moved to implement the above-cited policies with executive "ordinances," author- ized by Article 38 of the Constitution. Ordinances are a kind of govern- ment decree, decided and approved by the cabinet and signed by the prime minister. Article 13 of the Constitution says, ambiguously, that the president must also "sign" government decrees under Article 38. The ambiguity is to know whether the president signs automatically, merely as a guarantee of proper procedure by the cabinet, or whether the presi- dent's signature implies that he has a choice to make, whether to sign or not. And if he can choose not to sign, what happens then?

The potential use of this ambiguity of the Constitution's language as a real presidential prerogative had never been attempted before. But Mit- terrand now argued that Article 13 should be read as giving the president a choice of whether to sign or not. Chirac tried and failed to make Mitterrand concede that the president's signature was pro forma.[17]

Chirac, after all, was obliged to take his neoconservative, backlash legislation to Parliament.[18] In the National Assembly, the Socialists, now in opposition along with the "enemy brother" Communists, made sol- emn, not quite anachronistic speeches about the attitude of conservative "revenge" that historically followed every episode of left-wing govern- ment (until Mitterrand's second term).

The two years of cohabitation were also filled with partisan and personal jockeying for the 1988 presidential campaign. As is clear, François Mitterrand ended up well ahead of Jacques Chirac, illustrating the paradoxical logic of Fifth Republic cohabitation at the top: An insti- tutionally deflated president may prove to be electorally stronger than a suddenly dominant prime minister who looks like he is overusing his new powers. Mitterrand's care for both his own position and for a con- stantly stressful constitutional situation demonstrated political skill, a dignity of office, and a respect for the institutions of the state. This seemed especially so as he worked from a position of weakness (of course Mitterrand had had much experience in dealing from political weakness, beginning with his twenty-five years in the opposition and his devil's alliance with the Communist party). Cohabitation, contrary to what observers predicted, thus ended by enhancing Mitterrand's stature and his prospects for reelection in 1988. More than ever, French public opinion regarded him as a statesman and, in the Constitution's term, an "arbiter" in French political life. On the other hand, Chirac's constant attempts, which he thought necessary, to aggrandize himself and the prime minister's institutional control, intensified a perception of him as an "agitated" manipulator. Ten years earlier, when he suffered as Giscard's prime minister, people ironically had sympathized with his resignation from office in protest of Giscard's smothering authority.

Finally, in all the Cohabitation I struggles, Jacques Chirac undoubtedly gave substantial consideration to his own desire to be president one day. He would be careful not to destroy the prize he wanted one day to win, a Gaullist presidential office.

Cohabitation, all in all, showed that the Fifth Republic's institutions were flexible, and that their very ambiguity, as Georges Pompidou first argued, could be a source of strength in French politics even if such lack of clarity would be damaging in other ways. Cohabitation demonstrated that parliamentary government can indeed issue from the words in the constitutional text, even as modified by direct election of the president. Following the alternation from conservatives to the left in 1981, cohabitation tested one further institutional trope. In the "recentered" French Republic the possibilities of power sharing and government coalition are not yet exhausted.

In fact, the 1986–88 cohabitation showed more that this, that what had been constitutionally usual was not necessarily "normal," and what had been "normal" would not necessarily be usual in the future.

The whole issue of the future of cohabitation was reopened in 1993, with the election of a strong conservative majority to face President Mitterrand in his last two years in office. In preelectoral preparation for Cohabitation II, the conservatives vowed to be tougher, less pliant with Mitterrand than the Chirac government had been in Cohabitation I. Yet Edouard Balladur, Chirac's finance minister in 1986, in his first weeks as prime minister demonstrated little desire for direct confrontation with the president. The new conservative government's innovations—a selective, nonideological privatization of state-owned companies, and an ideological toughening on illegal immigration—couldn't hide the fact that the sluggish, recession-bound French economy, unemployment, and maintaining the agenda of European integration were the main problems. The Balladur government had little financial freedom. The major innovation in 1993 was thus budget cutting and raising money through a government bond issue, the "Balladur bond," and through privatizations, selling off state-owned companies.

Besides this, Balladur, with a much less aggressive temperament than Jacques Chirac, vowed to respect the Constitution "both in its letter and its spirit." In the first foreign sortie of the Cohabitation II partners—a Franco–German summit in early June 1993—Balladur allowed President Mitterrand to precede him and to do the business of the head of state alone. The prime minister then arrived for the substantive policy discussions, and the final press conference with Chancellor Helmut Kohl was conducted with three chairs. Yet if Balladur was clearly more courteous toward Mitterrand than had been Chirac, to some extent this was permitted only because the prime minister's policy preeminence was now unquestioned. Mitterrand was clearly accepting what he could not prevent.

Beyond the anecdotal aspects, the main conclusion of this analysis is to observe that continuing evolution of the party system (see the next chapter) conceivably could make cohabitation the norm in French government, or at least not more unusual than the situation of a Gaullist-type president resting his unchallengeable authority on a complicit parliamentary majority. This prospect is frankly worrisome in two ways: Either a parade of internally divided power sharing cohabitations could produce a new form of weak "stalemate" government, or a pattern of confrontational power sharing alternating with unchallenged Gaullist-style presidents could produce a destabilized institutional logic, careening in one election to another from one "system" to another. Like de Gaulle's charismatic leadership, cohabitation, an ingenious means of negotiating a dangerous passage in French institutional development, might become a dire threat to French politics—both despite and because of having first rescued it.

A saving grace, on the other hand, could conceivably be the consensus-making consequences of "the end of French exceptionalism" and the current disrepute of dogmatic ideology—that is, it is possible to envisage a "normalized" party system in which cohabitation of different political tendencies in the executive and legislative branches would mean no greater divergence of policy and purpose than in other consensus-dominant political systems in which control of the presidency and of the legislative branch (as in the United States) often resides in opposing parties. The Gaullist republic would then have entered its "postcohabitation" phase, in which the planned excesses of the Gaullist institutions would have been defanged, or rendered unnecessary, by the evolution of French parties and the French political culture.

Nevertheless, the dangers of cohabitation—the peculiar French form of power sharing created by the combination of a Gaullist constitution and French parties—are very real and very visible. The fact that cohabitation has thus far been more of a solution than a problem is not a permanent insurance policy for French government. The telos of French political development has not yet entirely pushed the nation beyond old demons and old nightmares. Yet just as for France's neighbors, Europeanization can in certain ways be both a curative purpose and a safeguard. Perhaps France's "responsibilities to Europe," as de Gaulle might have said, are the "great endeavor" whose pursuit will prevent cohabitation from turning into either "mediocrity" or some new "leap into the abyss."

The Condition of Parliament in the Fifth Republic

Beginning with an understanding of the "blocked vote" and Article 49.3, the French National Assembly's weak institutional clout and mediocre reputation during the Fifth Republic's first quarter of a century comes as no surprise. De Gaulle's intention in 1958 was nothing less than to extinguish the "games, poisons and delights" of the French parliamentary culture of the Palais Bourbon, the famous "house without windows" standing impressively—blindly—at the Pont de la Concorde's left bank.

First of all, de Gaulle and his advisors believed that changing the electoral law to majority voting would, over the long term, have a bipolarizing effect on the incoherent coalitions of the various and splintered Fourth Republic parties. And putting the president institutionally "above the parties," in effective control of the executive was another lever of change. The necessary corollary was to make Parliament as a whole the servant of the executive rather than its master. Parliament, to the Gaullists, was the habitat of irresponsibility, the center of partisan egotism, what de Gaulle called a "cracked mirror" representation of society. Parliament and the party system did not represent the people, but rather used politics for their own ends and interests.

Nevertheless every president has acknowledged the unjustifiably low standing of Parliament. Most recently, President Mitterrand, in announcing in November 1991 his intention to reform the nation's political institutions, recognized that, "despite my best efforts," the French Parliament remains "suffocated." Thus, parliamentary reforms were part of the series of constitutional changes he soon proposed to a constitutional committee (see below).

The Senate

The French Senate is the extreme example of this. In theory a partner in legislation, it bears no resemblance to the German Bundesrat or the U.S. Senate. It receives all legislation passed by the Assembly, but, similar to the British House of Lords, it can only amend or delay legislation. Most important, in the case of Senate–National Assembly disagreement, the government, under Article 45, appoints a reconciliation committee. Failure here allows the government to take the bill back to the Assembly for final passage, in the original Assembly version, or as amended by the Senate.

Only in the case of constitutional amendment can the Senate impose a veto. Under the two different procedures for amending the Constitution provided in Article 89, either a simple majority in the Senate and House is necessary if the president intends to submit the proposal subsequently to popular referendum, or a three-fifths majority if the president has called the Assembly and Senate together "in Congress" (a joint session), which doesn't require a subsequent referendum.

The Senate's most controversial moment came in 1962, when its speaker Gaston Monnerville, a distinguished Radical (i.e., centrist) politician from Martinique, resisted de Gaulle's referendum on direct election of the president because it was being presented unconstitutionally. The procedure was clearly unconstitutional since de Gaulle went straight to a popular referendum on the proposal, bypassing the Constitution's requirement of simple Assembly and Senate majorities on identical versions. Monnerville took the case then to the new Constitutional Council, which decided—showing how far the Council was from true judicial review—that "once the people have spoken in a referendum" the Constitutional Council has no competence to rule in the matter! This decision survived because 1962 was still a time of crisis, and because it was, once again, "a matter of de Gaulle."

President Mitterrand has had some trouble with the recent Senate. Its indirect mode of election makes it a strongly rural and conservative body. As opposed to the lower house, its partisan coloring has been traditionally more centrist than bipolar, which naturally means a practical conservatism. The Senate's progressive stands have usually come in defense of civil and political liberties ("republican liberties") or in defense of Parliament against Gaullist, neo-Fascist or Communist attacks on the institution. The conservative Senate was thus actually against the union of the left government policies, though powerless (see just above) to stop the Mauroy government's bills. On the other hand, the Senate was able to derail President Mitterrand's 1984 proposed referendum on expanding the constitutionally permissible subjects for referenda, and it had a part in defeating another constitutional idea to which Mitterrand has just returned: that access to the Constitutional Court should be open to citizens, not restricted to only the president, the speakers of the houses or a group of sixty deputies (see below).

The Senate in the Third Republic had been extremely powerful. It had an absolute veto in legislation, it could censure a government, and it was a hotbed of aspiring cabinet ministers and premiers. The Third Republic Senate took full part in the "games, poisons and delights" of the old parliamentary republic. When the party leaders wrote the Fourth Republic's Constitution in 1946, one concession to the bitter memories of interwar politics had been to reduce the Senate to a "Council of the Republic" and to give it only a delaying veto. Less responsible for the Fourth Republic's debacle, the upper house created for the Fifth Republic was thus given some minor new powers as compared with the Fourth Republic Council and, above all, a term of office extended from six to nine years. De Gaulle and Michel Debré expected the Fifth Republic Senate to be both grateful and conservative. To the contrary the Senate's conservatism—linked to agricultural, provincial and economically un-competitive regions of the country—was not Gaullist. De Gaulle's emphasis on industrial modernization, technological advance, the need for competitiveness, as well as his acceptance of the Common Market, put him at odds with the Senate. Not surprisingly, the Senate was much more sympathetic to Giscard, whose Independent Republican aristocratic–"peasant" origins seemed congenial.

In any case, as William Safran says, "Because de Gaulle could not dissolve the Senate, he attempted to neutralize it by reforming it out of existence." In the fatal April 1969 referendum, whose defeat brought the resignation General de Gaulle had threatened, the proposition was double: (1) a plan for political dismemberment of the Senate and (2) greater autonomy for France's regions.[19] The French Senate survived de Gaulle, but without finding any consistently influential and productive legislative role. The epitome of Senate irrelevance occurs when Article 49.3 is invoked, especially in voting the government's budget. Then the only pertinent question is whether the National Assembly votes censure of the government. If not, the bill is "considered as adopted" and the Senate's role is reduced to nothing.

The National Assembly

The National Assembly, called the Chamber of Deputies in the Third Republic, historically embodied popular sovereignty ripped away from the monarchy in the Revolution. British constitutional doctrine is, by contrast, built on the sovereignty of Parliament as such, whereas in French constitutional doctrine, the people are sovereign through their representatives in Parliament. Slightly different doctrines, but a similar result: Every law of Parliament is, in theory, of constitutional status. "Since only Parliament can enact a law, only another act of Parliament can rescind it."[20] This constitutional conception explains why the idea of judicial review until very recently found so little hospitality in France. In 1958, the new Constitution's aim was announced as the creation of a "true" parliamentary regime, one that would correct the weakness and abuses of the despised *régime des partis*. Michel Debré, the main drafter of the Fifth Republic constitutional document, took Britain as a model of proper government–parliament balance, though it seems the French didn't see how much the English system depended on party discipline. The Gaullists expected neither coherent majorities nor party discipline, except, of course, from the Communists with their "democratic central-ism." They therefore wrote a series of special rules, which not merely disciplined Parliament but enabled the "elective monarchy" to overawe it.

At the time the most controversial of these was Article 16, a classic "emergency powers" clause that allows the president, basically on his own decision, to rule by decree. Resembling similar articles in the Weimar and other constitutions that had permitted fascist takeovers, Article 16 seriously worried many politicians, who already were anxious about General de Gaulle's alleged authoritarian intentions. But remember the context: the Algerian crisis, with its danger of a military coup or civil war; the Cold War with its menace of land war or nuclear war in Europe.

The years 1958–62 indeed saw permanent crisis in Algeria. De Gaulle, between February 1960 and October 1961, did govern with extraordinary powers, first under Article 38 (Parliament giving the government authority to rule by ordinance), then, from April until October 1961, under Article 16. Article 16 has only been used this once.

But other constraints on the Assembly's work, all of which were still in effect in 1993, are glaring affronts to representative democratic procedure. First, the Parliament has little time. It meets twice a year for three-month sessions, very little compared to other democratic legislatures. Budget discussions in particular are time-constrained. The Assembly has only forty days for its first reading of the budget, and Article 48 allows the government to give priority to its own bills over those introduced by others. Thus the government rules the agenda of Parliament.

Another diminution of Parliament's role is a controversial constitutional distinction established between the "domain of law" (Article 34), within whose limits Parliament can legislate, and "rule making," the realm of government decrees (Article 37). A certain number of fields are set out

Rather than the other way around

for parliamentary legislation. The list is considerable, notwithstanding the fact that the very idea of limiting legislative competence in this way is unusual in a democracy. Moreover, laws passed by Parliament are usually "framework laws" *(loi cadre)*; the necessary "rules" for implementing framework laws are part of the government's rule-making responsibility under Article 37. (One is reminded of Stalin's sardonic dictum that what is *implemented* is the real decision, not what is decided.) Furthermore, any areas of rule making not expressly stipulated in Article 34's domain-of-law list are given over, ipso facto, to the administrative authority of the government. Article 37 says laconically, "Matters other than those that fall within the domain of law shall be subject to rule-making." Moreover, Article 38 authorizes the Parliament, if "asked" by the government, to give up its legislative power for a temporary period to the government. The necessary "enabling law" then permits the government to issue ordinances in domain-of-law areas normally reserved to a compliant Parliament!

Yet another Fifth Republic innovation, Article 40, neuters Parliament with regard to the power of the purse. *Deputies cannot propose legislation involving money!* "Bills and amendments introduced by members of Parliament shall not be considered when their adoption would have as a consequence either a diminution of public revenues, or the creation or increase of public expenditures." Strange but true.

The so-called blocked vote procedure completed the Gaullist Constitution's ligature of Parliament. Article 44 authorizes the government simply to refuse all amendments it doesn't like. In a blocked vote, the deputies are obliged to vote on a bill in exactly the form the government wishes, meaning, if the government so wishes, as originally introduced, without amendment. *The government can simply nullify parliamentary debate!* Even if used only moderately, the blocked vote is an outrage to the concept of parliamentary representative democracy. It can only be understood, not explained away. But as shown just below, today it is no longer even the major abuse of Parliament's normal role.

The blocked vote was most used, unsurprisingly, during the early years of de Gaulle's presidency. This was due less to his "authoritarianism" than to the facts of an unstable, dangerous situation and the requirements of rebuilding the state and constructing the new regime. Altogether the blocked vote was used 246 times in the first 20 years of the Fifth Republic to 1978. It was resorted to 28 times by the government of Raymond Barre, 1976–81, as a device to discipline his and President Giscard d'Estaing's difficult ally, Chirac's Rally for the Republic (RPR). Chirac, as noted already, had been Giscard's prime minister during 1974–76 and had resigned in bitterness.

In any case, during the 1980s the blocked vote, though sometimes still used, has been replaced as a government weapon by a different, even more stifling rule: Article 49.3 or, as the opposition says, "Government by Article 49.3." This rule permits a minority government to legislate even when it can't muster the odd votes to pass its bill.

The blocked vote is essentially a weapon by which a government can discipline its own majority in Parliament. The blocked vote wouldn't be needed if the government's majority controlled amendments to legislation. That is, whatever the minority proposes, so long as the majority votes in a disciplined fashion minority amendments and legislative proposals will lose all the time. So the blocked vote is a weapon to nullify dissent within the parliamentary majority, either in the junior partner party or within the party which is "the majority of the majority."

Article 49.3, an even more powerful weapon than the blocked vote, is a method of passing legislation without a positive majority. When it is invoked, it stipulates that government legislation, however important or insignificant, "is considered as adopted" *unless a motion of censure is introduced and successfully passed.* Article 49.3 is thus the favorite child of minority governments, meaning the several Socialist minority governments 1988–93. It has also been used occasionally as a precaution by conservative multiparty majority governments and even, as a few times in 1981–86, when the Socialist party alone had an absolute majority, if, on a specific bill or budget, the Communist "allies" or significant numbers of its own party intended to refuse to vote for the government's bill. In these cases the government appears suddenly to place itself "above the parties," and is in effect marking itself off from its political base in Parliament, which can become dangerous.

Before 1979, Article 49.3 had been used but six times. The Socialist governments used it a still rather modest eleven times in 1981–86, preferring the blocked vote when they needed help in getting their way. The Chirac cohabitation government used it several times in the two years 1986–88, while the Rocard minority government—the first minority government—had recourse to it sixteen times in 1989 alone, including using it to pass the government's budget. The Cresson government appointed in May 1991 did the same, getting its budget adopted not by a parliamentary vote on the budget, but because, having invoked Article 49.3, the thirteenth motion of "no confidence" since 1988 failed to get a majority. It had 264 votes when 289 would have forced the Cresson government to resign. The margin was that the Communist party abstained instead of voting against the Socialist government, whose budget it nevertheless rejected.

A neo-Gaullist leader, Bernard Pons, said to the prime minister during the debate, "Do you believe that, in a democracy, a government can long administer the country's business without having the confidence of the people and its representatives?" Arguing that the prime minister was governing with "a certain illegitimacy," Pons ironically quoted former deputy François Mitterrand's identical reproach of Prime Minister Pompidou during de Gaulle's presidency: "You have the duty·to obtain [the Assembly's] confidence!"[21]

Is there nothing to be said in favor of the blocked vote and Article 49.3? In a larger frame, are such measures completely undemocratic? The answer is a bit more complex than a simple yes. These sorts of rules do create a kind of stability and efficiency in lawmaking. They can limit weak government of the Fourth and Third Republic kind. Representative government is by definition a matter of governing as well as of representation. Democracy means conjoining the two, which are simultaneously both means and ends. The institutional issue is, in other words, a matter of striking a good balance among means and among ends, as well as between means and ends. There is no single correct solution, and therefore if the blocked vote and Article 49.3 are revised or fade away as the Fifth Republic continues to mature, they will be rightly seen as having served a useful purpose in their time, at least to the extent that their usefulness outweighed the harm they did.

Article 49.3 was, as said above, intended as a government's weapon to deal with a lack of a parliamentary majority; the 1958 Constitution writers supposed that French parliamentary politics would not change on this score. But 49.3 had two different modes of employment. For three decades it was a means for majority governments to discipline the troops by forcing resisters to contemplate overturning their own government. Then under the Socialist governments 1988–93, Article 49.3 became a means for minority government survival given opposition parties with a theoretical majority but in reality too divided, thanks to the Communist "problem," to form a replacement government. Socialist minority governments survived because the conservatives, taken alone, were short of a majority and the Communists wanted neither to ally with the conservatives, obviously, nor see the Socialists overthrown. In the latter case, they would have to face their shrinking electorate again, with the surplus handicap of being responsible for ousting a left-wing government.

Nevertheless, in this precarious situation the Communist party did keep a bit of leverage over the Socialists. It could threaten and sometimes actually vote for a conservative motion of censure instead of abstaining. After the 1988 Assembly was elected without a majority, the Communists in fact voted twice for a conservative motion of censure against the Socialists. The first time, in November 1990, involved the Rocard government's bill creating the generalized social contribution (CSG), a tax to finance social policies. Censure of the Socialist government was defeated by a mere five votes. In the second episode, in early June 1992, the PCF supported a conservative motion of censure facing the Bérégovoy government's bill accepting a reform of the EC's Common Agricultural Policy (CAP), the difficult issue that threatened to sabotage the Uruguay Round GATT talks. Communist speakers criticized "the capitulation of the [Europeans], faced with an American diktat," and demanded that President Mitterrand use "France's right of veto" in EC votes. The total vote in favor of censure—the Communists combined with the three conservative opposition groups—was unexpectedly close. The Bérégovoy government escaped by only *two* votes, the narrowest margin in the history of the Fifth Republic since the government of Georges Pompidou was ousted in 1962 (the only time a government has actually been voted out).

Yet the other side of the coin was that Socialist minority governments continued to survive with independent votes from conservative ranks, particularly among centrists, often including Giscard's prime minister, Raymond Barre. And, according to *Le Monde*'s reporting of the above incident, Jacques Barrot, leader of the Union for French Democracy (UDF), had used proxy votes to make certain a majority against the government would *not* be achieved, while the Communist Assembly group leader, André Lajoinie, had privately told Prime Minister Bérégovoy that the Communists were voting in favor of censure "in order to defend French farmers," but only in the knowledge that the government would not fall![22]

The large parliamentary majority of the new Balladur government in March 1993 transforms the government's position of being at the mercy of deputies and groups. But the unprecedented size of the majority—484 out of 577 seats—produces the opposite extreme, a government too strong in relation to Parliament unless the conservative parties, the RPR and the UDF, have a falling out. With 288 votes necessary for a majority, the UDF's 213 seats mean that it could threaten to bring down the RPR-led government.

And it is no longer merely arithmetic to say that a center–right, center–left, UDF–Socialist coalition is conceivable. One or perhaps two more electoral cycles may be required to clear the field for a party realignment, and the Socialist party (PS), needless to say, has to rebuild itself after its rout in 1993. The main cleavage in French politics would no longer be the old left–right division but a conflict between European and nationalist orientations, with a center grouping facing the anti-European part of the neo-Gaullists on one side and anti-EC Communists and Ecologists on the other side.

In the meantime, in any case, the National Assembly retains many of its peculiarities, most unfortunately its supine position vis-à-vis the Fifth Republic's overweening executive power.

Useful parliamentary investigating committees—if the French Parliament had them—would be one counterweight, and an effective means of making the executive branch accountable. But the Gaullist founding purposely gave Parliament only six standing committees in each house, as opposed to 19 in the Fourth Republic's National Assembly. With between 60 and 120 deputies each, the standing committees became, as the Gaullists intended, oratorical societies with huge memberships and little influence. Working groups in the committees have, to some extent, emerged as a quasi-committee system, but overall the government still manhandles Parliament's agenda and its working structure.

For three decades investigating committees were infrequent and passive, a seemingly natural feature of the parliamentary "house without windows." The French way of doing things was, when some special inquiry was wanted by the government, to create an ad hoc *comité des sages* (committee of "wise men") or blue-ribbon commission to conduct a study and present a report. This sort of commission, named by the executive branch, has no relationship to Parliament. Two typical examples have been the committee on problems of nationality and citizenship (discussed in Chapter 7) and the special commission to investigate the Greenpeace affair.[23] While a blue-ribbon commission is not, simply by virtue of being named by the executive branch, its instrument, only infrequently and recently have these commissions begun to demonstrate the genuine nonpartisan independence their prestige would imply.

Likewise only recently, as French ways of doing things have been scrutinized on the basis of European Community partner examples and on the example of U.S. congressional committee hearings brought to France through CNN World Television news, have French parliamentary investigating committees begun to have teeth, if not yet much bite. World television news coverage of U.S. congressional confirmation hearings, of cabinet appointments of the administration and of U.S. Supreme Court justices (especially the Robert Bork and Clarence Thomas hearings), have had a real "demonstration effect," though hard to measure empirically, within the French political class.

It was a quaint but unacceptable leftover from earlier times that, until 1991, French parliamentary committees of investigation were obligated by law to meet in closed session. Journalists were even forbidden to publish any information they might pick up unintentionally! A 1991 investigation of party finances was the first held in public session, according to a laudable reform of Assembly procedures. Witnesses, including all the party treasurers, were predictably close-mouthed, but the opportunity for publicity attracted the demagogue Jean-Marie Le Pen. He attempted to be called to testify in place of the National Front treasurer, instead being ousted from the session, in full view of the television cameras. The main conclusion of the commission was no surprise—that the campaign finance reform laws of 1988 and 1990 had not closed down the "hidden methods" of party fund raising. Furthermore the commission on campaign financing was limited by another long-standing rule, that investigating commissions must stay away from any issues that imply possible criminal prosecution, because, in the rigid French division of jurisdictions, that would be police and judicial business.[24] Nevertheless, an old taboo had been lifted by this first parliamentary investigation into the delicate subject of party finance.

The European Parliament and French Parliamentary Life

The European Parliament (EP) is the official parliamentary body of the European Community, though the EC's various councils of ministers are its actual legislating organs. The EP is connected to French political life, roughly speaking, in three ways.

First, until 1979 EP deputies were elected indirectly, by national methods in the different countries, for five-year terms. Since 1979, the French and all Community peoples vote in direct national elections for European parliamentary deputies. Contested by political parties much like national elections, the stakes are intrinsically lower (power is not at stake) and so is the level of participation. It has declined from about 60 percent to about 50 percent in the three elections in 1979, 1984, and 1989. In spite of this, the change in 1979 to direct, popular election of deputies has fostered legitimacy. The European Parliament, while not really loved, is no longer disdained. It has become an accepted, if mainly invisible structure in the average French person's mental political landscape. Certainly if given greater authority and powers the EP could become more significant to the average French citizen.

Second, for political parties the European Parliament has to varying degrees become an extension of national political life. Parties and states, for example, are known by whether they send strong or weak delegations. In the first case, it is a desire that the parliamentary aspect of European integration strengthen. In the second case, parties and governments neither expect nor want very much from the EP. As opposed to the German parties, or the former Italian Communist party (now the Party of the Democratic Left), which usually have sent high-quality delegations, French political parties, albeit with exceptions, have not sent their best or fastest-rising people to Strasbourg, the EP's home. Strasbourg is "out of the loop" and out of public visibility, sometimes a "political parking lot" or "honorable exit" for out-of-favor or over-the-hill politicians. There are notable exceptions, but few.

The third juncture of the European Parliament and French politics derives from the growing influence of EC rules on national legislation.

EP deputies will gain in domestic influence insofar as they become the best experts on increasingly significant Community affairs, and insofar as lobbies seek to influence them because EC, not national, laws are at stake. Still for the coming years, the most important effect of the European Parliament on national politics will be the influence European deputies can have inside their own national parties. If integration thickens and the European Parliament gains in stature, French national politicians, and through them French public opinion, will pay the Parliament more mind.

In negotiating Maastricht, the institutionally Gaullist French resisted the Germans, Dutch and others who wanted a quick, sharp boost in the EP's powers (see Chapter 9). But in the long run a balanced, decentralized, democratized European Union requires a stronger Parliament. French policy is likely gradually to accept more powers for the EP, which, after all, now has some parallel with Mitterrand's modest proposals, at the end of 1992, to strengthen Parliament's rights in the French system.

Judicial Review: France Changes, but Slowly

In France and England the idea of a supreme court with ultimate authority to determine constitutionality did not fit, as noted above, with the doctrine that Parliament was sovereign. But though its acts were vaguely sovereign in principle, the old Chamber of Deputies, unlike the House of Commons, didn't even believe in itself. So the French system had no high judicial review or supreme court, although the Council of State (see below) did, for example, decide conflicts of administrative jurisdiction among the branches of government.

Today the movement toward judicial review, encased in the growing authority of the Fifth Republic's innovative Constitutional Council, provides another example of French evolution toward international norms. French government remains parliamentary to the extent that the National Assembly can overthrow the government by a vote of censure. However, in other ways, first the Gaullist presidency and now the growth of judicial review, the Fifth Republic is moving away from, or joining an evolution of classic European parliamentarism. One could see the American presidency and the U.S. Supreme Court as "models" for France, but that is not exactly right. Great differences in the presidential offices, including their origins and intents, are quite evident. And with regard to judicial review the German Constitutional Court is a nearby example of how a strong supreme court can be added to a European parliamentary regime. (But of course the German high court, though anchored in a parliamentary system, does owe much to the U.S. Supreme Court's example.)

In the 1958 Constitution, the Constitutional Council was "conceived as not more than an auxiliary institution, indeed a helpmate of the executive in its efforts to police parliamentary behavior." But in the past two decades "the Council has assumed in its practice the role of a constitutional court."[25] In 1958 it was specifically intended *not* to create judicial review. The court's purpose was to be an advisory board on constitutionality, and, in the first years when the Gaullists were worried about being able to control the ex–Fourth Republic Parliament, this meant mainly protecting the executive against Parliament's attempts to get control of its own proceedings or to challenge the vast area of policy that the executive controlled by decrees and ordinances—that is, it meant mainly to enforce the new limits on Parliament written into the Gaullist constitution.

Predictably the Constitutional Council's membership was highly partisan. Its nine members were chosen, three each, by the president of the Republic and the presidents of the two houses of Parliament. This gave six Gaullist members a permanent majority against the three chosen by the anti-Gaullist president of the Senate, Gaston Monnerville. And only those three officials, plus the prime minister, could bring cases to the Constitutional Council! Until recently, most members of the Council even lacked legal training or experience. So the court was not even ready in its personnel to move toward judicial review. In the past decade appointees usually have had legal backgrounds, some distinguished, though genuine judicial specializations or extensive experience with constitutional law problems is still rare.

The trend toward judicial review began with a landmark decision in 1971, when the Council declared unconstitutional part of a tough bill amending the famous, liberal 1901 law on associations. Drafted in the wake of the May 1968 strikes and demonstrations, this section, as opposed to the simple 1901 registration procedure, would have allowed prefects to deny legal registration to an organization that they esteemed *likely* to act illegally. The Council's decision saw in this registration a kind of prior restraint, thus a basic violation of freedom of association, not only with respect to the 1901 law but also by virtue of liberal principles recognized in the preamble of the 1958 Constitution, which itself affirmed the preamble to the 1946 Constitution, including its extensive Bill of Rights. "For introducing judicial review in defense of civil liberties, the decision had been greeted by some as the French equivalent of *Marbury vs. Madison*."[26]

A notable difference from American practice is that the Constitutional Court deals with legislation under consideration, not with cases that come up through lower courts challenging established laws. This case arose after the bill had been passed by a majority in the Assembly, but not yet in the Senate. The operative rule of the Constitution states (Article 62) that any provision declared unconstitutional by the Court "may not be promulgated or implemented."

In 1974, President Giscard d'Estaing sponsored a liberal change in access, allowing, in addition to the four high officials, any group of sixty deputies or senators to bring cases to the Constitutional Court. This liberal reform in effect ensured the main opposition party, whichever it might be, access to constitutional adjudication.

At first there was a definitely partisan, but nonetheless parsimonious usage of the new procedure; forty-seven cases were brought between 1974 and 1981, mainly by the left-wing parties. Not quite one fourth of the bills in question were found to have unconstitutional characteristics, and the issues were important. The first was a test of the new law legalizing abortions; the others most often dealt with civil rights issues: "police search of automobiles, employment in private schools, union rights in the shop, and equality before the tax laws. Other decisions were concerned with conflicts between national statutes and international law."[27]

In the political "alternations" in power of 1981 and 1986, the court became a victim of partisan politics in a new way. As a means of obstructionism, both the conservative opposition in the 1981 Parliament and the Socialist opposition in the 1986 cohabitation Parliament began to refer all important bills to the Council. Only a few Council decisions declared the totality of a bill unconstitutional. Most often a Council decision fixed on specific parts and statutes, which, given the moment of intervention, became an instruction to rewrite the legislation so as to conform to the Constitution. In the early cohabitation period when President Mitterrand was trying to slow down Chirac, the Socialist party's use of this weapon, invented by the conservatives five years earlier against the union of the left program, led conservatives to charge that France was becoming a "government of judges," a victim of judicial activism. Of course they didn't mention their own use of the Council to harass "socialism" in 1981!

President Mitterrand's 1993 proposal to give individual citizens access to the Council seems designed to move France more quickly toward a genuine supreme court and international norms of judicial review. His earlier appointment of Robert Badinter as president of the Council was a sign of that intention. Badinter is a genuine legal scholar who had considerable experience as a trial lawyer on civil liberties issues before being named Mitterrand's Minister of Justice. (It is noteworthy that Mitterrand himself was a practicing lawyer early in his career, and that his best-regarded book—*Le Coup d'état permanent*—his polemical attack on the de

Gaulle republic for the 1965 presidential election, was built on constitutional arguments.) Despite all this, in its jurisdiction and methods of operation, and its judges and method of appointment, the French Constitutional Council's place in the system is still far from the German Constitutional Court or the United States Supreme Court.

The second high court, the Council of State, has a much longer pedigree (1799) and a much clearer role in the French system. First, it is a court to settle disagreements about jurisdiction among branches of the administration. Second, in its judicial role, the Council of State is a court for individual citizens to bring claims against the state administrations. And in this area, the Council of State long ago achieved a well-merited reputation for undoing arbitrary state actions against citizens.

The problem for individuals is that, even once given justice, enforcement is often the duty of the very administration that has been found in the wrong. Perhaps one third of these findings remain unenforced, especially faulty being the Ministry of Finance's noncompliance with tax decisions favorable to the taxpayer.

In the development of French constitutionalism, the Council of State's role as an institutionalized constitutional advisor in government legislation has recently grown significantly. According to a long-standing practice, all government decrees and regulations pass before the Council prior to implementation. In the past decade, in reaction to the parliamentary opposition's use of the Constitutional Council to challenge proposed laws, successive governments have adopted the habit of vetting all bills through the Council of State for an advisory opinion on constitutionality. The Council of State's role is not binding, as opposed to the Constitutional Council, but its prestige, competence and experience mean that its recommendations are almost never ignored.

Decentralization: A Socialist or a French Success?

Centralization of power has characterized most remakings of the French state from Louis XIV through de Gaulle's creation of the republican monarchy "synthesis" in 1958–62. The nineteenth-century historian Jules Michelet, for example, praised the Bourbon centralization of power as "a great historic undertaking" and a "great achievement"; the state propelled France, de Gaulle would write later, into the "first rank" of the nations.

Tocqueville, however, was of two minds about centralization. On the one hand he recognized its effectiveness as a political instrument of government but it was, more important, also a danger to liberty. *The Old Regime and the Revolution* performed the formidable intellectual and political service of showing that the despised Bourbon monarchy was succeeded, not by the Revolution's promised regime of "liberty, equality and fraternity," but by a Napoleonic democratic despotism whose centralized power *exceeded* in scope and intensity the absolute monarchy.

Napoleon replaced the Old Regime's *intendants* with the system of prefects and he redrew the administrative map of France to weaken the people's attachment to France's historic regions in order to better settle authority in the new *départements*. Along with the power of the prefects, appointed from the center of authority in Paris, the central state bureaucracies—above all the omniscient ministries of finance and interior—became the architecture of state authority during the 150 years of oscillation from one regime to another. For liberals, reform of the Napoleonic state became a permanent political cause, a measure of the attempt to create a genuine civil society in France, to close the gap that had been created between the citizen and the state. Even during the liberal Third and Fourth Republics, focused in Parliament rather than in the executive branch, power remained centralized in Paris and administrated by the central state bureaucracy. The difference—quite significant—was that there was less government power in society, less state control of individuals. Yet centralization remained the French way.

François Mitterrand, and the majority element of Socialist political culture, were part of the liberal bloc that hoped, from the Fourth to the Fifth Republic, to reform the Napoleonic state. Once elected in 1981, Mitterrand made the plan for a thorough decentralization of France's administrative institutions a high priority. One sign of his commitment was to put Gaston Defferre, longtime mayor of Marseilles and a Socialist party political heavyweight, in charge of getting the reform done. Socialist prime minister Pierre Mauroy, the longtime mayor of Lille and thus a longtime advocate of local power, also lobbied hard to get this change accomplished. Mitterrand and Mauroy even said later that decentralization, and not the program of nationalizations, was *la grande affaire*, the most important issue and success of Mitterrand's first term.

Was decentralization, however, really a "socialist" success? In a sense, the answer is yes. But did not decentralization fit badly with the Socialists' policy of nationalizations in industry and banking, of state control of the economy? Certainly so. But the matter is not so simple as merely to notice a "contradiction." Socialist party doctrine since the refounding Epinay congress of 1971 had espoused *both* nationalizations and *autogestion*, meaning self-managed socialism. The concept of autogestion was a party innovation that simultaneously gave the Socialists a doctrinal identity of their own and provided a weapon in their struggle in this period with the French Communist party's Leninist–Stalinist economic and political ideas.[28]

For the Socialists, decentralization was thus a double good: on the one hand, a classic French struggle, endorsed by all republicans, to liberalize the state; on the other hand, a Socialist battle against Leninism and Stalinism inside the French left. Decentralization would simultaneously undo the excessive French centralization of state power and impose their own Socialist conception on the Communists.

That said, in the long run the Socialists' large decentralization reform will be noted by historians as more a victory over Napoleon than Stalin. By giving the power of the prefects to the presidents of departmental and regional councils, and by allowing local governments to raise revenue through local taxes, the decentralization reform, according to one writer

> has not so much created local self-government as it has transferred admin-
> istrative responsibilities. . . . Thus the "democratization" in this reform lies
> essentially in the efficiency of having services provided at a level less re-
> mote from the people than the central government.[29]

The fact that this rapid reform succeeded so decisively indicates that it was an idea whose time had come, one Socialist change the conservatives do not even talk of undoing.[30] And the fact that decentralization has been a success, while the nationalizations and autogestion have not, seems to indicate that the French left in the Mitterrand era succeeded excellently at what was French in their program, above all in rallying and reforming the republic, but only poorly in what was Socialist.

Decentralization of the French state is a policy line whose course is far from run out. What has so far been done partially rebalances the French national domestic center and periphery. It also begins a preparation for France genuinely to accept a "Europe of the regions," whatever that will mean, sometime in the next century.

Mitterrand's Constitutional Reforms

Despite the emergency circumstances of its birth, the Fifth Republic survived. There is no need for a Sixth Republic and in 1993, as contrasted with the anxieties when de Gaulle suddenly resigned in 1969, when the left came to power in 1981, or when the first cohabitation began in 1986, speculation has almost ceased.

A few leading politicians, such as Simone Weil and François Léotard, have suggested making a full switch to U.S.-style presidential government. But few politicians make much of a case for a new regime, and the French people not more so. Moreover, the peculiar hybrid regime can be seen, as it is seen by many French people, as a new form of French singularity, a distinctively "French" solution (by definition desirable) to the classic problems of relating executive and legislative branches of government.

The French president is simultaneously de jure and de facto head of state, but only de facto head of government and then only when he has a compliant parliamentary majority. It is a unique status among democratic presidents. In international meetings, France thus gets special standing. For example, in the European Council's diplomatic hierarchy the French president, faced with "mere" prime ministers and chancellors, is given priority. At G-7 meetings, the French president is advantageously placed with the U.S. president, who is also head of state as well as head of government.

In spite of these symbolic advantages of presidential parliamentarism, the need for constitutional reforms has been obvious for years. Why did President Mitterrand wait so long—until the end of 1992, after fully eleven years in office—to put constitutional reforms on the agenda? There is no institutional answer, so the reason must have been political and partisan. Perhaps it was the wish to hold a card in reserve as the last great task in his presidency, to make the domestic sequel to the Maastricht Treaty or to have a big issue for Cohabitation II in which he could exercise some leverage on a conservative government. Some reforms even seem anachronistic today: In March 1993, a few weeks before the parliamentary elections, President Mitterrand said he would propose abolishing Article 16. The president of the Consultative Committee on Constitutional Reform, Professor Georges Vedel, said it "had no sense."

Two justifications for constitutional reform are most common. One is the perennial, generally agreed criticism of the Gaullist institutions' excessive concentration of executive power, manipulation of Parliament and influence of the judiciary. The second is that the EC's Maastricht Treaty of December 1991 obliged several minor constitutional changes at the national level.

In his first electoral campaign in 1981, Mitterrand had proposed four significant constitutional reforms: (1) "to restore [Parliament's] rights under the constitution," first of all by limiting the usage of the "blocked vote"; (2) to create judicial independence from government influence by changing the membership and operating rules of the Superior Council of the Judiciary; (3) to use a proportional representation electoral law at all levels, because "in France it is more democratic than majority voting"; and (4) to reduce the presidential term from seven to five years.

What has happened to these four reforms? The blocked vote has indeed been used more sparingly in the last decade. And, as Ehrmann and Schain assert, by "using its power to amend, Parliament has vastly expanded its role during the past decade. . . . [T]he amendments incorporated by either of the two houses into the final text are a better measure of the contribution which Parliament furnishes to the legislative output than what happens to laws proposed by deputies."[31]

Yet overall the French Parliament continues to matter much less than the legislative branch in England, Germany or the United States, particularly in the U.S. Congress's investigative and confirmatory roles.[32] While use of the blocked vote has diminished, Article 49.3 was used increasingly by the Socialists to pass even budgets as a question of confidence rather than as ordinary legislation. Article 49.3 in a situation of minority governments is no longer, as was originally intended, an emergency measure on bills of the highest importance. Socialist minority governments after the 1988 elections (Rocard, Cresson, Bérégovoy) were regularly obliged to obtain even ordinary legislation in this way. It works but is bad for the political health of the institutions. Rocard was seen as a politically weak prime minister because he couldn't get important legislation passed any other way. And in the long term, to operate this way is destructive of representative legitimacy.

By 1991 commentary about an "unloved" Parliament had become much amplified. While the Fifth Republic was unquestioned as a whole, the National Assembly and the deputies showed up in public opinion polls as largely discredited or even politically "useless," especially if a deputy did not also have a local position as mayor or regional councilor to act as a magnet for local projects. The National Front's antiparty demagogy added further to Parliament's bad reputation. And some deputies themselves, including several from the ruling Socialist party, went public with their sentiment of serving little useful purpose—as in one joint declaration signed by a cross-party coalition of twelve Socialist, UDF and RPR deputies, or in books calling for reform.[33]

With the landslide conservative RPR–UDF majority of March 1993, giving the coalition 80 percent of the seats (see Chapter 5), the problem of minority government has been ended for the moment. The RPR–UDF coalition will have ample votes to legislate whatever it wants through ordinary mechanisms. Will Article 49.3 and the blocked vote procedures be eliminated? The conservatives would have the political means to do so, but why should they? The costs in democratic legitimacy are evident, but so are the benefits. Which is worse: the risk of delegitimation or the risk of impasse? The long-term risk or the short-term deadlock?

Second, with regard to judicial independence, no fundamental reform has occurred either, although a bill may be presented in Parliament in 1993. The Superior Council of the Judiciary is still presided over by the president of the Republic, and composed, in addition to the minister of justice, of nine members, all appointed by the president. In the Gaullist years there certainly was political pressure on judges, thought of by them as unfortunate but necessary to stability after the recent crises. Gradually the judiciary has become more independent, and Mitterrand's general commitment to enforcing the rule of law was manifested in the tenure of the well-respected Robert Badinter as minister of justice. Jean-Claude Casanova's comment is to the point: "Either . . . the judiciary remains independent in spite of the Superior Council, or . . . it must be the president himself, not the institutions, who guarantees judicial independence."

Electoral reform is a mess of conflicting interests. As opposed to systems (such as the U.S.) in which the national electoral law is permanent and unquestioned, in France the electoral law, under Mitterrand's tenure, has been made once again instrumental, not fixed or quasi-constitutional. Mitterrand has used the electoral law, as in the former republics, as a partisan weapon for his own party or, at best, as the president's weapon to blunt institutionally or politically bad outcomes. For this he has been roundly criticized, even more so when his stratagem didn't work. By getting the Socialist parliamentary majority to change the electoral law to proportional representation for the 1986 parliamentary elections, Mitterrand did succeed in holding down the size of the conservative coalition's victory. And measuring at the lopsided 1993 conservative landslide—80 percent of the seats with 40 percent of the votes—Mitterrand opined to journalists that "some dose of proportional representation" should have been added this time as well.

One reform could eliminate partisan temptation by giving the electoral law constitutional standing. But changing the electoral law is a weapon French politicians don't want to give up.

Shortening the presidential term is the most popular reform in public opinion, with about 75 percent favoring it according to polls. The long seven-year term was set in the 1958 Constitution on the assumption that the president, at least after de Gaulle, would not be the real head of government. Sounding a bit worn out, Mitterrand himself in 1992 told an interviewer, "Fourteen years is too long."

Georges Pompidou, de Gaulle's successor, already had proposed shortening the term. The National Assembly at the time actually approved a bill, which, following Pompidou's sudden death in office, was never brought to a vote in the Senate. Mitterrand made presidential term reduction one of his "110 propositions" in 1981, and in a series of constitutional proposals made at the end of 1992, put forth the alternative—unexpectedly indecisive—of either a six-year term, renewable once, or a nonrenewable seven-year term. Most people had expected a simple six- or five-year term to be the proposal. The rest of his suggestions were to (1) increase use of the referendum; (2) limit use of Article 49.3 to the government's budget in order to improve the Assembly's balance against the government; (3) grant access for individual citizens to the Constitutional Council; (4) eliminate the provision for creating an emergency High Court of Justice; and (5) revise Article 16. It is not clear at this writing whether these proposals will be debated in the now engaged Cohabitation II.

Only a few influential leaders, such as Raymond Barre, have endorsed the seven-year term, on the argument that the long mandate preserves the desirable presidential "preeminence" over the Parliament. Mitterrand had opposed a five-year term, for the similar reason that identical presidential and parliamentary terms would surely weaken the president's preeminence. Equal five-year terms, he said at one point, would become consistently concurrent elections and turn the French president into "a German chancellor."[34] Mitterrand another time suggested that dual five-year terms would drive French institutions toward an American-type presidency. In any case it was Parliament, he noted in false presidential modesty, that had the constitutional power of decision about the presidential term. However this may be, François Mitterrand has become the longest-serving French president, surpassing even General de Gaulle.

On Using the Referendum Well or Badly

For President de Gaulle a referendum was the sacred instrument of a Rousseauist democratic conception, the means of the Great Legislator's "personal dialogue with the nation." Massive "yes" votes in four referenda (1958–62) legitimized his "heroic" leadership: creation of the Fifth Republic, his decision to accept Algerian independence, and the directly elected Gaullist presidency (see Table 3.1).

Though it may have seemed eccentric that de Gaulle resigned the presidency when he lost the modest April 1969 referendum on the Senate and regional administrations, the act was absolutely in character with his Rousseauist democratic conception. No other French president has wagered on referenda in this manner. For de Gaulle a referendum was, whatever the specific subject, always a plebiscite on his own legitimacy. It was an expression of his policy, and rejection of the referendum would be therefore, in his eyes, the peoples' rejection of de Gaulle. So de Gaulle each time promised, or threatened, to resign should he lose. By contrast, for his less heroic successors, winning a presidential election creates, as constitutionally it must, legitimacy sufficient for the whole term whatever political storms may arise. If "ordinary" French presidents resigned when a referendum is defeated, the result would be to "parliamentarize" the presidency and create increased pressure for a president to resign when his party merely loses parliamentary elections. This would elimi-

Table 3 ✦ 1 De Gaulle's Referenda
Source: Adapted from Ehrmann and Schain,
op. cit., p. 215.

	Yes Votes (as % of)	
	Actual Turnout	Registered Voters
September 28, 1958	79	66
January 8, 1961	75	56
April 8, 1962	91	65
October 28, 1962	62	46
April 18, 1969 (defeated)	47	37

nate cohabitation situations, but would amount, in effect, to a Sixth Republic. Mitterrand thus acted as a staunch defender of constitutionalism, the Fifth Republic and—surprise!—of the Gaullist presidency, in rejecting opposition calls for his resignation in March 1993.

De Gaulle used the referendum as a kind of politically holy moment in French democracy. Unsurprisingly, under his successors it, like so much else, has been routinized. The low 60 percent participation and very modest enthusiasm for Georges Pompidou's April 1972 referendum endorsing the United Kingdom's membership in the EEC (reversing de Gaulle's two stunning vetoes of the British) showed lukewarm public enthusiasm not only for the Community, but also for the practice of referendum or perhaps for Pompidou himself. With 40 percent abstaining, the 68 percent "yes" vote meant that only 36 percent of registered voters were with the president. Giscard d'Estaing didn't use the referendum at all and neither did Mitterrand until 1988, by which time fully sixteen years had elapsed between referenda. The return to the referendum was not made with enthusiasm. The Rocard government's referendum in November 1988 on new political structures for French-governed New Caledonia was constitutionally required. But the issue seemed to the metropolitan French a remote problem. True, the referendum was strongly approved, by 80 percent of those voting. But because the abstention rate was 63 percent, the bill in reality was approved by only 26 percent of registered voters!

On the other hand, the 51 percent victory in the Maastricht referendum on September 20, 1992, indicated not public disinterest, but, given the high turnout, exactly the contrary. Opinion polls show that approximately three quarters of the French deem the referendum a valuable institution, and that they rank it, with the presidency and the Constitutional Council, among the few most highly regarded institutions. The problem seems therefore not whether to use the referendum, but how to use it well.

A referendum, we have said, is not mandatory, but is one possibility among several of deciding constitutional questions. For example, President Mitterrand could have had the Maastricht Treaty approved by Parliament alone, in which case the three small constitutional amendments would have required two-thirds majorities in the two houses. Parliamentary ratification was probably even his preference. A French referendum approving Maastricht was decided to counteract the narrow but devastating "no" in Denmark's summer 1991 referendum.

Maastricht and French Institutions

The Maastricht treaties on monetary and political union asked for three minor amendments in the French constitution. The most important was required by the creation of European citizenship. France, like all EC countries, must permit residence and the right to vote in local and European Parliament elections for a citizen of any other EC country. The principles governing local government were duly revised to permit EC foreigners to vote, but unlike other countries the French withheld the right of EC foreigners to run for mayor or to hold departmental or regional office. The three amendments for Maastricht compliance were vetted by the Constitutional Council, voted by a big margin in Parliament and then approved in the narrow 51 percent victory in the referendum of September 20, 1992 (see also Chapter 9).

In the future, fleshing out the European Union's political system will surely have more institutional spillover effects. One good example is increasing the powers of the European Parliament, which will make it harder to resist similarly revalorizing the French Parliament's role in the French political system. To now, French resistance to an enhanced EP, as advocated by Germany in particular, expresses basic differences: centralized, unitary, presidentialist France versus federal, decentralized, parliamentary Germany. In this light, French acceptance, at Maastricht, of a limited veto power for the EP indicates that more than one French institution will ultimately be reformed in a European direction—a combination of banalization and improvement. A similar argument could be made, for example, about the effect that the increasing authority of the European Court of Justice is having on the development of judicial review in France, with the Constitutional Council as its supreme court.

Conclusion

France doesn't need a Sixth Republic. French constitutional history is changing, and the French constitution is no longer, according to the postwar joke, a subspecies of periodical literature. Or, if a Sixth Republic were wanted, two new factors—"cohabitation" and European integration—are already creating it. Cohabitation is turning out to be an unexpected teacher of political liberalism—first in practice, then gradually in partisan thinking. Cohabitation may eventually become so domesticated that it will have forgotten its origin and even its own name. A French bipartisanship may one day be something other than an oxymoron.

On the other hand, the less likely but more worrisome possibility is that cohabitation may become the norm *without* a broad consensus regime of partisan politics. In that case the ambiguity of simultaneous presidential and parliamentary majorities could lead to constitutional trouble, deadlock, gridlock, or worse.

On the other hand, European integration, which challenges the French ability to compete, also creates, as we have seen, indirect levers for useful domestic economic and political change, including the reform of France's political institutions. In sum, de Gaulle seems to have been right about the logic of French institutions, but several vital reforms are necessary.

Endnotes

1. De Gaulle is quoted in Alain Peyrefitte, *The Trouble with France* (New York: Alfred A. Knopf, 1981), p. 48, as requoted in Ehrmann and Schain, p. 21. Mitterrand is quoted from a 1992 interview with journalists.

2. See, for example, Maurice Duverger, "A New Political System Model: Semi-Presidential Government," in Arend Lijphart (ed.), *Parliamentary vs. Presidential Government* (New York: Oxford University Press, 1992), pp. 142–150. General de Gaulle's important "Bayeux Manifesto" speech of June 16, 1946, demanding strong executive government, is also excerpted in this anthology (pp. 139–141). The main passage is this:

   In the present period of transition [i.e., following France's liberation from Nazi rule] it was undoubtedly necessary for the constituent National Assembly to elect the president of the provisional government because, with a clean slate, there was no other acceptable method of selection. But this can only be a temporary arrangement. Truly, the unity, the cohesion, and the internal discipline of the French government must be sacred, or else the very leadership of the country will rapidly become powerless and disqualified.

But how could this unity, this cohesion, and this discipline be maintained in the long run, if the executive power emanated from the other power, with which it must be in balance, and if each member of the government, which is collectively responsible to the entire national representation, held his position solely as the delegate of a party?

Hence the executive power ought to emanate from the chief of state, placed above the parties, elected by a body which includes the Parliament but which is much larger. . . . The chief of state . . . must serve as arbiter above political contingencies.

3. Gordon Smith, *Politics in Western Europe*, 5th ed. (New York: Holmes & Meier, 1989), p. 134.

4. See Smith, *Politics*, Chapters 1 and 5. In certain corrupted parliamentary regimes—Italy's, for example—the parliamentary parties repeatedly connive to bring down governments. But this is done for other reasons than to change the real political composition and policy of the government. The parties in question are actually already in the governmental majority, and they use fabricated cabinet "crises" as a normal way to fight interparty, or even intraparty battles for position and office. Most of the same people (often including the "defeated" prime minister) are reappointed after a government "crisis"; a few new appointments reveal the extent of the change (or the lack thereof).

5. Quoted in *Le Monde*, November 8, 1991, p. 14.

6. Raphaël Hadas-Lebel, "La Ve république et la guerre," in *Pouvoirs*, no. 58, special issue, *La France en guerre*, pp. 6–7.

7. See Ehrmann and Schain, pp. 290ff. De Gaulle's man Michel Debré looked to the English model, yet the constitution for which he was responsible ended up much more an American or even Ancien Régime French model! For Debré's thoughts, first in 1958 and then twenty years later, see William G. Andrews, *European Political Institutions: A Comparative Government Reader* (Princeton, N.J.: Van Nostrand, 1966), and then "The Constitution of 1958, Its Raison d'être and How It Evolved," in William G. Andrews and Stanley Hoffmann (eds.), *The Fifth Republic at Twenty* (Albany: State University of New York Press, 1981). Another valuable early analysis is Nicholas Wahl, "The French Constitution of 1958: The Initial Draft and Its Origins," *American Political Science Review*, vol. 53, no. 2 (1959), pp. 358–382. The following de Gaulle quotation is from Ehrmann and Schain, and is originally found in André Passeron, *De Gaulle, 1958–1969* (Paris: Bordas, 1972) p. 114.

8. See, for example, Roger-Gérard Schwartzenberg, *La droite absolue* (The absolute right) (Paris: Flammarion, 1981).

9. From a speech to the National Assembly, December 27, 1979, quoted in Raphaël Hadas-Lebel, "François Mitterrand et la fonction présidentielle" (François Mitterrand and the presidential office) in *French Politics and Society*, vol. 9, nos. 3–4 (Summer/Fall 1991), p. 3.

10. Ibid. Hadas-Lebel, p. 2.

11. *Le Monde*, July 2, 1981, p. 1.

12. The most dramatic example related to state financing of parochial schools. In July 1984, a Socialist bill to phase out state financing of parochial schools was passed, but it created an unforeseen outrage. (See page 31).

    Giving in to public pressure, President Mitterrand three weeks later unilaterally announced that the bill, which still needed to pass the Senate, would be withdrawn. Mitterrand's education minister, Alain Savary, and the prime minister, Pierre Mauroy, both resigned (though Mauroy, politically worn-out from the "union of the left's" battles since 1981, had been looking for an appropriate moment to resign for months already). Mitterrand's personal withdrawal of the bill did appease public opinion. But his act was a flagrant institutional coup, aligning his behavior—and not for the only time—with the "regime of personal power" he had long criticized when in opposition.

13. Pompidou is quoted in Safran, op. cit., p. 132. For conflicts in decision making involving the president and prime minister, see two books by Thierry Pfister: *La vie quotidienne à Matignon au temps de l'union de la gauche* (Daily life at Matignon at the time of the united left) (Paris: Hachette, 1985) and *Dans les coulisses du pouvoir: La comédie de la cohabitation* (Behind the curtains of power: The comedy of cohabitation) (Paris: Albin Michel, 1986).

14. By naming Chirac prime minister, Mitterrand indicated he would bow to the underlying parliamentary framework of the Constitution. There were three reasons for this. First, Mitterrand was bound by democratic morality—the need to respect the result of the ballot box. Second, by respecting the letter of the Constitution Mitterrand was also respecting its obvious spirit. To act differently would have raised a powerful doubt about the overall legitimacy of the Gaullist presidency. Finally, there were several tactical calculations. President Mitterrand, entering new institutional territory, wanted to avoid being responsible for turning the beginning of cohabitation into a constitutional crisis. If there was to be a constitutional crisis,

better that Jacques Chirac be the instigator, in which case public opinion would favor the president. At the same time, for Mitterrand to name his main adversary as prime minister in the awkward, untested cohabitation situation was a poisoned gift: It placed Chirac in a dangerously exposed political position. And the ups and downs of cohabitation did end up weakening Chirac's presidential prospects, resulting in Mitterrand's reelection in 1988.

15. On cohabitation see Vincent Wright, *The Government and Politics of France*, 3rd ed. (London: Unwin Hyman, 1989); Maurice Duverger, *Bréviare de la cohabitation* (Cohabitation manual) (Paris: PUF, 1986); Julius W. Friend, *Seven Years in France: François Mitterrand and the Unintended Revolution, 1981–1988* (Boulder, Colo.: Westview Press, 1989), Chapter 5; and also Pfister, *Dans les coulisses,* op. cit.

16. The idea for mobile land missile launchers was borrowed from the Reagan Administration's program at the time. Other borrowed ideas were monetarism, deregulation and (from the Thatcher government's policy) a big emphasis on privatization as a way to "push back socialism in the economy."

17. In late June 1993 came Mitterrand's first use of a technical power to frustrate the Cohabitation II Balladur government, making use of the president's control of Parliament's agenda in special session. Mitterrand refused to put on the agenda of the National Assembly's special session, called by Balladur, a conservative bill reforming the Falloux Law (the original law putting limits on state financing of parochial schools). This meant it would have to be voted in the fall session, when the French would be back from vacation and opposition would be better mobilized.

18. Because French judicial review is still underdeveloped, Chirac couldn't take the case to a supreme court. Such a heady conflict would have been too rich for either the Council of State or the Constitutional Council to take on. See below in this chapter on the two courts.

19. Safran, *The French Polity*, p. 175. For the Senate, half its members would have been elected in the old way (indirect election, by regional and local officials), and half would now be chosen in a corporative fashion (by trade unions, business groups, etc.) The Senate's legislative purview would have been reduced, from everything the Assembly considered to only certain social, economic and cultural matters. The Senate was to be totally excluded from "general" political matters, to be defined by the government. To de Gaulle the existing Senate had shown itself to be useless or, worse, opposed to his constructive initiatives. He thought "corporate" representation

would be political progress, following on the example of the consultative Economic and Social Council (itself a largely irrelevant institution).

The voters found the April 1969 referendum overly complex and not of first importance. Everyone understood on the other hand that only a year after the "events of May" this was a referendum on de Gaulle: yes or no. De Gaulle's perennial threat to resign was taken seriously, so this vote was a real exercise in Rousseauist democracy. Defeat and instant resignation were for de Gaulle a dramatic, politically aesthetic and democratic way to leave office. But a few Gaullists did chastise him for "leaving the field," as in January 1946.

20. Ehrmann and Schain, p. 326.

21. See *Le Monde*, November 20, 1991, p. 10.

22. See *Le Monde*, June 3, 1992, pp. 1, 9.

23. See Ehrmann and Schain, op. cit., pp. 340ff. The comité des sages practice reflected a long governmental distrust of Parliament. Whereas, for example, it was Congress that investigated the Iran–Contra affair in the United States, in France the Greenpeace affair, which might have involved crimes, was given over to an ad hoc blue-ribbon committee. The Commission on Nationality and Citizenship, headed by Marceau Long, was set up by the Chirac cohabitation government when the latter's new bills restricting naturalization and immigration created high controversy. The Commission's report was published as *Etre français aujourd'hui et demain* (To be French today and tomorrow) (Paris: La documentation française, 1988), 2 vols. See also the related report by the Haut Conseil à l'Integration (High Council on Integration), *Pour un modèle français d'intégration* (For a French model of integration) (Paris: La Documentation française, 1991). The whole issue of immigration and "foreigners" is discussed as a problem of public policy in Chapter 7.

24. See the reporting in *Le Monde*, November 22, 1991, p. 10.

25. Ehrmann and Schain, op. cit., p. 354. Several points in this discussion come from this source. The most complete study of the Constitutional Council is now Alec Stone, *The Birth of Judicial Politics in France: The Constitutional Council in Comparative Perspective* (New York: Oxford University Press, 1992).

26. Ehrmann and Schain, op. cit., p. 352–353.

27. Ehrmann and Schain, p. 353.

28. Socialists perennially were at loggerheads with Communists over

whether centralized power was a good thing. They fought Leninist "democratic centralism" (inside the party), "dictatorship of the proletariat" (in society) and "proletarian internationalism" (within the international communist movement), as well as Stalinist centralization in the economy (nationalizations, planning). Communists, in reply, perennially mocked Socialists for not being genuine revolutionaries, not being willing to do what had to be done, whatever violence, in order to "build socialism." The accusation did intimidate French Socialists for decades. See Ronald Tiersky, *Ordinary Stalinism: Democratic Centralism and the Question of Communist Political Development* (Winchester, Mass.: Allen & Unwin, 1985).

29. Friend, op. cit., pp. 146–147. The most complete study in English is Vivien A. Schmidt, *Democratizing France: The Political and Administrative History of Decentralization* (New York: Cambridge University Press, 1991).

30. An exception is the Socialists' 1991 decision to relocate the ENA—the famous Parisian National School of Administration which since 1945 has given a graduate education to much of the French elite—to Strasbourg, the capital city of Alsace and home to the European Parliament. Geographical "delocalization" of such an important French institution would, the Cresson government argued, not merely boost the prestige of Strasbourg and the government's commitment to decentralization, but also demonstrate the French state's commitment to a future "Europe of the regions" within the European Community. However in June 1993 the Council of State, in agreement with the Balladur government, reversed the Cresson government's decision. Delocalization of ENA had naturally been seen by students and alumni (many in top government positions) as an "exile."

31. Ehrmann and Schain, op. cit., pp. 332ff.

32. For example, see the book by a Socialist deputy, Jean-Michel Belorgey, *Le Parlement à refaire* (To rebuild Parliament) (Paris: Gallimard, 1991).

33. See, for the deputies' declaration, *Le Monde*, December 27, 1991, p. 7, and Belorgey, op. cit.

34. Pierre Favier and Michel Martin-Roland, *La Décennie Mitterrand* (The Mitterrand decade), 2 vols. Vol. 1, *Les Ruptures, 1981–84* (The innovations, 1981–84); Vol. 2, *Les Épreuves, 1984–88* (The challenges, 1984–88) (Paris: Seuil, 1990 and 1991).

4
✦

Political Parties: The Centering of Right and Left

Consensus or Impotence?

Gaullism's victory in 1958–62, its positioning of the presidency, quickly affected French political parties and the party system. Parties, an ideological and programmatic lever of politics, have become less important than they were in the parliamentary Third and Fourth republics. Furthermore, the combined presidential and parliamentary characteristics of the Fifth Republic's institutions have permitted various party structures and party purposes. There is no more variety today (perhaps less), it is just different. French politics is overall much less a "party regime" than had been the case for a century.

French political parties today are of two kinds: (1) the major parties, or those that can hope to elect a president, and (2) the minor parties, which cannot. There are three major parties—the Socialist party (*Parti Socialiste*, or PS), the neo-Gaullist Rally for the Republic (*Rassemblement pour la République*, or RPR), and the Union for French Democracy (*Union pour la Démocratie Française*, or UDF), which is itself a federation of three small center–right parties. The major parties have become increasingly routinized organizations whose main goals are (1) to win the presidency and (2) to control the majority in Parliament, thus winning the right to supply the prime minister and most other key ministers as well. In policy terms there are still important differences among the three large parties, but pragmatism reigns amid occasional seizures of doctrine and genuine enthusiasm.

The minor parties operate more like parliamentary than presidential parties, but they also differ greatly one from another. They are not so mesmerized by presidentialism's premium on consensus and victory. There are two kinds of minor parties: the ideological parties on the extremes and the old-style parliamentary cliques in the center. The fascist-sounding right-wing Front National (FN) is, naturally, highly ideological. Yet, because of Jean-Marie Le Pen's personal control of the movement and his electoral popularity, it is also quite focused on presidential politics, if only to make a good showing on the first ballot. The French Communist party (*Parti Communiste Français*, or PCF) generally runs its own presidential candidate, even though it does especially poorly in candidate-centered elections and will normally support the Socialist candidate on the second ballot. But it operates today mainly as a parliamentary party whose political strategy, if it any longer has one, is to influence the Socialists and President Mitterrand. There are two small ecological groupings, usually categorized, ambiguously, on the extreme left. The fundamentalist "Greens" have been a permanent opposition single-issue group, whereas "Ecological Generation," whose leader, Brice Lalonde, was minister for ecology, belonged to the Socialist governing coalitions. Each group runs its own presidential candidate, to "count the troops," and they have maintained a stormy coalition in parliamentary elections although they tend to split up noisily in between.

The other small parties are the historical centrists, vestiges of the parliamentary parties of the Third and Fourth Republics. The Social Democratic Center (*Centre des Démocrates Sociaux*, or CDS) and Movement of Left Radicals (*Mouvement des Radicaux de Gauche*, or MRG), operate as old-style parliamentary parties, allied to either the majority or opposition coalition. Their leaders aspire to cabinet positions at most, and these tiny parties have no permanent agenda. That they survive at all is due to local implantation and the legal possibility of accumulating positions: mayor, regional councillor, parliamentary deputy.

The fierce ideological and organizational party machines that fought the battles of French political history are thus largely gone. Because of the Fifth Republic's presidentialism, the major political parties, as parties, are less significant in policy making and governance than in the Third or Fourth Republics. In the centrist republic the major parties have largely abandoned ideology for consensus, and party headquarters is less interested in a parliamentary majority than a presidential majority. "Cohabitation" is any ambitious politician's second preference, and the most efficient way to move on your first preference is to focus on the presidency. Thus, whereas in the old parliamentary republic a leader's fortunes depended on his party's strength as a party, in French politics today a leader's personal popularity can be largely distinct from the popularity of his party.

The result is, as stated above, a decline in the significance of parties in constructing governments and wielding power. The leaders of French politics still come mainly from the parties, but the parties, as parties, have less say than before. Presidentialism has turned the major parties, at least, into adjuncts of the presidential process. The union of the left's 1981–83 experiment with Socialist policies seems to have been the last gasp of party program government, and then only because the new president, Mitterrand, chose to try it.

To discuss French political parties used to be a shortcut way of discussing French politics as a whole.[1] Today, the main French parties have become footnotes to the Gaullist institutions, to a media-influenced political culture and public opinion focused on the presidency.

Where has all the power gone? The answer is fairly clear. As in any technologically advanced democracy, part of the traditional work of parties is now done by television, radio and print media. Another part is hardly done at all: the cultivation of citizenship and political sociability, of interested, informed public opinion, of serious, dignified conduct of public business.

Television and the press increasingly determine the nature of political campaigns in France. French leaders today are asked difficult and probing questions, a great change from the staged press conferences of General de Gaulle. But print and electronic media journalism also is beginning to imitate the American obsession with "feelings" and with the private lives of elected officials. Politics is being turned more and more into news, and one result is a malaise in representation. If a political party ought to be a school of democratic thought and civic commitment, French parties today are falling short. As the French commentator Jacques Julliard puts it, "[O]utside of electoral periods, the political parties have almost no implantation in the population . . . [constituting a] renunciation by parties and trade unions of their traditional role of structuring participation [*encadrement*]."[2] This might seem to be a description of American politics rather than of France, and justifiably so. Overall, differences still are more salient than similarities, but the French and American political party cultures no longer sit on opposite sides of an abyss. Indeed, cosmopolitan French politicians regularly assert that the French Socialist party is, or should be, cousin to the American Democratic party (as well as to the German SPD), and that the French right should unify to create a "modern conservative party" either like other European conservative parties or like the American Republican party.

Compared with the past, the decline of partisanship is not only a decline of pernicious ideological illusions. Among the major parties there is a decline of partisanship as such, of healthy public debate and the taking of sides in a thoughtful, forceful manner. The sudden partisanship in the September 1992 Maastricht referendum was the exception that highlighted the rule. This worrisome growth of apoliticism is partially masked by the bubbles of nationalist enthusiasm on the neo-Fascist right and the primitivist part of the Ecologist left.[3] But it is unmistakable, and it expresses a new "malaise in representation" in France, which the French commentator Pierre Rosanvallon attributes to "the misery of pragmatism" that has replaced principles and ideals in the major parties.[4] Reinvigorating this weakened articulation and aggregation of partisan issues will be a major task of French political parties in the coming years.

What has just been said is not meant, however, to heap nostalgic praise on the old ideological parties. They had grave defects and contributed mightily to political immobilism, corruption, failure and even, in the 1930s and 1950s, to the coming of wars and defeats. Jacques Fauvet, then editor-in-chief of *Le Monde*, in 1957 gave the following description of French politics:

> [T]here are two fundamental principles—that of the right and that of the left; three main tendencies, if one adds the center; six "political families"; ten parties, small and large, each composed of multiple factions; fourteen parliamentary groups, highly undisciplined; and forty million different opinions.[5]

This was either political folly or true proportional democracy, or both.

Enough has been said already to give a general idea of the stalemated, immobilist Third and Fourth Republic party systems, the Parliament-dominated regime of "plenty of brakes and not much motor." We might call this the "unreformed" French party system. From the end of the Fourth Republic to the 1970s—that is, from the recall of General de Gaulle in 1958 to the systemic changes engendered by the events of May 1968—was a time of transition when the old party system had been broken apart by Gaullism and the rise of a Gaullist party, but the reform initiated by presidentialism had not yet come to fruition. The full victory of presidentialism would not be achieved until the 1980s, when the Socialists won the presidency and a supporting parliamentary majority.

A brief sketch of that system will do. On the far left was the Communist party. Beyond it on the extreme left was an array of Maoist, Guevarist,

Trotskyite, anarchist, "situationist" and still other revolutionary *groupuscules*. These revolutionary sects did not define themselves in reference to mainstream politics, about which they cared little, but in relation to the PCF. They (correctly) considered it to be bureaucratic and Stalinist but, like it or not, the PCF was the major force claiming to be revolutionary and working-class–based. These groupuscules, which ended up at the head of the May '68 student revolt, argued that the Communist party sold out the possibility of revolution in 1968 because the general strike had gotten out of their own control. Such leaders as Daniel Cohn-Bendit ("Danny the Red," a French–German student), Alain Krivine and Alain Geismar became momentary cult figures, leaving behind several books and pamphlets that tell less about French society than about the young revolutionary left's frustration with the PCF's remarkably conservative reactions to what looked like a revolutionary situation.[6] To be sure, the PCF's leaders also had to reckon with two international controls. Moscow didn't want to foment trouble in Western Europe, because that would legitimize Western assistance of anti-Soviet movements in Eastern Europe. The second factor, bluntly put, was NATO.

Nevertheless, strong with its 20 percent-plus electoral vote and its great trade union power in the CGT, the Communist party in the 1960s and 1970s continued to intimidate the French left by limiting the Socialist party electorally and the far-left-wing groupuscules ideologically and organizationally. The Communist veto power in French politics worked in two ways. First, by its attitude toward the Socialist party it determined whether the left had a chance to gain power. Second, by emphasizing either a "soft" or a "hard" face, it strongly influenced which conservatives would control government policy, the authoritarian or the progressive-liberal elements.[7]

The SFIO (*Section Française de l'Internationale Ouvriere*) Socialists, the PCF's rivals on the left and a key party in the Fourth Republic, were weakened and dispirited by the end of the 1960s. Heirs to the same European social democratic tradition that produced strong postwar governing parties in Sweden, West Germany and England, in France social democracy was an ideology of "reformism" that dared not speak its name. Communism's dominance required the Socialists to be, at least rhetorically, anticapitalist and revolutionary. The Socialists were intimidated, when not ridiculed, by Communist leaders. The Communists, it became clear, cared less about uniting the opposition to win an election than about "staying in power" inside the left itself. Yet because de Gaulle attracted the center parties into a conservative coalition, the Socialists were also denied their Fourth Republic alliance with them. So, in a celebrated quip, the SFIO had become "like the slice of ham in a sandwich, and getting thinner all the time."

The SFIO's electoral nadir came in the 1969 presidential election, forced suddenly by President de Gaulle's resignation on his defeat in the April referendum. Disorganized and dispirited, the Socialist party mustered but 5 percent for a reluctant compromise candidate, Gaston Defferre, mayor of Marseille. Two years later, in 1971, this demoralized party was taken over in a remarkable coup by François Mitterrand. Merging his own little party with the grand old SFIO, he became leader of the retitled "Socialist party."

Mitterrand's strategy was simple and daring. The presidency had become the main prize and focus of government; it required an electoral majority to win. Parliamentary alliances were now subservient to alliances for presidential elections. Mitterrand's risky bet was that French voters would reinflate the Socialist party to avoid a Communist-dominated left-wing government. Voters would not fail to make the Socialist party stronger than the Communist party the closer the left came to power. Thus in 1972 Mitterrand signed the "union of the left" alliance, a Marxist-sounding coalition of (1) the Socialists, (2) the Communists, and (3) the tiny centrist MRG wing of the old Radical party. The coalition's "Common Program" called for new nationalizations of corporations and banks, and large-scale economic planning by the government.

Ups and downs ensued in the 1970s. For a few years the French Communist leaders unexpectedly joined the Spanish and Italian Communists in "Eurocommunism," an apparent Europeanization and democratization of Soviet-style communism. For this short period the Communists seemed genuinely to be reforming themselves and to be benefiting from the union of the left alliance along with the Socialists.

But then various local and national elections showed the Socialists gaining ground and the Communists standing still. In 1976–77 the Communists, seeing that their strategy was working better for the Socialists than for themselves, smashed what seemed like a winning combination, hypocritically blaming the Socialists for the split.

For the next three years there was only more trouble on the left, until Mitterrand's unexpected presidential victory in May 1981 against the incumbent Giscard d'Estaing. The Socialist leader's victory put the Communists in the very spot they had created havoc on the left to avoid. The PCF's leaders believed that they had to accept Mitterrand's offer to join the government now, because otherwise they would provoke a large-scale "exit" by their own Communist rank and file. So the PCF wound up in June 1981 as junior partner to a newly dominant Socialist party in the union of the left government headed by Pierre Mauroy. Over the next decade the Communists went from decline to decline. The collapse of communism internationally then orphaned the PCF, one of the few communist parties not to change its name. François Mitterrand won his daring wager on allying his Socialists with the Communists, and the Mitterrand years marked the change from the old "exceptionalist" French left to today's "recentered" left. Not only the parties but also the substance of left-wing voting and political culture has been changed.

French Parties Today

The French party system today is neither a Third or Fourth Republic–style multiparty parliamentary system nor a two-party or two-coalition presidential system. It is a hybrid, and this results both from the hybrid presidential–parliamentary national institutions and the fact that most parties still organize themselves into two coalitions, which the French still call, perhaps incorrectly, "the right" and "the left." Above all the nature of the Fifth Republic's parties and party system has been determined by the Gaullist presidency, a directly elected president with enormous powers whose victory requires a majority. This has a bipolarizing effect—the victory of majority logic over proportional representation logic—which guarantees the survival of *la droite et la gauche*. In short, institutions count. Changing the institutions changed the party system.

As said by way of introduction, there are basically two kinds of parties, the big three presidential parties and several parties of influence or protest. The latter are the centrist parties (CDS, the Radical party, the Movement of Left Radicals), the Communist party, the National Front, and the two "Ecologist" groupings. The centrist groups are parties of influence, junior partners in governments, whose leaders may hope for ministerial posts. The other parties—PCF, FN, Greens, Ecological Generation—combine goals of influence and protest. The Communists had government posts during the union of the left period (1981–84), and the Ecological Generation leader, Brice Lalonde, was a much-in-view ecology minister in the recent Socialist-led governments. The National Front and the "hardline" ecologist Greens are more important factors of public protest than of policy influence. But they do, to varying extents, influence the terms of public debate: the more striking example is the National Front's exacerbating influence on public controversy about "foreigners" and about the linked issues of race, ethnicity, religion, unemployment and national identity.

The next chapter will analyze party coalitions and electoral alliances, in which party positioning is crucial. But a diagram of the conventional party positioning (Figure 4.1) is already useful here to facilitate the discussion of individual parties. The three major parties are in bold. Conventional party labels are used, but they deserve a skeptical reading. This is not the place to debate what is *really* politically left and right.

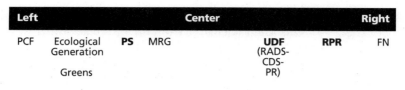

Left				Center		Right
PCF	Ecological Generation	**PS**	MRG	**UDF** (RADS- CDS-	**RPR**	FN
	Greens			PR)		

Figure 4 ✦ 1 French party positions

The Presidential Parties: PS, RPR and UDF

The Socialist Party The French Socialist party might intensely be debating the question, What is "socialism" today? What can a socialist program be, given European social democracy's failure to get beyond capitalism, and the demise of communism, with whose Stalinist idea of "socialism" it had for decades to contend?

Few Socialist leaders any longer give the impression that these are important questions. The experience of governing disillusioned the idealists of 1981. Dreams of massive social progress have become an awareness of the limits, and dangers, of having power. Few French Socialists believe any longer that a "socialist society" is plausible. A whole generation of Socialists—the so-called Mitterrand generation—has been educated to reality, put to use, and worn out by the attrition of a decade in office. Set against what might have been the party's fate fifteen years ago, this is a pretty good balance sheet.

The Socialist party, especially after its devastating losses of March 1993, is already entering the post-Mitterrand era as their indomitable, aging leader finishes his second seven-year term, left alone to "cohabit" with a crushing conservative parliamentary majority and government. Mitterrand's personal authority and prestige dominated the Socialist renaissance for two decades, and without him the faction-ridden PS would surely have split apart, never regaining its place as the main party on the left. On a historical scale Mitterrand was no de Gaulle, but he successfully refounded the French left.

Since most of the policy discussion in this book already concerns the Socialist-led governments of 1981–93, there is no need for a summary here. Better to discuss straight away the main ideas and broad options in the party today.

Michel Rocard, the Socialist prime minister in 1988–91, and likely future presidential candidate, has said for years that the PS is, or should be, roughly in France what the Democratic party is in the United States. Most of the successor Socialist party leaders—Rocard, Laurent Fabius, EC Commission president Jacques Delors, former minister Lionel Jospin—would agree that any return to hardline ideology would sink the party. Mitterrand for years has set the tone on this point. He rarely speaks of some different kind of society, and he hardly mentions socialism at all, wanting to be "the president of all the French," not merely president of the Socialists. He is not fond of class struggle imagery. His distrust of capitalism is not a crusade against private property or industry, but a profound suspicion of the corrupting power of money in society. Mitterrand sees himself in the mold of pre–World War I socialists such as Jean Jaurès and Edouard Bernstein, for whom socialism was a moral and political struggle for human dignity, not the playing out of scientific theories of violent class struggles.

Mitterrand has tried to update socialism's relevance. For example, asked before the Maastricht EC summit meeting whether he would rather be known in history as a Socialist or a European, Mitterrand replied, "If you said both you would have it right. I am a European very much because I am a Socialist."[8] This modernized conception, if tenable, nicely links the traditional Socialist value of internationalism with the real contemporary issues of European integration.

In terms of domestic policy, an ideologically thin, pragmatically battle-hardened social democracy is what remains of the PS's visionary socialist self-management (autogestion) program of the 1970s. Social democracy in the 1990s, after a century of total failures and partial successes, seems to be basically an egalitarian, humanist adaptation of capitalism. The French Socialist party moved willy-nilly with its times, strongly influencing developments in the Spanish, Portuguese and Greek Socialist parties in the decisive decade of the 1980s.

During Mitterrand's presidency the French PS made its accommodation to market economics and blended with the traditional Colbertian, Jacobin statism that any French governmental party inherits with the keys to the offices of power. François Mitterrand, who will be 78 years old when his term expires in 1995, will probably be the last Socialist leader with a heartfelt connection to pre–World War II French society. Though his socialist commitment came late in life, though it was ambiguous and had to be reconciled with his "Florentine" political craftiness, Mitterrand has been a successful combination of Jean Jaurès and Machiavelli. Against this, Ehrmann and Schain's assessment of the rising generation of PS leaders is very hard:

> For Socialist leaders who have occupied power since 1981, the ideological differences among the various factions have become relatively meaningless and have deteriorated into personal rivalries. Shorn of ideological pretensions, these rivalries have sharpened as the end of Mitterrand's second term in 1995 draws near and has opened, quite prematurely, the question of his succession. . . . At the 1990 party congress seven rival factions engaged in a struggle mostly designed to position themselves favorably for the greatest possible influence in the next administration.[9]

The relevant question in this factionalism is, unfortunately, not which ideas will win out, but whether the next presidential candidate will be able to unite a fractured party. Party organization used to matter—for the worse—a great deal to the Socialists, because, faced with PCF organizations in the workplaces and in neighborhoods, the PS was in a position of permanent inferiority. Today, not only has the equation changed with respect to the Communists, but also, in a more media-driven political process, the importance of party organization itself has changed.

How many members does the Socialist party have? How many "enterprise sections" and auxiliary groups? These used to be important questions, when the Socialists had to face off with the Communists for dominance in the workplace and the street. Today the number of those with membership cards—perhaps 100,000 after the 1993 Socialist electoral defeat, with various degrees of commitment—matters less than the size of its campaign chest and the persuasiveness of its candidates in the media, especially on television. French election campaigns, following the American example, are increasingly waged not in rallies and grassroots debate, but on television. Not by accident, fewer French people are partisan than in the old days of left and right politics. And the political culture of French public opinion—once an example to the world—has become anemic, more forgetful, less demanding.

For the Socialist party this is both a gain and a loss. The gain is that the Socialists, at least under Mitterrand's leadership, have proved themselves a modern, even contemporary party. The loss is that decline of genuine partisan engagement and purpose of which something has been said above.

The huge defeat of March 1993 has thrown the Socialist party into a crisis. Internal struggle and realignment is natural after such a large loss. But this does not make it less vicious, especially after a long period in power. As the conservative Balladur government was taking the reigns of power, the PS's Michel Rocard—the party's designated candidate for the next presidential election who nonetheless lost his own seat as deputy in the election—engineered an internal party coup. He ousted Laurent Fabius as party leader with the promise of a "big bang" recreation of a social democratic party, encompassing the PS and willing Communists, Ecologists, and others. Rocard was certainly taking a risk, and he was accused of destroying the PS in the service of his presidential ambitions.

The Neo-Gaullist RPR To understand the neo-Gaullist party still requires that one begin with de Gaulle. Not that much remains of de Gaulle, but the reader's understanding of French politics will be helped by measuring what has been lost.

Charles de Gaulle was a controversial army colonel with a sense of destiny when, in May–June 1940, the Nazis destroyed the French army, overran the country and uprooted the regime in six shocking weeks. Along with a few others, de Gaulle rejected the French government's acceptance of the German terms of armistice. He escaped to London and from June 18, 1940 organized French resistance. The Resistance movement opposed both the Nazi invaders and the so-called Vichyite French state, set up under Marshal Philippe Pétain. Succeeding in a long struggle against tremendous odds, de Gaulle emerged at the time of the Liberation as the "savior" of France and president of the provisional government. De Gaulle resigned in January 1946, frustrated by the "ferments of dispersal" that had reemerged among French politicians. He stayed out of politics for twelve years, until, again as a "savior," he was called back to deal with the war in Algeria. As his price, he demanded the creation of new national political institutions, the Fifth Republic. After eleven tumultuous years in power, President de Gaulle resigned a second time in April 1969, following a losing referendum that seemed essentially a pretext to leave the historical stage in a flash of high political drama.

Charles de Gaulle's legacy was difficult for "Gaullists" to live up to. As an electoral force, Gaullism has always refused the label of "party," preferring to be called a "rally" or "movement." De Gaulle had wanted the presidency to be permanently "above" the partisan melee of the parties, and he himself never was a member of a party, not even his own. Gaullism had to be more genuine than a party. It would be a rally of like-minded people, whose goals would be patriotic and genuinely political rather than merely to find careers and advantages for themselves.

In the Fifth Republic's first decade 1958–68, between de Gaulle's sensational return to power and the "events of May," the Gaullist UNR took about one third of the vote. The Gaullists were the majority force on the political right and the largest single electoral grouping. In the wake of the events of May 1968 the Gaullists, this time called the Union for the Defense of the Republic (*Union pour la Défense de la République*, or UDR), won 37 percent of the vote, producing an absolute majority in the National Assembly. This was a first, not only in the Fifth Republic, but in the entire parliamentary history of France. This was also the first time that the president of the Republic was supported by an absolute majority of his own party in Parliament, revealing that the Fifth Republic's institutional strength was not dependent entirely on de Gaulle himself. It was, of course, a prefiguration of Mitterrand and the Socialists' situation in 1981.

During Georges Pompidou's presidency (1969–74), the Gaullist movement became more of a permanently organized and administered party in the traditional sense. It had more members and paid more attention to party structure and constituency work, and its parliamentary deputies voted with party discipline, unlike the traditional "parties of notables" on the French right or center. Yet, with the General gone, factionalism ran free and the Gaullist vote declined. In the 1974 election to succeed Pompidou, Jacques Chaban-Delmas, although a *compagnon de la Libération** and by virtue of that a "historic Gaullist," got less than 15 percent. Valéry Giscard d'Estaing thus became the conservative candidate in the runoff ballot, ending Gaullism's monopoly of the presidency.

The inevitable transformation of the "historic" Gaullist "rally" into a presidential party began as the next leader emerged. But Jacques Chirac's style and goals accelerated the process. A neo-Gaullist kingpin since taking over as secretary-general in 1974, Chirac has always seemed motivated mainly by the desire to be president. All the rest, however much wrapped in neo-Gaullist rhetoric, is secondary. Through personnel changes and centralization of the organizational structure, the Gaullist party under Chirac began to turn into an up-to-date electoral machine. At the same time, President Giscard d'Estaing, in an apparent deal, named Chirac prime minister. For this, the ambitious Chirac had apparently pledged he would not support his fellow Gaullist, Chaban-Delmas; thus Chaban's very poor showing on the first ballot.

A tumultuous relationship ensued for two years within the "two-headed" French executive as Jacques Chirac's vigorousness collided with the ambition and the presidential supremacy of Giscard d'Estaing. In 1976 Chirac, claiming he didn't have the "necessary authority" to govern as prime minister, resigned the office on his own initiative. In addition to demonstrating his own determination, Chirac's innovation—prime ministers had always served purely at the president's pleasure—signaled that the Fifth Republic's constitution was more than a simple elective monarchy. How much more the president's power could be limited was proven, again by Chirac as prime minister, in the right–left "cohabitation" regime of 1986–88, with President Mitterrand from one day to the next obliged to accept parliamentary government in domestic affairs as well as in much of foreign affairs.

Out of office, but more than ever running permanently for the presidency from his position as mayor of Paris, Jacques Chirac in 1976 launched a second overhaul of a now neo-Gaullist party, renamed, as it still is called, the Rally for the Republic (*Rassemblement pour la République,* or RPR). (Once again we notice the Gaullist refusal to think of itself as a mere "party" like other parties.) Chirac quickly put the old guard Gaullist "barons"—such as Michel Debré, Maurice Couve de Murville and Olivier Guichard—into the role of elder statesmen, pushing them and their now

---

*"Liberation comrade," a Gaullist Resistance decoration

sometimes inconvenient Gaullist ideas away from power. Remarkably, almost half of the RPR's new national executive in this year, handpicked by Chirac, had never belonged previously to any Gaullist organization.[10] This neo-Gaullism has really been the end of Gaullism as a vital idea embodied in a political movement. In one sense, obviously, there could never have been a Gaullism without de Gaulle, because, as Stanley Hoffmann wrote not long after the General's death, "Gaullism was a stance, not a doctrine; an attitude, not a coherent set of dogmas; a style without much substance—beyond the service of France and French grandeur, itself never defined in content, only by context."[11] And to the extent that Gaullism consists in a small set of well-known values, François Mitterrand has certainly been more Gaullian (if not Gaullist) than any other post–de Gaulle president.

When the conservatives defeated the left in the 1986 parliamentary elections, Jacques Chirac, as leader of the largest conservative party, was named prime minister by President Mitterrand. The period of political "cohabitation" lasted for two years, until the presidential and parliamentary elections of 1988. Mitterrand, as president, maintained control in matters of high foreign policy, security and defense policy. But the self-proclaimed French conservative "neoliberal" coalition initiated a wave of tax cuts and privatizations. These privatizations undid several of the 1981–82 left-wing nationalizations in industry and in the banks, and went farther to privatize several long-standing state-owned corporations, such as TF1, the flagship national television station. Chirac seemed to have given up General de Gaulle and Colbert for Ronald Reagan and Margaret Thatcher, the heights of *étatisme*** for the melee of the market. "Neo"-Gaullism had certainly not turned out to be a Gaullist rose by any other name!

Then, contrary to the conventional wisdom of spring 1986 that argued Mitterrand's reduced power would finish him politically, the battles of cohabitation turned out to profit Mitterrand rather than Chirac. President Mitterrand, contrasted with the "agitated" Chirac, seemed a statesman caring for the long-term interests of the country and the political institutions. As his 1988 electoral advertising put it, Mitterrand during the cohabitation had become *la force tranquille*, the man of "quiet strength." Chirac, on the other hand, emerged weakened by cohabitation. As a prime minister always fighting his president for place, he could not shake the reputation of being a pugnacious manipulator motivated by presidential ambitions rather than by worthier goals.

Mitterrand defeated Chirac in the presidential election of 1988, and the PS defeated the right in snap parliamentary elections called by the

---

** statism

reelected president. Unsurprisingly, the RPR dove into an internal crisis, and between 1988 and 1991 Chirac's preeminence was tested by a younger generation of leaders. But Chirac held on, and he remains the RPR's favored presidential candidate.

In October 1991 the RPR party convention came up with the surprise proposal for some alliance with the Ecologists. What was the logic of this call across the political spectrum? First, the RPR leaders had decided to avoid alliance with the National Front, betting that most FN voters will vote RPR no matter what on the second ballot of both the presidential and parliamentary elections. Second, the appeal was banked on Ecologist disappointment with Mitterrand and the Socialists. So there seemed little to gain and much to lose in any formal agreement with the National Front, and on the other hand by tempting the Ecologists they can show, as Mrs. Thatcher did in Britain, that order-minded conservatives can be "green." But although there is an authority-minded wing in the Ecologist movement, most Greens are uninterested in the RPR.

Yet, for the neo-Gaullists even to risk ridicule by appealing across the left–right divide is additional evidence of two themes in French political evolution. The first is the presidentialization of the major parties, and of national politics in general. As the RPR has become more and more a presidential party, it has become less and less a Gaullist party, less and less a party of principle. It is a pragmatic party whose raison d'être is electoral and whose founding ideals have become malleable and negotiable. In policy terms, it is a managerial rather than doctrinal party, whose key instincts (Gaullist nationalism and resistance to supranational European integration) no longer are sure signs of what the party's policy actually will be. The clearest example is the RPR's split regarding the 1992 Maastricht referendum on the next stage of European integration, with followers of Jacques Chirac in favor, and those led by Charles Pasqua and Philippe Séguin against. The RPR is, in sum, a vivid example of the decline of ideology in French politics.

The second theme, the RPR's pragmatism, along with the Socialist party's evolution, illustrates how in entire areas of public policy the traditional meanings of "right" and "left" have become ambiguous. Clear and consistent differences between the major parties may well exist at the margins of policy making, but this is the exception. The rule is consensus on parameters in broad areas of policy. This leaves ample room for incremental party differences, but the era is now past when the entire structure of society seemed at issue in an election. Specifically, the left is no longer committed to nationalization as a matter of principle, and the right is no longer ideological about reprivatization (if the RPR had ever, during the mid-1980s enthusiasm for Reaganomics, genuinely abandoned its Colbertism and statism). François Mitterrand's popular slogan in the

1988 presidential election—*Ni . . . ni* ("Neither . . . nor")—meaning no more nationalizations and no more privatizations—was an apt conclusion to the ideologically tumultuous 1980s. The privatizations promised in 1993–95 by the conservative Balladur cohabitation government are no relaunching of ideological war.

Yet as the parameters of policy choices narrow, marked particularities, often traditional characteristics, still differentiate the sociology of the various party electorates. Change in voting patterns has lagged behind party policy convergence, a striking example of cultural steadfastness in the face of public policy change. The main differentiating factor, as for a century, is religion. Religious belief and practice still seems to be the founding principle of the electorate of the right, while secularism underpins the left (see Chapter 2).

During its true Gaullist period, the UNR–UDR was supported by a "catchall party" electorate embodying de Gaulle's own broad, charismatic popularity. But after a fast start in the 1970s against then-President Giscard d'Estaing, the neo-Gaullist RPR under Chirac's leadership shrank to a classic conservative clientele. The RPR today overrepresents older, wealthier voters and farmers, those who define themselves as "right" and "anti-left," those espousing the interests of business, those endorsing state financing for parochial schools, those who vote "personality" rather than "ideas" and those opposed to abortion.[12]

In opinion polls in 1990–92 the RPR became the single largest party preference. As a result of the 1993 elections, in which the RPR was the largest vote-getter, Edouard Balladur was named prime minister and Alain Juppé the foreign minister, in an RPR–UDF–CDS government. Jacques Chirac took no governmental office, avoiding the troubles of cohabitation and reserving himself for the already looming 1995 presidential election.

The Union for French Democracy (UDF) Among the "big three" presidential parties, the RPR by convention occupies the position of "right-wing," with the Socialists (flanked by the Communist party and the Ecologists [see below]) on the "left." In the center–right position is the Union for French Democracy, a liberal–conservative grouping that is actually a somewhat fragile federation of smaller parties. These are the Republican party (*Parti Républicain*, or PR), the Social Democratic Center (*Centre des Démocrates Sociaux*, or CDS), and the Radical party.

Valéry Giscard d'Estaing, president of the Republic in 1974–81, has been its main leader since the UDF was created to support his presidency. After two decades he is still, like Chirac in the RPR, the leading UDF leader against a series of younger rivals, and he maintains a slim hope to be elected president once again in the coming election. Unsurprisingly, the UDF, like the RPR, has been struggling internally over succession and a conflict of political generations.

As a federation, the UDF is less of a self-standing organization than either the PS or the RPR, which are unitary parties. The PS contains many factions, and one or more could even split from the party. But the parent organization would remain. The UDF, on the other hand, as a federation of three separate parties, could one day break apart. The UDF's political coherence—on this point it always was what the other two major parties have become—is not some precise program or set of principles. Unity was built on loyalty to a leader, the young and rising Valéry Giscard d'Estaing, who tried to resemble John F. Kennedy, even to the use of a nickname: VGE, like JFK.

Today, coherence is provided only by a general ambition for office and the fact that, in a French maxim, the UDF "has the merit of existing." The raison d'être of the UDF is, in other words, the weakest of the three major parties.

Valéry Giscard d'Estaing had a precocious, even meteoric career. He was a young finance minister (appointed at 35 years old) in the governments of both de Gaulle and Georges Pompidou. He won the presidency in 1974, against François Mitterrand, at the age of only 46. However in 1981, VGE's career was short-circuited when his bid for reelection was unexpectedly defeated by Mitterrand. Since then he has persistently, single-mindedly, often awkwardly, maneuvered to regain office. In opinion polls he ranks continuously last among the major candidates. But his former prestige, his perseverance, plus the ambiguous publicity of his continuing rivalry with Jacques Chirac, has blocked the way to a successor generation of UDF leaders, as has Chirac in the RPR.

Giscard's own party, the largest of three in the UDF and worth close to 10 percent to 15 percent of the parliamentary vote, is the Republican party (PR). Created in 1962 with the name Independent Republicans (RI), it was a small group of non-Gaullist conservative deputies and ministers. Seeing de Gaulle weakened by the events of May 1968, VGE, in a shocking act of lèse-majesté, called for a "no" vote against de Gaulle in the 1969 referendum, helping to put the General into retirement. The new president, Georges Pompidou, who had been de Gaulle's prime minister in 1962–68, reappointed Giscard to the powerful and prestigious office of finance minister, which he held from 1969 to 1974. On Pompidou's untimely death in April 1974, Giscard then made his successful run for the presidency.

Giscard's plan, guided by his electoral mentor Michel Poniatowski, was to transform French politics by turning the small RI into the most important party in France. It didn't work. Renamed the Republican party in a new look for the 1978 parliamentary elections, the Giscardist current, despite VGE's attractiveness to business and to young people, failed to change voting patterns very much. The PR remained mainly a personalistic clique of ambitious Paris deputies and a coterie of rural bourgeois and aristocratic local government leaders. Many were simply free riding on Giscard's political coattails.

In defense of Giscard, it must be said that his presidency began with the first oil price crisis and international recession in 1974 and ended on the heels of the second crisis in 1979–80. French consumers, under Giscard and his second prime minister, Raymond Barre ("France's best economist," said Giscard the former finance minister), were shielded from the recession's worst effects. But this required artificial support of the franc and putting off adjustment to the higher price of oil. What this meant was that Giscard d'Estaing followed a political and electoral economic policy rather than adjusting to the new oil situation as was done by the German and Japanese governments. Both he and the French economy paid the price a few years later.

The UDF was put together for the 1978 parliamentary elections. Ehrmann and Schain comment on this:

> [A] better organization seemed necessary, not only because of the threat from the Left but also because the RPR under Chirac had given Gaullism a new *élan*. Since it appeared hopeless to balance the forces within the majority by emulating Chirac's organizational effort, the way chosen was the one which parties of the Right and center have always found opportune: an alliance among groups and personalities, however heterogeneous and unrepresentative of major political currents these groups might be.[13]

Besides the Republican party, the largest UDF organization is the CDS, which consists of remnants of the old Christian Democratic party, the MRP, one of the three large parties (with the Socialists and the Communists) in the Fourth Republic.

The third component of the UDF is the majority right wing of the Radical party (3–5 percent), the remains of the historic Third Republic Radical–Socialist party. Its main attributes are local roots and a long tradition of parliamentary expertise. It is a centrist party in policy terms. The Radical party broke apart in 1972 over the question of whether to join in the new Socialist–Communist union of the left alliance. The minority in favor of joining the left (1–2 percent of the electorate) split off under the name Movement of Left Radicals. Since 1972 the MRG minority group has been aligned with the Socialist party.

Why have the UDF's component groups not merged into a single party? It is not ideological or program differences that prevented a single party, but the desire to retain separate influence in a collective leadership. Factionalism helps in waging the battle for offices and prizes.

Like the RPR the UDF has been going through a struggle for the leadership. Giscard's main rival inside the Republican party has been François Léotard, a younger, "successor generation" personality who was named defense minister in the 1993 Balladur government. Léotard, who has presidential ambitions, takes few distinctive positions. He is yet another example of the new-style French politician who offers not ideology but competence, not a connection to historical traditions but a modern look and personal attractiveness.[14]

Some "progressive" centrists, however, moved away from the UDF after Mitterrand's reelection in 1988. They tried, and failed, to create a substantial center–left grouping, with two goals. The first was to counterbalance the PCF's voting importance for the Socialists in Parliament. Without sufficient centrist votes, a Socialist minority government always needed Communist votes, unless it was willing to govern by permanent use of Article 49.3. The second goal of this sputtering center–left was to become a political bridge from the Socialists to the main part of the center, to the CDS. This would bolster Mitterrand's post-1984 strategy of compensating for the Communists' disappearance by widening the Socialist parliamentary majorities toward the center. François Mitterrand and Giscard d'Estaing thus pursued similar "recentered" strategies, another instance of the centrist evolution of French politics.

Despite this modest record the UDF and centrist movements can offer several other political personalities besides Giscard d'Estaing. The key center–left leader has been Jean-Pierre Soisson, a former conservative government member. Soisson was one of four CDS leaders to take the controversial step of cooperating with Mitterrand's strategy of opening to the center by joining the Edith Cresson government in May 1991. Caught in unfounded accusations, he resigned from the new Bérégovoy government in 1992, retreating to a general council presidency in his home region. But he returned rapidly as agricultural minister, an important position as the crucial GATT negotiations were heating up. Raymond Barre, prime minister under Giscard (1976–81) and then a presidential candidate, is another major leader. Simone Weil, who was president of the European Parliament and for decades was the outstanding female French politician, is a third important figure, now minister for social affairs.

Despite Simone Weil's perennial popularity in opinion polls, the center parties never had more than small electoral bases in the Fifth Republic. But this fact does not invalidate the hypothesis of a "centrist" republic. Rather, the new centrism has arisen from a decline of ideology, and from a convergence of right and left. Indeed, the "center" parties may be condemned, paradoxically, by the very emergence of the new centrist republic! For decades the center parties defined themselves precisely against the old ideological left and right. Today the small center groupings seem to have only a tactical importance in French politics. Whether they survive does not depend on their ideas. It depends on how useful their political existence, as junior partners and buffers, will be to others.

The Nonpresidential Parties

The physiognomy of the other parties recapitulates French political development. The other parties are a mixture of old wine in old bottles, old wine in new bottles, and new wine in old or new bottles. Some of them—the Radicals, the Communists, the so-called peasant grouping in the Senate—are hoary beasts who don't know how to give up the ghost. Others, such as the National Front and the two ecological parties, are very contemporary, at least in appearance.

The French Communist Party Before the French Communist vote collapsed below 10 percent in the early 1980s, Jean-Marie Le Pen, as an outsider, used to rail against "the gang of four." He meant the two two-party coalitions that dominated French politics: the PS–PCF on the left, and the UDF–RPR on the right. But even prior to the Soviet Union's collapse in 1989, the French Communist party already had been passed by the National Front, leaving a gang of three, the presidential parties.

After a half century, the French Communist party has become a political cripple. No longer a millenarian movement, it is now mainly a manifestation of the persistent French tradition of protest voting and of the entrenchment of a subculture.

The French Communist party used to be known as the most faithful Communist party, the "eldest daughter of the church" within the international Communist movement, just as France was within the Roman Catholic Church before the French Revolution. Since the Soviet Union's collapse, the PCF is one of the few Communist parties not to have changed its name or its commitment to "a French kind of socialism." It has been stuck for years with obdurate, neo-Stalinist leaders, first of all the top man, Georges Marchais. It has kept only one third of its Fourth Republic vote, and less than half its vote when de Gaulle resigned from office in 1969. Its vaunted capacity to mobilize rank and file and sympathizers has dwindled. Its trade-union link, the CGT, has likewise lost much of its membership and its capacity to mobilize workers, in addition to being less under the Communist party's influence (see Chapter 6). If presidential elections are now to be considered the high point of the struggle for political power, Communist presidential campaigns in the last twenty years have been uniformly disastrous, whether the PCF candidate was the now ridiculed Georges Marchais (general secretary since 1968) or his lackluster 1988 stand-in, André Lajoinie. Hidebound orthodoxy is challenged, unsuccessfully, inside the leadership by a couple of groupings: the "inside" faction is led by party economist Philippe Herzog; another is the so-called *Refondateurs** grouped around the 1981–84 PCF government ministers (Charles Fiterman, Anicet Le Pors, Jack Ralite). There are also outright dissident movements, called *renovateurs* or *reconstructeurs,*** who have established contacts with Socialists and other left-wing groups to promote a new broad left-wing "rally." This alphabet soup of French Communist dissent is very complicated, but also very marginal and anachronistic. It will take at least a few more years, it seems, before the direction of French communism's transformation is decided, including the replacement of the top leadership.

In the meantime the Communists still have modest political assets to manage. In tests of voting strength, the PCF prefers parliamentary to presidential elections. More people vote for the PCF in parliamentary elections, and the party wins more seats, because Communists and Socialists, despite all their animosities, still step aside for each others' front-running candidates (mainly Socialists) at the runoff ballot. A presidential election, by contrast, is for the Communist party basically an exercise of "counting the troops" on the first ballot, since a Communist presidential candidate will never make the runoff, let alone be elected.

On the other hand the PCF, unlike the other nonpresidential parties, still can play a real if modest role in government. Much reduced from the union of the left period of 1981–84, it was still of significance when Communist votes were necessary, as they often were, to fill out a Socialist minority government's majority in Parliament in 1988–93.

From 1981 to 1984 there were four well-watched Communist government ministers, as well as many lesser Communist officeholders, in the union of the left Socialist–Communist coalition government headed by the Socialist Prime Minister Pierre Mauroy under President Mitterrand's general supervision.[15] After quitting the government during the change-over from Mauroy to Laurent Fabius in 1984, the Communists tried to bargain with their votes in Assembly dealings with the three Socialist minority governments after 1988.

The Communist leverage and strategy in Parliament was simple. The Socialist minority governments required either Communist or centrist

---

*refounders
**renovators or rebuilders

votes to pass legislation. So the Socialist prime minister must negotiate either with the disciplined Communists or with amorphous groupings of centrist deputies. (And even Laurent Fabius's majority government negotiated for Communist support, because this maintained a semblance of political legitimacy of the union of the left.) The alternative for the Socialists was the politically weak one of Article 49.3 of the Constitution, by which, as was seen in Chapter 3, a government bill is "considered as adopted" unless a motion of censure defeats it (and, it goes without saying, brings down the government!). This allowed the Socialists to govern, because the requirement for censure—an alliance of the right and the Communists—was unlikely.

Obviously, the Communists would not lightly overthrow a Socialist government, if only because the Socialists would refuse to ally on the second ballot of ensuing elections. To vote out a Socialist government could thus have reduced the Communists almost to zero in Parliament.[16] In the 1993 elections this paid off. The Communist party got fewer votes than in the previous elections in 1988, but because Socialists cooperated, the PCF surprisingly won 23 seats, enough to form a parliamentary group.

The French Communist party was once a great if not a good story. Today it is a rump of world communism's demise, having missed many occasions to reform itself before change had become pointless.

The National Front The National Front, because of its spectacular anti-immigrant and xenophobic attitudes, is the one French political party that foreigners are sure to know about. It is a poisonous political operation that has been an unquestionable public relations success. Its profile merges with European-wide racial, ethnic and religious problems. The FN is one means of expression for two-decade–old controversies concerning "foreigners" and immigrants in French domestic society, and, unfortunately, it is a natural political megaphone for concerns about the upsurge in post–Cold War, post-Communist Europe of nationalism, xenophobia and ethnic conflicts. A decade ago foreigners might have believed that the National Front's surprising level of support confirmed what has often been alleged about the French—that they are a chauvinist, racist people. In the 1990s the French are less likely to be singled out on this score.

Forgotten is the fact that France has been a country of significant immigration off and on since the thirteenth century. In the past century alone successive waves of immigrants (Italians, Poles, Portuguese, Armenians, and so on) were integrated and more or less well accepted into French society. Furthermore, because of the Third Republic's geopolitical policy of filling the interwar French demographic deficit, France in

1930 had, on one calculation, the highest percentage of new immigrant population of any country, slightly higher than even the United States at that moment.[17]

Nevertheless, the tapestry of French history has also been stained by persistent currents of anti-Semitism and anti-Arab racism, of which the Dreyfus Affair, Jean-Paul Sartre's *Anti-Semite and Jew* and Frantz Fanon's *The Wretched of the Earth* are vivid exclamation points. French nationalism strictly speaking, whether anti-British, anti-Italian, or anti-German, is on the other hand more geopolitical than cultural in origin. Since the 1960s, when a booming French economy offered jobs to hundreds of thousands of migrant workers from Algeria, Morocco and Tunisia, social and cultural prejudices and problems have enveloped the resulting second- and now third-generation North African Muslim communities, as well as the much less numerous black African immigrants and clandestine workers. Thus, while the French state historically was neither politically nor officially *anti-immigrant* (to the contrary, assimilationist Polish, Italian and Portuguese immigrants served the geopolitical goal of a larger population in a culturally digestible way), in the past twenty years the French state, and by and large the French people, have become so, along with most other European Community countries. There are two obvious reasons: high domestic unemployment and the growing racial and religious presence of brown and black Afro-French, concentrated in Paris, Marseilles and a few other cities and the French Midi (the Mediterranean south).

Leading the popular uprising against immigration and racial and religious mixing, the National Front perfectly demonstrates the steadfast relevance of "protest" politics in French political culture. Its main characteristics—racial and religious prejudice, antiestablishment rhetoric, populism, know-nothingism—recall the antitax Poujadist movement of the 1950s, the postwar France prototype of protest insurgencies. At the same time, there is in France today a genuine and very practical debate all through the political system, from the political parties down to the neighborhoods and schools in big cities, about the desirability of multiculturalism as opposed to the long-held public philosophy of assimilation to French cultural and social norms. While the National Front is not to be trusted with the country's problems, Le Pen speaks truth when he asserts that the FN "says aloud what many French people say under their breath."

Paradoxical as it may seem at first, the right-wing National Front has inherited a significant number of voters deserting the Communist party. How so? For decades a "protest" vote for the Communist party was a serious way for many French people to send a message to the establishment. But the PCF no longer is a very threatening presence in French politics, and many protest voters consider the National Front a better political megaphone for their discontent. Protest voters aren't really committed to the Communist or National Front programs and don't want these parties in the government. With the Communists it was a protest against "international capitalism" or against "American imperialism"; with the FN today, it is "French" anger about "immigrant workers taking French jobs," or about the Arab communities in French cities and towns, or about "illegal" immigrants benefiting from French medical insurance and social security programs. And since the French Communist party, notwithstanding its supposed internationalism, always had an undercurrent of chauvinism, racism and anti-Semitism in its internal party life, differences between the extreme left and right are sometimes less than they seem from the outside.

The FN also inherits disappointed voters from the major parties, including the Socialists as well as the RPR and UDF. The FN has, in fact, made inroads in various degrees into every sector of the electorate. Nevertheless the statistically typical FN voters are male, from the upper part of the working classes, making a reasonable living, and inhabiting the troubled urbanized and industrial zones of big cities (big-city suburbs, Lorraine, Nord, Lyon region), as well as the Provence–Côte d'Azur. They tend to be nonpracticing Catholics, who think of themselves as centrists as often as right or extreme right. Generally they feel closest to the RPR and believe French democracy "functions badly." Thus most of the FN's voters are neither extremist themselves nor made up of society's most disadvantaged. The FN has a rather large area in which it might grow (people who say they *might* vote FN), and its electoral base tends to be an active and dynamic part of French opinion. The FN's success, according to one analyst, is the product of economic and social crisis in declining industrial areas more than a genuinely Fascist turn. The two key issues for FN voters seem to be violence and insecurity in their own communities, and the new visibility of immigrant communities and culture in France, even when these people have little personal contact themselves with so-called foreigners.[18]

The National Front's surge in the 1980s was built on Jean-Marie Le Pen's charismatic, demagogic leadership. For Le Pen the movement is a national platform from which to influence French opinion and to refloat his presidential candidacy. But the movement's worrisome successes—between 10 and 15 percent of the national vote, up to 25 percent in places like Marseille, which has a 25 percent Muslim, North African population—are due in significant measure also to the two-ballot electoral system. Given a runoff ballot to decide winners, the first ballot is made into a "primary" election, a kind of proportional representation voting in which protest or favorite-son voting can be used to send a message to

Paris. The French say that on the first ballot you vote your heart and on the second you vote your wallet. Most National Front supporters are first-ballot voters who would not want the FN to run the government.

The National Front was founded by Le Pen in 1972. For the next decade it had little success, never getting more than 1 percent of the vote. Suddenly in the mid-1980s its vote skyrocketed. The FN list got 10 percent in the 1984 European Parliament elections, and Jean-Marie Le Pen took almost 15 percent on the first ballot of the 1988 presidential election.

In the 1986 parliamentary elections the FN's quick electoral rise, on French fears about immigrants, briefly touched the bottom of the Communist electoral decline. Then in local elections in the early 1990s the historic change occurred: The FN and PCF electoral curves crossed. The once-mighty French Communist party had been eclipsed not only by its Socialist rival but also by a "surge movement" on the neo-Fascist right. In the most recent 1993 parliamentary elections the FN topped the PCF by more than three points, 12.4 percent to 9.2 percent (see Figure 4.2). This reversal (even if the FN's rise may collapse) constitutes a historic setback for those who still bank on class politics in France.

In addition, the FN vote has gradually become more working class, winning over disillusioned Communist "protest" voters and younger voters, including a French jingo and "skinhead" contingent. In 1988, the FN had 15 percent of 18-to-24-year-old voters, some openly placing themselves "on the extreme right." The National Front's youth electorate indicates that establishment parties have at least temporarily lost their hold on young people. François Mitterrand himself was partially responsible for this, since his 1986 electoral change—a proportional representation law that successfully held down the conservative parties' victory—in the process gave the National Front 35 seats and a political shot in the arm. In majority voting in 1988 the National Front got but one seat. Yet opinion polls continue to give the FN 10–15 percent of the global electorate and its local and regional elected representation is becoming well implanted. Unhappily, the FN seems no longer a "surge" phenomenon, and it is trying, like established parties, to set up a permanent network of secondary groups (workplace, church, schools, universities).

The National Front's growth and durability (at least thus far) was generally not foreseen. Most observers didn't predict the persistence and worsening of conditions that make people vote FN. In addition, observers, probably including President Mitterrand, underestimated Le Pen's capacity to mature as a leader, as a crowd pleaser and as a media personality. And they also didn't foresee the FN's capacity to stabilize Le Pen's presidential electorate.

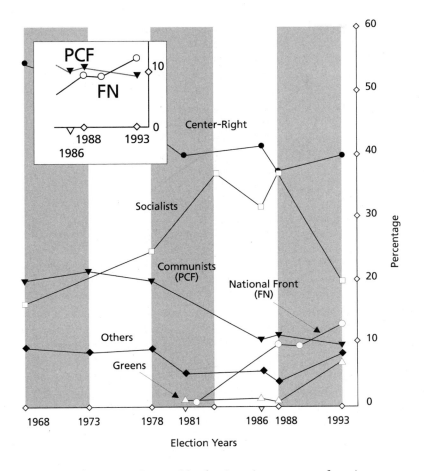

Figure 4 ✦ 2 National assembly elections (percentage of vote)

Will the National Front endure? Will the worry, fear, racism and hope for a providential leader grow or decline? The FN, like all national-populist movements, is focused on its Great Leader. Whatever Jean-Marie Le Pen's private peccadillos or even crimes, his people love him in the excessive way party militants want to love their leaders, very much as analyzed eighty years ago in Robert Michel's classic *Political Parties* (1911). Le Pen's rallies are staged as evenings of communion of the faithful, of revelation and of adulation. Le Pen walks spotlit into an FN rally as if he were a savior arriving on a beam of light. His trademark arms-raised, V-for-victory salute is meant to make people think of de Gaulle, and thus to associate Le Pen with the idea of saving France. Le

Pen was 60 years old in 1991, so for better or worse he is likely to be a factor on the French scene for at least another decade.

To most people, the National Front's program is about immigration and foreigners. Its views on other subjects—economic policy, foreign policy—do not matter much. What is the FN's program on immigration? For years there was no special list of proposals. People knew only that Le Pen wanted to "send the foreigners back" and to have "France for the French." In November 1991 the National Front's ideological spokesman, Bruno Mégret, finally presented a list of fifty measures concerning immigration. It was a sobering catalog of what the hard right would do if it had power. These measures, he said, "obviously don't concern EC citizens, and, in addition, those of our European community of destiny, of culture, of religion and of civilization, as well as those countries with which we might create particular arrangements." The FN immigration policies, in other words, would not violate EC agreements, but would favor whites and Christians, and might agive preference, recalling France's colonial obligations, to people from former French possessions.

Among the fifty measures were the following: Create a government monitoring agency and a "ministry of population"; cut off government financial aid to organizations of foreigners in France; establish the *jus sanguinis* (blood tie) as sole criterion for French nationality; prevent marriages whose purpose is to obtain nationality; reexamine naturalizations made after the cutoff of immigration in 1974; expand the possible reasons for withdrawal of nationality; ban "cosmopolitanism" (multiculturalism) from national education; create quotas for a maximum number of immigrants per school class; end the policy of family reunifications of previous immigrants; end "fake" tourism, whose real purpose is illegal immigration, by requiring a high return bond posted on departure; repudiate the European Schengen Agreement, which is to completely eliminate EC internal border controls on persons; require a health examination at the French border, including a recent test for AIDS; give French people priority in jobs, public housing, family allocations, and so on; create a manufacturing label of origin that reads, "Made In France by French People"; create certain special rules limiting the property rights of immigrants; abolish the ten-year residence permit for foreigners, now renewed almost automatically, in favor of a two-year permit with no automatic renewal; organize special transportation for returning immigrants to their country of origin; expel clandestine immigrants and clandestine workers; use chartered ships and chartered air flights for their return; systematize the search for illegal immigrants and illegal workers in France.[19] An American journalist wrote in 1991, comparing Le Pen to David Duke and Pat Buchanan in American politics:

Le Pen has cleverly exploited the real social and cultural problems posed by immigration to legitimize xenophobic, anti-Semitic and racist appeals to voters caught in an economic squeeze. Mr. Le Pen does not win the national elections, but his National Front party has taken the campaign vocabulary of French politics hostage.[20]

By the time of the 1993 elections, hardline RPR–UDF talk about immigration had stolen some of the National Front's uniqueness. Yet the conservatives boycotted the FN on the second ballot, and the FN lost even the one seat it had won in 1988. Shut totally out of Parliament (including Le Pen's own defeat in Nice), the FN will have to concentrate efforts in its local government positions and perhaps take more to the streets. In any case, the FN popular vote increase was of some consolation to Jean-Marie Le Pen, who plans to run for president again in 1995.

The Ecologists The French ecologist groups are, as in the United States, simultaneously an example of the possibility of the good fight in a single-issue group, and, on the fringes of the movement, an example of a fanatical sense of mission, sometimes an antihumanism in the guise of respect for animals and trees.

In the 1970s, during the "limits to growth" hysteria provoked by the first oil price crisis and the Club of Rome's celebrated report on declining world resources, the French Green party made its electoral appearance. It won 3 percent in the 1978 parliamentary elections (split equally between women and men voters) with 6 percent of the votes of people between 25 and 34 years of age and almost no votes in the over-65 category. In 1988, the Greens got only 1 percent of the vote. In the 1989 European Parliament elections, on a proportional representation vote, the Greens suddenly got more than 10 percent, looming large because 51 percent of the voters abstained. In those same elections, a right-wing populist "Hunting" party got 4 percent largely in protest of a European Green campaign to ban hunting!

The most intense political drama of the Ecologists in the 1980s was the *Rainbow Warrior* Affair, in which the international Greenpeace movement's antinuclear activism led to a death and a political scandal. In July 1985, French intelligence agents blew up the Greenpeace ship *Rainbow Warrior* in the harbor at Auckland, New Zealand, in an attempt to sabotage a Greenpeace campaign that, by sailing into target areas, was trying to frustrate French nuclear testing in the South Pacific. Though his death was not intended, a Portuguese photographer, apparently slow to evacuate the ship after a warning, was killed by the explosion. Reporters revealed first that the saboteurs were not "bandits" but French DGSE (secret service) agents, then that the Elysée military chief had authorized funding, and finally that either President Mitterrand had known about the operation or his staff was involved without his knowledge. Both possibilities were bad, and the New Zealand government protested the fact that French agents were operating in its territory.

President Mitterrand deplored the unquestionably unintentional death of the photographer, but he insisted that the DGSE policing of Greenpeace was a legitimate national security action, because regular testing maintained the French nuclear force. The French state, furthermore, could not allow a citizens' group, however well-intentioned, to block its military policy. Following a bitter internal debate at the highest levels of the French government about who, if anyone, would take responsibility, Defense Minister Charles Hernu, one of the president's oldest political friends, finally resigned. But it seemed clear he was not the only one who might justifiably have done so. The DGSE agents (the so-called false Turenge couple) were put in a minimum security prison in New Zealand for a relatively short sentence before being quietly returned to France for "medical reasons." The episode did not change the government's nuclear testing policy, but it did provoke rethinking the rules of "war" regarding this practice of civil disobedience in defense of the environment.

In any majority voting system—presidential or parliamentary—a few percent can sometimes tip the balance between the parties or candidates. In the French combination of presidential and parliamentary direct elections such is particularly true. This brings the Ecologists considerable attention, particularly as a major election approaches. But many of the green-oriented voters who prefer to vote for a major party vote Socialist, because the PS has seemed the most willing to listen to their concerns and because the "socialist" party is somehow still their natural home. Thus President Mitterrand has included the Ecologists in his political spoils system.

For several years there have been two organized ecologist groups. Ecological Generation, whose spokesman Brice Lalonde has been minister for the environment, is considered by the other group as having joined the establishment. The best known spokesman of the *Verts* (Greens), Antoine Waechter, exemplifies the uncompromising, ascetic mentality in the green movement. The Greens' November 1991 convention decided, prompted by Waechter and a few others, to seek "more responsibilities"—to emphasize political organization, vote getting and power sharing in local government. In local and regional elections they would consider alliances "case by case" with parties across the board, no longer limiting themselves to their "natural" Socialist party big brother. So the Ecologists, meaning their voters, are now courted by the other major parties, meaning the RPR and UDR. Green voters could be decisive in any two-ballot election runoff. Even as low as 2–3 percent, the Ecologist vote could be crucial in the next presidential election.[21]

In the 1993 parliamentary campaign, the two ecologist groups first fought, then made up to run as a tandem. Opinion polls misleadingly gave the Ecologists first 10, then 15, then 20 percent of the vote until a few weeks before the actual ballot. At their zenith, the Ecologists' polls beat the Socialist party! In the end the Ecologists received but 8 percent. Because of the majority electoral system in two ballots, like the National Front they won not a single seat.

Conclusion

French political parties used to be significant and fascinating "stories" in themselves, whether or not they were in power. Today, the major French parties—the Socialists, the Gaullists, the UDF—have become electoral machines more than anything else. They are the nexus of power around which circulate several smaller parties of influence and of protest. This "electoralization" of the major parties is yet another aspect of the normalization of French politics and of the end of French exceptionalism.

Normalization naturally creates its own problems. The public interest is seriously injured when parties no longer embody real philosophies of public policy and important partisan alternatives. French political parties, like French institutions, are in need of renewal. Partisan identities have eroded. Not only the number of floating voters, but also the rate of abstention has increased significantly. Campaign financing (see the next chapter on elections) is one important aspect of party reform. But the fundamental problem is political: It stems from the party system's subordination to presidentialism. De Gaulle's revolution of the institutions turned out to be too much of a good thing. An appropriate equilibrium of powers and rebalancing of the idiosyncratic French constitutional framework is a major task for the post-Mitterrand decade.

Endnotes

1. For example, see François Goguel, *La Politique des partis sous la IIIe république* (Party politics in the Third Republic), 3rd ed. (Paris: Collection Esprit, 1958), and Duncan MacRae, Jr., *Parliament, Parties, and Society in France, 1946–58* (New York: St. Martin's Press, 1967).

2. Julliard, in François Furet, Jacques Julliard and Pierre Rosanvallon, *La République du centre. La Fin de l'éxception française* (The centrist

republic: The end of the French exception) (Paris: Calmann-Lévy, 1988), p. 122.

3. See Thierry Pfister, *Lettre ouverte à la génération Mitterrand, qui marche à côté de ses pompes* (Open letter to Mitterrand's generation, the one that lost its track) (Paris: Albin Michel, 1988), and *La République des fonctionnaires* (The civil servants' republic) (Paris: Albin Michel, 1990). Pfister, Prime Minister Mauroy's advisor and speechwriter, has played a gadfly role criticizing the decline of left-wing politics and the pluralism of spineless consensus.

4. Rosanvallon in *La République du centre*, op. cit., p. 182, and passim.

5. In *La France déchirée* (France torn apart) (Paris: Fayard, 1957), p. 22, quoted by William Safran, *The French Polity*, op. cit., p. 56.

6. The best known, in English translation, was Daniel and Gabriel Cohn-Bendit, *Obsolete Communism: The Left-Wing Alternative* (New York: McGraw-Hill, 1968).

7. See Ronald Tiersky, *French Communism, 1920–1972*, op. cit., Part 2; Annie Kriegel, *The French Communists: Profile of a People* (Chicago: University of Chicago Press, 1972); Georges Lavau, *À Quoi sert le parti communiste français?* (What is the purpose of the French Communist party?) (Paris: Fayard, 1981).

8. *Le Monde*, October 23, 1991, p. 10.

9. Ehrmann and Schain, op. cit., p. 248.

10. Ehrmann and Schain, op. cit., p. 265.

11. Hoffmann, *Decline or Renewal? France since the 1930s*, op. cit., p. 217.

12. Ehrmann and Schain, op. cit., p. 266, citing material from Gérard Grunberg et al., in *Le Monde*, April 27, 1988, p. 12.

13. Ehrmann and Schain, op. cit., pp. 270–271.

14. Léotard once studied to be a priest, and his brother is a well-known movie actor, Philippe Léotard. Unexpectedly, in 1992 Léotard was investigated on charges of fraud and corruption in land and construction deals as the mayor of Fréjus. In February 1993 a trial judge found the charges unsubstantiated and issued a *nonlieu*, meaning the evidence was insufficient to move to a trial. Léotard immediately announced his renewed candidacy for mayor of Fréjus and for the March 1993 parliamentary elections.

15. The most important of the four Communist ministers was Charles Fiterman, minister of transport. Fiterman, getting beyond a long career as a pure party loyalist, has been the internal party opposition's unofficial leader and its hope to replace Georges Marchais. Cer-

tainly in almost any other kind of party, Marchais—who announced his retirement in 1993—would have long ago been replaced.

16. For example, in October 1991 the Cresson government brought a bill before Parliament to squeeze illegal immigrant workers and residents by more intense investigation of employers' official hiring and housing certificates. Before debate began, the Communist parliamentary group said it was in favor but would *vote* in favor only if its own amendments were incorporated. If not, the Communists would abstain, in which case the bill still would pass. See *Le Monde*, October 10, 1991, p. 8.

17. See Patrick Weil, *La France et ses étrangers: L'aventure d'une politique d'immigration 1938–1991* (France and its foreigners: The adventures of an immigration policy, 1938–1991), pp. 23–24 passim. In 1930, according to Weil's source (Gérard Noiriel, *Le Creuset français* [The French melting pot], p. 21) France had 515 immigrants per 100,000 population as against 492 in the United States.

18. See Pascal Perrineau, in the magazine *Commentaire*, no. 55, Autumn 1991.

19. In *Le Monde*, November 19, 1991, p. 8.

20. Jim Hoagland in the *International Herald Tribune*, December 23, 1991, p. 4.

21. The Green convention holds to rules such as absolute male–female parity and speakers limited to two minutes. Waechter's prominence may be problematic for the first round of the 1995 presidential election, since according to parity the next Green candidate is supposed to be a woman.

5

✦

Elections and Electoral Strategies

Games of Presidential and Parliamentary Majorities

Every democracy, while remaining a system of fair play, displays characteristic electoral strategies and partisan ploys. Every set of institutions likewise has its natural bias, just as every nation maintains a collective memory of its electoral history. Fairness and advantage somehow manage to coexist. Democracy, while never completely equitable, is certainly distinguishable from authoritarianism; and the distinction is all-important.

France for over two centuries has been a classic "case" in the running and studying of elections. France has been a society in which a layered and textured political culture suffused the people, where "political families" ran intensely over generations, and where the stake in politics counted so much that victory at the polls often meant the opportunity to use government power for revenge before anything else.

In the last twenty years, by contrast, meanings and commitments in French political culture have been shaken up, and voters have become less predictable, meaning less committed to political families—communism, socialism, Gaullism, and so on—than in the past. The March 1993 parliamentary elections showed again that there are increasingly more independent voters in French politics, as well as more abstainers. Even if most French people still vote consistently left or right as a habit or principle, more and more voters are willing to switch party allegiances, and more than a few—now—will even cross the once unbridgeable left–right divide.

Evolution of French elections is, in short, another symptom of the fading of French exceptionalism. Party ideologies, once visceral, today touch voters less and for shorter periods of time. The vibrancy of Gaullism and communism have been replaced by the shrillness of the National Front and the fundamentalist Ecologists. People perceive that, among the three major governing parties, there are marginal differences, in office if not in principle. Voters have learned that limited resources and the intricacies of international interdependence sap any government's margin of initiative. They are more allergic now than forty, or even twenty years ago, to revolutionary language and are aware, with disgust or satisfaction, of the recentering of left and right.

The loosening of generational ties to parties along with the increase of floating, independent voters raises an old, troubling issue in French political discussion: whether "normalization" and relative depoliticization of political life is all to the good.[1] The fading of France's "silent civil war" raises the question whether there are not prices to pay for consensus, civil apathy rather than civic-mindedness.

Parties are the electoral machines and political loudspeakers of a modern democracy. Political parties, seen as a party system, are also a sort of living fossil record of a nation's historic political struggles. The number, type and age of the parties are a political genealogy.

But a list is not an analysis. Even a *catalogue raisonné*,[*] such as the previous chapter's study of French parties, needs a dynamic analysis that explains how the party system "works," the logic of electoral coalitions and the characteristic partisan formulas for winning power.

In early 1973 a young American political scientist had the opportunity to ask François Mitterrand in private how the newly recreated Socialist party would resolve itself on President Pompidou's 1973 referendum on France's participation in the EEC, over which PS factions were bitterly divided. To outside observers the issue seemed intractable, because the different left- and right-wing factions inside the party were worked up in full political and ideological battle dress. The Socialists who argued for a "yes" party policy wanted to vote in favor of European integration even though it meant having to support the conservative Pompidou government. Those who argued for a "no" vote—mainly the ideological Marxist

---

[*] descriptive catalog

and self-management (*autogestion*) Socialists, whose strength at the time was much larger than today—wanted to vote against the EEC because it was "capitalist." Mitterrand hesitated before answering, seeming to consult with himself about how much to reveal. His amused look intimated that this "intractable" problem should not have been so difficult to figure, even for a professor. Roughly recalled, his answer was: "French people are about evenly divided for and against Europe. The Gaullists and the Communists are against Europe and thus the referendum. If the Socialist party calls for a "no" vote in this referendum, it will speak for 50 percent divided three ways with the Gaullists and Communists. On the other hand. . . ."

Mitterrand hesitated anew; the professor succeeded in drawing the conclusion about how the future president posed the problem of positioning the Socialist party. At the same time, let me add, Mitterrand did not mean that policy making is *only* calculation. On the other hand. . . .

Ambiguous Majorities: The Gaming of Presidential and Parliamentary Elections

French national elections bathe in the ambiguity of the presidential–parliamentary institutional dualism. The first fact about French electoral politics, despite usual presidential dominance, is permanent ambiguity, the permanent "intershock" of the different possible combinations of presidentialism and parliamentarism.

De Gaulle set up, perhaps inadvertantly, an innovative liberal democratic regime by superimposing direct popular election of the president, established in his 1962 referendum, onto the nominally parliamentary government set up in the Constitution of 1958. This, as shown in Chapter 3, creates a "bicephalous," two-headed legitimacy in the national government, which may require a difficult "cohabitation" of presidential and parliamentary leaders. Even though so far avoided, a constitutional crisis, a presidential–prime ministerial struggle with no obvious institutional outcome, cannot be excluded. The consequences for French electoral politics are complex.

Presidentialism incites in top party leaders a loyalty to themselves, as perpetual candidates, above loyalty to party. This is a change from the old French party system in which party ideology, program and loyalty were much stronger values, and in which leaders permanently needed their parties more than in today's presidential popularity contests. Today, party leaders who should logically be focused on parliamentary elections and parliamentary power, are instead driven primarily by their own presidential ambitions. Top leaders perpetually think in presidential terms, even though, as shown above, the representative system described in the constitution is basically parliamentary. The conservatives have suffered on this score particularly, insofar as Jacques Chirac and Valéry Giscard d'Estaing have battled each other for two decades, often to the detriment of RPR–UDF conservative alliance.

On the left, the Communist party's lack of legitimacy has meant its presidential candidates are always symbolic, like the Ecologists. This has left the field open to a Socialist presidential candidate and from 1965 to 1988 François Mitterrand ran largely unchallenged in this open field.

A second effect of presidentialism has been to reinforce all other recentering tendencies affecting presidential parties. Because presidential elections are majoritarian and won by gaining an extra margin in the center rather than on the extremes, leaders who want to make the presidential running will not allow their party's policies to stray very far from what might command a majority at the polls. Yet centrism, as we saw already, is not exactly the same as consensus. A broad centrism of party outlooks—compared to past wars over institutions, the nature of the economy and foreign and defense policy—does not necessarily mean rigorous policy consensus or left–right bipartisanship. But the gradual *recentrage*[*] of the three major French parties has been dialectically a cause of rising *anti*consensus voting, generally for the National Front and the Ecologists. At 10–15 percent each, the anticentrist vote is nearly 30 percent on the first ballots of parliamentary and presidential elections. With abstentions added in, the effective voter turnout in France today is at a record low (see below), though still much higher than in the United States.

The Logic of French Elections

Politicians of the Third (1875–1940) and Fourth (1946–1958) Republics (with Nazi occupation and the Vichy state during World War II) bequeathed a sometimes scurrilous record of manipulating electoral laws for partisan purposes.[2] De Gaulle believed that majority voting in both the presidential and parliamentary elections would make the Fifth Republic a less abused system, or at least that stable government (as contrasted with the parliamentary republic systems) would be favored.

In 1986, however, to limit Socialist party losses and to avoid an overwhelming conservative parliamentary majority, President Mitterrand and the PS parliamentary majority changed the parliamentary electoral law

---

[*] recentering

from majority voting back to proportional representation; this was the first backsliding in the Fifth Republic. After winning the 1986 elections, Jacques Chirac's conservative cohabitation government immediately returned the law to majority voting. Nevertheless the old French electoral law genie had been let out of the bottle.

In 1991–92 President Mitterrand again discussed changing the electoral law, and once again the reason was that the conservatives threatened a rout of the Socialists (which happened in 1993). Mitterrand's idea this time was to mix an element of proportional representation into the majority system by having a certain number of seats, perhaps a third or even half, elected on a proportional basis. (The German mixed electoral system has shown this can work very well.)

In the end, however, Mitterrand did not seek another reversal for the 1993 elections, but perhaps only because his Socialist party was now a minority government, meaning a bill might have led to the government's overthrow even if Article 49.3 were used.

Changing or manipulating electoral laws, for better or worse, seems again a live option for French governments. Mitterrand in principle preferred majority voting to proportional representation. But his larger view, quoted in his Special Advisor Jacques Attali's recent memoir, is that, since each system has its own biases, "there is no good system. It's necessary to change from time to time."[3] At the least this is the thinking of a parliamentarist rather than a presidentialist. At the most, it is one of Mitterrand's rare political blind spots.

As the Partisan Wheel Turns

The history of national elections in the Fifth Republic 1958–1993 is quickly sketched, thanks to the clarifying effects of majority voting.

Political parties, needing majorities to win seats, have been persistently drawn into coalitions. This normally has reinforced the historical "right" and "left" positionings of parties established in the several pre-1958 regimes. Electable presidential candidates, needing a national majority of voters, begin on the right or the left but move toward the center to seek a winning margin. Thus majority voting has paradoxically both bipolarized and moderated the party system. And presidential platforms, at least those of electable candidates, have also been moderated by the need to seek a majority.

On the other hand, parties and candidates whose main purpose is not to win but to act as pressure groups or protest campaigns—the Communists, the National Front, the Ecologists and so on—have tried to remain immune to the moderating, recentering effects of majority voting. The

Communists in the 1970s and 1980s were seduced by the vision of joining the government. The National Front has remained anathema to any putative coalition partners on the right, and so has avoided a similiar fate, at least thus far. The Ecologists have split in two on exactly this point: Ecological Generation (Brice Lalonde) choosing a government role and the Greens (Antoine Waechter) trying to be "neither on the right nor the left."

In Parliament, for almost a quarter century, from 1958 to 1981, the right ruled, in fractious conservative coalitions of Gaullists, Giscardians and assorted conservative centrists. The secret of conservative rule was simple: So long as the Communist party was loyal to the Soviet Union and had 20 percent of the vote, the French left was paralyzed and the right was in power permanently. Thus one spoke of a "tacit alliance" between the French right and the Communist party, in which the PCF remained in "splendid isolation" on the left, while its revolutionary posturing sent a majority into the arms of the conservatives.

François Mitterrand in the 1970s took the risk of allying the Socialists with the Communists. He won his wager, and from 1981 to 1993 the left governed, with the exception of the two cohabitation governments, 1986–88 and the current 1993– Balladur government. From 1981 to 1984 the Communists were junior partners in the union of the left's PS–PCF–MRG coalition government, but the Socialists were always the main force. From 1988 to 1993 the Socialists governed more or less by themselves, in minority governments, while the French Communists withered. Whatever strategy the Communists tried in the last twenty years failed: alliance with the Socialists, breaking the alliance, joining the Socialist-led government, leaving it, being loyal to the old Soviet Union, criticizing the new Commonwealth of Independent States (CIS).

Of the Fifth Republic's presidents, the first two were Gaullists: de Gaulle himself (1958–69) and then his former prime minister, Georges Pompidou (1969–74). The third president, Valéry Giscard d'Estaing (1974–81), was a conservative (UDF) but not a Gaullist, the first step away from "the Gaullist republic." François Mitterrand (1981–95) was the first left-wing and first Socialist president of the Fifth Republic. He is also the first Fifth Republic president to win reelection; Valéry Giscard d'Estaing was the first, in 1981, to run for reelection, being defeated by Mitterrand.

Table 5.1 shows the results of Fifth Republic parliamentary elections, giving two indicators: (1) the percentage of a party's vote on the first ballot and (2) the number of seats won overall—that is, in both the first and runoff ballots.

How will the partisan wheel turn now, moving toward European monetary and political union at the end of the century? What is the next

Table 5 ✦ 1   Parliamentary Elections in the Fifth Republic

Source: Adapted from Ehrmann and Schain, op. cit., pp. 242-243.

Party	1958 Vote (%)	1958 Seats	1962 Vote (%)	1962 Seats	1967 Vote (%)	1967 Seats	1968 Vote (%)	1968 Seats	1973 Vote (%)	1973 Seats
	Registered Voters (millions)									
	27.2		27.5		28.3		28.3		29.9	
PCF	19.1	10	21.8	41	22.5	73	20.0	34	21.2	73
PS	15.5	47	12.5	66	}19.0	}121		41	18.9	89
MRG	—	—	—	—			}16.5	8	1.5	12
Radicals	7.3	33	7.8		}12.6	}41				
Center[a]	22.1	118	9.6	}39			}10.3	}33	}12.4	}31
MRP	11.6	64	9.1	55	—	—	—	—	—	—
UDF[b]	—	—	4.4	36		42		61	10.6	77
Gaullists	17.6	212	32.0	233	}37.7	200	}43.7	293	23.9	184
FN	—	—	—	—	—	—	—	—	—	—
Total	100	487	100	478	100	487	100	487	100	490

Party	1978 Vote (%)	1978 Seats	1981 Vote (%)	1981 Seats	1986[c] Vote (%)	1986[c] Seats	1988 Vote (%)	1988 Seats
	Registered Voters (millions)							
	34.4		35.5		36.6		37.9	
PCF	20.5	86	16.2	44	9.7	35	11.3	27
PS	22.6	107		267	31.6	208	34.8	274
MRG	2.1	10	}37.6	14	0.3	2	1.1	2
Radicals	—	—	—	—	—	—	—	—
Center[a]	—	—	—	—	—	—	—	—
MRP	—	—	—	—	—	—	—	—
UDF[b]	21.4	119	19.2	63		129	18.5	130
Gaullists	22.5	155	20.8	87	}42.0	145	19.2	128
FN	—	—	—	—	9.9	35	9.8	1
Total	100	491	100	491	100	577	100	577

[a]Outside government majority   [b]PR and other center parties in government majority
[c]The 1986 election was by proportional representation. Unaffiliated deputies and splinter groups are not included.

likely phase in French electoral politics? Will the establishment right and left wings hold firm? Will the extremist parties stay outside? Will the center parties merge completely with the left–right framework, or will a new center emerge, built on a PS–UDF bargain? Or, alternatively, will the completion of a historical phase in French political history, the end of French exceptionalism and the recentering of the republic, mean new parties and new partisan alignments?

It is hard to know what would be worse: perpetuation of the left–right establishment? a mushy centrism? a new polarization? the eclipse of national politics by European politics? or the failure of Europeanist politics because of the "new nationalism" in post–Cold War Europe?

All this is a brave new menu for French politics, and only a reckless futurist would make specific predictions. What is legitimately worthwhile, on the other hand, are some comments concerning the environmental conditions within which the next phase in French partisan politics will evolve.

Majority voting, perhaps combined with some share of proportional representation as Mitterrand has suggested, will probably stay in place. (Notice that mixed systems, combining advantages and defects of different rules, may be the long-run future of European domestic politics and of the EC political system.) This will keep the necessity of seeking majorities in both parliamentary and presidential elections and the nearly irresistible drive to the center where the winning vote margins are found.

For the governing parties of right and left, two other factors lead toward centrism. The first is all the levels of international interdependence: the effects of European integration, the homogenizing effects of international competition, the desire to emulate others' successes in facing common problems, the seepages or avidly sought influences of international culture. The second is the constriction of domestic policy possibilities because of tight money and national resources in the face of endlessly multiplying problems.

A third influence creating centrism and consensus is the individual factor, elements of personality and character. Candidates and leaders try to imitate one another's successful gambits, nationally and increasingly—thanks to CNN—internationally. Politicians across borders come to resemble one another, or they try to. The French, as always, have been among the world's best resisters of this kind of influence. But the departing generation may be the last of France's "historic" leadership groups, those with a vivid connection to the political culture of historic France. "CNN-ization" may, although probably less so than in other countries, contribute to the homogenization of a post–Cold War French elite as well as to policy consensus and political centrism. In this sense François

Mitterrand may soon be missed as, among other things, the last "really French" president.

Rising Abstentions:
A Normal Aspect of Recenteredness?

Abstentionism in French elections is in some ways a clear trend, corre-lated with an overall partisan decline and depoliticization in French po-litical culture. But there are different kinds of elections and voting, and there seems a certain voter intelligence at work.

Abstention is not rising in all kinds of elections. In fact there are contradictory trends. On one hand, voting in parliamentary elections is significantly down.

> In both the Third and the Fourth Republics general disenchantment with parliamentary institutions never prevented a high turnout at na-tional elections. Since the consolidation of republican institutions in 1885 . . . electoral participation never fell to less than 71 percent of regis-tered voters, and in most elections was much higher. Constituency inter-ests and an individualized appeal to the voters kept tension, and hence interest, high.[4]

The 1988 abstention of over one third of registered voters was the high-est in the history of French republican parliamentary voting. Though it had been nearly equaled once, by the 1962 election at the end of the Algerian crisis, the 34 percent abstention rate in 1988 far exceeded those of other previous elections (23 percent in 1958, 19 percent in 1973, 29 percent in 1981 and 22 percent in 1986). An appropriately mediocre political result ensued: the first minority government (Rocard) in the history of the Fifth Republic.

Yet, just one month previously, May 1988, the abstention rate was minimal in the two ballots of the presidential voting, which produced Mitterrand's strong reelection. It was about the same as in 1981 (just 19 percent on the first ballot and 14–15 percent on the second) and not much different (3–4 percent) from the other two Fifth Republic direct presidential elections of 1974 and 1965. On the other hand, abstention rates have gone through the roof (reaching U.S. levels) in voting for the "faraway" European Parliament: between 40–50 percent in each of the three elections so far, 1979, 1984 and 1989. And on a referendum the French people considered of little importance—the November 1988 Ro-card referendum on a new governmental structure for New Caledonia—the abstention rate was 63 percent. What these different rates of absten-tion seem to mean is that French voters have "elected" the presidential election, which they correctly perceive as the keystone of the Fifth Republic's constitutional and political edifice. The president's preeminence and the decline of party differences seem to have combined to devalue parliamentary elections, except when, as in the 1986 election that produced Cohabitation I, voters want to punish the president and sanction his party's policies, even though they can't vote him out of office.

In addition, abstentions rising from 40 percent (1979) to over 50 percent (1989) indicate declining or wavering enthusiasm for the European Parliament. During the 1980s, despite institution of direct election in 1979, the European Parliament did not much gain in importance, either in its real powers or in the eyes of French voters. If it does gain in significance, French voters will surely respond by turning out in greater numbers, especially if the French parties run more attractive candidates, which will occur in proportion to the parliament's increased importance.

As for abstentions on referenda, each referendum is different. Turnout varies heavily most of all with the subject. French voters no longer troop obediently to the polls for the mere fact of a referendum. De Gaulle's two crucial referenda in 1962 (Algeria and the directly elected presidency), as well as the third in 1969, all had very high (80 percent) participation. In 1969 the two issues—reducing the powers of the Senate and creating administrative regions—did not impress voters. But they knew from de Gaulle's usual warning that to defeat the referendum would provoke the president's immediate resignation, which of course it did. Georges Pompidou's Europe referendum in April 1972, asking for approval for the EC's enlargement to include Britain and other countries, was, even though it succeeded, a political failure both in turnout and in the narrowness of victory.

Following this mediocre result, the referendum lay in disuse until Michel Rocard's minority Socialist government presented the 1988 referendum on New Caledonia: As pointed out just above, only one third of the voters turned out.

The most recent use of the referendum was Mitterrand's perilous exercise in ratifying the December 1991 Maastrict Treaty. Prior to the Maastricht referendum campaign in summer 1992 French public opinion polls registered little recalcitrance about European integration. In particular, substantial majorities, varying between 55 percent and 65 percent, said they accepted the two big ideas of a single European currency and a common foreign policy, while 70 percent agreed that European integration is good, or at least necessary, for France. However, during the campaign, popular support suddenly plummeted, and the Maastricht referendum was approved by a bare 51 percent majority. What happened? Was a near majority of the French genuinely against European integration?

Many voters voted not on Maastricht, but to register a protest: either an anti-Mitterrand, anti-Socialist party protest, or a generic protest of unemployment or the problems with "foreigners." Since Maastricht was the government's bill, voting against it was voting against the Socialists and Mitterrand. President Mitterrand later said he had never expected more than 52 percent in favor, meaning a result similar to a parliamentary or presidential second ballot. But this rings false. He would not have risked a referendum that might actually be lost, especially since the point of the exercise was to regain momentum lost when the Danes voted against Maastricht. In France the Parliament itself could have approved Maastricht alone. The referendum was constitutionally unnecessary and a near disaster politically, which shows how even the shrewdest, most experienced political calculators can be wrong. Thus, while the electoral map of the Maastricht referendum outcome (see Figure 5.1) seems to show that the French are about evenly divided for and against Europe, that is surely erroneous. There is certainly a recognizable division, as the map shows, of "European" and "nationalist" geographical variations in the voting public, although rather than the simple 51–49 split that the referendum seemed to show, it is surely a much larger majority in favor of European integration in general, with different size majorities on specific questions.

What the map of the Maastricht referendum really shows is that the French electorate, as always, is about evenly divided between right and left: The 51–49 split looks like nothing more than the result of a presidential or parliamentary second ballot! The French voters changed the issue on Mitterrand in 1992, turning the Maastricht referendum into an ersatz national election or plebiscite.

The cause of European integration is safer in France than it appeared in the September 20, 1992 vote. Mitterrand's referendum, with the incomprehensible Maastricht Treaty to ponder, strongly resembled de Gaulle's unloved 1969 referendum on the Senate and the regions, which the General lost to a 53 percent no vote, a "presidential" margin. The difference was that in 1992 the voters decided, even if narrowly, to "keep" their president (Mitterrand, though asked about it, had made sure *not* to threaten to resign), whereas they had voted crashingly to chase de Gaulle from office one year after the antigovernment, antistate events of May had ended in such a paradoxical Gaullist parliamentary victory in June 1968. If electorates can be said to possess wisdom, the French voters showed it: Their narrow yes vote meant that they voted up Maastricht while still administering a grand remonstrance to Mitterrand. This permits the president to finish his term with legitimacy and a modicum of political grace in Cohabitation II rather than struggling all alone against

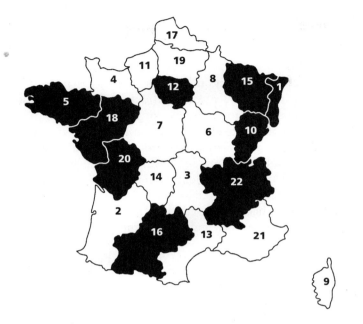

Vote Percentages on Referendum

	Yes	No		Yes	No
1. Alsace	66.2	33.8	12. Ile-de-France	54.1	45.9
2. Aquitaine	49.6	50.4	13. Languedoc-Roussillon	47.0	53.0
3. Auvergne	49.4	50.6	14. Limousin	46.6	53.4
4. Basse-Normandie	48.9	51.1	15. Lorraine	54.4	45.6
5. Brittany	60.3	39.7	16. Midi-Pyrénées	52.1	47.9
6. Burgundy	48.7	51.3	17. Nord-Pas-de-Calais	44.6	55.4
7. Centre	46.1	53.9	18. Pays de la Loire	54.1	45.9
8. Champagne-Ardenne	49.3	50.7	19. Picardy	42.9	57.1
9. Corsica	43.7	56.3	20. Poitou-Charentes	50.2	49.8
10. Franche-Comté	50.3	49.7	21. Provence-Alpes-Côte d'Azur	44.8	55.2
11. Haute-Normandie	44.8	55.2	22. Rhône-Alpes	54.8	45.2

Figure 5 ✦ 1 Electoral map of September 1992 referendum on Maastricht Treaty
Source: Adapted from *Le Monde.*

a repudiation of the major work—the construction of Europe—of his presidency and his long career.

Abstention is different from protest voting, but often not less significant for electoral outcomes. French politicians and electoral analysts have long cultivated a concern for its ups and downs. France has traditionally produced high voter turnouts, so the recent upward trend in legislative election abstentions is of significance.

Two explanations stand out. First, the trend confirms that political parties have lost public prestige, loyalty and confidence. Parties are much less powerful organizers of voters and issue thinking than they used to be. But this decline in party partisanship and depoliticization vis-à-vis the old party political culture is not necessarily a desertion of politics as such by the public. The logic of the Fifth Republic's institutions has just worked its will. The preeminence of the president, except under cohabitation circumstances, puts the elections for Parliament under the presidential shade. But cohabitation may become more frequent, reinvigorating parliamentary voting, as political culture and party structure evolve farther away from France's exceptionalist past.

The current problem is that, given the global recentering of policy options in France today, presidential voters choose a candidate and, presumably, a policy emphasis. But they do not opt for an entire way of life, a "new society." In France, as elsewhere, voters increasingly are asked to vote for character rather than programs. They realize that electoral programs are rhetorical or at least very changeable once politicians must deal with the problems of governing and the temptations of being in power. They sense, more or less acurately, the limits of policy choice on any president and any government. So the increase in abstentionism in parliamentary elections does not yet signal a vital political decline, so long as presidentialism sufficiently renews political culture and so long as party purpose can, at some point, be reinvigorated.

The European Parliament and French Parties

The European Parliament is the parliamentary institution of the European Community. Its members were indirectly chosen, through various methods in the different countries, until 1979. This was a manifestation of the EC's early stage of development and intergovernmental structure. Direct elections were held first in 1979, with each country choosing its own electoral law. The reason for direct election was to develop a democratic legitimacy for the European Parliament as well as public consciousness of its potential importance. The Parliament's powers remained extremely limited through the end of the 1980s—essentially the power to discuss and to propose amendments to Commission proposals. Until the European Parliament clearly had won legitimacy among the various

European country electorates, it was not at all antidemocratic to keep its powers under firm control. This was all the more so because parliamentary delegation quality and seriousness of purpose varied much from one country to another.

French parties, unlike in certain other countries such as Italy or Germany, have generally not sent high-powered delegations. For influential but defeated French politicians, the European Parliament has served as a kind of exile or limbo, or even as the last post for second-rank politicians. Former president Giscard d'Estaing, for example, took a seat in the EP while he tried to work his way back to the top of the French domestic political scene. The French disregard for the EP is contrasted most significantly with the Germans, whose EP delegation features politicians of influence and meets regularly with the chancellor. German enthusiasm for the EC Parliament flows logically from the German Parliament's great domestic influence, and the desire for more balanced political institutions in the Community than is now the case. The French disregard for the EP in a similar way reflects the Fifth Republic's centralization and the low prestige and power of the French Parliament in the French system.

Elections, Centrism and Consensus

The concept of the "recentered" French republic, it is now clear, does not focus on the small parties known formally as center parties. Formally "center" parties have small electorates; in the 1989 European Parliament elections, a "center" coalition led by the popular Simone Weil, former president of the European Parliament, got only 8 percent of the vote.

In the recentered republic a basic fact is that the presidential election, which determines the political landscape, is won in the center, not on the right or the left. French voting in presidential elections has become suffused with majoritarian tendencies, roughly balanced between right and left. The right and left have now accepted each other's legitimacy, a fact of historical importance. Because individual candidates can increasingly hope to win votes across the right–left divide, either can win a majority. By winning the presidency in 1981, François Mitterrand made the historic proof that the Fifth Republic was not a permanent government of the right. Thus, as in consensual republics everywhere, a "swing" vote becomes key. And this swing vote in France is only partly located in the nominally centrist parties.

An important characteristic of French elections is the growing number of independent, noncommitted, floating voters. This may be a conservative voter who switches to the left, or vice versa. But since there are many parties, not just two, in a parliamentary election, and since there are perhaps six first ballot presidential candidates, a floating voter always has more than one place to jump on the first ballot. A disaffected Socialist or a conservative may equally well decide to vote ecologist. Or a disillusioned Communist voter might vote for the National Front (a recent internal party controversy in fact concerns PCF members with affinities and contacts with the nationalist right). Or a disappointed Mitterrand supporter might plausibly vote for a conservative, a centrist or an ecologist presidential candidate. In any case, it is clear that there are more alternatives for an independent, floating voter than in, say, the American system.

The floating voter in the new French electorate may transgress with insouciance the once-sacred line between left and right, right and left. An old taboo has been broken, and in this new partisan landscape the nominally "center" parties lose their strategic and tactical reason for being, which was to serve as both buffer and a stake in the negotiation of coalitions. The republic has been "recentered," but it is not a republic governed by the so-called center parties.

The French electorate does overall seem to want centrist government. Public opinion does not ask that problems be solved in extreme ways, or with extreme means. The old days are gone of ideological promises and programs to "change society." French voting patterns over the past two decades have enhanced all the other centripetal forces dragging parties to the policy center.

Of greatest symbolic value, it has now been demonstrated that the French are willing to accept as president either a right- or left-wing politician. In fact, what will seem surprising to newcomers to things French is that it used to be different. For students whose intellectual and historical frame of reference is essentially post–Cold War Europe, an effort of imagination is required to understand how, for example, as late as 1981 many responsible officials genuinely worried that François Mitterrand's election, putting Communists in the French government, would trigger a disastrous situation. For more experienced observers, a different effort is required: to remember all we once knew, to keep our sense of history intact.

In short, the major policies of the government left and right parties lie within a rough consensus. In terms of policies, left and right are, roughly speaking, "centrist." Their differences are nuances within a tacitly agreed framework, a framework that is simultaneously French, EC and international. Moreover, it is no longer certain which party will espouse which ideas within the consensus. As young peoples' responses to political polls suggest, what is "left" and what is "right" is no longer obvious.

The left, at least in the Mitterrand presidency, has been strong on defense and very conservative in fiscal and monetary policy. The consensus has been made by the left joining the conservatives on the economy, on defense, and on the institutions. The Fifth Republic was created by Gaullists, and it could survive only by winning legitimacy also on the left. This it has done. The policy limits of both right and left seem increasingly to be set by European norms of fiscal, monetary and social policy behavior.[5]

What to do about unemployment, immigration, social security and public order may be the main issues in French politics (as in other European Community countries). The domestic debate allows for differences, but differences within limits. As Jacques Delors puts it, "a little higher (or lower) interest rate policy, a more hardline or more understanding government policing of clandestine immigration," and so on. Political decisions concern setting priorities among the same set of problems, given their varying severities. Is fighting inflation (keeping interest rates high) more important than fighting unemployment (lowering interest rates to stimulate investment to create jobs)? Is reducing government spending more important than maintaining government benefits, for example, in health care? Should spending for defense be slashed in order to reduce government deficits?

Le Pen, on the other hand, embodies the French people's protest about a problem to which there is no clear policy solution, for it is more than a problem of money. His electoral success is one way in which people can pressure the major parties—from whom they do not want dramatic solutions and would be (most of them) shocked if such were attempted.

In 1984–85, looking at a probable Socialist defeat in the 1986 parliamentary elections, Mitterrand's consideration of changing the electoral law had much to do with the newly important National Front. To keep majority voting would minimize the FN's National Assembly presence, whereas a change to proportional representation would maximize it. Mitterrand opted to change the law, and the FN entered Parliament for the first time, with a large group of 35 deputies. It was a political scandal.

What was Mitterrand's electoral gaming here? Did it make sense?

Proportional representation maximized the National Front's electorate and victories. Why? Because PR meant National Front votes would be "useful," would not be wasted as in a majority system where the FN would lose almost everywhere because it had no allies with whom to seek majorities. With 15 percent of the votes in a PR system, a party gets 15 percent of the seats. With 15 percent in a majority system a party with no allies will be beaten in every district.

But why would President Mitterrand give the FN an electoral success, putting it in Parliament with a significant group of deputies, for which he was sharply criticized on all sides? There were several reasons.

Mitterrand hoped that the PR law, by maximizing the National Front's success, would split the right-wing vote enough to prevent an RPR–UDF victory. This failed, though the size of the RPR–UDF parliamentary majority was considerably less than it would have been under a majority voting system. Second, never conceding any election as beyond reprieve, Mitterrand believed a PR system would also maximize the Socialist vote, the centrist vote and the Ecologist vote, perhaps allowing a government with those three parties. If the left pulled the election out, the Communists might even rally. However, PR only minimized the Socialist party's losses and created the cohabition government coalition of RPR and UDF.

Finally, Mitterrand believed that, since the National Front's popular support was a social fact that had nothing to do with electoral laws, to have the FN and Le Pen inside Parliament, constrained by the rules of the game, was safer than having him outside in the streets, free of institutional responsibilities. Nevertheless, Mitterrand was criticized for legitimizing Le Pen and his nationalist–racist discourse. Quoted by his Special Advisor Jacques Attali, Mitterrand summed up the 1985–86 electoral situation:

> We have four objectives, which we have to put in priority if we can't have them all: no absolute majority for the RPR; no absolute majority for the RPR–UDF; help the center to emerge; give the largest number of seats possible to the PS. Majority voting in two ballots favors the RPR. It must be eliminated. If the left has only 41 percent, whatever the electoral law, the last three objectives are unattainable. As a result, given that all the possible electoral laws will give an UDF–RPR majority, they are identical for us. And we shouldn't try to work it so they have a narrow majority. The narrowest are the strongest. Except with national proportional representation, with every other electoral system you get a majority of seats with 45 percent of the votes. . . . Our choice is thus only between having national proportional representation or having 60 deputies more (through a system of remainders), realizing that in any case no system will stop the RPR–UDF coalition from obtaining a majority.[6]

A return to majority voting was one of the Chirac government's first laws in 1986, but cohabitation worked out poorly for the conservatives, and the Socialists in May 1988 looked to achieve another smashing absolute majority following Mitterrand's big victory in the presidential election and his dissolution of the Assembly. In fact the June 1988 parliamentary elections, on the basis of the reinstated majority electoral law, looked likely to produce such a large Socialist majority that, remarkably, President Mitterrand cautioned the voters, saying that "it isn't good when one party rules alone."

Sometimes voters think ahead and opinion polls are misleading! The June 1988 parliamentary elections produced not a Socialist party landslide, even with a majority electoral law, but only a small plurality. The result was minority government, since the Communist party was kept out and an attempted centrist movement failed to produce. On the other hand, because of the reinstated majority system the National Front got only a single seat.

Did Mitterrand commit a grave error by manipulating the 1986 electoral law, increasing the clientele for the National Front? Or would the FN have grown in society anyway? And if Mitterrand did commit an error, was it political (i.e., a miscalculation of the outcome) or constitutional and moral (i.e., it is bad to manipulate institutions for partisan purpose)? An argument can be made both ways.

In an analytical sense, however, Mitterrand's strategy of splitting the right in order to keep the left in power is, after all, nothing more than the exact inversion of the right's strategy of 1958–1981, of counting on the Socialist–Communist split in the left to keep themselves in office. At this "macro" level, French electoral politics is simple to grasp! As for Mitterrand's "promotion" of the National Front: No one argues that the president wanted this. Yet strategies can backfire, and policies can produce wrong or unintended consequences.

A recent text on France asserts that "it now seems clear that parties are the principal organizers of political life in France, both within the institutions and among the voters."[7] Perhaps or perhaps not. But what seems even more pertinent about contemporary France is that political life as such is *less* organized than in the past, and that overall political parties in France have declined in importance, not increased. There are fewer party members, fewer clear party sympathizers, fewer militants and less party ideology. The French today seem to care less about political parties per se, and about the differences between them, than at any time in a century, since party organization by the left made parties the key to parliamentary elections, obliging the right to organize in response. The already noted rise in electoral abstention is a confirming trend, running parallel to the decline of party memberships and to the decline of membership in labor unions. A pattern emerges of partisan disengagement.

The loss of partisanship has been sharp in the Communist party and in the Gaullist party. But the disappearance of party activists is heavy also in the Socialist party—partially as a secondary effect of the decline of communism. The decline of the PCF is a practical permission for the

Socialists to relax without fear of being "white-anted" or "drowned" by their "enemy-brother." Even the Ecologists have less intense, less militant public support than 5 or 10 years ago.

The sole exception is the National Front. But the FN is the exception that proves the rule. The FN is a protest party. It is precisely the kind of populist politics made possible when established parties lose their organizing grasp of public opinion and political activism. The success of the National Front is, in other words, hard evidence that the major parties are not representing and organizing French political opinion very capably—except that, *faute de mieux*, they still win the elections.

The 1988 legislation on financing of political parties is consensus that the party system needs serious reform. It is possible to argue that this governmental concern with party money is a sign of the parties' preeminence in politics.[8] More precisely it seems to be a concern with the preeminence of elections in producing the prizes that politicians vie for and the division of power on the basis of National Assembly groups. Of course it is true that the parties organize the elections by providing the candidates. But particularly in the all-important presidential election, candidates are not limited to money from the parties. Current scandals rage about political financing. Illegal corporate and other private money is alleged, concerning President Mitterrand's reelection campaign in 1988, and in Socialist party financing generally.[9] Despite the new party finance law the old methods, not unique to France, will be sturdy resisters to change. Accusations of unscrupulous campaign financing have for decades been hurled across the entire spectrum of Fifth Republic politics, from the "secret treasuries" supposedly held by semiobscure, proto-Fascist Gaullist political operatives, to various charges about Valéry Giscard d'Estaing's campaigns run by Michel Poniatowski, to the current allegations against the Socialists and also the National Front (Jean-Marie Le Pen is alleged to have become personally well off financially through a suspicious inheritance of a murdered colleague's estate).

On the other hand, Socialist party financial corruption is a kind of proof of the normalization of the differences between right and left. Twenty-five years in opposition made it easy for the left-wing parties to be critical of the right. Now the Socialists, after a decade in power with the temptations and corruptions of office, can no longer claim to be the party of clean hands.

Not to mention the browbeaten Communist party, whose alleged "gold from Moscow" was the perennial party finance scandal of the Cold War. In October 1991 the PCF faced the awkward disclosure by a glasnost-minded Soviet journalist that the old stories about Moscow gold were true (and only the credulous had doubted it!). Secret receipts were published, signed by none other than PCF treasurer Gaston Plissonier, for amounts of $1–2 million annually, continued even into the late 1980s. French Communist leaders continued to deny the story, incredibly and, in post–Cold War Europe, laughably.

The 1993 Parliamentary Elections and Cohabitation II

The Union for France (*Union pour la France*, or UPF) conservative coalition of the RPR and UDF crushed the Socialists in the March 1993 parliamentary election. This inaugurated Cohabitation II, the second instance, after 1986–88, of divided government: a Socialist president facing a conservative parliamentary majority and cabinet empowered to govern by Article 20 of the Constitution. The conservative victory was a landslide of no less than 80 percent of the seats (see Figure 5.2).

Combined with incumbent control of the Senate as well as of most regional and departmental governments, the conservative landslide left President Mitterrand alone at the top as the only counterweight to conservative policies. Does this landslide victory mean that ideological war has returned? The answer is, paradoxically, no. The 1993 elections, beyond the landslide in numbers of seats, confirms the tendencies we have found underlying the recentered republic.

The hidden hand in the 1993 electoral outcome was not party appeal, but the electoral system itself: majority voting in two ballots. With 40 percent of the first ballot vote, the RPR–UDF coalition had *exactly* the same score as it did in 1988—when it lost to the Socialists! What made the difference? How could the conservatives, with the same percentage of the vote at the first ballot, move not merely from defeat to victory, but to a majority larger than any in the history of the French republics?

The key was the collapse of the Socialist party, which fell from almost 40 percent in 1988 to 20 percent in 1993. Conservative UPF candidates won almost everywhere, not so much because of their own popularity but because the opposition, of whatever stripe (Socialist, Communist, Ecologist), was divided, demoralized, deflated. The logic of majority voting is that, in the most extreme case, if one side wins 51 percent in each district it will get 100 percent of the seats, because it wins 51–49 percent in each contest. And for the conservatives it was obviously easier to advance from first ballot results to a majority on the second ballot. So the left was routed because the majority electoral system intensified modest majorities of votes into a historically unprecedented majority of seats.

Where did the Socialists' 20 percent loss go? Basically to the minor left-wing parties, meaning the two green parties—Ecological Generation

The Left

Party	% National Vote*	Seats
Socialists	28.25	54
Communists	4.61	23
Radical left }	3.32	6
Other left }		10
	****36.18**	**93**

The Right

Party	% National Vote*	Seats
RPR	28.27	247
UDF	25.84	213
Other right	3.56	24
NF	5.66	0
	****63.33**	**484**

Total number of seats: 577
Electorate: 37.5 million

*Second round
**Omits minimal vote for Ecologists and fringe candidates

The new parliamentary alignment, 1993, . . .

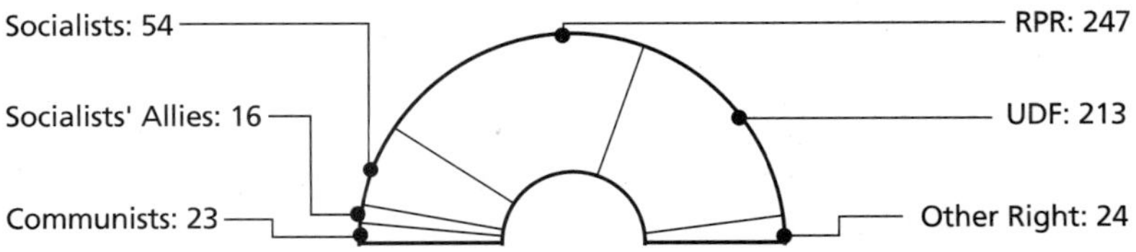
Socialists: 54
Socialists' Allies: 16
Communists: 23
RPR: 247
UDF: 213
Other Right: 24

and the old, 1988

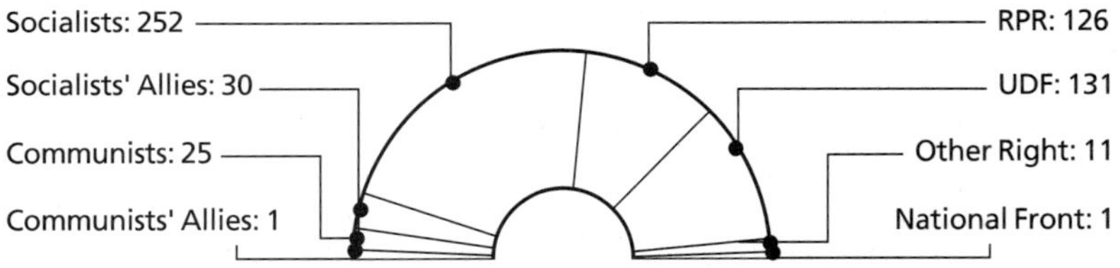
Socialists: 252
Socialists' Allies: 30
Communists: 25
Communists' Allies: 1
RPR: 126
UDF: 131
Other Right: 11
National Front: 1

Figure 5 ✦ 2 Electoral results and parliamentary alignment from March 1993 elections
Source: The Financial Times, March 20, 1993, p. 2.

and the Greens—and the Communists, as well as to the "various center–right" category. Because the Socialists and Communists as usual stood down for each other's better-placed candidates for the second ballot, the Communists were able to win twenty-three seats. Because the National Front had no electoral allies at all—that is because RPR–UDF shunned it—the FN, in spite of winning a few percentage points more than the PCF, won no seats at all, losing even the single seat it had won in the previous election.

On the second ballot runoffs, the missing 20 percent of 1988 Socialist voters either stayed home or voted massively for other parties. The right won in a landslide, even though the first-ballot result showed a wish to kick out the Socialists more than to plebiscite the right. Voters had little reason to believe the conservatives would be more successful than the Socialists in solving France's major problems, and Balladur quickly told the French that unemployment would get worse before it got better, which it did.

Indeed, unemployment, the EC-wide dilemma of the 1990s, in this election finally replaced immigration, "foreigners" and racism as the dominant issue in French politics. Even though high unemployment was continent-wide, voters' patience with the minority Socialist government's "conservative" emphasis on low inflation and the "strong franc" seemed finally to snap. Exasperated citizens wanted a shift in emphasis, which the Mitterrand–Bérégovoy government was not promising. (Moreover, lowering the unemployment rate requires new growth to create new jobs, which depends on the German and U.S. economies over which the French government has little leverage.)

Politically worn out and mired in corruption scandals after a long decade in office, the Socialists were in effect shrugged off by the French electorate in 1993 though there was little reason to believe the cohabitation government of Edouard Balladur would, by its policies alone, make a big difference. On the other hand, the Balladur government is bringing a different emphasis in certain social issues—law and order, illegal immigration, government subsidy of religious schools—in which a different tone amounts to a different policy.

The 1993 election result, according to a venerable French political adage, manifested the urge to *sortir les sortants*, to "get rid of the incumbents." The next bunch of rascals may not be better, but at least they will be different. It would be a mistake, however, always to exclude the possibility of a change for the better.

Conclusion

In terms of long-range tendencies, pessimists will see the effect of the recentered republic on the parties as basically negative, the political expression of a thin complacency. Underneath the long Socialist years in power and underneath the misleading conservative landslide victory of 1993 lies the truer fact: depoliticization and decline of partisan spirit in France, a decades-old concern, now a reality. It is not only a decline of interest in partisan politics in favor of a fixation on standards of living (what General de Gaulle contemptuously called "the price of bread"), but also a deeper distancing of citizens from "the idea itself of the republican state as arbiter and protector," a consequence, says François Furet, of "the confiscation of politics by the technocrats of economic growth."[10] If so, it is not a political malady peculiar to France. But it certainly distinguishes contemporary France from postwar France.

Endnotes

1. See Depeux, *La dépolitisation*, op. cit.

2. Sophisticated study of electoral laws and behavior has long been a French specialty. A good study of how electoral laws affect politics is Peter Campbell, *French Electoral Systems and Elections since 1789* (Hamdon, Conn.: Archon Books, 1965). In French, see Raymond Huard, *Le Suffrage universel en France, 1848–1946* (Universal suffrage in France, 1848–1946) (Paris: Aubier, 1991), and Alain Lancelot, *L'Abstentionnisme électoral en France* (Electoral abstentionism in France) (Paris: Armand Colin, 1968).

3. Jacques Attali, *Verbatim* (Paris: Fayard, 1993), pp. 43, 690.

4. Ehrmann and Schain, op. cit., p. 200.

5. See my essay, "Mitterrand, France and Europe," *French Politics and Society*, 9 no. 1 (Winter 1991): 9–25.

6. Attali, *Verbatim*, op. cit., pp. 785–786.

7. Ehrmann and Schain, op. cit., p. 288.

8. Ibid.

9. See an account written by a police inspector, Antoine Gaudino, *L'Enquête impossible* (The impossible investigation) (Paris: Albin Michel, 1990). In fall 1992 the treasurer of the ruling Socialist party, Henri Emmanuelli, was indicted after the PS headquarters was searched in an unannounced raid. The Socialists claimed they were being singled out because they were the governing party. True or not, this incident shows French investigating judges can have real independence. (There is also new interest in reforming the institution of the investigating judge, which critics say is out of control.)

10. Furet et al., op. cit., p. 51.

6
✦

Interests and Groups

Post-Marxian Bases of French Politics

Burke failed to realize how things were in the kingdom which the monarchy (whose downfall he deplored) had bequeathed to its new masters. Under the old order the government had long since deprived Frenchmen of the possibility, and even the desire, of coming to each other's aid. When the Revolution started, it would have been impossible to find, in most parts of France, even ten men used to acting in concert and defending their interests without appealing to the central power for aid.

—Tocqueville, *The Old Regime and the Revolution*, Part 3, Chapter 8, p. 206

If political liberty is to be something other than an anarchist-type spontaneity, it requires an attachment . . . a belief which guides its use.

—Valéry Giscard d'Estaing, *Deux Français sur trois* (Two of three Frenchmen), p. 153

French politics revolves around pressure groups . . . be they groups of farmers, lorry drivers or students.

—*The Economist*, December 12, 1992, p. 13

The French "Partenaires Sociaux"[*] and the Single European Market

French social and associational life was long criticized as lacking the strong cooperation and healthy pluralism necessary to a democratic society. Underneath a thin coating of bourgeois formalities simmered antisocial attitudes and, among the working classes, the "ruled" in society, a persistent anarchism, a permanent tendency to explosive rebellion. A rooted "civil society" was what France lacked, and to contemporaries May 1968 seemed merely the latest confirmation of the fact.

Already 150 years ago Tocqueville had made the impoverished associational life among the French a major theme of *The Old Regime and the Revolution*. French society was a fragile stretch, he said, along the bifurcation between an all-powerful state and a privatist bourgeois and petit-bourgeois social structure, in which one elemental social motivation was what Michel Crozier a century later aptly called the "horror of face-to-face relations." No healthy civil society, no democracy, can function on such a poor social foundation. For those Frenchmen whose political convictions were neither statist nor Marxist, democracy in France over the last century has thus meant the struggle to build civil society, a crucial part of which had to be the renovation of the group structure, the construction of a healthy pluralism.

The old France is much changed. The Tocquevillean analysis of an impoverished civil society still applied to France well into the postwar decades when Crozier, Stanley Hoffmann and others brilliantly updated and elaborated on his basic insights. In France today, to the contrary, a perceptive journalist, immersed in the daily occurrence of strikes, demonstrations and bargaining, can plausibly assure his readers that "French politics revolves around pressure groups—be they groups of farmers, lorry drivers or students."[1]

Have interest groups and lobbies in fact become the pivot of the politics of French public policy? Has France changed so much in this respect? The answer is in a certain sense both yes and no. Civil society has been largely created, but the inner sinews of French politics and of the state, policy making in the deepest sense, remain more insulated from group lobbying than, for example, in the United States or in Germany. But the difference now is more one of degree than of kind. France has joined the ranks of pluralist, group-oriented, lobbying liberal democracies, but to a French degree and with Gallic emphases.

---

[*] Social Partners

From the point of view of a journalist who has just observed how French farmers' protests—blockading streets, sequestering government officials, dumping crops to waste, pelting ministers with manure—could drive government policy in the GATT Uruguay round negotiations in 1991–92, a "group theory of politics" understandably seems to explain the guts of French public policy. But in a statist and tutelary political culture that was simultaneously highly class-conscious and Marxist or reactionary, the group theory of politics is still far from explaining French public policy as a whole.[2] Organized and representative pressure groups are, on the whole, certainly more effective and legitimate than ever in French political and economic life. But that said, it is important to notice that, in the past twenty-five years since the great strike wave of 1968, certain kinds of groups, such as farmers and truckers, have gained in influence while others, most notably the traditional confederal "umbrella" trade unions, have shrunk in numbers and political clout.

The "1992 Project," the "Single European Market" (SEA), came legally into existence on January 1, 1993. The single market means that, albeit with some gaps, French corporate business, labor and agriculture now really operate in a single, integrated, barrier-free Community-wide economy in the technical sense of the term. The European Economic Community (EEC) is, technically speaking, a customs union, meaning an internal free trade area among member states, plus a common external tariff vis-à-vis all third states. By contrast, the new single market eliminates all remaining internal, *informal* barriers to movement of the factors of production, creating a free flow of goods, services, capital and, for all but three nonsignatory countries of the Schengen Agreement (Britain, Ireland and Denmark), the free movement of people. Implementation of the Schengen Agreement on the free movement of people, signed by France and eight other EC states, is to lift any remaining border controls within those states as of mid-1993. In addition, the signature of an agreement between the European Free Trade Association (EFTA) and the EC in November 1991 has created the so-called European Economic Area (EEA). The EEA agreement gives free trade and certain other EC privileges to the EFTA countries (Scandinavia and the European neutrals), most of whom want to become EC members (see map on inside cover).

This is an ambitious program of monetary, fiscal, social and political goals that will place French economic and social actors yet further into a Community-wide and EEA-wide competitive setting. In some respects old French patterns will no doubt survive, but, overall, European integration is forcing French ways of doing things toward European and international norms, which necessarily will reduce the traditional specificities of French economic habits and group structures. Observers who have not looked closely at the French situation recently, or those with a stereo-typed view of the old "Gallic" France, may well be surprised at the extent of contemporary French toleration and even acceptance of international standards. Outdated images of French industry—on the one hand, a sort of *capitalisme sauvage*** practiced within hidebound, uncompetitive family-owned firms, and, on the other hand, a militant, fundamentalist anticapi-talism in the labor unions—hardly fit the French industrial sector today.

On the management side, from the 1960s on, the diploma of choice of France's industrial management elite became an American business school MBA. Today, while not abandoning Harvard and Stanford, France's fu-ture business class can do quite well enough with training at the INSEAD, HEC and other French business schools, whose methods originally were American-inspired, but who have been developing their own curricula and case studies now for twenty years. After the diploma, daily life for the typical French international business executive in the 1990s involves the usual time spent in jets and foreign countries. They live in a contemporary transnational business culture, making them part of an international busi-ness class, both of whose common languages, English and computers, they are required to speak. The French industrialist has evolved far from his postwar provincialism, put under scrutiny when Jean-Jacques Sérvan-Schreiber rocked the business and political classes in 1959 with *The Ameri-can Challenge*. As for the French labor movement, with few exceptions the attitude of workers and unions has become reconciled to what Marxist thinking used to vilify as "bourgeois capitalism." The level of strikes has declined sharply over the past decade. The strength of anticapitalist, an-tiprofit-oriented thinking has also declined precipitously, both despite and because unemployment is so high.

In the past, the long-time major union organization, the Communist-dominated General Confederation of Labor (*Confédération Générale des Travailleurs*, or CGT) often didn't sign collective-bargaining agreements, though it implemented them when signed by others. The purpose was to put the onus of "class collaboration" on the Socialist, Christian Demo-cratic, and independent unions, who could be portrayed as "traitors from a working-class point of view." With the demise of communism, the CGT no longer can play this old game. So long as French communism remained a massive force, and so long as the Soviet Union remained a plausible ideological icon, French labor relations were mired in a contra-diction: The main labor union was out, not for collective bargaining, but to overthrow the capitalist system. It would tolerate collective bargaining by others, to keep its own political hands clean. But to the extent possi-ble, the CGT leadership and cadre structure kept its second iron in the

---

* savage capitalism

fire, the hope of somehow coming to power and sweeping away French capitalism and French bourgeois society.

The *partenaires sociaux* in France, the "social partners" as unions and management are called in today's sanitized vocabulary, have largely to become normalized negotiating adversarial cooperators in a market economy collective-bargaining relationship. Some old French particularities remain, due either to history (e.g., a residual anticapitalist mentality in some trade union circles, or the old aristocratic–bourgeois snobbing of business), or to sociology (the large contingent of North African Muslim Arab workers, especially in certain key industries such as automobiles). But both business and labor understand that what they can reasonably refuse or demand of the other is fixed, within increasingly narrowed parameters, by what is being demanded and accorded in other European countries, with Germany—*das Modell Deutschland*—the usual reference.

The December 1991 Maastricht Treaty agreements for deeper economic and monetary union were thus welcomed by most spokesmen for the French social partner organizations. François Périgot, the head of the French business confederation CNPF (the National Confederation of French Business, the counterpart of the National Association of Manufacturers in the United States and the Confederation of Industry in Great Britain), said French business is "very much in favor of a single currency because it means a very high level of concertation among [the different national] economic policies." Only a decade earlier, the CNPF would have vigorously opposed being forced by the government to attempt to meet German standards! On the labor side, the moderate Workers' Force (FO) union, which in recent years has strengthened enough to rival the CGT, was also positive. Its Secretary-General, Marc Blondel, said FO was very much in favor of deeper European integration. He objected only that the meager "social chapter" of the Maastricht Treaty (which Britain's Conservative government rejected completely), was a "minimum," and that social gains for workers had to become a larger part of the EC's agenda. Other labor unions—the French Democratic Confederation of Labor (CFDT), the CFE–CGC and the French Confederation of Catholic Workers (CFTC)—all were positive. Only the CGT, more than ever willing to bargain collectively but still anticapitalist and suffering the French Communist party's political influence, opposed the Maastricht accords outright, as of course did the PCF itself.

French Business Today and the German Model

Still, things don't change so quickly and completely. French business historically, as we saw already, was quite ambivalent about industrialism and commercialism, especially about mass production and selling, which were considered low activities. Pockets in French society did plunge enthusiastically into business. But other sectors of the French bourgeoi-sie, contrary to Marxist theory, disdained capitalism even more than did Marxism itself, which saw the redeeming feature in capitalist production of hastening the revolution! The classic image of the reluctant French capitalist was not totally false to the spirit of early French industry: Better to sell 10,000 bottles of fine (and expensive) cognac than 1 million bottles of inferior (and inexpensive) wine.

French business today to some extent still shies from the toughest competitive markets. Where this is so, however, it is not because of snobbery but because the French business class lacks the confidence and drive to sell in the hardest markets. A telling commentary on French business's weak commercial combativeness is that President Mitterrand several times has publicly lamented French industry's lack of drive, add-ing that this holds back France's international influence as well as its standard of living. At the same time, irony was not absent from the fact of a Socialist president exhorting French businessmen to try harder for new market shares!

Nevertheless, French industry's traditional weaknesses have clearly been changing for the better. After decades of global industrial trade deficits, particularly severe with its most industrialized trading part-ners, France's trade balance in the last months of 1991 went positive, including with its major European Community partners. With the lowest inflation in 1990–1991 among EC partners, plus currency sta-bility, France was gaining market shares abroad and starting to regain them in the French domestic market. Thus, given trends that seem likely to be reinforced by the single market, traditional wisdom about French business needs to be reexamined.

"Saint-Gobain," as one analyst wrote, "is an apt paradigm of French industry,"[3] a classic example of Colbertism, of the state's leadership role in creating French industry. Founded in 1665 by Colbert to benefit a French mirror maker (using know-how stolen from the Venetians), Saint-Gobain was given a state monopoly and protected by the state from foreign competition. Today, on the other hand, Saint-Gobain is a model of the reformed French economy. It is a private-sector, quoted company, thoroughly international and deeply involved in and influenced by Ger-many:

> Saint-Gobain's foreign work force, management and sales are now dou-ble those in France. Its German sales are two-thirds of its French sales—and, in motor-industry glass, twice as large. It has further strengthened its presence in Germany by buying the former East German plate-glass maker *Kombinat*. It is opening factories in Eastern Europe to match the spreading investments there of the German car industry. Its chief execu-

tive, Jean-Louis Beffa, speaks with enthusiasm of worker-participation in management: "Saint-Gobain decided to open the books to its unions to the same degree as in Germany, so that they can judge how we raise our money and how we use it. Instead of blind discussion with the unions, we greatly profit from the transparency. All the managing boards of our group now feature two representatives elected by the work force."

Saint-Gobain is undoubtedly a shining example of modernized French private-sector attitudes. Yet the Saint-Gobain case also shows how "German" industrial attitudes have been no less encouraged and perhaps even more so by Mitterrand and the Socialist governments of the 1980s, than they would have been by conservative governments. To be sure, it was the Chirac cohabitation government of 1986 that announced a spectacular break with Colbertist statism and *dirigisme*. But the Socialists were converted during their years in power. The French Socialist "Bad Godesberg"—the famous German Social Democratic party's 1959 congress that gave up Marxism—was less an official ideological renunciation than a gradual, hard acceptance of the rules of market economics and of European integration.

The 1991–92 Edith Cresson government was supposed to tack against this trend, to refurbish the Socialists' left-wing, industrial policy reputation, as well as to sound a protectionist note against Japanese trade competition. In fact the Cresson experience showed the limits on French maneuver in economic policy.

Cresson, who had been both minister of industry and minister for European affairs, proposed to create a French superministry of economics and finance something like the Japanese Ministry of Trade and Industry (MITI), to use Japanese means, in other words, to face down Japanese competition. Mitterrand sidestepped Cresson's idea, because it was too radical, too statist, too different from what France's partners—especially Germany—were doing. Cresson also started to resuscitate the 1970s idea of "national champions," conglomerates that can be technology innovators and export leaders. It is controversial because it assumes the state can pick winners, because it raises the stakes in key corporate sectors, and because it can fail grandly, producing terrifically costly losses.

Cresson first eyed a merger in the computer and aerospace industries but then tried a new state conglomerate in nuclear, semiconductor and consumer-electronics firms to have a French equivalent of Germany's Siemens and Japan's Toshiba. The company, to be called Thomson CEA Industries (TCI), would be put together from broken-off loss-making parts of Thomson (defense and electronics), combined with CEA Industrie, part of the Commissariat de l'Énergie, France's state-owned nuclear giant. The state would have a majority ownership share in the new TCI company. (An unspoken aim in this project, it must be added, was to use state ownership to get around the EC's extremely tight rules on state subsidies to industry.)

But this lurch back toward statist intervention in the evolution of corporate development probably does not indicate the road to the future. Any idea of reinventing French Colbertism—say, by the conservative majority elected in 1993 (which in any case seems more interested in privatization)—will be blocked by the need of French business to have the freedom to compete internationally, and by more liberal European Community rules limiting state intervention. In addition, state-obliged industrial mergers are controversial because they are open to state abuse of power. There is natural suspicion today whenever the French state moves heavily in industry, merging bits and pieces of huge industrial companies. Thus a renewal of privatization and a basically hands-off state industrial policy was in the conservative UPF electoral program in March 1993, after Pierre Bérégovoy, Cresson's successor as prime minister in 1992–93, had already eased off the Socialists' neo-Colbertian return.

In sum, French business has broken with its traditional ambivalence about the culture of capitalism, entrepreneurship and commercialism. "Money" no longer carries the stigma it carried in a more aristocratic and Catholic society. Capable French students are flocking to business schools and, like their American counterparts, are usually interested in success and affluence more than in politics or ideology. Longtime francophiles are shocked to realize that lycée and college students no longer feel an instinctive identification with the "right" or the "left." And when young people are committed to politics at all, the focus is likely to be public interest issues (ecology and antiracism) or threats to French jobs and prosperity, rather than the old class struggle discourse of left and right. France, most people know, has been "greened" electorally as much as other European countries. More surprising is the degree to which France has also been "businessified." Maintaining business dynamism has become vital to all French governments and to any idea of maintaining France's political, economic and cultural rank. Although it was forgotten, de Gaulle had said repeatedly that there was no other way to "rank" and "prestige" than to rebuild France's economic base. In this sense de Gaulle could be called an unabashed modernizer, "a man of the day after tomorrow," as André Malraux said, as well as "the day before yesterday."

Textbook discussions of French business emphasize the National Council of French Industrialists (CNPF), as well as the organization of small and medium-sized French enterprises, called the CGPME. Size and structure are detailed, and their lobbying activities are described in pluralist terms.

Another kind of analysis emphasizes the venerable practice of *pantouflage*, the "in and out" career patterns of French elite managers, who alternate government service, with its enviable lifetime tenure in the administrative *grands corps*, with high-paying jobs in industry, for which these managers are "detached"—that is, put on leave, often for long stretches, from their government civil service corps. Pantouflage is a sweet system for insiders and scandalous when revealed to the rest of the world.[4] Pantouflage gives French business perennial inside influence on government decisions as well as experienced, well-connected lobbyists.

At the beginning of the Fifth Republic in 1958 the CNPF was already important, as French economy recovery went forward. The government planning and economic bureaucracies had been much more modernist than Fourth Republic parliamentary politics as a whole. This was accelerated in the de Gaulle Republic, whose commitment to modernize France industrially and economically was especially clear. The CNPF had very wide membership (1 million firms), not to mention the deep pockets one would expect from an encompassing business confederation.

For two reasons, however, the political significance of CNPF and CGPME has become less obvious in the last ten years. First of all, in de Gaulle's time and through the presidencies of Pompidou, Giscard and even the first years of Mitterrand's tenure, business organizations were a natural counterweight to French unions. The CNPF put itself forward, and was so used by governments, as the business respondent to the trade unions' anticapitalist bias. Successive CNPF presidents were prominent media spokesmen for the business point of view, allowing government to appear as a mediator or third force between business and the unions. Moreover, the strongest unions until a few years ago were the Socialist and, above all, the Communist-dominated union, the CFDT and the CGT. The sharp decline of union membership in the last ten years, and the equally remarkable shift in the union balance of power away from the CGT to the formerly minority independent FO union (see below), with the CFDT still as the middle power, has paradoxically weakened the CNPF's prominence as the official spokesman for business in the country. Twenty or even ten years ago the French "attentive public" knew well the cast of characters in union–business relations: François Ceyrac and Yvon Gattaz for the CNPF, Georges Séguy and Henri Krasuki for the Communist-dominated CGT, Edmond Maire for the Socialist-leaning CFDT, André Bergeron for the independent FO. This was the generation that negotiated May '68 and the recessions of the 1970s. Today's business and union leaders are, however, much less well known. Among the general public, particularly young people, they may hardly be known at all. Not only a generation, but also the concerns of a generation, have passed from the French scene.

European economic union is a second reason for CNPF and CGPME lack of visibility. Until business organizations unite across the EC and collective bargaining becomes community-wide, French business organizations will remain caught between the old national prominence of the CNPF and the not-yet-established effectiveness of the UNICE, the European Community employers' organization. One role of UNICE, for example, will be to advise multinational corporations, often with plants in several EC countries, on national and Community social legislation.

Deregulation and declining statism means that French business must make its successes under purer market conditions. In addition, the writing of European-wide rules in the single market framework means that increasing numbers of French regulations and policies are the result of European decisions. Altogether the French business confederations are somewhat in the background in the present transition phase, even if they are still a source of valuable industrial information and support for business in French collective-bargaining negotiations. The CNPF is also occasionally asked by the government to negotiate "framework" collective-bargaining agreements with one or more unions, but these general agreements are not binding in particular situations. Seemingly, the pantouflage method of personnel management is, along with rather successful lobbying of government (often its own people!), the main business of business organizations in France today.

The question today is which sort of capitalism—German, American, Japanese—French industry should take as a model. For perhaps the first time in French history, the future of French capitalism is often debated with enthusiasm rather than with trepidation.[5]

Whither French business? One best-selling French commentator on the economy argues that the French choice lies between German-style and American-style capitalism, a choice of a kind of national economy (see Chapter 8) as well as a kind of business enterprise. The German model, according to Michel Albert, emphasizes several particular characteristics: (1) extensive training in industry and a widely admired system of apprenticeships, (2) small and medium-sized export-minded companies, (3) linking of industry with the finance and huge blocks of shares that banks and insurance companies can provide, and (4) overall, a sense of "collective success, consensus and attention to the long term." The American model, on the other hand, is based on extreme individualism and the shortsighted goal of profit in the short term. The French tradition, by contrast, still practices a "social Colbertism: The State commands the economy in the name of a political ambition and a desire for social progress. . . . [It is] a Colbertist State which has not given up its tutelary relationship with the economy: protectionist and dirigiste on the one hand, but on the other hand an investor, an entrepreneur, a Saint-Simonian."[6]

At the level of the individual firm, French business should embrace the collective spirit, transparency of accounts and mutual respect that, for Michel Albert, is characteristic of well-run German firms. The wide French centralist tradition was, he says, "translated into absolute monarchy inside the enterprise. The principle of the all-powerful president-director-general was not a German idea, but a French one." Albert's worry is that the European Community's development will not be "German" enough to oblige French firms to make the right choice. Exaggerated as this may be, his book is an indication that French business is attempting to make the transition from its historic biases to a competitive, Europeanized outlook.

Workers and the Decline of Labor Unions

At the level of the labor unions, this alternative of American and German models is the choice between the American unions' historic refusal of a corporatist, partnership model, in the name of autonomy in collective bargaining, and the contrary postwar German model of *Mitbestimmung*, meaning union codetermination, coresponsibility and codecision. What have French unions historically tried to do, and where are they headed today in the post-Communist, post-Marxist, post-Socialist European situation?

French labor unions were remarkably calm during the Socialist governments of the 1980s. Rising unemployment, from Giscard's 2 million in 1981 to Mitterrand's 3 million in 1993, was surprisingly tolerated by the French work force, and by the unions, until the run-up to the 1993 elections. This was due partly to a natural union sympathy for Socialist governments, and partly to compensatory economic achievements—low inflation and strengthening of the French franc. Conceivably, unemployment had been less and more severe than statistics indicate: less severe, because some people counted as unemployed were not really seeking jobs; more severe, because many not counted as unemployed had given up trying to find work. In 1991, in any case, workers' patience with Socialist economic "rigor" began to ebb, and unions and professions again were able to mount street demonstrations on issues of jobs and working conditions. The relative peace of labor relations in the 1980s in France has been broken in the past few years, and groups ranging from farmers to fishermen to hospital personnel to students are leading the way to what looks like a new adversarial decade in the 1990s.

Historically, Marxist thinking was simultaneously the glory and the bane of French workers. Marxism and French communism were the cause of much of French unionism's weak representativity, and of its bad industrial relations, so deeply mistrustful of owners and management. The decline of Marxism is one reason for a sharp shrinking of union membership, a fall from France's already low levels due to politicization and ineffectiveness. About 20 percent of salaried workers used to belong to the various and politically divided unions. Today the number is less than 10 percent. This should be pitiful, yet it is not much discussed. The significance of this historically low membership is masked because agreements negotiated by the unions are accepted by nonunion workers, and because job security is often so precarious that nobody wants to be a worker militant.

Yet French workers as recently as twenty years ago might still mistake themselves for Marx's mythical proletariat, dissatisfied with mere bread-and-butter collective bargaining, always on the verge of a lunge for the State apparatus in a *grand soir** that would "put the working class in power." For almost a century French workers were imbued with class struggle ideas, and the great cleavage occurred between those who believed in working-class unity for socialism and those who preferred a Christian, Catholic view of life, whose purpose was not to overthrow the exploiters but to reconcile people of goodwill. Like so much else in French society, worker and union politics were deeply marked by Marxism, then marked again by the 1920 split between Socialists and Communists.

The great strike wave of May–June 1968, so astonishing at first, turned out to be the last hurrah for revolutionary worker and trade-union thinking. No one—not the political leaders, not the commentators, not the scholars—expected the so-called events of May. (A single—in retrospect, overrated—*Le Monde* editorial noted, just before the explosion, that "France is bored." But this insight was a clever and often-reprised nineteenth-century headline that had appeared likewise just before an earlier revolution, that of 1848.)

Though hard to imagine today, faculty and students struck together to close nearly all universities in the country, except for a few natural science departments, business and law schools, and so on. Even harder to imagine, almost half the entire French work force was out on strike a few days later. This meant, literally, 9 million out of 20 million salaried people. There was minimal television news, because even in the state television and radio organizations most of the newspeople, including the broadcasters, joined the strike. For a few days an old-style revolution seemed possible in an advanced society—not to mention in a NATO country.

---

*triumphal night

Table 6 ✦1 Unionization in Industrialized
Countries, Percentage of
Salaried Population (estimated
1989)

Source: Ehrmann and Schain, op. cit.,
p. 177.

Country	Rate of Unionization (%)
France	10
United States	18
Japan	28
West Germany	43
Great Britain	40
Italy	39
Belgium	75
Sweden	83

France, one could have said with justice, was being herself. Why did so many people, union militants and the previously apathetic alike, go out on strike? And why didn't the French Communist party, still fearsome in 1968, try to seize power? Why was President de Gaulle, who at one point seemed on the verge of quitting power (his ministerial staffs actually packed their papers), finally able to recapture control of the situation? And why did French workers settle for bread and butter in the reformist Grenelle Accords instead of seizing power? How could the Communist-run union, the CGT, have secretly negotiated with the government at Grenelle?

These questions, especially after communism's collapse, are basically of historical importance. For our purpose, what is important is to observe that May '68 seems, in retrospect, to have had a paradoxical effect. By pushing the limits of politics without plan or organization, the "people of 1968" unwittingly struck a blow for doing things in an organized way. The entire union of the left strategy of the left-wing parties, and the careful testing of the Fifth Republic Constitution's possibilities—*l'alter-nance, la cohabitation*—are in a general sense a dialectical legacy of May '68's chaotic and unsuccessful "revolution of the imagination." The ano-rexic condition of the major trade unions today—all supporters of the May strikes if only for fear of being left behind—is, at least to some extent, another aspect of this legacy. With a work force of about 30 million, France's current unionization rate is the lowest among the indus-trialized countries (see Table 6.1). This may still partially reflect a his-toric French aversion to joining organizations; it may be, as just suggested, a legacy of May 1968; but it is certainly a practical reflection of whether union membership brings benefits.

French union membership has gone up and down significantly over the decades, shooting up as a result of crisis (World War I, the Popular Front, World War II, May 1968), then dropping precipitously. French workers joined unions at the rate of approximately 50 percent in the post–World War II period, the highest French level, which made the unions truly representative for a period. This rate dropped then over the long term, despite a temporary reversal from 1966 to 1977. By the end of the 1970s, the end of conservative governments and the prelude to the victory of Mitterrand and the left in 1981, the unionization rate was down to between one fourth and one third of salaried blue- and white-collar workers.

In the Mitterrand presidency one might have expected, given that the left was in power, a rebound of union membership and influence. The reverse occurred. Why this happened is important for an understanding of French politics' basic developments over twenty years.

True, unionization rates have declined almost everywhere in the industrialized countries. But that does not explain France's singularly steep decline, except that France began from an already low figure. One factor particular to France and a few other countries such as Italy, Spain and Portugal has been the collapse of communism. The Communist-dominated CGT used to be the most powerful union because, whether or not one liked the PCF, the CGT got results. The CGT, even according to its own, usually rigged figures, has lost half its membership in the past fifteen years. Half or more of CGT members, as before, vote non-Communist, which illustrates again that the CGT is known to produce results.

The Workers' Force (FO) union was born out of the CGT in 1947 in a split against Communist control. During the Cold War it was always the poor third cousin of the three main union confederations. To its satisfaction, the FO has gained much of what the CGT has lost in recent years. Workers' Force policy is patterned on American unions' collective-bargaining traditions, the main point of which is to refuse, in the name of autonomy, German-style codetermination and sharing of management responsibility. Codetermination is based on the idea of union–management mutuality and shared, collective interest. Free collective bargaining is, on the other hand, a doctrine of independent and self-interested negotiation, in which unions are one part of a balanced confrontation of interests in industry, rather than part of joint management of a collective good. It is in character with postwar French political culture that the "American" FO union should have lagged behind the outright anticapitalist unions. FO's "free collective bargaining" ethos had little attraction for a working-class culture suffused with anticapitalist, class struggle ideas. And the recent workers' swing to FO member-ship also reflects the turn of the past decade to market, capitalist and European integration–oriented ideas.

CFDT

The third and smallest of the major unions, the Socialist-leaning CFDT, with perhaps half a million members, resulted from a split from the Christian CFTC union in the 1960s. Its Christian socialist origins were overlaid in the 1970s with a very popular *autogestion* or self-manage-ment Socialist idea, which provided the PS with much-needed doctrinal ammunition against Communist ideas during the union of the left strug-gles in those years.

The CFDT was a very important political and ideological force in the 1970s and 1980s. And although today it is the smallest of the three trade-union confederations, it may yet play an important role again in the larger trade union and political cultural scene. The CFDT was crucial, for example, in formulating the idea of a "recentered" left. And it was a key part of the so-called second left, the non-Communist left based in "civil society," which, following Socialist leaders such as Michel Rocard, argued against statism and dirigisme. In 1992, the CFDT innovated in a different way by electing the first woman, Nicole Notat, leader of a French union confederation.

The CFDT's Christian socialist and collectivist inclinations tempt it, on the other hand, toward the views of German and Japanese trade unions, which see industry and the economy as a naturally collective and hierarchical undertaking, for whose success unions, as well as manage-ment and ownership, must take responsibility. The CFDT is thus the French labor union whose political culture is closest to the German or "Rheinish" codetermination economic model, as opposed to the Ameri-can model of liberal collective bargaining. Which one will become the European Community standard remains to be determined. In sum, French trade unionism changed sharply in the Mitterrand decade, not due to "Mitterrandism" alone, but to exterior trends well underway when the left-wing alliance finally came to power in 1981.[7] The transformation of French unionism is still incomplete, however, and further alterations will occur, due to French factors and European factors alike.

Rather than taking the ambivalent stance of negotiating agreements while combating the structure, French unions are now willy-nilly inside the system. With the collapse of socialism as an idea, there is no other tenable place to be. Moreover, French management is changing as well. International norms have infiltrated old French particularisms, and, on both sides, to accept normalized relations is more and more irresistible. French management no longer exhibits such a provincial worldview. An-other aspect of the changing scene is the Maastricht Treaty's so-called social chapter, which is designed to implement the European Social

Charter through Community-wide legislation on working conditions, social security, and so on.[8] As EC social legislation expands, even if less rapidly than single market and monetary union measures, EC country trade unions and trade-union movements, already loosely organized on the Community level in the European Trade Union Confederation (ETUC), will become more alike, or at least operate with similar principles. Transnational unionization in multinational EC firms and EC-wide collective bargaining are some years away, yet they seem to be a logical outgrowth of the single market. And as with economic harmonization generally, EC-wide collective bargaining is likely to be modeled on the most successful model, which means that the French and others will move toward the German example. There might be a crossnational amalgamation of unions or even direct founding of new EC-wide unions in new industries. Trade-union "unity," meaning mergers, has been on the agenda for decades not only in France, but also in Italy, Spain and the other European countries where a politically divided union movement persists. To the extent communism was responsible for trade-union splits, reunification of labor organizations, both nationally and EC-wide, could be a further result of communism's demise and the end of the Cold War. This, plus renewed economic growth, could create new members, even a new life, for a reformed, post-Marxist labor union movement.

French Farmers, the CAP and the GATT

French "peasants"—the anachronistic reference to *les paysans* is a not altogether insignificant relic of feudal culture—are dying out as a species. In a few years only genuine "farmers," modern commercial agricultural entrepreneurs, will remain. Their sharply declining numbers, which threatens the very survival of the traditional small farmer, *le vrai paysan*,[*] gives farmers' self-defense and collective action extra passion and legitimacy. French farmers are thus partly, as the world knows, successful farmers defending cushy state subsidies, and partly small farmers defending not just their incomes, but a way of life. Successful French farmers live well; the small-holding paysan struggles to survive. French farmers wield political clout, far more than their numbers would justify. "They have," as one journalist described a recent farmers' demonstration, "a bad reputation. . . . They tend to do things like spraying government ministers with liquid manure, burning sheep alive and attacking lorries carrying imported meat with crowbars."[9] Defense of farm subsidies in the EC's Common Agricultural Policy (CAP) produces classic episodes of

---

[*] the true peasant

French maneuvering in European Community negotiations. The above-cited farmers' march on Paris coincided with the conclusion of a European Community negotiation giving Poland, Czechoslovakia and Hungary less-expensive access to EC country markets. At the last minute French negotiators vetoed a part of the deal, involving small amounts of meat imports from Eastern European countries. The British representative accused the French of "living on another planet"; they were blocking a large agreement because of a small amount of meat imports, when so much else in the way of mutual concessions had already been set. A day later, a complex compromise suddenly was reached. The French had successfully proposed that the Eastern European meat in question instead should be sold, with EC financial aid, to the Soviet Union, which for decades had been a market for Eastern European meats, and which would be facing a very hard winter requiring massive food aid. The French also agreed that, if the Eastern European meat could not be unloaded on the Soviet market it could then be imported into the EC. The Socialist government of Edith Cresson, and President Mitterrand, appeared, if only for a Sunday afternoon, as implacable defenders of conservative French beef and sheep farmers, and by extension of conservative French paysans in general. French unity, and electoral interests, demanded no less!

Beyond the spectacle, though, how significant is French agriculture in the French economy, and how important is the agricultural foreign trade surplus to French government policy? More than one measure is needed to give an estimate.

Remarkably, France today is the second world exporter of farm products after the United States. And for an economy that had been in chronic global trade deficit, France's agricultural success has been all the more significant, explaining its tenacity in current GATT negotiations which focus on reducing French, and EC CAP export subsidies. France, which until the 1970s had a deficit in agricultural trade, in 1990 produced a $9 billion agricultural trade surplus. An EC breadbasket, France's anxieties about the entrance of Spanish, Greek and Portuguese agriculture into the Common Market have not been borne out. French agricultural land is about one-quarter of the total cultivated in the EC. "France produces almost 40 percent of the wheat and corn in the European Community, almost 20 percent of the meat and eggs, and almost 30 percent of the milk. To the domestic economy, agriculture and agricultural products contribute about 6.1 percent of the gross domestic product, down from 15 percent in 1959, but compared with 2.9 percent in the United States."[10] Overall agricultural productivity tripled in the past three decades, in the 1980s growing twice as fast as in the economy as a whole.

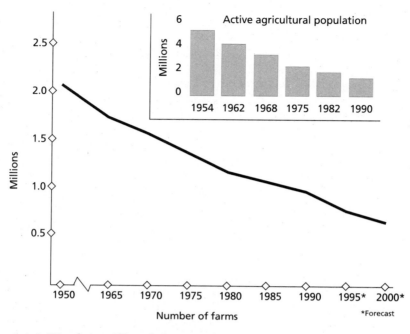

Figure 6 ✦ 1 Numbers of French farms and agricultural workers

Source: French Ministry of Agriculture and INSEE

Between the world wars, there were almost 4 million farms in a general population about one third less than today. In the 1960s the number of farms dropped below 2 million, and by the early 1980s there were only 1 million. With attrition of age and with many farmers being forced to sell out, there will be only 400,000 to 500,000 farms at the turn of the century (see Figure 6.1).

The demographic decline in the French peasantry, let there be no mistake, has been deep and brutal. Nevertheless, while working farmers represent only 4 percent of the electorate, the farming lobby and rural population is 15–20 percent of the vote, including farm families, nonowning farm workers and other rural voters. This is enough electoral power to make or break electoral fortunes in Paris, and it is why French governments are so responsive to farm lobby pressure.

French farmers historically have voted, not surprisingly, for the conservative parties. They vote in particular for the neo-Gaullist RPR. Today's Gaullists have both the General's heritage and their own rural conservatism. Their longtime leader, Jacques Chirac, though the mayor of Paris, is from the Corrèze, called by one journalist "the Appalachia of

France." Former president Valéry Giscard d'Estaing also has rural roots, but the Giscardist Union for French Democracy has a reputation for economic modernism, won when the young Giscard was finance minister in the first Fifth Republic governments. Yet French farmers understand the neo-Gaullists can't save them from all economic forces either, because reform of the Common Agricultural Policy and French subsidies is inevitable in internal EC negotiations and in the GATT negotiations.

By one calculation, the huge subsidies from the EC and French governments account for—astonishingly—three quarters of French farm incomes.[11] The French are, naturally, the EC's largest agricultural producer, with about one fourth of total farm output, about the same as its percentage of cultivated land in the EC. Because France benefits most from EC farm-support policies, French farmers' incomes are inevitably the main potential victim of making farm subsidies less irrational.

The size of farms is a key factor in the problem. In French farming, as in American farming, small farmers have progressively been pushed out and swallowed by bigger, more economically efficient farms. Thus, the total cultivated land in France has declined only slightly since World War II while the number of farms, and farmers, has dropped radically. Productivity increase has benefited most the relatively small number of large farms. Income differences between small and large farms have remained at a ratio of about 1 to 10 for 30 years. Nevertheless, the majority of French farms in 1990 were still 60 acres or less, economically at the margin of survival. Thus among the 1 million remaining farmers in France there is still much room for "economic consolidation." The human and social pain will persist a bit longer in "solving the problem of the peasantry."

The hardest hit French farmers in the current crunch are the small and medium-sized breeders of livestock—beef and sheep farmers—who produce a quarter of EC meat supplies. Many of them made large investments in modern equipment when prices were high. Badly indebted today, they are particularly threatened by cuts demanded in EC support prices, and by the possibility of free Eastern European country meat exports in the future, as was the issue in the demonstration just described.

On the other hand, the EC's CAP is still hugely profitable for the largest, most efficient French farmers. Because their subsidies are not lowered but increase with production, the most efficient farmers often specialize to take more advantage. The paradoxically greater subsidy provided to larger production is, as in the American farm price-support system, a bizarre result of the original intention to aid farmers most in need.

There is no straightforward "good" policy for a French government to follow regarding the future of the agriculture sector. So long as the farm vote is large enough to be politically crucial, it is no use encouraging elected politicians to do only what is right. Furthermore the "right" solution is not simple, and any policy must distinguish between small and large farmers, as well as take account of international EC and GATT commitments as well as French domestic problems.

Most of the remaining small farmers seem fated to be forced to give up, as so many already have. In the name of what principle might they get, as the new "Rural Coordination" organization demands, special subsidies to survive? Not from the ministries of purely economic affairs, but perhaps from the Ministry of Culture? or the Ministry of "Solidarity," on the principle that saving rural France is part of what de Gaulle called "a certain idea of France"? Would French voters agree that this was a good use of the taxpayer's money? Second, France faces demands from EC partners to reduce further the CAP's cost; and yet more demands, from the United States and other countries in the GATT negotiations, for the EC to reduce CAP subsidies even more in the name of liberalized trade.

These are strong pressures to withstand in the long run. Perhaps there is in France only a tacit agreement among the party leaderships to restrain farm subsidy and CAP reform as much and as long as possible, until the French paysan has further disappeared and, thus, rural France will have become less capable of political revenge at election time.

SOS–Racism: Human Rights Activism in the Post-Marxian Age

The human rights organization SOS–Racism was one of the most exciting innovations in French political life in the 1980s, not merely in itself but also as a harbinger of a new breed of crosspartisan, nonparty, public interest pressure groups that have grown up outside the old party system.[12] Surely the fortunes of such public interest groups—Greenpeace and Doctors Without Borders (*Médecins sans Frontières*) are other examples—were increased by the decline of ideological war in French politics. The key was probably the transformation of the French left, meaning the deflation of the Communists and the liberation of the Socialists. SOS–Racism was to a great extent in sympathy with the Socialist party. Its popularity can also be interpreted as a political compensation of the racist National Front. Many people who would not have joined a political party, even the PS, to fight against racism, joined or marched with SOS–Racism.

SOS–Racism's leading spokesman in the 1980s was Harlem Désir, a young, politically charismatic man of color. A second-generation immigrant, his father was born in Martinique, arriving in Paris at the age of fourteen. The other SOS–Racism spokesman was a young antiestablishment Socialist deputy, Julien Dray, who is Jewish. This leadership combination was very striking, as was the innovation in French politics of SOS–Racism's overtly mixed-race and mixed-religious appeal.

Established in November 1984 with Harlem Désir as president, it seemed a direct response to the National Front's first electoral break-through in the June 1984 European Parliament elections, when the FN won 11 percent. SOS–Racism rapidly, in the next few years, became a political and media success. It suggested, in a French context, the Rain-bow Coalition in the United States, an alliance of a liberal, generally young white majority element with the rainbow of French minority groups, "black, brown and *beur*."[13] Fighting the good antiracist fight with rock concerts, badges, demonstrations, and political sympathy for Mitterrand and the Socialist governments, SOS–Racism was one of the prominent and most original "new forces" in French politics of Mitterrand's heyday.

SOS–Racism began on a combination of deep antiracist feeling combined with practical political calculation. One of the first successes was its famous "Hands off my buddy!" badge *(Touche pas a mon pote!)*. As a slogan of interracial solidarity, the badge was bought by hundreds of thousands of people and worn by Parisian political and media personalities as they had worn the Polish "Solidarnosc" badge in 1980–81. Of equal importance, other human rights organizations of venerable standing in France rallied their support, including the Masonic organizations, as announced by the Grand Master himself of the huge, historically powerful Grand-Orient Lodge of France; the CFDT trade-union confederation; the Federation of National Education; and the League for Human Rights.

In June 1985 SOS–Racism, with large donations from the government and from several large progovernment firms (the RATP subway, Thomson, the UAP insurance company, BSN), organized its first big media event, a rock concert at the Place de la Concorde. And around this time SOS–Racism became an official part of the "Génération Mitterrand," a political campaign centered on mobilizing the youth vote for the 1988 presidential election. Harlem Désir made a public appearance tour around France, with the theme of registering new voters, 2.7 million potentially for the 1988 election. Needless to say, the two SOS–Racism leaders, Harlem Désir and Julien Dray, were welcomed at the Elysée Palace, and in August 1987, Désir, the erstwhile grassroots beur leader, was consecrated by the media as a serious French national leader by an invitation onto France's prominent evening television political interview show, "The Hour of Truth."

With the double-edged sword of power, both SOS–Racism leaders were taken up by President Mitterrand as unofficial advisors on social questions and, obviously, as hoped-for protégés. Mitterrand watchers spotted the danger of cooptation in this special attention from the president, such as had happened, for example, with Isabel Thomas, a firebrand leader of 1986 demonstrations by lycée and university students for school reform, who was hired for the presidential staff as an advisor on these very problems.

When Mitterrand won reelection in 1988, the two founders of SOS–Racism shifted into more traditional political roles, with unfortunate consequences for the movement. Dray won a parliamentary seat as a Socialist deputy from the Essonne, resigning from SOS–Racism and taking most of its leaders into the Socialist party, creating the "New Socialist School" faction in the PS. Désir was named, by a presidential decree, to a seat on the Economic and Social Council, a sinecure—it provides an income for a small investment of time—for Mitterrand protégés.

In the next months, President Mitterrand and the new prime minister, Michel Rocard, seemed to switch gears on their earlier liberal views concerning the immigration problem. In particular, Mitterrand, in a statement playing to French fears, now said that the "threshold of tolerance" for new immigration had been reached. Prime Minister Rocard added, in another much-quoted phrase, that "France cannot take in all the world's misery." To their credit, Dray and Désir, in spite of being in power's favor, continued to be critical of the Rocard government (1988–91), and by implication of Mitterrand, on the immigration issue. But SOS–Racism lagged in other ways, notably in an attempt to shift from rock concerts and street demonstrations to establishing interracial friendship houses (*maisons des potes*).

SOS–Racism encountered yet leaner times when, along with the French Communist party, Trotskyites and others, it demonstrated against the Gulf War in January 1991. There had already been bad internal arguments over Israeli–Palestine issues—beurs strongly identified with the Intifada, for example—and the Gulf War created another such internal split. France's participation in the coalition's war against Iraq had widespread support in the country, and by miscalculating or ignoring its supporters' sentiments, SOS–Racism's leadership lost political legitimacy. There was much rank and file exiting from the movement, and a sudden scarcity of political and media personalities who had earlier been glad to get on a bandwagon.

In the past few years SOS–Racism has been out of public favor and down in membership and contributions. Harlem Désir, still seeking a more traditional political career, was among the many well-known PS candidates defeated in the March 1993 parliamentary electoral rout. SOS–Racism since has naturally protested the Balladur–Pasqua hard line on immigration and illegal aliens, with little success other than being received at the Elysée by President Mitterrand.

While this particular organization may be in decline, remarkable as it was for several years, the antiracist sentiment it has embodied, and the youth culture it has mobilized, certainly are not. But will parties, presumably of the standard left, be up to the job of representing the massive antiracist, anti–National Front feeling in French public opinion?

SOS–Racism's problems exemplify not only the new centrality but also the hard paradox of human rights politics in France today. A French consensus on human rights has emerged as one of the bridges spanning the old left–right ideological gulf. Yet human rights can be a vague democratic abstraction, with much rhetoric and few changes. To join a march takes only a little time, just as to admire the handsome, activist, globe-trotting minister for humanitarian efforts or the heroic Doctors Without Borders may only require watching the television news.

Paradoxically, the very popularity of generic human rights as a cause in France today, especially among young people, may be a symptom of a growing, worrisome depoliticization. Democracy requires healthy partisanship and genuine civic commitments. On the other hand, depoliticization to some extent is the logical aftermath of the two-century French revolution, garnished by four decades of Cold War and Soviet threat.

The fading of political partisanship, of civic direction and loyalty, takes on a yet more somber tone when cast against the backdrop of an increasingly deracinated, uprooted society. The character of French social structure, thus the social bases of politics, has changed profoundly in a short time. Depoliticization plus deracination will mean a grave new world of problems.

Urbanization and suburbanization has come later and faster in France than in Britain, Germany, Northern Italy or Holland. Three of four French people today live in cities; 8 of 10 live in urban ecosystems; 1 of 2 lives in a *banlieue,*[*] which often means less a residential suburb than a poor neighborhood stacked with others up against an urban ring road. Most striking of all, 80 percent of the French today are concentrated on 20 percent of the territory; if trends continue, soon 90 percent will live on 10 percent of the Hexagon.[14]

All sorts of traditional community structures have gone far in breaking down. Eighty percent of the French still say they are Catholic, but less than 15 percent are practicing. The decline of "atheistic" left–wing culture—in the PCF and the CGT—is to some extent a parallel phenomenon: the agony of France's traditional "two churches," the black and the red.

---

[*] suburb

The extended family, as in comparable societies (although France used to be different!), has also faded sociologically. And the traditional nuclear family has not resisted, though it has stood up better than either communism or the Church. Nevertheless, rates of divorce, single parentage and out-of-wedlock births have skyrocketed in France over the past three decades. Deaths occur less and less at home, more and more (70 percent) in a hospital. The most evocative statistic of all in this "newest" France: the number of French people living alone seems to have literally doubled since 1968. In a total population of 57 million, as many as 18 million adults live alone. Of these, 1 of 2 say that they suffer seriously from loneliness.[15] A related French singularity, France has the world's highest per capita consumption of tranquilizers.

This alienated, increasingly deracinated society seems no longer the old France, whose classic bourgeois characteristics were still only a few decades ago plainly visible to scholars and tourists alike. "Bourgeois" France continues to fade, the France of vibrant, deeply defined family, social and religious groupings, and also of stiflingly conformist rules of life, as well as the world's exemplary petit-bourgeois culture of envy and resentment. The French visage today seems modernized, yet socially and culturally poorer. Only having started from such a fabulously rich heritage gives foreigners the false impression that things are still basically the same. But it is an illusion. To connect only two facts of contemporary French sociology—the number of people living alone and the emptying out of rural France—is to measure what has been lost, not to be remade except in a new form and on a secular timescale.

Conclusion

France is today (as it was in May 1968) a prime example of what Raymond Aron, in one of his conceptual books about industrial society, called "the disillusions of progress."[16] The old bourgeois French society had grievous faults to be sure, but a thinness of social structure, a lack of sense of belonging and place, were not among them. In the new France, standards of living have metamorphosed for significant numbers of people. But psychologically and morally—that is, in human terms—society has become, to use one of Aron's favorite terms, "infernal" for too many people. France, like other contemporary societies, is producing a brutally homeless underclass of the street; in other societies it seems less unexpected.

The sheer human suffering is anguishing in itself. And the danger of political depoliticization and social atomization is well known—the social basis for populist authoritarianism, a menace fortunately still well over the horizon.

But what combination of individual engagement, social creativity and political reform will push this danger back decisively? Can the French, this time necessarily with partners, first of all Germany, cope with the problems of modernity, with the "disillusions of progress"? And if so, *pace de Gaulle*, would France's way this time not necessarily mean the *full* association of European integration with national renewal?

Endnotes

1. *The Economist*, December 12, 1992, special survey on agriculture, p. 13.
2. The important early studies in English of French interest group politics were Henry Ehrmann, "Interest Groups in France," in Ehrmann (ed.), *Interest Groups on Four Continents* (Pittsburgh: University of Pittsburgh Press, 1960), and Val Lorwin, *The French Labor Movement* (Cambridge: Harvard University Press, 1954). See also Suzanne D. Berger (ed.), *Organizing Interests in Western Europe* (Cambridge: Harvard University Press, 1981).
3. For this and several points in the following section see Nico Colchester, "L'état c'est l'Europe," special survey on France, *The Economist*, November 23, 1991, pp. 14ff.
4. See Pfister, op. cit. and two studies by Ezra Suleiman, *Politics, Power and Bureaucracy in France: The Administrative Elite* (Princeton, N.J.: Princeton University Press, 1974) and *Elites in French Society: The Politics of Survival* (Princeton, N.J.: Princeton University Press, 1978).
5. See Guy Sorman, *Demain le capitalisme* (Capitalism tomorrow) (Paris: Editions du Seuil, 1986).
6. Michel Albert, the head of Assurances Générales de France, in *Capitalisme contre capitalisme* (Paris: Editions du Seuil, 1991). Quotations are from Chapter 7.
7. See Mark Kesselman in Kesselman et al., *European Politics in Transition*, pp. 206ff, and Kesselman (ed.), *The French Workers' Movement* (London: Allen & Unwin, 1984). Because of its size and importance we should note a fourth big union organization: the Fédération de l'Éducation Nationale (FEN) (National Education Federation). For decades the conglomerate FEN organized well over half the teachers and nonteaching staff in the massive public education system. In 1993, after years of internal conflict, it split. In a way a civil servants' union, since teachers and staff in the French educational system have civil servants' status, the FEN talks a radical public rhetoric but in fact is usually a corporatist partner in the educational system with the government bureaucracy. It is deeply involved in the rules of promotion, tenure, transfer and salary. The FEN's suc-

cess as an organization makes two points. First, in France it is easier to organize public-sector workers (especially those with tenure or the possibility of it) than private-sector workers. Second, the FEN's high rate of organization indicates that it is a union's lack of success in securing benefits that is the cause of low membership.

8. See Peter Lange, "The Politics of the Social Dimension," in Alberta Sbragia (ed.), *Euro-Politics: Institutions and Policy Making in the "New" European Community* (Washington, D. C.: The Brookings Institution, 1992), Chapter 7.

9. *The Economist*, October 5, 1991, p. 28.

10. Ehrmann and Schain, op. cit., p. 42.

11. *The Economist*, October 5, 1991, p. 28.

12. On race and immigration issues in France, see R. Brubaker, op. cit., and J. Hollifield, op. cit.

13. *Beur* is "Arab" in Verlan, the argot of kids in the suburbs and streets who are of North African origin.

14. See Alain Duhamel, *Les Peurs françaises* (French Fears) (Paris: Flammarion, 1993), pp. 132ff.

15. Ibid., p. 140. For the original study see Michel Hannoun, *Nos solitudes: Enquête sur un sentiment* (Our Solitudes: Inquiry about a Feeling) (Paris: Editions du Seuil, 1992). The figure of 18 million seems too high, perhaps by a lot. But the radical trend toward adults living alone—divorced persons, widows, bachelors—is not open to question.

16. See Raymond Aron, *Progress and Disillusion*, op. cit.

7

✦

Public Policy:
Some Key Issues

France, like other countries, has finally tamed the formidable strength of the people's will within regularly elected institutions, and rendered it compatible with a strong executive branch of government. [France] presents the same spectacle as the other European countries, and has the same problems to resolve: the educational system, reform of the tax system, problems of the security of persons, agricultural prices, the adequacy of social spending. Her citizens fight over distribution of the nation's wealth, and no longer over the legacy of the nation's history. Along with its revolutionary stakes, French politics has lost its theatrical dimension.

—François Furet, *La République du centre* (The centrist republic), p. 55

"Ordinary" Public Policy

Public policy debate in France used to be, like most aspects of French political life, a hostage to the left–right ideological war, above all to the supposed choice between capitalism and socialism. Only in the past decade—so recently, since the union of the left governments of 1981–84—has French public policy debate emerged, and not yet entirely, from the old ideological struggle.

There is of course a serious danger in "ordinary" public policy think-ing: a lack of imagination, an entrenchment in merely marginal alterna-tives. On the other hand, a new and fruitful pragmatism may develop, capable of unleashing heretofore pent-up energies and inventiveness. Rather than a sterile confrontation of rigidified doctrines, a post-Marxian French left is free to reconceive a realistic and plausible agenda derived from the left's core values—egalitarianism, justice, generosity. The French right is in its turn pressed to liberalize and update the conserva-tive touchstones of order, the nation, and the rights of property. And, more than ever, both the left and the right in France are obliged to measure themselves against international standards; so references multi-ply to how things are done in Germany, the United States, Japan and yet other neighbors and partners.

The campaign regarding the September 1992 Maastricht referendum may have marked a historical turning point in the structure of French partisan politics. Neither the right nor the left was united. Both were divided internally over whether to approve or reject the Maastricht Treaty, and these splits may indicate a deep-running evolution in French politics.

The left–right cleavage in France is no longer a kind of French Berlin Wall. It is no longer a zone of mortal political danger and no longer an unerring map of partisan divisions: The recentered, centrist republic is a reality. The vote on the Maastricht Treaty referendum seemed to show France once again divided in two: 51 percent in favor, 49 percent against. But this was illusory in two respects. A large part of the anti-Maastricht vote was a punishment of an unpopular President Mitterrand and an unpopular Socialist government. And unlike the highly ideological past, voters' feelings, whether for or against Maastricht, were on the whole not very intense. The project for European Union was too vague and com-plex, and economic times too close to the bone for French people to have been wildly enthusiastic about a major new step in European integration. Yet, precisely for the same reasons, only ultranationalists believed that Maastricht was the devil's work against the French nation. And several months earlier opinion polls showed about 70 percent of the French as favorable.

The parliamentary vote on Maastricht was a better indicator than the referendum of the degree to which the issue of Europe spans the old left–right gulf in French politics. In favor was a broad center–left, cen-ter–right consensus. It was made up of the Socialists on the left, the UDF and CDS in the center–right, and—*pace de Gaulle*—even a majority of the parliamentary neo-Gaullist RPR, including Jacques Chirac, the party's presumptive presidential candidate. Chirac said that it was "inconceiv-able" that France, after a long negotiation, should reject its partners by rejecting such an important agreement. General de Gaulle, who vetoed Britain's application, recognized mainland China and pushed the NATO command out of French territory, would have rejected being so tied up by circumstances and partners. But three decades of intensifying European integration would perhaps have cut down the room to maneuver even for a de Gaulle.

Arrayed against the Maastricht Treaty was no unified ideological bloc, but rather a hodgepodge combination of right and left groups with nothing in common except a vague, self-contradictory nationalist demiurge. The minority of the parliamentary RPR, led by Charles Pasqua and Philippe Séguin, was against, along with about half the neo-Gaullist electorate. Outside the RPR was Le Pen's National Front far-right party, and, inside the governing Socialist party, a small "Jacobin-Republican" faction led by Jean-Pierre Chevènement was also against. Finally, on the far left were the French Communists and the Greens, the more fundamentalist group in the ecologist movement.

Considering not only the great issue of Europe but also other problems of domestic and foreign policy, it is clear that party realignment— some ideologically unprecedented change—is both desirable and conceivable. Whether, or how soon, new alignments occur will naturally depend on many things: party histories, electoral calculations and personalities as well as values and policies. But as the March 1993 parliamentary elections ended, observers said that the "union that begs to be created is one embracing the UDF and the Socialist party, campaigning for France to remain the driving force behind European integration." Its strategy would be to make the central cleavage line in French politics "Europeanism versus nationalism, Brussels versus Astérix le Gaulliste."[1]

Already in his 1981 reelection campaign, President Giscard d'Estaing had tested, unsuccessfully, the opinion poll–based theme that on most important public policy issues "three out of five Frenchmen want to be governed in the center." (A few years later, after his 1981 defeat, he upped the figure to two out of three Frenchmen.[2]) Giscard d'Estaing, despite losing to Mitterrand, was probably not so much wrong as ahead of the political wave. His attempt to incubate a political culture of centrist values was frustrated because the French electorate turned out to be interested first in testing Mitterrand and the left in office. Nevertheless, as this book attempts to demonstrate in several ways, the long-term, longitudinal opinion polling on which Giscard d'Estaing relied for his centrist conclusions was substantially correct. The "recentered" republic is a reality of French public opinion.

This chapter is not a general survey of problems; it focuses on a few key domestic policy issues selected either because they are perennially fundamental or because they are pivotal issues today. Each is "French."

But as with French social issues generally—the rise of unemployment and the decline of unions; nationalization and privatization of industry; immigration and racism; women's issues; AIDS—it is a matter of European and international policy dilemmas expressed in French accents and with Gallic emphases. There is still a recognizably French public policy "style," a French kind of public administration. But it is less idiosyncratic than before, less based on statist, tutelary national traditions and on French cultural habits and prejudices. And French public policy elites, though still largely the product of the *grandes écoles* such as the ENA and the École Polytechnique, are no longer quite so homogeneous, or at least so "French," as before. Still, public policy and partisan politics have evolved more in the past fifteen years than has the corps of high civil servants in France. Successive Socialist governments of 1981–93 did no better, and often worse, than conservative governments in democratizing political and administrative-bureaucratic elite recruitment.

Economic Issues

Unemployment

In the 1993 parliamentary electoral campaign, unemployment, as opposed to immigration and racism, reemerged as the pivotal issue in French domestic politics. On the day before Prime Minister Bérégovoy handed over power to the new prime minister, Eduoard Balladur, his government finally admitted that the symbolic roof of 3 million unemployed had been broken. This confirmed that over 10 percent in the French work force were officially unemployed, with hundreds of thousands more underemployed in part-time jobs, precariously employed in temporary jobs or in one of a series of government apprenticeship programs. Various categories of self-employed workers—farmers, fishermen, truck drivers—staged blockades, dumped produce, and sometimes struck violently in defense of their livelihood. Other categories of salaried employees—medical and hospital personnel, primary and secondary teachers, and so on—took to the streets to lobby not only for better working conditions, but also for the survival of their jobs.

To long-time observers of France, these seemed familiar scenes. Yet the resurgence of resistance to unemployment was anything but a renewal of the class struggle labor actions of the 1950s and 1960s. For one thing, those took place with unemployment at historically low levels, say 2 percent, and with prosperity broadly increasing. For another thing, labor unions were a lot stronger than now. Today workers and the self-employed demonstrate not against French capitalism, but against foreign competition. They don't want to overthrow the government, they want the government to protect or to subsidize their livelihoods. And they rise up against a Socialist government as quickly as against a conservative government. They see little difference, and rightly so, between economic and financial policies of the left and the right.

Yet in the late 1980s immigration and the question of "foreigners" had been the most explosive issue in French politics. Given high and increasing unemployment—7, 8, 9 percent—the question is why, especially given France's history of labor militancy, did so many French people accept painful, prolonged unemployment without major rebellions? Where were the labor unions, traditional defenders of jobs and benefits? In the country of May 1968, why did such widespread personal and family hardship not produce more violent consequences?

As indicated just above, unemployment in France used to be, twenty or thirty years ago, a smaller economic problem but a larger political problem. Precisely when the level of unemployment was low, during *les Trente Glorieuses* to 1973, levels of union membership, numbers of strike days, and management's fear of the working class were all much higher than today. At that time, even slowly rising unemployment in the Cold War years always was portrayed in terms of capitalism's "contradictions," threatening the perennially forecast "general crisis of capitalism."

On the other hand, the French labor movement was during these years feared much beyond its actual numbers. Compared with West Germany, Great Britain or Sweden, where 40 percent to 80 percent of workers were union members, in France only about 20 percent belonged. So few workers joined precisely because of the French labor movement's politicization, which made unions as much or more political as professionally interested; on the other hand, *le Patronat*, French business owners and managers, tried to limit unionization, because they feared it and because the labor movement's internal divisions made the unions weak partners for management.

French business and the French state feared the Communist CGT more than they feared labor as such. And they were not wrong to do so: The CGT was tied up with the PCF, and the PCF was tied up with the Soviet Union. A large part of the 20 percent of French union members belonged to the CGT (although many joined not because they wanted to be Communists but because the CGT was the strongest, most feared and combative labor union).

The end result for French workers was a labor movement riven with all the conflicts in French politics as a whole and thus weakened. The vibrancy of such a labor movement certainly depended a lot on the healthy economic growth of the period. There was low unemployment, for which unions could take some credit, justified or not, and productivity gains allowed the success of union demands for greater benefits. Only now is it possible for some in the French labor movement to realize why the 1950s and 1960s really were a golden era for the unions. It could have been a disaster.

French unemployment in early 1993 was, as indicated above, about 3 million in a work force of some 30 million. Ten percent unemployment—a new, unhappy record since the Depression—twenty years ago would have been considered a time bomb waiting to go off. But, barring the unforeseeable, today's social and professional job actions indicate a continuing and perhaps worsening period of social struggles over unemployment and threats to current employment. But there are few signs of some general strike, some social explosion as in 1968. (But there were not in 1968 either.)

During the postwar period until the early 1970s, the French economy was in a condition of technical full employment. There was even a chronic shortage of workers, which had three significant effects. First, the need for labor stimulated a large influx of foreign workers, mainly from North Africa—that is, from France's colonial possessions. Second, on the independence of Algeria, Morocco and Tunisia in the early 1960s there was rapid absorption of the French *pieds-noirs* repatriated from these Maghreb countries. Third, consequently there was a natural, continuous domestic inflationary pressure in the French economy because of the high cost of relatively scarce labor.[3]

Before 1967, French unemployment was remarkably low, never higher than 1.7 percent, descending as low as 0.9 percent. Unemployment began to climb gradually thereafter, reaching 2.8 percent in 1974 at a time when technical definitions of full employment were still higher, about 3 percent to 4 percent. Furthermore, in this period, and especially during the exceptional growth years of 1969–73, unemployment generally was a kind of "adaptation," meaning a short period of unemployment while moving from one job to another.

The oil price crisis of 1973–74 and the ensuing recession marked the beginning of a time of high unemployment. From 2.8 percent in 1974, unemployment rose to 7 percent in 1981. This was due to continuing international recession, which had become "stagflation" (a combination, rather than a trade-off, of high unemployment and high inflation), and to the second oil price shock of 1979.

This was the situation when François Mitterrand and the union of the left government came to power in 1981, with their countercyclical Keynesian Socialist reflation. As was said already, this government stimulation of demand ended quickly and chaotically, because French consumers bought vastly more imports than noncompetitive domestic products. The initial Mitterrand–Mauroy program thus created jobs, but unfortunately they were in other countries. And stagflation, the double penalty of Keynesian socialism, showed that willingly increased domestic inflation not only did not reduce unemployment but also augmented it. This was hardly what the first "workers' government" since the 1936 Popular Front intended!

The successive Mitterrand policy corrections of 1982 and 1983 gradually put the French economy back in sync with the business cycle in the G-7 economies. But several years were required for all the penalties incurred in 1981–82 to be paid off. For example, only in 1985 did the French franc hit its (shocking) low point—10.5 francs—against the overvalued Reagan dollar. More significantly, French unemployment, as in most countries belonging to the Organization for Economic Cooperation and Development (OECD), continued to rise: from 8 percent in 1983 to 10.5 in 1987, back to 9 percent in 1990, then up again to 10 in 1992 and over 11 percent in 1993. In 1991, French unemployment was, among the G-7 countries, exceeded only by that of Canada and Italy. Things have not improved since.

But unemployment has risen beyond formerly "acceptable" levels in most of the G-7 countries. Britain's unemployment during the last years of the Thatcher government had even exceeded France's, for example. And U.S. unemployment edged closer to France's in the last years of the Reagan presidency. Nevertheless, the level of French unemployment, while not the worst, has been, by a significant degree, worse than the average G-7 unemployment over the past seven years.

Heading toward 1994, forecasts indicate a worsening of the situation. The economy's weak growth, hurt by Germany's recession, slid into contraction—that is, outright French recession. The French INSEE economics institute predicted a 1.2 percent fall in gross domestic product in 1994, and the OECD said the French recession would likely be even worse than expected.

Unemployment in France thus would get significantly worse beyond the 3 million and 10 percent figures of March 1993: perhaps another 500,000 before the trend turns around. This might mean 12 percent unemployed by the time of the 1995 presidential election, a social time bomb and a bad record on which to run (see Figure 7.1). For human and political reasons it was thus reasonable to suppose that the Balladur government would take significant countercyclical steps by the beginning of 1994.

During the same period, on the other hand, the French inflation rate was, at 2–3 percent, the lowest among the G-7 countries, and the French franc was made "virtually" into a strong currency. The franc is attacked periodically in the markets because speculators doubt the sufficiency of hard currency reserves or the French government's political will to defend the franc with high interest rates (or both), but under Mitterrand

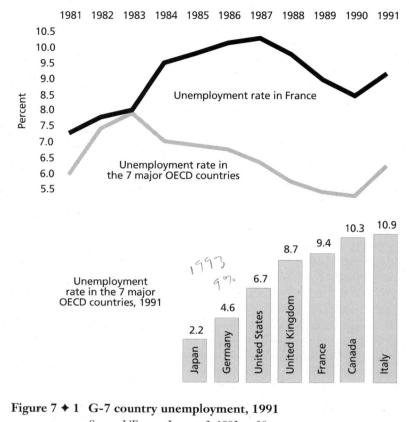

Figure 7 ✦ 1   G-7 country unemployment, 1991

Source: L'Express, January 2, 1992, p. 38.

and Pierre Bérégovoy as finance minister, old questions about French economic fundamentals were answered. The exception was the 1992–93 budget deficit slide, following Bérégovoy's replacement of Edith Cresson as prime minister. Conservative parties successfully focused on this in their 1993 electoral campaign, arguing that Bérégovoy had lightened up because a big election was near. Bérégovoy, the "Pinay of the left," was apparently deeply affected by this attack on his integrity and competence.

According to Phillips curve–type reasoning, the very high level of French unemployment over half a decade has been the price of low inflation, a strong currency, and enviably low public-sector deficits and debts. As was to be expected, the government's 1991–93 shift to a higher priority for fighting unemployment, even if unsuccessful, more than doubled the government's budget deficit, which is still comparatively not excessive.

Successive governments have tried to lower unemployment, with mainly moral rather than practical success. Job training and government-subsidized apprenticeships have provided several hundred thousand temporary jobs, usually no longer than a year. While the results of this so-called social treatment of unemployment are limited, even temporary jobs are worthwhile, especially for young people, the largest category in French unemployment, above all—worst off among the worst off—for first-generation immigrant youths. In three years up to 1991, about 440,000 young people passed through the so-called job-solidarity contract program created by the Rocard government in 1988. It replaced a slightly different program, called TUC, the working principle of both being government tax reductions to businesses hiring young people. Another program created by the Cresson government in 1990 was a tax reduction for hiring household help. The government gives a tax credit for half the salary, up to a limit of 25,000 francs per year. (The benefit to the government treasury is that some of what would otherwise be totally black market wages is legally declared and, therefore, taxed.)

The upshot of these youth-oriented and other programs for the unemployed is that, unfortunately, the tendency has not yet been reversed. The government's job programs create low-paid, highly subsidized and economically unnecessary or otherwise unaffordable jobs. They are half-gestures, sometimes useful and hope-sustaining, but on the whole, temporary social-security "parking lots" for unemployed young people entering the job market with little or no job qualification.

The French programs to deal with youth unemployment take as their inspiration the often-admired German system of apprenticeships, which at any one time supports 1.5 million regularly placed apprentices for periods of up to three years. The system of apprenticeships has become the normal way for a large percentage of German young people to join the labor market and the normal way for most large German companies to replenish their work force. But the German system, whose huge costs are shared by *land*, local, and federal government payments, as well as by business, has been operating for decades. It has become a wide-reaching, highly regulated and subsidized career-training and placement system. Any such French programs were long delayed or limited by working-class ideological hostility against capitalism and by the social irresponsibility of French business.

OECD recommendations concerning French unemployment regularly prescribe a combination of three policies: (1) tax cuts for business investment, (2) more flexibility in the labor market (meaning fewer restrictions on layoffs and greater willingness of workers to relocate for new jobs), and (3) predictably, additional job training and apprenticeships.

This very orthodox list could fit almost any European country. But there is general agreement that, as in other countries, only significant new economic growth, rather than government programs, will reduce the French unemployment level to a significant degree in the short to medium term. And yet, even a turnaround of the international economic slowdown of the early 1990s, which the U.S. economy appears to be leading in 1993, may not generate the degree of economic growth that could substantially, rather than marginally, reduce unemployment, not only in France but also throughout Europe. A reduction of unemployment from 10 percent to, say, 8 percent, would surely be welcome. But 8 percent unemployment is far higher than the 4–6 percent that the strongest Western economies perceived as "normal" in previous decades. What would be the social and political consequences of a failure, in the long term, to bring unemployment levels back down to the acceptable levels of earlier prosperity?

The generalized stymie of French public policy on the unemployment issue was revealed in a striking moment of the 1988 presidential campaign television debate between President Mitterrand and Prime Minister Chirac. Although unemployment was then, according to opinion polls, the main concern of the French, the candidates discussed it only briefly. Neither had a convincing public policy plan, and the entire subject could make both candidates look bad. President Mitterrand at one point said laconically that "There has been a continuity of failure." Chirac replied "No, we haven't all failed in the same way."[4] In its own way, this was a remarkable moment of the new French consensus.

In sum, the best remedy for unemployment is strong economic growth to create good, new jobs. A government policy for the "social treatment of unemployment" is a palliative, not a solution. It has its place, and this impulse of generosity is, in partisan terms, more characteristic of left-wing governments than of conservative governments. But the significant understanding implicit in the new French consensus on the parameters of economic and social policy is that economic well-being will be more a matter of economic growth than of redistribution.

The relative quiescence of the French labor movement and patience among the unemployed must result, at least in part, from the simple lack of convincing alternatives. Also, the new French willingness to look around at one's partners, to measure France's problems and successes by cosmopolitan standards, is a growing characteristic of French policy making. What unions, business or any group can demand of government or of the social partners in French society is increasingly measured against what happens in Germany, in the other strong EC countries, and also in the United States and even in Japan. Most startling of all, in the perspective of French history, is that French business—corporate capitalism—is gradually being seen by unions and workers as "one of us," part of the international corporate industrial mechanism, the hope, not to say the necessity, of French prosperity.

Nationalizations: The "Neither–Nor" Solution

Nationalization and its opposite, the privatization of industry and banks, became highly ideological issues for one last time in French politics in the 1980s, as in a few other European countries, above all in Britain under Margaret Thatcher's government.

President Mitterrand's first government carried out a significant nationalization program in 1981–82. This has been discussed already above. Were the Mauroy government's nationalizations part of a "leap" toward socialism?[5] The answer is no, or else that socialism is just unattainable. However one decides, the nationalizations between July 1981 and February 1982 are an impressive list, concisely described by Peter Hall:

> Although the largest French banks were already under state control, the Government nationalized 36 smaller banks, two investment banks, Suez and Paribas, and the remaining minority of private shares in the Crédit Lyonnais, Banque Nationale de Paris, and Société Générale. It acquired 100 percent of the shares in six industrial conglomerates . . . [CGE, CGCT, Thompson-Brandt, Rhone-Poulenc, Péchiney-Ugine-Kuhlman, St. Gobain]. . . . State debt in the two major steel firms, Sacilor and Usinor, was converted into a majority shareholding, and the government acquired 51 percent of the shares of two arms and aeronautical manufacturers, Dassault-Breguet and Matra, as well as control over the computer firm CII-Honeywell-Bull, and the pharmaceutical house, Roussel-Uclaf . . . The state now owned 13 of the 20 largest firms in France and a controlling share in many other French companies. State holdings accounted for 24 percent of the employees, 32 percent of the sales, 30 percent of the exports, and 60 percent of the annual investment in the industrial and energy sectors of the French economy.[6]

It is of some interest, if only historical, to ask how much influence the French Communist party had in this affair. Some background is necessary to make a judgment. First, Mitterrand would surely have avoided committing himself to such a large nationalization agenda at all had he not been obliged to bargain for Communist party support from the time of his first run for president, in 1965, and continuously thereafter. In 1981, despite the Socialist party's unexpected absolute parliamentary victory following his election to the presidency, Mitterrand felt obligated to keep his two-decade-long pledge to form a government including the Communists and to implement several of the 1972 Common Program's policies. He even chose the most extreme method of nationalizing companies, at 100 percent, instead of the less radical, less expensive way of buying state controlling interests at 51 percent, as Socialist party "realists" such as Michel Rocard advised. Nevertheless, Mitterrand rejected the Communist maximalist demand to nationalize *subsidiary* companies as well as parent corporations. This Common Program "ambiguity," which would have expanded the nationalizations to a much larger level, had been left unclarified for a decade! It illustrated that the Socialist–Communist coalition was based on ideological rhetoric, which would be clarified only after power had been achieved. In 1972, when the program was first written, the Communists were much stronger. By 1981, François Mitterrand had won his risky bet with the Communists that the French would only elect the left to office if the Socialist party had become stronger than the PCF.

To avoid any appearance of a Bolshevik-style "confiscation" of property, the Socialist-led government paid expropriated company shareholders considerably more than prevailing market prices. Shares of Rhone-Poulenc, for example, recently trading below 50 francs were exchanged for a bond worth 126 francs, which in addition paid 16 percent interest!

What was the point of the nationalizations? There was never one single goal, several targets were aimed at simultaneously. In spite of all the rhetoric, first and foremost, neither François Mitterrand nor the Socialist party was out to lead a revolution. And the Communists, whatever Georges Marchais and the other top leaders discussed or thought, never had much say over what the government did. Instead, there was an ambiguous mix of genuine policy aims and purely political and ideological goals. Some industrial policy enthusiasts of nationalization stressed the practical rescue of important "national champion" elements in France's industrial base. Other, more doctrinal Socialists hoped that nationalization was a prelude to widespread autogestion experiments in workers' control gradually to weaken capitalism, strengthen unions, and so on.

Opponents of the nationalizations worried less about the various takeovers in industry than about near-complete nationalization of credit created by the new bank takeovers. Jacques Chirac, for instance, asserted that the industrial nationalizations were virtually "a detail," because by nationalizing credit and using it to plan the economy, the state—that is, the Socialists—would direct French industrial development entirely. The Socialist government, exactly to the contrary, said that the nationalization of credit would better "guarantee" capital to truly strategic industries by reducing the dependence of investment on "business confidence"—that is, capitalist motives. French companies were self-financing in 1981 at a rate of about 50 percent; the state therefore would now control about 50 percent of company financing in the entire economy.

The conservative parties and the Patronat (the peak association of business) forecast a disastrous politicization of business investment and the ruin rather than the renewal of French industrial competitiveness.

What happened? The practical outcome of the 1981–82 nationalizations was costly, but it hardly revolutionized the French economy, let alone French society. The Mauroy government rapidly stepped back from trying to decide investment and a state-led industrial plan, and the Socialists got cold feet rather quickly in the face of the giant project they had seemingly launched.

On the other hand, the Patronat's dire predictions of bankruptcies and permanent ruin of French industry did not come true either. The nationalization plan ended in mid-1982, and the Mauroy government, in two steps in 1982–83, abandoned its pump-priming Keynesian policies. In the face of skyrocketing inflation, a fiscally conservative policy of economic "rigor" was adopted.

Yet Prime Minister Mauroy and Finance Minister Jacques Delors could not avoid three humiliating devaluations of the French franc in the short space of two years. Business commentators termed this a devastating verdict by the markets on the grand French experiment with socialism. Mitterrand said, with some bitterness, that the French Socialist program had been predictably attacked by international capitalist speculators.

In 1984, politically, intellectually and morally exhausted by the tumultuous union of the left years, Pierre Mauroy was replaced as prime minister. The three-year union period thus came to a close. Mitterrand said to an advisor that Mauroy's departure from office, marking the clear end of Mitterrand's left-wing phase, was "the most painful day of my term."[7]

Mauroy's successor, Laurent Fabius, was a protégé of President Mitterrand. But what did that now mean in policy terms? Whatever other qualities Fabius brought to the job—Mitterrand emphasized his youth, which would counter one of Jacques Chirac's advantages in public opinion—he was basically a technocrat and a modernizer, an establishment *enarch*, rather than an ideological Socialist. Mitterrand, the moving force behind the construction of governments, had made his intention clear: to maintain conservative financial and economic policies, with modernization replacing socialism as the principle of public policy. In reaction, the French Communists, since three years quite powerless, quit the government coalition, formally rupturing the union of the left and ending the period of formal Socialist–Communist alliance. When the cohabitation conservative Jacques Chirac government of 1986–88 took power, the Socialists' nationalizations were not surprisingly attacked.[8] Chirac, following the model of the Thatcher government's privatization of Labour nationalizations in Britain, quickly put on the market several corporations from the 1981–82 changeovers. The stock market was weak and the government's shares were sold in bad conditions, but this money-losing attack on "socialism" was thought imperative for ideological and political reasons. After a rush to privatize and launch other "rollback of socialism" policies—frenetically done because the next presidential election, which would pit him against Mitterrand, was in less than two years—Chirac abruptly stopped the program only about 40 percent completed.

During the 1988 presidential campaign, François Mitterrand came up with what was in effect a peace proposal—*Ni . . . ni* (neither . . . nor)—which finally broke the cycle of political revenge by succeeding governments on the issue of nationalizations.[9] Mitterrand promised that, if reelected, a second term would bring no new nationalizations, no more privatizations. In proposing to bury this historic issue, Mitterrand sought to appear as a "president of all the French," not just of the left or the Socialists. Above the partisan fray, Mitterrand would be, as his campaign posters said, *la force tranquille* (the quiet force), a pillar of strength. It worked. Mitterrand, opposed by a strident Jacques Chirac, was elected to a second seven-year term.

The neither–nor pledge remained unscathed during the first three years of Mitterrand's second term. At the end of 1991, Prime Minister Edith Cresson got Mitterrand's approval for a renewal of state industrial policy, to involve buying and selling parts of government ownership in companies. But significantly, there was no question of new nationalizations. The first Cresson move was, in fact, not for new state ownership but for a small state sell-off, a partial privatization in which money would be raised to hold down the budget deficit and to finance the government's "social treatment" programs designed to hold unemployment down.

The first miniprivatization, a 2 billion franc (Fr) ($360 million) sale of shares in Elf-Aquitaine, France's largest state-owned company, was scheduled for the end of 1991. Demonstrating how difficult the timing can be, it had to be held back because the Paris stock market suddenly slumped in response to the Wall Street "minicrash" in mid-November. To go ahead would have involved no small potential loss: Elf-Aquitaine stock dropped from Fr 435 per share on November 15 to Fr 350 by December 15. And the decision to delay the Elf sale looked even better when compared with the Chirac government's costly 1987 decision, in the wake of the October Wall Street crash, to go ahead for political reasons with the privatization of Compagnie Financière de Suez, which was, everyone agreed, badly sold.

Elf, an oil and chemicals conglomerate, was the first move in the Cresson government's plan to sell off minority holdings in several public-sector companies, including insurance companies and other industrial groups. By selling off about 2 percent of Elf's equity, the French state's holding was reduced to 51.5 percent from 53.8 percent. At the end of October 1992, Cresson's successor as prime minister, Finance Minister Pierre Bérégovoy, announced a second privatization. Ten percent of Rhone-Poulenc, France's most profitable company, would be put on the market for the same dual purpose of raising money for the government to finance unemployment programs and to hold down the deficit.

A second aspect of the Cresson program was to return to an activist industrial strategy. Several state-owned companies in difficulty would be reorganized through government-directed mergers and infusions of new capital from the state. This was a throwback to the Gaullist and Giscardist "national champion" industrial policy, favored by Edith Cresson during her earlier jobs as minister of foreign trade and minister for European affairs in the 1980s. It was not only, or merely, a variety of Socialist planning, but also a Colbertist, étatiste approach to economic policy—as French as it was Socialist.

French government plans for nationalizations or privatizations increasingly have become technical operations chronicled in the business pages. Mitterrand's neither–nor formula has ushered in, or perhaps merely recognized, the "postnationalization" era in French politics, in which privatization is not, ipso facto, a right-wing proposal nor nationalization, ipso facto, a left-wing proposal. *La guerre des nationalizations est finie.*

The Balladur government, as expected, almost immediately, in May 1993, issued a list of possible privatizations (see Table 7.1), from which it would choose those actually to be put up for sale. The government hoped the stock market would be sufficiently healthy to realize $1–2 billion from the first year's privatization sales. In addition to fulfilling its commitment to get the state out of unnecessary economic activities, privatization revenues would help plug the suddenly rising budget deficit left by the Socialists. (In a traditional conservative action to raise cash, the government floated a hugely successful tax-free bond issue—the 6 percent "Balladur bond"—aimed at individuals as well as institutions; it sold out, oversubscribed three times, in a few days in July 1993, raising almost $19 billion as opposed to the $7 billion initially projected.)

Despite its impressive size, the Balladur list is a good example of the decline of war rhetoric over privatization and nationalization. There is some, but little talk of revenge—a conservative desire for revenge, a Socialist fear of revenge—or of making a new "change of society." President Mitterrand and the Socialists are unhappy, but the left has accepted that some amount of privatization is, or can be, a good thing. The privatization list is, moreover, not a single-minded attack on the union of the left's nationalizations, but a composite view of twentieth-century French economic history, containing companies that were already on the 1986

Table 7 ✦ 1 The Balladur Government's Privatization List, May 1993
Source: Adapted from a table in Le Monde, May 27, 1993, p. 24.

Company	Number Employed	% Public Ownership	Date Nationalized
Aérospatiale	45,000	74	August 1936
Air France	64,000	99	June 1945
Banque Hervet	1,380	55	February 1982
BNP	58,000	73	December 1945
Central Reinsurance Fund	160	100	April 1946
Bull Honeywell	35,200	72	Febuary 1982
Compagnie Générale Maritime	2,500	100	July 1933
Crédit Lyonnais	70,000	52	December 1945
Péchiney	61,000	55	February 1982
Renault	146,600	80	January 1945
Rhone-Poulenc	83,300	43	February 1982
AGF	22,000	65	April 1946
GAN	49,000	79	April 1946
UAP	40,000	53	April 1946
Seita	5,500	100	January 1959
Société Marseillèse de credit	2,368	100	February 1982
SNECMA[a]	25,300	97	May 1945
Elf-Acquitaine	87,000	51	November 1941
Thomson	100,000	82	February 1982
Usinor Sacilor	90,800	80	November 1981
National Contingency Fund	2,000	42	July 1868

[a]Société Nationale d'Entreprise de Construction et Materièle Aéronautique

Chirac government's list, some that were nationalized by the Socialists in 1981–82, and others that appear for the first time, such as the Renault automobile company. Renault, which was nationalized in January 1945 by the provisional government consequent to its owner Louis Renault's collaboration with the Nazi occupiers, had for four postwar decades been a workers'—especially a Communist CGT and Communist party—bastion. Strikes of Renault unions, especially at the suburban Paris-Billancourt factory, were particularly fraught: "When Renault sneezes," went the political proverb, "France catches cold." Jean-Paul Sartre's mistaken and paternalist maxim had it that the truth about the Soviet Union should not be told, because "we must not throw Billancourt into despair."

Privatization of Renault would be highly symbolic, whatever its economic result. Renault's workers and unions, except for a rearguard disgruntlement of Communist and Jacobin enthusiasts of state ownership, are not opposing privatization, seeing certain advantages and some disadvantages, and little change in the way the firm is run internally. A reconciled Billancourt, for so long a focal point and barometer of anticapitalist working-class feeling, is, for any long-time observer of France, a singularly impressive sign of deep-going changes.

Immigration, Racism and "Foreigners"

Immigration is a pressing issue today in most of the wealthy Western countries. But *immigration* is not the right name for problems of racism and tolerance, which have been the most explosive social dilemma in French life for a decade, feeding the rise of the National Front and uneasiness about "French identity." France's problems in this regard need to be put into context. The issues are European-wide, but the problems in France have their singularly French aspects.

Immigration involves a concatenation of conflicts. Involved are race, ethnic and religious prejudice; unemployment and hard times; social, cultural and political pressures; and vague yet potent nationalist worries about "an invasion of foreigners which is threatening French identity." There is, at its most extreme, a hoary nationalist alarm: "The nation is in peril." It is an old, worrisome story with a new cast of "others."

One fact should dominate French controversy about immigration, even though it doesn't: Legal immigration into France was practically closed off in 1974, except for family reunifications with already successful immigrants. In other words, since 1974 French government policy has nearly shut down new immigration.

How was the policy implemented? It was, of course, unthinkable to write a law that simply excluded all foreigners forever. So the Government's squelching of new immigration, except for family reunifications, was implemented by almost entirely eliminating residence permits of long enough duration to entitle a foreigner resident in France to apply for naturalization.

The important exception was, as mentioned, to permit reunification from abroad with family members who were or were becoming naturalized French citizens. It was an important proviso: On this basis, plus high immigrant birthrates, the North African Arab Muslim population in France grew considerably after 1974 in spite of the general French ban on immigration. A few statistics convey the dimension of new legal North African immigration to France: Altogether currently there are only about

15,000 new legal North African immigrants per year, and this small number is easily outdistanced by the number of voluntary departures returning home.[10] Altogether the total number of new legal immigrants into France is now about 100,000 per year, in a population of approximately 56 million. The simple conclusion must be that new legal immigration, immigration as public opinion tends to think of it, is not an "invasion." There are real social and political problems concerning immigrants in France—no one denies this—but the issues are elsewhere.

It was the legal right to family reunifications that created large immigrant communities and largely unforeseen social problems, as the original ghettoized dormitory buildings of socially isolated, single, male foreign workers of the 1950s and '60s became permanent neighborhoods of "foreign French" families and community groupings. And because of family reunification and the neighborhood and community building it engendered, there arose the additional delicate issue that, because fertility rates are higher among the immigrant population than among the French, disproportionate claims by new arrivals were created on social services: on state family allocation, on schools and on all the other forms of government support that go with children in France.

But even family reunifications have been squeezed, off and on, since the 1974 halt of new immigration, for example, by restricting the number of times reunification can be claimed (the 1993 Balladur government is proposing to limit reunification to a single time), or by limiting the extent of kinship permitted, to the nuclear family or beyond. Another restriction has refused family reunification to polygamous marriages, while yet others tried to limit "marriages of convenience," requiring, for example, a year's marital residence before a residence card and citizenship procedure can be requested.

The Balladur government wants to mark itself off from the previous Socialist governments by adopting, or appearing to adopt, more restrictive policies on family reunifications. But we have seen that, given the numbers, even a reduction of 10 or 25 percent from 100,000 persons per year would not amount to a visible change in society. The real problems are elsewhere, in two places: illegal immigrants and the consequences of legal immigration.

The first issue is how to deal with illegal immigrants. Here it is possible to point to a notable difference between conservatives and Socialists in public policies. Socialist governments during the Mitterrand years tried to act with greater concern than conservatives for the human and political rights of even illegal immigrants, whereas conservatives, both in the 1986–88 Cohabitation I government and in the Balladur Cohabitation II government, have adopted a policy of cracking down.

Practical manifestations of this difference in attitude were seen early on in three conservative bills. In the first, the Balladur parliamentary majority voted, in May 1993, a law making it technically more difficult for French-born children of foreign parents to become French citizens: Whereas citizenship had been automatic at the age of 18, children born in France to foreigners would now have to "manifest their wish" for French citizenship sometime between the ages of 16 and 21. The conservative argument was that, for many such young people, *dual* citizenship—a second, French citizenship—is a mere political convenience, for travel and in other ways. Otherwise they identify wholly with their ethnic citizenship. In June the National Assembly overwhelmingly voted a second law authorizing the police to make random identity checks, even where no suspicious behavior is involved, to put pressure on illegal immigrants. Legal immigrants deemed a threat to public order could be deported, and legal immigrants whose papers are not in order could be denied public health care. A third bill was soon to be debated, restricting the right of foreigners (as had just happened in Germany and in other EC countries as well) to enter France as political refugees.

Socialist deputies objected, justly, that random identity checks—a policy reprised from Cohabitation I—were in themselves a blow to human rights, and that certainly they would be misused, against young Arabs most of all. This concern was not shared, however, by a public moved by fear and by racism, as opinion polls showed wide public backing for the strict conservative government policy. And Balladur's interior minister, the hardline, disciplinary RPR Charles Pasqua—who had held the same job in the Chirac Cohabitation I government—said that the government's goal was to move "toward zero immigration." He said, "France has been an immigration country, but it no longer wants to be. It no longer has the means."[11]

This sounded like a harsh, new public policy turn. However, because Socialist governments had already limited family reunifications, and because the conservatives are merely intensifying a consensus policy, Pasqua's "goal" was news only in public relations terms, not in fact. Pasqua himself soon admitted he really meant "zero *illegal* immigration," but the tone was clear: "reassurance to the white French public, deterrence to would-be immigrants."[12] How far the Balladur government will go remains to be seen. But it is likely that visible police pressure on "foreigners" will remain a tried and true way of showing that conservatives are in power and that, therefore, "things" have changed. A difference in emphasis, here as elsewhere, constitutes a significant difference in policy between conservatives and Socialists, between right and left, in France. It is no longer a war between two kinds of society, but it is significant.

So the paradox of legal immigration is that it has produced the multicultural French dilemma today. But there is also a paradox of the paradox: French demographic weakness indicates that by the year 2000 there will suddenly be a new need for immigrant workers! How, and which way, will French attitudes toward foreigners change then? The answer is hard to predict. Five to ten years is longer than officeholders normally look out on their graph lines. Besides the sheer number of future immigrants, and what their legal status will be, a third question is whether French immigrants of the twenty-first century will continue to come from North Africa or rather from a pool of skilled, culturally closer migrants from Eastern Europe, whose workers—Polish, Balkan, and so on—have come to France in the past. In 1970, three quarters of the foreigners living in France were European. Today, Europeans are about 40 percent, while Arabs and Africans are nearly 50 percent. Will the trend continue or reverse? The necessary immigration of the twenty-first century will raise hard questions for the French, complicated by historical migratory patterns and juxtaposing France's obligation to its colonial past and North African domestic minority, with its European Community past and European Union and Confederation future.

Illegal immigration certainly is a continuing problem, for France as for nearly all the EC countries, because even the poorest EC country remains attractive to African and Middle Eastern emigrants seeking new opportunities. Yet illegal immigration is not the "invasion" imagined by the typical French populist xenophobe. Estimates are between 35,000 and 100,000 illegal immigrants per year, a significant number but not an invasion. And at the end of 1991 the French High Commission for Integration reported that the number of foreigners resident in France had actually declined slightly during the 1980s.[13] There were 3.7 million resident foreigners in 1982, and 3.6 million in 1990, in a total population that rose slightly in the decade to 56 million, about 7–8 percent of the population. Given the chance, moreover, immigrants and their children rapidly become French citizens, as Figure 7.2 strikingly shows.

Thus, the greatest tension over "foreigners" in France is the native white French frustration about legal Arab immigrants, large numbers of whom are now citizens like any other. The French problem with foreigners and immigrants, in other words, concerns people who are now themselves French citizens. They remain foreigners and immigrants only historically, and, of course, in native French peoples' minds. Legally and morally they are French.

France is therefore face-to-face with a multicultural social reality that will not disappear, which must be dealt with. French multiculturalism is very different from the vast sociocultural diversity of American society,

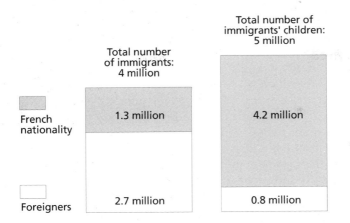

Figure 7 ✦ 2 Immigrants and their children in France in January 1986

Source: The Economist, November 23, 1991, p. 8.

and also from, say, Germany's Turkish minority, which, though it is as large as the North African minority in France, has long been denied reasonable access to citizenship and real cultural hospitality.

The French problem with foreigners is, beyond its universal aspects, therefore singularly French. Particularly intense is antiforeigner feeling combined with racial and religious prejudice. This means French prejudice against Arab Muslims from former French colonies in North Africa's Maghreb region: Algeria, Morocco and Tunisia. Because they are by far the most numerous foreigners, and because of France's colonial past and expulsion from these countries, especially the Algerian war, prejudice against Arab Muslims is far more intense than against black Africans. The latter—few in number, concentrated in a few big cities and able to demand much less from national and local governments—are perceived as a less ominous presence, both despite and because they are more "other" than the North Africans.

Native French resentment, to put it differently, is not really focused on illegal immigrants and workers, but on the increasing presence and visibility in a white, Christian, European nation of legal brown and black immigrants and their families, the bulk of whom are becoming naturalized, thus permanent in the population.

French society is seeing its composition and complexion permanently changed before its eyes. North African and other foreign communities now constitute, as every visitor sees, very visible parts of French society. Paris may be the example most encountered by tourists, but in several

Mediterranean coastal cities—Marseille, Nice and others—North African communities are even more concentrated and visible. Marseille today is perhaps 25 percent North African, and an "Arab market" no longer means a small grocery shop but a real souk in the central city.

North Africans in France today are often second- and sometimes even third-generation French, the so-called beur population, which is already large enough to have electoral significance.[14] These beurs are beginning to surface in sometimes quite visible public jobs, for instance, as television journalists or leaders in union and professional organizations. Naturally, the beurs also have their own popular music stars and songs, and an internationalist multiculturalist political slogan: "Black, brown and beur."

Intolerance is often the result of sheer propinquity, and prejudice can be engendered by the simple fact of culturally different populations living and working in close proximity. But native French resentment of foreigners can also be a sublimation of one's own problems. Unemployment, forced early retirement, insufficient income and family problems easily can be transformed into resentment of foreigners, who, for vague reasons, seem to be the cause of social problems. And another field of resentment of foreigners is often found—only an apparent paradox—among French people who in fact have little contact with North Africans or other immigrants. This is prejudice derived from television, the newspapers and the neighbors, a classic provincial, xenophobic reaction that seems to explain what's wrong with France.

The government's Commission on Nationality has documented a substantial change over time in the immigrant population's countries of origin. In 1975, for example, about 46 percent of the resident immigrant population came from outside the EC area. In 1990 this figure was 64 percent, mainly from Algeria, Tunisia and Morocco. The North Africans, who were a vast scatter of immigrants in the original foreign worker rush of the 1960s, were by the 1980s substantial ethnic populations within French society. French unemployment in the 1970s and 1980s basically doubled, from 5 to 10 percent, from under 1,500,000 to over 3 million in early 1993. Unemployment sharply increased resentment and animosity about foreign workers, both despite and because they were legal immigrants, most of whom were becoming naturalized. As "French" unemployment increased, French opinion worried that "'they're taking our places." Few French people were in fact squeezed out of jobs, given those usually held by foreign workers. Aside from some working-class factory jobs, French people shunned the street sweeping and other menial occupations done by foreigners.

Nevertheless, high unemployment among native French and joblessness in the immigrant work force both are correlated with antisocial or criminal behavior. Among the immigrants, almost 30 percent of young people were unemployed in 1991–92. While immigrants constitute 6 percent of the French work force, in 1992 almost 20 percent were unemployed, as opposed to 10 percent overall. To provide a full understanding of the depth of the social and cultural problems produced by immigration is beyond the range of this discussion. Such factors as the difficulty of reconciling Islam with secular society and political democracy, the phenomenon of anomie among young people, the full underlying causes of delinquency, and so on would each need extended analysis.[15]

The Arab Muslim immigrant population rightfully protests discriminatory treatment. When the French economy needed labor in the 1950s and 1960s, the French government was glad to "welcome" foreign workers and immigrants. Now, in the face of high unemployment, primitivist calls to "send the foreigners back home" need to be resisted. But if the economy is not producing new jobs, public policy is limited to palliative "social" bandaids. In terms of public order and justice, French governments must protect the rights of "others," most of whom are, let us remember, French citizens, against native prejudices, as well as protect foreigners against the government's own temptation to curry public favor or to give in to popular prejudice through police harassment or unfair enforcement of the law.

Historically, the left has emphasized generosity as a public policy principle, whereas the right has stressed the need for order and the protection of society. In reality, both are stumped in dealing with immigration, because the combination of difficult economic conditions and inflamed public opinion have left little margin for governments to innovate in one direction or another. The rhetoric has been very different at times, but the Socialists were unable to create affordable housing for foreigners, and a conservative government obviously could not send naturalized foreigners home, even if it wanted to do so.

France used to be a beacon for foreigners. When it was a matter, in the postwar decades, of a few people of color—mainly in Paris, and mainly black Americans playing jazz, writing novels or doing art—the French were attracted to them, and were welcoming. In the 1950s, Dexter Gordon, James Baldwin and Billy Holliday were the "children" of Langston Hughes and Josephine Baker. And when it was a matter of accommodating large numbers of immigrants who were not so different by color and religion, as with Poles, Italians and Portuguese, in spite of a period of transition that included a certain amount of violence, the French accepted integration and assimilation of the foreign populations. With Vietnamese immigrants and "Vietnamized" neighborhoods, there has also been remarkably little violence, because of their cultural affinities with France, because of their social discretion, and partly because Vietnamese self-help has meant Vietnamese full employment.

In any case, the French, like other peoples, are finding race to be more divisive, and more socially explosive, than other social differences. The current French problem with race is double: On the one hand, the legacy of France's colonialism is that these are the very countries that have been the recent sources of immigrants; on the other hand, time has not yet been sufficient for adjustment to the 1960s and '70s wave of North African and black African immigration. The very perceptible racial change in the populations of French cities has occurred, as Tocqueville would have emphasized, "within living memory." With approximately 4 million foreigners in a total population of about 56 million, France has an immigrant population that is, in percentage terms, as high as any country in the world, including the United States. The great debate is, to quote the consecrated phrase, whether immigration will be "a grave peril to the nation or, on the contrary, a great opportunity for France."

One pivotal issue here is the question of multiculturalism: Should immigrants assimilate, become French, or should they remain culturally what they are, which would gradually change the meaning of what is French? By extension, sociologically the issue is a matter of what the future French society should be. Should immigration result in a melting pot in which immigrants are "Frenchified," just as earlier generations of immigrants to the United States were "Americanized"? Or should immigration be permitted gradually to transform the French nation into a very visible multicultural, multiracial society in which foreign cultures, races and religions will have their permanent place in a new national equilibrium?

Interestingly, the term *intégration* has acquired more than one meaning in France, showing the extension of alternatives, or rather the uses of persuasion, in public policy dialogue. The term used to mean an immigrant's full assimilation into society, to become culturally as well as legally French. Then, *intégration* began to be used by some people to mean an endorsement of multiculturalism—that is, integration but not assimilation. In the past few years, those who want France to become a more multicultural society and who therefore resist the traditional demand that immigrants become French have been asking that immigrants be guaranteed *une simple insertion* into French society. This implies according the rights and privileges of French citizenship and nationality, especially job and home, without the moral and cultural burden to become French in the older meaning. Traditionalists reply that France is not like, for example, the multicultural United States, and that, as a singular nation whose people look back on a 1,000-year history, France cannot be, and should not try to become, a multicultural society. At the antiforeigner extremes of both right and left, this view holds that France is a homogeneous culture that can only be ruined by what the National Front stigmatizes as "miscegenation." Notwithstanding, scholars such as Fernand Braudel,

Theodore Zeldin and Eugen Weber have shown how mistaken it is to think of the French historically as a homogeneous people with a single language and a single culture. The French are a composite nation, built up historically from various components; remarkably, at the end of the nineteenth century the national language had not yet spread thoroughly throughout the national territory. In the late 1800s, the first and often sole language of much of rural France was still a dialect. *Yes, but a French dialect!*

The integrationist-multiculturalist view, found at least sentimentally in the Socialist party, and in organizations such as SOS-Racism and France-Plus, was not always the basis of Socialist government policy since 1981 on these issues. A remarkable example was the Socialist government's black undersecretary of state for integration, Kofi Yamgnane, who insisted that Muslim immigrants to France must accept republican secularism and the separation of church and state, and must respect republican rules in the educational system. His view was that Muslim girls from fundamentalist families should not be allowed to wear a *chador*, or veil, in school. This, said Yamgnane, is not just a matter of the freedom to dress how you want, or a symbol of a religious belief such as a crucifix or a star of David. To wear the chador is an open rejection of the lay, secular nature of the public school system, an imposition, as a matter of principle, of Muslim fundamentalism inside the republican school. One newspaper even labeled Yamgnane, an immigrant from Togo whose new hometown is a Breton village, "a republican in the Third Republic tradition of Jules Ferry"! (Yamgnane was defeated, with most Socialist government ministers, in the March 1993 parliamentary election.)

Dominique Schnapper, a sociologist who was a member of the Commission on Nationality that produced the 1988 report *Etre français aujourd'hui et demain* (To be French today and tomorrow) reaches two conclusions on this subject: First, generally speaking, "the French are unaware that France has been a country of immigration," and second, that the choice between a policy of assimilation or one of multiculturalism doesn't exist for France. "The fabrication of a pluricultural and plurilingual State, without the predominance of one language and one culture in particular, is a pipedream," because, whatever the changes in governments and statements of principle, "The [French government's] policy of Frenchifying immigrant populations, despite gestures such as some school work in the languages and cultures of origin, has not fundamentally changed."[16]

A second issue concerning whether immigration is to be considered a "grave peril to the nation" or an "opportunity" for France is demography. The size of a national population has complex geopolitical and other ramifications, especially on a crowded, dangerous continent such as old Europe. In a period of "limits to growth," high unemployment and general worry about the future, the idea of limiting population may seem attractive as a way of reducing pressure on scarce resources and opportunities. On the other hand, a society that wants to be politically powerful, economically competitive, and culturally influential will value a dynamic birthrate and a large, expanding population. From this point of view, immigration must be considered an opportunity. It is, so to speak, good fortune for the receiving country. But geopolitical concerns are in contradiction with racialist concerns about French identity. And the same people—let us call them nationalists—want both. So, ultimately, they will be in a bind, even if, lucky for them, it is one or two decades off.

Birthrates all over Community Europe, and in most of the wealthy societies generally speaking, have for several years now been below the population replacement rate. The lowest EC birthrate a decade ago was the West German, at 1.6 children per woman, with 2.1 necessary to replace the population. Remarkably, in the past few years, Italy, in spite of Catholicism and the Italian love for children, has taken over the dubious honor of the lowest EC country birthrate. French governments, on the other hand, have a long tradition of promoting population growth; France's generous postwar family-allocation benefits, which begin with the second child, have expressed this policy in financial terms.

France in 1991–92 had the highest (1.8) birthrate in the European Community. But this is still below the statistical replacement level. At the same time, unification in 1990 sharply increased the population of Germany, France's neighbor and geopolitical partner and rival, from 62 million to 78 million. (At unification, the former East Germany was one of the few European societies to have positive population growth, but in the mere few years since, the new eastern German Laender already show a stunning demographic decline to below replacement level.)

Without immigration, French economic development since World War I would have been severely retarded, and today, what some French people think of as overpopulation is confined to Paris and a few other large cities into which immigrants, along with former rural French, have crowded. On the other hand, huge parts of the French countryside have been emptied, draining the old rural France, and it is not clear how the French countryside can be usefully repopulated. The compulsion to compete with Germany, plus the desire to have a balanced territorial development, should ultimately be good reasons for a more positive French attitude to immigration and even to foreigners. But this, if it happens, will take time.

Such problems are not just French, but EC-wide concerns today. The French debate over immigration occurs simultaneously with controversy about overall European Community integration, about the wisdom of the Schengen Agreement to abolish national frontiers within the single unified market, and about the liberation of Eastern European and former

Soviet peoples, which is the freedom, among other things, to immigrate westward. Ultimately, to ask "Are the French a racist people?" is a naive question, because it implies that there is a simple answer. Better questions would focus on the extent, the variety and the intensity of racism, as well as the extent to which racism leads to actual discrimination. Better questions would also be comparative.

In the end, perhaps decades off, the workings of demography will decisively affect France's racial and ethnic problems. The number of mixed couples in France, for example, is on the rise, just as one would expect given a permanent mixing of populations. In 1989, according to official sources, nearly 1 in 10 marriages in France united a French-born person with a foreigner by birth. And the percentage seems to be increasing significantly, 18 percent between 1988 and 1989, for example.[17] Also increasing, but at a slower rate, are marriages involving a foreign woman and a French man. This seems to be due to the arrival in significant numbers of foreign girls in the public school system. Previously, when most new foreigners were male foreign workers, there were more marriages between a French woman and a foreign man. Immigrants from North African countries largely replaced Spanish, Italian and Portuguese new arrivals in France, and the trends in mixed marriages have reflected the successive waves of immigration. For example, the number of intermarriages involving a Spanish or Italian foreigner in France has declined significantly in recent years.

In absolute terms the number of these intermarriages is not yet impressive—for example, approximately 2,000 Algerian women per year marry French men. Nevertheless, even this number, and above all its persistence, indicates that integration in French society is to some extent an established fact, and that various constraints—religious, family or other—are giving in to propinquity and the other reasons for the usual historical mingling of populations. What this means is that, gradually, the racial difference between large numbers of immigrants and native French is being transformed into a racial difference among French people, because most nonwhite children born on French soil are either French at birth (most Algerian children and children with at least one parent who is a French citizen) or become so on their eighteenth birthday.

The limits on genuine integration remain strong, however. For one thing, many intermarriages are in reality only "white" marriages, made so that one partner can obtain citizenship. For another, the social upheavals created by all the problems of foreigners suggest a rough ride ahead for years, all the more so if there is further immigration pressure from Eastern Europe and the former Soviet Union.

What are the policy alternatives facing French governments on the immigration question? As with other problems in the centrist republic, the margins of choice have narrowed. Regarding potential immigrants, the issue seems to be finding a just, or at least a legitimate and acceptable, limitation of new arrivals. Regarding foreign workers, the problem is to find the right length and obligations to attach to the work visa, including some tolerable opportunity for foreign workers to apply for permanent residence or French citizenship. Within France, the "security" issue seems to be the practical guarantee of constitutional rights of citizens and legal foreign residents, as well as a just policing and pacification of social troubles. In addition, French immigration debates will have to take into account the policies of EC partners, and in particular the Schengen Agreement, which means not throwing the doors of the country open, but nevertheless having the obligation to discuss immigration questions among the twelve EC states, in addition to the national debate.

Otherwise, the government can push the levers of three kinds of policy: (1) trying to reduce illegal border crossings through more intense surveillance of frontiers; (2) reducing the number of visas given in certain countries, first of all in North Africa; and (3) restricting political asylum through stricter criteria and more investigation in order to distinguish genuine cases from disguised hopes of "economic immigration." As far as the EC's Schengen Agreement is concerned, the main issues are first, to strengthen border enforcement in the most porous member states such as Greece, Portugal, and Italy; and second, the long-term hope that, through aid to development, potential economic immigrants will find increasing reasons not to leave their home countries.

Dissuasion of new immigration will have to be European-wide, and the European Community countries have declared often and in many ways that they are no longer countries of free immigration. On the other hand, no EC country will want to be singled out by third countries as unfairly closed, or as xenophobic or racist, and no EC member, in the other direction, will want to be accused by its Community partners of being a sieve, or a revolving door that admits and passes on unwanted immigrants. Some policy makers are advocating that the EC's rules should regard all emigration-producing countries equally, meaning that old colonial, geographical, cultural and historical ties should be eliminated in favor of equality and fairness in distributing benefits. But this false "justice" is advocated as a way to discriminate in a new way, to prefer culturally close, highly motivated young workers from Eastern Europe to North Africans.

Women and Politics in France

Because Simone de Beauvoir was French, misconceptions abound outside France about French women's rights and culture, about the importance of feminist concerns, and about the intellectual status of French feminism. The most glaring is the erroneous perception that a culture that produced such a seminal, widely read book on the situation of women as *The Second Sex* (1949 in French, 1952 in English) must have built an unassailable feminist movement. Relatively speaking, the French women's movement and French feminism are, in fact, less widespread and less powerful than their American or even British and German counterparts. *The Second Sex* was, so to speak, a minor miracle in its time and place, due as much to existentialist philosophy as to feminism, and obliged to struggle, often unsuccessfully, with the overweening Cold War Communist party ideology, in which the problems of women were treated as a mere subcategory of the grand struggle for socialism.

Moreover, like contemporary French feminist theorists such as Julia Kristeva and Luce Irigaray, de Beauvoir was far more influential outside France, especially in the United States, than at home. On the other hand, more practical contemporary feminists—one could cite activists such as novelist Benoîte Groulte, psychologist Evelyne Sullerot, lawyer Giselle Halimi, historian Elisabeth Badinter, and even President Mitterrand's wife, Danielle Mitterrand—are well known in France but generally ignored by the mainly university-based audience for French feminism outside France.[18] Needless to say, French feminists, like their American and European counterparts, would not agree on exactly what feminism is, nor on who is authentically feminist or feminist enough. This, however, is not an issue here.

What is the status of French women in politics? A few basic points need to be emphasized. First, with respect to the issue of women in government positions, François Mitterrand, without making grandiose public claims, has named many women to high positions during his presidency, probably more in the executive branch bureaucracy than in the several Socialist governments. In addition to advancing women to important positions, Mitterrand's actions (an ambivalent feminism at best) seemed part of a broader intention on Mitterrand's part to break certain taboos. Several examples can be cited. First, Mitterrand the Socialist gave crucial support to NATO's Euromissile deployment in 1982–83. He even spoke in favor of it in a famous speech to the German Bundestag, against the policy of his German SPD "comrades" and against the West German peace movement's huge street demonstrations. Contrary to expectations of a left-wing French president, he took a hard anti-Soviet political line from 1981 to 1985, before the arrival of

Gorbachev as Soviet General Secretary. In the Middle East, Mitterrand became the first French president to visit Israel, symbolically making it his own first trip abroad as president. During this visit, Mitterrand openly appealed to the Knesset, the Israeli Parliament, for recognition of the Palestinian right to a homeland. He then went to Jordan, where he broke another taboo by asking the Jordanian Parliament to recognize Israel's right to exist within secure boundaries.

In naming his prime ministers, Mitterrand also acted with an agenda beyond merely finding good people. His first prime minister had to symbolize left-wing alliance, and Pierre Mauroy, a true social democrat and mayor of the northern industrial city of Lille, filled the bill admirably. The next three prime ministers were, successively, a Jew (Laurent Fabius), a Protestant (Michel Rocard), and a woman (Edith Cresson). Even if Mme. Cresson's nomination was controversial for extraneous reasons (rumors abounded of a onetime romantic relationship with Mitterrand), and even if Cresson fit the bill in other respects—for example, having a reputation as a leftist and a protectionist—Mitterrand's intention to break taboos and advance the cause of women in politics was clear.[19]

In the various governments since 1981 there have been more than a token number of women appointments. Valéry Giscard d'Estaing claimed in a recent memoir to have consciously promoted women to important positions in his term 1974–81. But he never, either by numbers or by his own attitudes, got beyond tokenism.[20] Edith Cresson in 1991 told an American newspaper that "There are three places where women have always been excluded: the military, religion and politics. I would say that, today, it is still in politics where they have the least access."[21]

Whatever the number of women in high government positions, the movement for women's nondiscrimination rights in France has been, and remains sparser and much less visible than in the United States, where women's issues are high on the agenda of national and local politics alike. Why should this be so?

French women did not obtain the right to vote until 1944, at the time of the Liberation, and unsurprisingly first voted in a most traditional fashion. They voted more conservatively on the whole than did men, and they abstained more often than men.[22] In the 1965 presidential election, for example, 51 percent of French men voted for François Mitterrand versus only 39 percent of French women.

By the 1970s, however, women's voting behavior was clearly changing, due to familiar factors of economic, social and political modernization. In the 1986 parliamentary elections, the postwar "gender gap" in French elections finally closed, with both men and women voting 44 percent for the left. Since 1986 women have even voted *more* left-wing than men, largely because more men than women have shifted to the

National Front (about 10 percent of the female vote to 17 percent of male voters).

French women as a group are rarely political feminists in the American sense of organization and partisan activism in the electoral and political arena. But French women have certainly come a long way in becoming conscious of "ordinary sexism" and of the consequent value to them of an "ordinary feminism." Until recently, French women probably were more organized in church groups or in the French Communist party (the "Union of French Women") than in secular women's groups. As the Communist movement fades in France and the Catholic Church grudgingly accepts new kinds of women's activism, women are surely organizing themselves more and in new ways.

As in nearly all countries, left-wing political parties speak for the goals of women's liberation, or "ordinary feminism," more loudly than do conservative parties. François Mitterrand, for example, in the 1965 presidential campaign became the first major French politician to call for the legalization of birth control. Socialists and Communists in 1979 helped the liberal–conservative Giscard d'Estaing pass the French law permitting abortion, which succeeded with the votes of only 70 of 290 conservative deputies. The National Front has campaigned in this area on a traditionalist platform. Jean-Marie Le Pen has appealed for the repeal of legal abortion, for example, and the FN proposes that a woman who has both children and a job should go back home with public support— "Wages for Motherhood."

This conservative praise of traditional women's roles in 1989 became an issue in a different way in the famous "affaire des foulards" (the *foulard* or *chador* is the Muslim female's scarf or veil). Three young immigrant Muslim girls were expelled by the principal of a secondary school in a small town north of Paris for wearing the chador.[23]

Surprisingly, the French left didn't know what to think in this matter. Some commentators sprang to the defense of one of the nineteenth century's great left-wing victories—France's hard-won liberal, secular, "republican" education system—against a threat of religious fundamentalism. Well-known left-wing intellectuals argued, with remarkable passion, that to allow the Muslim veil, which the girls were obliged by their traditionalist father to wear, would legitimize fundamentalism and inevitably encourage further demands, the risk of which would be a public school culture absolutely opposite to the assimilationist, integrationist French ideal. To accept the veil would also countenance the submission of women, and thus the affair became divisive among women and feminists as well.

What was remarkable was that the traditionally right-wing idea that immigrants constitute a threat to French cultural identity and institutions was suddenly shown to be shared by a good part of the French left. In addition, French feminists were divided between, on the one hand, their passion for women's liberation and, on the other, respecting others' traditions and beliefs—that is, multiculturalism. This intermeshing of gender and ethnic issues, far from played out, defies any definitive conclusions. The most relevant point, for now anyway, seems to be precisely the interpenetration of values, goals and strategies; to observe how such issues as the political and social situation of women and the clash of ethnic and religious values make for unexpected realignments of historic political allies.

What, finally, was the government decision in the chador affair? Education Minister Lionel Jospin, backed by President Mitterrand, Prime Minister Rocard and a further confirmation by the *Conseil d'État* (state counsel), provided a liberal lesson to Jacobin hysterics, right and left, who believed that the "entire republican secular educational enterprise" was at stake. (Indeed, the fact that such eminences had to decide this matter shows how centralized policy making in the French educational system remains.) Wearing the chador would be permitted, the ruling came down, just as other religious symbols, such as the Christian cross and the Jewish kippoh, had long been. But religious proselytizing would be strictly forbidden in schools, by which the government assuaged the republicans' worry about Muslim fundamentalism. In addition, no pupils would be excused from school programs such as sex education and athletics—which was precisely what the parents of the three girls had requested on religious grounds, and which required lifting the veil. Muslim or any other parents who could not accept this secular, inclusionist school policy, had the alternative of sending their children to a private school. Ironically, of course, the Socialists saved themselves on this issue by means of the very private educational sector they had attempted to wean from the state with the education reform of 1984!

One last issue in this short account of women's issues in France is the problem of sexual harassment. In the United States sexual harassment has become a major public concern, both in the sense of its allegation by women and in its effect on various aspects of life from human relations in the business office to the process of examining the qualifications of presidential candidates and nominees to the Supreme Court. Is the French situation "ahead" of or "behind" American developments? Such a question is hard to answer.

On one hand, radical French feminists would like France to track every American feminist achievement, especially on issues such as sexual harassment and wife battering. On the other hand, many moderate French feminists and other advocates of women's rights think of American society as extremist, no social model for France. French feminists, and in a general way French society as a whole, are often very much aware of American developments. From the Clarence Thomas–Anita Hill Supreme Court hearings to prosecution of the Navy's Tailhook Association, the pace-setting American struggles over women's issues have become, both through CNN and French news reporting, part of the attentive public's daily fare. But what about French government policies dealing with "ordinary" sexual harassment?

Two recent French laws illustrate the state of affairs. Within a June 1991 broad reform of France's penal code, a section defining sexual harassment and its punishment—one year's imprisonment and a fine of Fr 100,000 (about $20,000)—was voted by the National Assembly. And in April 1992, State Secretary for Women's Rights and Consumer Rights Véronique Neiertz won government approval for an addition to the French labor code prohibiting sexual harassment in the workplace.

In a recent analysis, "Is There a French-style Sexual Harassment?," two French feminists say that these first laws on sexual harassment are grossly insufficient because they are based on an "extremely restrictive" definition of harassment.[24] They point out that the workplace law deals only with sexual harassment in situations of unequal authority in a hierarchy, ignoring that sexual harassment in fact often occurs among colleagues—that is, people of equal authority—because, they say, sexism is more powerful than collegial status in a work environment. It seems that, to the extent France's future is a continued loss of exceptionalism and further homogenization in the ranks of EC and G-7 cultures, French public policy concerns here, as elsewhere, will be internationalized. The "French difference" will be harder to maintain, but probably all the more guarded for that.[25]

AIDS as a Public Policy Issue in France

France's connection to the American debates over AIDS (Acquired Immune Deficiency Syndrome) first arose with the controversy between Dr. Luc Montanier of the French Pasteur Institute and American Dr. Robert Gallo over whose laboratory first successfully isolated a strain of HIV (human immunodeficiency virus). Montanier's team, it is now established, was first (by a few months), and the virus Gallo's team "discovered" was really a sample of the French virus Gallo had requested from Montagnier's laboratory. After adjustments of patents, financial rights, and collegial prestige, international controversy over the affair has abated. Montagnier, with the agreement of the U.S. government investigating team and the international medical community, says "there is only a Gallo problem," referring to the ethics of Gallo's own actions and those of his laboratory. In any case the quality of top areas of French medical research was resoundingly reaffirmed in this matter, and when an AIDS cure is found, no one will be surprised if the researcher is French.

At the level of epidemiology and thus of public health policy, France is the European country most affected by AIDS. This is surely due to the character of Paris and its large, diverse, urbane population. At the end of 1991 about 8,500 people had died of AIDS-related diseases. Another 16,000 were known to have developed full-blown AIDS in a known population of 70,000 HIV-diagnosed people. Estimates of unknowing carriers of the virus in France ran as high as 130,000.

AIDS has become a public issue in France in several internationally familiar ways. First is the large number of infections for a European country. Second is the stigmatization of homosexuals and of AIDS as "a homosexual disease," though HIV homophobia has been much less severe than in the United States, as has been homophobia generally speaking, for historical reasons. In any case, HIV infection in France has been a more heterosexual disease than in the United States and statistically more related to drug use.

The key episode of public concern in the French AIDS struggle has involved a series of tragic, accidental, irresponsible HIV contaminations through blood transfusions administered by state-run blood banks. Settled in October 1992, the case concerned blood used in transfusions for hemophiliacs during a short period in 1985, blood that, as was proven in a sensational internationally observed trial, public officials knew was contaminated and could have been decontaminated using a simple heating process recently invented in the United States but not yet accepted in France. The trial showed that more than 1,250 hemophiliacs had been infected by the use of tainted blood, whose blood-clotting factor they required, and that almost 300 had already died as a result. Three former health officials were convicted of authorizing distribution of the contaminated blood, and the court sentenced Michel Garsetta, former head of the National Blood Transfusion Center, to four years in prison, as "without doubt the creator and overseer" of the country's blood transfusion policies.[26] Garetta's deputy was sentenced to four years with two suspended, and the two men were ordered to pay $1.8 million in compensation to the victims and their families.

The case brought troubling questions to public debate. Lawyers for the victims wanted the case tried in a criminal court on a charge of "poisoning," rather than in a lower court that usually deals with commerce-related misdemeanors and in which the accusation was "fraudulent description of goods," the maximum penalty for which is four years. The third official convicted, a former health official at the justice ministry, was given a four-year suspended sentence for "failure to assist a person in danger." In

French law, the charge of poisoning could apply only if there was intent to kill.

But most of all, French opinion was angry that former cabinet ministers were not held accountable for their oversight responsibility in the period of May to October 1985. In particular, Edmond Hervé, deputy health minister in 1985, shocked the court by admitting that he and others in the government knew that the blood-clotting factor was contaminated more than four months before it was ordered withdrawn. Government and health officials apparently pacified their worries with half-belief of a then-current hypothesis, plausible at the time but since shown to be totally wrong, that only a small percentage of HIV infections become full-blown AIDS. Lawyers for the victims had wanted to bring three former cabinet ministers to trial, including the health minister, Georgina Dufoix (who said she was "responsible but not guilty"), and even the prime minister at the time, Laurent Fabius. But this attempt failed in a parliamentary commission hearing. Even at the trial's end it was not entirely clear why the tainted blood supply had remained in use for five full months, until October 1985. Certainly money and glory were involved, in petty, murderous measure: Either $40 million worth of blood stocks would have had to be destroyed or expensive, just-marketed blood-screening and decontamination technology would have had to be bought from the United States. The French National Blood Transfusion Center was under pressure, it was revealed, to become profitable and to compete better with foreign centers. In addition, it was alleged that certain public health and political officials wanted to wait until the French Pasteur Institute developed its own screening method, which they believed—rightly, it turned out—would happen within a few months. The French could then "buy French" in this dramatic medical research race, which had already opposed French and American research teams. Acceptable motives, one might argue, except that they become intolerable when lives are at stake.

This terrible episode in the French AIDS struggle, which took four years to come to trial, throws a harsh light on the French health care bureaucracy but also, obliquely, on the larger issue in France of corrupt or delinquent political manipulation of public policy. This is not a uniquely French bad habit, nor is health care the most egregious French example. As in other countries, public contracts for construction, and not just for national defense, have sometimes been found in violation of responsibility for the public good. It is just that in France, where for historical reasons investigative journalism and parliamentary scrutiny have been slower to develop than in other liberal democracies, the governance of public policy has been less often subject to public scrutiny and investigation.

In this case French health care officials, and certain government officials up to cabinet level, allowed financial and political considerations to overrule their knowledge of probably lethal dangers posed by the contaminated blood. In their defense, Garetta and the other health officials could argue only that the higher-up government officials, those not on trial, were also involved in the decision making that had created such a human tragedy. The court, in fixing the blame directly on Dr. Garetta and a few other health care officials, no doubt did find "the one most responsible and most guilty" person. And no one suggested that Garetta intended murder. But if a guilty public official was found out and convicted, there remains a larger and continuing issue of bureaucratic ethics and the responsibility of government, at all its levels, for the public interest and the public good. In February 1993, an extraordinary trial before the High Court of three high officials—the ministers of health and social affairs and the then-prime minister Laurent Fabius—ended in a ruling of inapplicable procedure. The three officials, at the time of this writing, may be retried before the High Court, with a different indictment.

Compensation for victims is the final element of this tragic episode. In a state-run health care system, public money must pay not only the costs of HIV and AIDS treatment, but also the awards of compensatory damages to the victims of these tainted public-administered blood transfusions. The government quickly accepted responsibility for paying all medical costs incurred by the victims and then agreed to pay a sum in damages for the accidental loss of life that had been caused.

The issue then became a cheerless fight over how to fund this extra financial burden on the state health service. First a plan to impose a special surtax on medical insurance salary deductions was rejected in the Cresson government, because new taxes in economic hard times are politically dangerous. Then Cresson said the cost would be financed by overall budget cuts, and a "solidarity fund" was created from which to pay the victims.

In this tragic dilemma, as in so many other issues, French public policy has become "ordinary." This may seem bland, but ordinary does not mean easy. It is easy to build castles in the sky; it is hard to alleviate human suffering on earth.

Endnotes

1. *The Economist*, March 27, 1993, p. 15.
2. Valéry Giscard d'Estaing, *Deux français sur trois* (Two of every three French people) (Paris: Flammarion, 1984; 2nd expanded edition, 1985). See also earlier hints of his idea of a new French consensus in

Démocratie française (French democracy) (Paris: Fayard, 1976). Two useful books on the Giscard presidency are J. R. Frears, *France in the Giscard Presidency* (London: Allen & Unwin, 1981), and Jean Bothorel, *Le Pharaon. Histoire du septennat Giscardien* (The pharaoh: History of Giscard's seven-year term) (Paris: Grasset, 1983).

3. Michel Pérébeau, "Les enjeux économiques de la fin des années quatre-vingt," in Lévy-Leboyer and Casanova, *Entre l'état et le marché: L'économie française des années 1880 à nos jours* (Between the state and the market: French economy from 1880 to the present) (Paris: Editions Gallimard, 1991), p. 623.

4. Pierre Favrier and Michel Martin-Roland, *La Décennie Mitterrand* (The Mitterrand decade), Vol. 2, *Les épreuves* (The challenges), p. 737.

5. Two socialist-inspired analyses of this issue are Daniel Singer, *Is Socialism Doomed? The Meaning of Mitterrand* (London: Oxford University Press, 1988), and Mark Kesselman, "Socialism without the Workers: The Case of France," *Kapitalstatte* (Summer 1982): 11–41.

6. Peter A. Hall, *Governing the Economy: The Politics of State Intervention in Britain and France* (New York: Oxford University Press, 1986), Chapter 8, pp. 203–204. Hall's is a particularly well-balanced study of the 1981–84 economic program of the "union of the left" government.

7. The best-informed account of the Mauroy government, written by an inside source, is Thierry Pfister, *La vie quotidienne à Matignon au temps de l'union de la gauche* (Paris: Hachette, 1985). Mitterrand's "special advisor" Jacques Attali's *Verbatim* (Paris: Fayard, 1993) is highly informative but must be checked against other sources. See also the collection of Mauroy's speeches and declarations, *À Gauche* (Paris: Albin Michel, 1985). In English, a good summary analysis is found in Julius W. Friend, *Seven Years in France: François Mitterrand and the Unintended Revolution, 1981–1988* (Boulder, Colo.: Westview Press, 1989). See also George Ross, Stanley Hoffmann and Sylvia Malzacher (eds.), *The Mitterrand Experiment: Continuity and Change in Modern France* (New York: Oxford University Press, 1987).

8. A detailed history of this episode is in Pierre Favier and Michel Martin-Roland, *La décennie Mitterrand*, op. cit.; see Vol. 2, parts 8, 9, 10. See also Friend, op. cit., in English.

9. "Neither–nor" recalls at least the rhythm of the anarchist motto, *Ni dieu ni maitre* (Neither God nor master).

10. One specialist gives an approximate figure of 75,000 departures annually for the years 1975–82, slightly more for the period 1968–75. See Patrick Weill, *La France et ses étrangers. L'aventure d'une politique*

d'immigration, 1938–1991 (France and its foreigners: The story of an immigration policy, 1938–1991), p. 209. Another excellent new study, more sociologically than policy oriented, is Dominique Schnapper, *La France de l'intégration. Sociologie de la nation en 1990* (France and integration: The nation's sociology in 1990) (Paris: Gallimard, 1991). See also Catherine Withol de Wenden, *Les immigrés et la politique* (Immigrants and politics) (Paris: Presses de la F.N.S.P., 1988); Gerard Noiriel, *Le Creuset français: Histoire de l'immigration XIX–XXe siecles* (The French melting pot: Nineteenth- and twentieth-century immigration history) (Paris: Editions du Seuil, 1988). In English, see James F. Hollifield, *Immigrants, Markets and States: The Political Economy of Postwar Europe* (Cambridge: Harvard University Press, 1992), and Martin A. Schain, "Immigration and Politics," in Peter Hall, Jack Hayward, and Howard A. Machin (eds.), *Developments in French Politics* (London: Macmillan, 1990).

11. See *Le Monde*, May 6, 1993, p. 1, and *The New York Times*, June 12, 1992, p. 2.

12. *The Economist*, June 12, 1993, p. 57.

13. The *International Herald Tribune*, November 8, 1991, p. 4.

14. See Alec Hargreaves, "The *Beur* Generation: Integration or Exclusion," in Howorth and Ross (eds.), *Contemporary France* (Vol. 3) (London: Pinter, 1989), pp. 147–159.

15. See, for example, the prize-winning book by Gilles Kepel, *Les Banlieues de l'Islam* (The suburbs of Islam) (Paris: Le Seuil, 1987).

16. Op. cit., pp. 12, 86–87.

17. The statistics are from a 1991 ministry of social affairs report: Michèle Tribalat and Francisco Muñoz-Perez, "Les mariages d'immigrés avec des français. Leur évolution depuis quelques décennies" (Immigrant–French marriages: Their evolution in the past few decades) in *La Nuptualité: Évolution en France et dans les pays développés* (The marriage rate: Evolution in France and in developed countries) (Paris: PUF, 1991), cited in Philippe Bérnard, "L'envol des couples 'mixtes' " (The rise of interracial couples), *Le Monde*, December 21, 1991, p. 10.

18. Useful accounts in English of women in contemporary France are found in Howorth and Ross, op. cit.: Janice Windebank, "Women and Domestic Labour in France," pp. 71–96; David Gascoigne, "French Feminist Fiction Since 1945"; and especially Jane Jenson, "The Varieties of French Feminism," pp. 114–146.

19. A chatty but informative account is Marie-Therèse Guichard, *Le President qui aimait les femmes* (The president who loved women) (Paris: Robert Laffont, 1993).

20. See Chapter 6, "Les femmes dans la vie publique" (Women in public life) in *Le Pouvoir et la vie* (Power and life) (Paris: Editions Compagnie 12, 1988).

21. *The New York Times*, May 16, 1991, p. A3.

22. On this and following points see Janine Mossuz-Lavau, "Women and Politics in France," *French Politics and Society*, 10 no. 1 (Winter 1992): 1–8.

23. See David Beriss, "Scarves, Schools, and Segregation: The *Foulard* Affair," *French Politics and Society*, 8 no. 1 (Winter 1990): 1–13.

24. Sylvie Cromer and Marie-Victoire Louis, "Existe-t-il un harcélement sexuel 'à la française'?" (Is there a French style of sexual harassment?) in *French Politics and Society*, 10 no. 3 (Summer 1992): 37-43.

25. See the broadly informative article by Amy G. Mazur, "The Formation of Sexual Harassment Policy in France: Another Case of French Exceptionalism," *French Politics and Society*, 11 no. 2 (Spring 1993): 11-32.

26. See *The New York Times*, October 23, 1992, p. 1. Appeals are still being heard.

8
✦

Political Economy

The French Economy and European Integration

In order to establish a living bond between us, I decided to visit every département in France. . . . On the immutable surface of France and the abiding bedrock of its human substance, I saw with my own eyes the transformation that was being wrought by the rapid development of industry, the mechanization of agriculture, the growing birthrate, the bulging student population, the proliferation of motorized transport. Although our country, compared to others such as Germany, Britain, Belgium and the Netherlands, is particularly resistant to change, on account of its geography, its lack of raw materials, the low density of its population, and its contentious and at the same time conservative character, this necessary transformation was nonetheless everywhere in progress, though with considerable differences in speed and scale between the regions, which are also much more diverse than elsewhere.

—Charles de Gaulle, *Memoirs of Hope: Renewal and Endeavor*, 1971, pp. 291, 293–294

[Economic development and the spread of prosperity in society] can explain why, in the second post-war period, French history has shown a tendency to banalization.

—Maurice Lévy-Leboyer, in Lévy-Leboyer and Casanova (eds.), *Entre l'état et le marché*, p. 11

The Fading of French Economic Particularity

With a high standard of living combined with high unemployment, two specters have increasingly haunted the French economy in the last decade: international competition and European integration. And, in a certain sense, both carry the imprint of Germany.

However, unlike the past, French fears of German economic superiority no longer make for a global retreat into protectionism. Economically as well as politically, France, with notable exceptions, has chosen European integration and international competition over political and economic nationalism—and has been winning the struggle, though not without difficulties and setbacks.

True, France's commitments to the EC—to the single integrated market (the SEA, "the 1992 Project") and, ostensibly, to the second and third stages of monetary union (the December 1991 Maastricht Treaty)—make economic nationalism illegal, as well as difficult to bring off politically. A powerful case in point is French farmers and the General Agreement on Tariffs and Trade (GATT)—the French attempt of 1992–93 to stave off additional cuts in EC Common Agricultural Policy (CAP) farm subsidies in the GATT Uruguay Round. To protect French farmers, French negotiators invoked the so-called Luxembourg Compromise of 1966. This was an agreement among EC governments to bring an end to de Gaulle's 1965–66 "empty chair" policy, a French boycott of Community decision making in order to impose national sovereignty on an expansive EC Commission. For twenty-five years the Luxembourg Compromise, though without constitutional standing, has protected the veto power of any member government that invokes a vital national interest in a negotiation. But, as the ongoing debate over farm subsidies and EC–U.S.–GATT negotiations has shown, whether the Luxembourg Compromise still holds, or for how long, has become an open question. National sovereignty in certain policy areas such as external trade has been at least legally superseded by "pooled" EC authority.

French economic actors, both private and public, both by choice and by necessity, increasingly follow the maxim "Do what you fear." This means, in one commentator's apt image, that France's surprisingly market-driven industrial and monetary policies have been overhauled "to emulate Germany and to compete abroad," rather than "to repose foppishly, like Shakespeare's *dauphin* (heir) in the courts of a fortress Europe."[1]

But a hard agricultural protectionism remains one glaring French economic particularity, even as the size of the farm population is in rapid decline. The joint conservative and Socialist government protection of French agriculture by resisting reductions in the EC's CAP subsidies is a rearguard action. Its goal is to delay and cushion the human costs of an agricultural conversion that the French themselves regard as unavoidable. The problem is how to save *le monde rural*, rural society as a whole, when the economic activity on which it is based is disappearing in much of the countryside. And for French politicians and parties, the political struggle over the economics of agriculture is also a fight over the rural vote, remembering that a few percentage points can spell the difference between victory and defeat, especially in closely contested, all-important presidential elections.

Traditional sectors in France's "dual economy" are growing smaller and sometimes moribund.[2] Opening France's economic borders in the service of European integration has brought commercially vigorous, but often socially damaging effects. Uncompetitive industrial firms have closed, small agriculture has been decimated, and the countryside as a whole—rural France, the culture and society of *la France profonde*—has emptied. Unemployment and early retirement have become as characteristic of contemporary France as the "bon chic bon genre" ("BCBG") ("good proper families") success stories, the French equivalent of 1980s Reaganite yuppieism in the United States.

Three factors—international competition, European integration and technological innovation—are continuously transforming traditional characteristics of French industry, agriculture and services. The same forces are also constricting the old domineering role of the French state in French economic life, a French particularity since Louis XIV accepted Colbert's plan to fill the king's treasury, to finance Louis' desire "to govern, not just to rule," by involving the state in manufacturing.

In the French export sector, one still finds a unique predominance of luxury goods, wines and foods. Food and luxury goods exports are, in profit terms, still France's most lucrative foreign earners. But this cultural and culinary production, plus the air of sophistication and joie de vivre that goes with it, are still too often all that foreigners associate with French products. To the contrary, French business today exports an impressive range of high quality industrial and technical goods and services. Yet, despite the many successes, French production is still on the whole not competitive with the highest quality goods—German, Japanese or American—in the most intensive markets. The French therefore frequently must focus on less-competitive markets, often due also to French failures at sales and after-sales service if not to inferior products. Overall, France's large agricultural sales, along with the export of services, have been the most consistently positive elements in the French trade balance.

The French economy exports nearly 20 percent of its gross domestic product (GDP), a very high level internationally but about average for the major EC countries. In terms of the value of its exports, France shows

Table 8 ✦ 1   Per Capita Volume of Exports (Constant Dollars)
Source: Adapted from data in *Libération*, December 3, 1991,
p. 10.

	1910	1970	1980	1990
France	29 (2)	353 (2)	2,072 (2)	3,211
Germany	27 (3)	563 (1)	3,141 (1)	5,578
Great Britain	48 (1)	323 (3)	2,056 (3)	—
United States	19 (4)	208 (4)	985 (5)	—
Japan	5 (5)	185 (5)	1,114 (4)	2,244

Relative rank is indicated in parentheses. The 1990 figures are Germany
$5,578, France $3,211, and Japan $2,244, according to the Japanese
Institute of Economic and Social Affairs.

up as the fourth ranking exporter in the world after Germany, the United
States and Japan, and it precedes Great Britain and Italy. Considering
industrial exports alone, however, Germany and Japan pull away from
France, exporting nearly twice as much. Yet, if population differences are
factored in and if one measures the volume of exports per capita (see
Table 8.1), then France surprisingly is the world's second largest exporter, trailing only Germany.[3]

A long-recognized trend in France's foreign trade since the 1950s has
been its progressive concentration inside the European Community area.
France moved away from its pre-EC emphasis on the empire, and then,
after colonial independence, the so-called French Union and French
Community. Until the early 1960s, French trade with the franc zone—
comprising essentially its former colonies in Africa—was over one third
of France's exports. But by the end of the 1970s this had been gradually
reduced to less than 10 percent, a result of three readily apparent factors:
the liberalization of international trade through the GATT system, rapidly increasing intra-EC trade and the well-known fact that trade increases relatively faster among industrialized nations than between rich
and poor countries.

From about 25 percent in 1958, France's trade with other EEC states
had climbed to 50 percent by the late 1960s. It was at 56 percent by
1972.[4] Today, Germany is France's single biggest trading partner,
though the French are unhappy with the persistent large German industrial trade surplus with France. In any case, French trade has become
overwhelmingly "localized" within the European Community, and the
EC has produced overall exactly what its French advocates hoped, and
what economic theory predicted: first, a remarkable stimulation of
French industry and of export sales skills (albeit faced with the continued

superiority of German industry), and second, the phenomenon of "trade diversion," meaning the growing concentration of trade of all EC countries within the Community. In habits of design and sales, certain eccentricities of postwar France—unusual or odd product designs (e.g., the old Citroen cars, such as the frog-looking luxury DS, and the hugely popular, inexpensive tin-can "Deux Chevaux"[*]), weak foreign sales networks, poor after-sales service—have gradually given way to international standards and tastes. At a more basic level, the old French patterns of state intervention in the economy have been adjusted, especially in fiscal and monetary policy. French financial policy beginning with the Raymond Barre government under Giscard d'Estaing in 1976 (and excepting the 1981–83 Socialist experiment) tried to reach rigorous European Community and European Monetary System standards. This of course meant German government, Bundesbank standards. In the 1980s, this new "strong franc" policy contributed to significant Phillips curve trade-offs between inflation and unemployment: on the one hand, very high unemployment (as discussed in the previous chapter) and, on the other hand, the lowest inflation rate (2.5 percent in 1992) among the big EC countries, not excluding Germany (see Figure 8.1).

German unification, of course, has brought unwelcome changes in the Federal Republic's economic and financial position: (1) an inflation rate nearly doubled in 1991–93 to about 4 percent; (2) a sharply increased budget deficit, requiring large government borrowing in the markets; and thus (3) high Bundesbank interest rates to attract sufficient capital to German government bonds. The French, while immensely satisfied to have a lower inflation rate than Germany, have been squeezed by high German interest rates since German unification. And they have, with other EC partner governments, bitterly protested. The German mark (DM) continues to be the EC currency of choice. The continued attractiveness of DM bonds in the markets, in spite of Germany's problems, forces the French to keep their own interest rates higher than economically necessary, in order to attract sufficient capital themselves. High German interest rates thus inhibit French economic recovery. French credit markets and new investment are squeezed, and French unemployment is kept higher than necessary. In this regard, as in many other respects, France continues to have a German problem as well as a German partner.

Despite all this, *The Economist* magazine, in a striking testimonial, wrote in 1991 that France could have been given an award for "the most improved economic management over the past decade" among the G-7

---

[*] literally, "two horses"

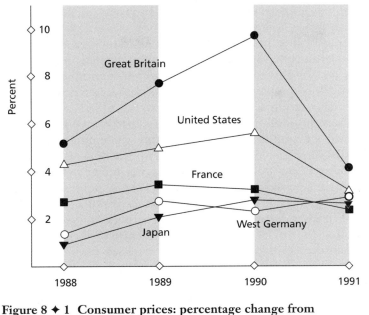

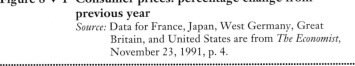

Figure 8 ✦ 1 Consumer prices: percentage change from
previous year

Source: Data for France, Japan, West Germany, Great
Britain, and United States are from *The Economist,*
November 23, 1991, p. 4.

countries.[5] Historians would have blinked not twice but thrice to find
France—let alone the French Socialist party—at the head of the 1980s
class for economic and monetary rigor! As in other respects, French
affairs can no longer be summed up as a matter of *plus ça change, plus c'est
la même chose:* "the more things change, the more they stay the same."

Traditions of dirigisme and étatisme—of the state-led economy and
state ownership of key industries and businesses—have both diminished,
along with the French state's formerly standard use of wage and price
controls. Exchange controls, first established in 1939, lasted much longer
in France than in West Germany or Great Britain and finally were put in
the way of extinction in 1986, along with price controls. (De Gaulle and
Pompidou tried and failed, in 1968–69, to end exchange controls.) As
part of preparing for the 1992 Project single integrated market, French
exchange and price controls were progressively dismantled, leading to
complete abolition—something of a silent French revolution—in 1990.

What is more, France's low levels of government debt and low deficit
put it, as of 1992, among the few EC countries that would qualify, under
the Maastricht Treaty's so-called convergence criteria, for Stage 3 of

monetary union, the establishment of a single currency and a "Eurofed." (This changed in 1992–93, however.)

Altogether these were impressive achievements for France, and for Socialist-led governments. However, high unemployment, the devastating black mark for Socialist government, was an uncompromisable factor in the 1993 election campaign, in which the conservative RPR–UDF coalition won a devastating victory.

In the medium and long term, it matters less that France in the early 1990s temporarily became the EC's low inflation champion—which can change and will—than that the French economy has demonstrated it is capable of a durable low inflation rate, low government debt and low annual government borrowing—in short, that French politcal economy has changed from the period when France was considered a "sick man of Europe." The French industrial economy is today, with no greater exceptions than in other EC countries, open and competitive. To say that it is not as strong as the German economy is not to say it is not strong. Furthermore, the French economy has abandoned or is shedding most of its erstwhile special cases, even if in certain sectors, especially farm subsidies, the French remain quite "particular" (while far from unique, as Americans, Belgians and Japanese will know!).

The concept of French economic "particularity,"[6] however, is not the same concept as the exceptionalism of French political history that we have used in this essay. French exceptionalism derives, as discussed at several points already, from the uniqueness and drama of France's political history. Exceptionalism stems from a history of "grand moments" and "great undertakings" as contrasted with the more mundane, less brilliant, or at least less traumatic political developments of other peoples and nations. The concept of French exceptionalism also implies the "exemplary" character of modern French political history and political culture. Other peoples, without doubt, often looked to France (and occasionally still do) for inspiration, for a model or at least for an example of vibrant political and intellectual life or of a bureaucratically efficient, dignified state. France's economic *spécificité*, on the other hand, refers to the national characteristics, often enough disabling rather than elevating, of French economic structure and economic culture. France's economic particularities are distinguishing, but they have rarely made the French economy internationally distinguished.

Overall, France, from the disastrous end of the economically booming Second Empire in the Franco–Prussian War until the postwar boom of the 1950s and 1960s, was regarded as a case of perennially retarded economic development. French industrialization began early, in the 1780–1830 period along with England's, and the two countries led the way into the Industrial Revolution. However, whereas England became industrialized and urbanized early, rapidly and thoroughly—already in 1850 over 50 percent of English people lived in cities of more than 100,000 population—French industrialization faltered after its early start.

French industrial development was a matter of patchy growth—in Paris, Lyon, Marseilles and a few other areas—rather than across-the-board industrialization accompanied by transformation of the social structure. The French peasantry survived, unlike English peasants squeezed out by the "enclosure acts," and France until World War II was justifiably called "a country of peasants and shopkeepers." And the French bourgeoisie was notoriously ambivalent regarding industry, business and moneymaking.

After 1850, the French industrial lag was cemented by sluggish demographic growth. Slow population growth eventually became thought of as a national worry and even a national calamity, when it was magnified by the huge population losses of World Wars I and II. Contrary to the experience of other industrializing societies, there actually was a slight absolute population decline in the 1930s. In the 1870–1914 period, the glory years of the Third Republic, France once again became a "country of immigration." Otherwise the French population would not have grown at all. Sizable immigration from Italy and Poland maintained French hopes, vain as they turned out, of remaining a world power of the front rank. In France still today it is not surprising to hear the geopolitical argument that, by decimating each other's populations in World War I, France and Europe stupidly destroyed their geopolitical strength and their capacity to remain the focal point of international relations.

In any case, EEC membership in 1958 brutally confronted France's economic "particularities," mainly competitive weaknesses, with the various strengths of its main partners, especially West Germany. Four major French characteristics stood out in the 1958–88 period: (1) an usually large and politically powerful agricultural sector, which insisted, successfully, on maintaining the huge subsidies of the Common Agricultural Policy; (2) a perennial industrial trade deficit; (3) a growing and increasingly export-oriented service sector; and (4) a currency perceived by the markets as weak, in spite of sporadic periods of French government rigor to build a strong franc. During the last half of the 1980s, by contrast, a whole series of deflationary policy changes matured, carried out by Socialists and conservatives (during the Cohabitation of 1986–88) alike. They have produced wide effects, not merely economic changes but also political and social changes, leading France to join the technologically most advanced countries.[7] The end of the twentieth century is no doubt bringing the full rounding off of the edges of France's historical economic particularities.

Broad Characteristics of the French Economy

One defining aspect of French economic development has been *dualism*, meaning a strong traditional sector surviving alongside sectors of rapid modernization. Another dualism was the coexistence of a market sector with a state-run sector. The various defining characteristics of French economic growth developed, therefore, from the interplay of classic market forces with the unusually strong dirigiste state role. The state's leaders were "enlightened minorities, Saint-Simonians, or the technocratic industrial class of the 1920s and their successors." In either case the interplay of market and state economic elites, in addition to the effects of France's wars, made for "the very peculiar roads and stages followed by the French economy, as well as the sense of French backwardness at certain historical moments."[8]

Germany and Italy created genuine economic "miracles" in the decades after World War II. Britain, on the other hand, lagged behind the 4–6 percent boom growth rates in these countries, with 2 percent growth. France, measured against these partners and rivals, did very well, not so well as to be considered an economic miracle on the German scale, but well enough for a new middle class of socially mobile, urban and internationally oriented French people to see extremely attractive economic prospects rapidly open before them in the 1960s and 1970s. In a much read and quoted book, the distinguished economist Jean Fourastié baptized the period *les Trentes Glorieuses* of postwar French economic growth.[9]

In gross terms, several statistics give a quick picture of French economic progress. France in 1960 had less than half the U.S. gross national product (GNP) per capita, for example, whereas by 1987 the figure was over 80 percent.[10] France's GNP doubled between 1960 and 1978 in real terms, and the French growth rate in 1965–1973, averaging 5–6 percent per year, was surpassed only by Japan among the industrialized countries. Similarly, industrial production in 1969–74 rose 37 percent, and productivity also increased at high rates, reaching a remarkable 7.5 percent annual growth in 1968–73. French productivity increases for these several years outdid West Germany, which contributed to an overall French lead over Germany in GNP growth of 26 percent during this particular period. However, over the longer term these French accomplishments were either not kept up or shown to be aberrations. For example, production and productivity increases were abnormally high after the lost production of 1968 due to the strikes of May–June. And the low average rate of GNP growth in 1980–85, only about 1 percent per year, was due to the Socialist government's zigzag policies. It is ironic that the French union of the left government in 1981–82 had counted on an American-led international recovery to stimulate French exports. The problem was that the Reagan boom arrived 18 months later than the Socialists had hoped, and the consequences were devastating.[11]

For the "socialist" year 1981–82 French economic growth was higher than average growth in the EC, but it was more due to the Keynesian increase in French consumption, especially to increased imports, than to new domestic production and exports. As a consequence, the years 1983–86 produced growth much below the EC average. The French economist Michel Pérébeau concluded that Socialist economic ideas had received a coup de grace:

> The lesson was very hard, but it was well understood. No important [French] political leader still believes that international competition is a myth fabricated to justify hardline salary policies, nor that a policy of sweet insouciance towards inflation can in the long run promote growth and full employment.[12]

As with the decentralized Jacobin state administration, the Colbertist state economy has also been reduced, with minor conservative–Socialist battles over reprivatizations and renationalizations. The "mandarin" conception that France could be guided economically only by a dirigiste government has also fallen before certain facts. The French have, in effect, been left little choice if they would be fully at the center of European integration. Looking back from 1991, a British commentator wrote:

> Centralized state planning tends to be overwhelmed by the complexities of rich economies. State control of finance is brushed aside by international flows of money, and state protectionism by Europe's common market. The result has been little short of a silent revolution. Pinch yourself today to remember that in late 1981 the . . . Socialist government . . . controlled the price and allocation of credit, controlled wage rises and many prices, applied exchange controls, controlled the electronic media and had a dirigiste industrial strategy. . . . Remember, too, that this same government was then bent upon nationalizing much of French business . . . and that those two old handmaidens of centralized power—inflation and exchange-rate devaluation—were deployed to leach away the savings that the French were not allowed to move abroad.[13]

French External Accounts

The trends in France's external accounts demonstrate the competitive constraints on French national economy policy. Table 8.2 gives the French trade balance (in millions of constant francs) and the percentage of imports covered by exports.

Table 8 ✦ 2   France's Balance of Trade

Source: Casanova, in Lévy-
Leboyer and Casanova,
Entre l'état et le marché,
p. 551.

Year	Trade Balance ($ million)	% Coverage
1949	−1,030	85
1950	452	99
1955	797	102
1956	−3,330	83
1957	−4,038	83
1958	−1,879	92
1959	1,811	124
1960	2,643	120
1965	−1,615	105
1970	−6,895	100
1975	−6,358	103
1980	−87,628	89
1985	−69,435	97
1987	−65,909	97

Jean-Claude Casanova's analysis shows that, in 1946–1987, exports covered imports in the French trade balance only in sixteen out of forty-two years. On the other hand, the degree of imbalance was steady, in that increases in imports were generally balanced by an equivalent increase in exports. The French trade weakness thus has not been cumulative, even if it has been constant. In another data series showing three different external accounts, Casanova demonstrates that in the thirty-three years 1950–1982, the French trade balance was in deficit eighteen times, the balance of payments was in deficit seventeen times and the overall balance (including long-term capital movements) was in deficit nineteen times. This indicates how persistent foreign trade weakness emphasized France's general economic inferiority vis-à-vis Germany, which had perennial trade surpluses, and why the "exterior constraint" on government policy in general has weighed more heavily in France. Table 8.3 shows that in the period 1980–89, France accumulated a total deficit of $76.5 billion with its EC partners, most of it with Germany.

Among the major EC economies, France has only been in a stronger intra-EC trade position than Great Britain. Given Britain's economic

Table 8 ✦ 3 French Trade Deficits

Source: IMF, *Direction of Trade Statistics: Yearbook, 1987, 1990*, in David R. Cameron, "The 1992 Initiative: Causes and Consequences," in Alberta M. Sbragia (ed.), *Euro-Politics*, p. 69.

	West Germany	France	Italy	Netherlands	Belgium-Luxembourg	Great Britain	Ireland	Denmark	Greece	Spain	Portugal
1980	7.5	−5.0	−5.7	10.8	1.2	0.8	−1.6	−0.9	−1.8	0.2	−1.5
1981	6.4	−5.4	−4.1	13.5	0.9	−1.0	−2.1	−0.8	−2.6	−0.1	−2.1
1982	11.7	−10.1	−1.9	13.0	0.5	−3.7	−1.1	−0.7	−2.7	0.0	−1.9
1983	7.4	−8.4	−0.4	13.1	−0.2	−5.6	−0.2	−0.2	−2.4	0.3	−0.8
1984	9.2	−7.0	−3.2	13.8	−1.4	−5.9	0.3	−0.8	−2.0	2.3	−0.2
1985	10.9	−7.7	−4.8	12.6	−1.5	−4.3	0.5	−1.4	−2.4	1.6	0.1
1986	23.9	−7.8	−3.1	12.0	0.7	−14.0	1.3	−2.0	−3.0	−1.2	−0.7
1987	34.8	−9.6	−5.5	10.9	1.5	−16.6	2.8	−0.9	−3.6	−5.0	−2.6
1988	46.3	−7.1	−6.2	13.2	1.0	−26.6	3.6	0.1	−4.2	−7.9	−3.7
1989	50.3	−8.4	−7.3	15.1	3.2	−26.9	4.0	0.9	−5.4	−11.1	−3.7

Cumulative Totals, 1980– 89

West Germany	France	Italy	Netherlands	Belgium-Luxembourg	Great Britain	Ireland	Denmark	Greece	Spain	Portugal
208.4	−76.5	−42.2	128.0	5.9	−103.8	7.5	−6.7	−30.1	−20.9	−17.1

problems and its love–hate relationship with the EC, this is small consolation for the French.

It is consistent with the above-cited trends that French economic growth historically should have been less oriented toward export than has been economic growth in partner countries. This long entrenchment in the domestic market was, as Casanova says, among European countries "really a French singularity." And it seems to fit with France's cultural tradition of self-absorption, self-satisfaction and insularity—of the French finding all that they needed in the Hexagon. Like the ancient Persians and Chinese, the French long inhabited a mental "middle kingdom," in which travel and foreign commerce were acquired tastes, adjuncts to, but not necessities of the good life.

Such attitudes are no longer possible. As the two Germanies were unifying in 1989–90, concern arose over whether France could remain economically compatible with the "new" new Germany, and whether it could stay a genuine partner in the Franco–German tandem.

One reason for concern was that the French industrial trade balance has deteriorated in the past decade. From 1970 to 1982 a surplus was sustainable because of two particularities: French arms sales (France is the third-ranking arms merchant in the world after the United States and the former Soviet Union), and the so-called *grands contrats*, contracts for huge construction and infrastructure projects—road and rail networks, subways, public utilities—in less-developed countries.

Deficits suddenly appeared in 1987 (Fr 11 billion) and 1988 (Fr 42 billion). French industrial trade, as noted above, had already been in deficit with the industrialized countries. Surpluses came from French sales in the "soft" markets of the Third World, often, in the 1970s, thanks to Third World governments' recycling of petrodollars. At first the new weakness was masked by increased earnings of services in the French trade balance. In 1960 services were 38 percent of French commercial exports, in 1970 the figure was 37 percent, but in 1980 services had risen sharply to 60 percent. Part of this was soft, a rise in tourism; but the major part was the sale of French technical expertise, connected with industrial and engineering projects, and business administration.

A second factor causing concern about French competitiveness today is France's loss of market share internationally. Between 1979 and 1987, in volume France's share of OECD markets dropped from 12.6 to 11.6 percent, in developing country markets from 11.1 to 10 percent, and in former communist country markets from 12.1 to 11.1 percent. France does not import, so to speak, too much; the problem is that exports are weakening. Exports as a share of French GDP declined in the 1980s. The key factors seem to be, first, that French industry is not as intensively specialized and sales-driven as are exporters in other countries, and second, that traditional areas of French comparative advantage (agricultural and food products, metal and chemical industries) have progressed only weakly in the last twenty years of international trade. Thus, to the extent that economic success and influence in European integration requires competitive industrial exports, France must not merely maintain its place, but also reverse a trend.

Table 8 ✦ 4 **Unemployment Rates for Five Countries**
Source: The Economist, March 13, 1993, p. 119.

	January 1993	January 1992
France	10.5	10.0
Germany	7.5	6.2
Great Britain	10.6	9.2
Japan	2.3	2.1
United States	7.0	7.3

Unemployment and Tax Burdens

Almost every EC country suffered high unemployment in the 1980s. The French particularity was that France's unemployment was a few points higher than elsewhere, the mirror of its low inflation rate. This "anti-worker" inflation–unemployment equilibrium was not, certainly, what had been expected of Socialist governments.

To understand the significance of French unemployment and inflation, as with trade balances and other indicators, requires a comparative measure. Given international trends, in the 1980s rising unemployment was practically unavoidable. Government policies—both Socialist and conservative—marginally increased the number of jobless. But there were the simultaneous gains of a low inflation rate, an increasingly solid currency, and new esteem for French economics and for the French left's capacity to govern. In early 1993, comparative unemployment statistics were as shown in Table 8.4.

Table 8.4 and others in this chapter demonstrate that France's broad economic indicators were quite competitive, given one or two black marks, with those of its partners, who each have their own black marks. Britain, falling into recession in 1992, does as poorly as France, or worse on unemployment. German inflation, because of German unification, is worse than France's, and German unemployment is also rising, being especially high in the former East German territories. Nearly all the major European countries were falling into recession in early 1993, just as the United States seemed to start recovering from the statistically mild but socially very damaging recession of the Bush years. In any case, no one, on a comparative basis, could call France a "sick man of Europe."

But the disaster is unemployment, where the cost is so immediately human rather than monetary in nature. When Giscard d'Estaing left

Table 8 ✦ 5 French Unemployment,
1967–1994

Year	No. Unemployed Workers
1967	500,000
1974	1,000,000
1981	2,000,000
1993	3,000,000
1994	±3,500,000 (±12%)

office in 1981, defeated by Mitterrand, unemployment had already risen from 2.6 percent in 1973 to 7.6 percent. The Socialists between 1981 and 1993 certainly failed to keep unemployment down, as Table 8.5 shows. But three factors, in addition to the 1981–82 fiasco of "Keynesian socialism," account for France's strikingly high unemployment rate as the Balladur Cohabitation II government took over in March 1993: (1) the legacy of the 1970s, (2) the policy of low inflation, and (3) the policy of the "strong franc." By 1994 the unemployment rate was pushing 12 percent.

France's high unemployment (and underemployment) rates of the past decade have had horrible social costs, as any regular visitor to the country is painfully aware. Young, middle-aged and older workers have, to varying degrees, had their lives and life chances changed for the worse. Salaried workers and executives (*cadres*) in their fifties have unwanted early retirement forced on them while still in the prime of their working lives. Middle-aged workers and employees are suddenly deprived of family incomes and thrown into desperate, humiliating family situations in addition to the pain of losing a job with no good prospect of finding another. Young people, especially those who have never had a job, are, in a well-known scenario, set adrift between school and . . . what? How long they remain adrift, and whether they can ever achieve what used to be called a steady job, is one of the great social struggles of the 1990s.

The ravages of unemployment have increased social and political xenophobia, including voter susceptibility to the rhetoric of the National Front. Particularly high unemployment correlates with the particularly large (10–13 percent) anti-immigrant vote for the National Front. Yet unemployment among the immigrant population, as already noted, is worse than among the French—about 20 percent overall, 30 percent among immigrant young people as opposed to about 20 percent among French youth. However this may be, certain categories of French opinion continue to believe that immigrants, most of whom are now French citizens, are the cause of French unemployment.

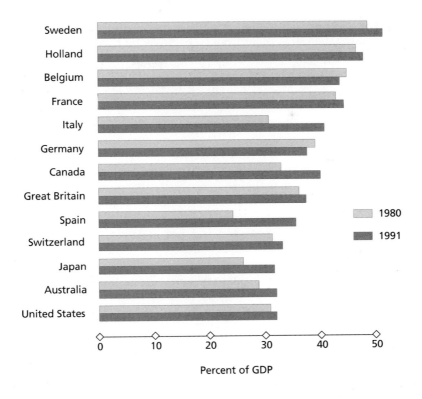

Sweden
Holland
Belgium
France
Italy
Germany
Canada
Great Britain
Spain
Switzerland
Japan
Australia
United States

☐ 1980
■ 1991

0   10   20   30   40   50

Percent of GDP

Figure 8 ✦ 2 Tax revenues as percentage of gross domestic product (1992)
Source: The Economist, March 13, 1993, p. 19.

As for income levels, the 1980s in France were a time of widening disparities between the poor and the well-off, again contrary to Socialist promises. The top 25 percent had a 20 percent increase in real income in the 1980s, while the bottom quarter had stagnating incomes. President Mitterrand has said that the failure of his various governments to reduce French inequality is his "biggest regret."

One important cause of the French economy's failure to provide more jobs is that the massive administrative French state remains bloated, eating up resources that could be used for growth. Of every 100 workers in France, 23 are on national or local government payrolls, compared with 18 in 1970, and with an average of 15 in other industrialized countries. (Figure 8.2 shows how French government tax revenues compare with other countries.) In 1970, the French government, through all forms of taxes, disposed of 35 percent of GDP; by 1990 this figure was 44 percent. (In the 1981 presidential campaign against Mitterrand, Giscard d'Estaing warned that at 40 percent France would be on the "threshold of socialism!").

If high unemployment and comparatively low growth (1 percent in 1992–93) are the main symptoms of France's new economic problem, the cause is "that France's economic revolution is only half-complete. . . . Despite all the changes, France still runs the most state-dominated economy in the G-7."[14]

The out-of-date French tax structure explains why the huge state bureaucracy works to hold back employment and to disadvantage lower-paid workers. The main issue is that social security (meaning health care, unemployment and pensions) is isolated from the rest of government's finances. It is funded mainly by high, flat-rate contribution payments from both employers and workers, and is a pay-as-you-go system that, rather than incurring debt, simply raises contribution levels.

French government revenues depend heavily on social-security taxes. Since 1970, income and other national taxes have gone down from 18.4 percent to 16.4 percent of GDP, and local taxes have risen from 3.4 percent to 6 percent. Social-security taxes jumped from 13.1 percent to 20.3 percent of GDP. So, just as happened in the United States during the Reagan years, social-security taxes rose to compensate for other areas. And this, the biggest, fastest-growing burden of government thus fell largely—and regressively—on wage earners and company contributions, which discouraged business from hiring new workers.

Thus a major public policy issue for several years has been to find ways to control social-security costs. French health care spending has been rising faster than in any other G-7 country (the French, for example, are the world's leading consumers of medicines), with some exceptions for the profligate United States. And the French pension system, which like the American system is operated on a pay-as-you-go basis, soon will face the classic demographic fear: too many benefits owed to too many retirees paid for by too few contributing workers—that is, insolvency.

One proposed change would fund social security partly from the tax system. But this would simply shift the burden without reducing social spending. As in the United States, reducing social spending seems unavoidable, with the proviso that vital services must be saved. Furthermore, the income-tax system itself ought to be reformed, or else low-income people might in any case end up paying more than a fair share. The top French tax rate is 57 percent, which seems a hard hit at the rich. But only half of French families pay any income tax at all! The French income-tax system only produces 20 percent of central government revenue, whereas fully 40 percent comes from the value-added tax (VAT), a

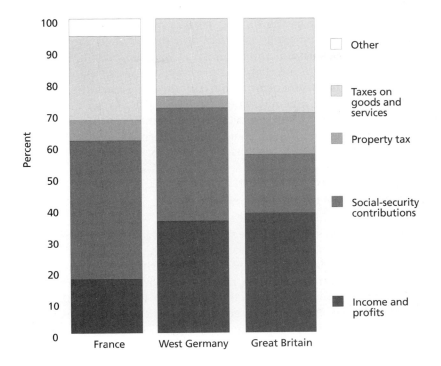

**Figure 8 ✦ 3 Tax structure comparisons: France, West Germany
and Britain**
Source: The Economist, November 23, 1991.

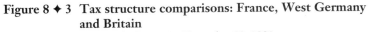

tax on consumption (see Figure 8.3). The VAT adds an overall 18.6 percent to the price of consumer items and, like all indirect taxes, disadvantages those with lower incomes who are obliged to spend more to live.

As public policy specialists say, the entire French public sector "remains overweight. It is, moreover, financing itself in a way that aggravates unemployment, social frustration and probably, therefore, xenophobia."[15] The "social treatment" of unemployment—government-sponsored apprenticeships, training schools and the like—has had small effect on the unemployment rate, whether under Socialist or conservative governments. The minimum wage is, as always, good for those who would otherwise be paid less but damaging for those whose potential jobs are prevented by it. The so-called Minimum Income for Reintegration, a combination of minimum income and workfare ideas introduced in 1989 by the Rocard government, has likewise had only a marginal effect.

In the past few years, social critics have even begun to speak of "the new poverty" in France, post-Marxist and without the class struggle. It is a bitter concept, particularly so for the Socialist governments on whose watch most of the new poor were created.[16] For the defeated Socialists in 1993, it was some consolation, and explanation, that high unemployment is an EC-wide, G-7–wide international phenomenon, attributable to no particular country, government or party. Yet the marginal difference is very significant between unemployment at 10–11 percent, as in Britain and France in 1992, and 7 percent, as in neighboring Germany in 1992: "3 percent" contains a lot of people and much suffering.

France's Economy and the EC's Single Integrated Market

Completion of the EC's single market as of January 1, 1993, plus the goal of full monetary union by the end of the century, again indicates that French economics today must be set in an international frame. The meaning of the single market is that, in addition to no internal tariffs, all informal barriers to internal EC economic activity must be dismantled. In addition to the free movement of goods, there is to be free movement of capital, services and people. The goal of a single EC currency, built on the ECU, and a European central bank, the Eurofed, has been set for 1997 or soon thereafter, as the third stage of monetary union.

No one expects all this to happen either completely or on time. But that is beside the point. For believers in the benefits of integration, continuation of movement forward is what counts. Jean Monnet compared European integration to riding a bicycle: Either one moves forward or one falls off.

France is the largest EC agricultural producer and agricultural exporter. And its farm-export surplus, in recent years around $9 billion, more or less compensates for its industrial trade deficit. But the industrial trade deficit is a persistent issue in itself.

Historically, the French state developed two industrial policy strategies to try to remedy the weaknesses of French industry. One used tax incentives to spur mergers in order to create large businesses, partly to promote industrialization as such, and partly for the international trade benefits of economies of scale. Often this policy worked, but sometimes government-promoted mergers failed disastrously because they didn't make business sense. The other strategy was sectoral development, special treatment for technologically promising "national champions." A designated national champion was either a firm capable of significantly increasing the volume of French exports, or one embarked on massive capital projects, such as the telephone system, nuclear plants and rapid-transit systems. Results from the national champion policy were often positive, in the sense that exports grew and the French economic infra-structure was dramatically improved. On the other hand, the consumer-goods sector of the industrial economy remained vulnerable to import competition. The situation in the 1970s was summed up by political economist Peter Hall:

> While France sold arms to the OPEC nations, the Germans and Japanese were penetrating French markets for automobiles, electronics, and consumer durables. Furthermore, pitfalls and errors of a state-led industrial policy were not always avoided: for example, big failures in the computer field, overextension of the steel industry requiring salvage by the state, and the commercially disastrous supersonic Concorde.[17]

In the past decade the French tried to sell their EC partners on a similar strategy of merging different national firms in order to create "Community champions." France's EC partners have demurred, both because the German example argues against industrial dirigisme, and because private-sector reliance has become the preferred European policy. Moreover, French industrial policy was often protectionist, spending lots of public money rescuing "lame duck" enterprises.

As already noted, France and Germany are each other's single largest trading partners. French industrial inferiority to Germany has resulted in a persistent, demoralizing industrial trade deficit. Germany has for decades maintained a large surplus in industrial goods trade with the French, and German industrial exports have been successful in the toughest export markets, whereas French business has generally assumed its products would lose in the most competitive markets. Therefore, French business has concentrated its effort in soft markets, especially Third World markets in Francophone countries.

French business strategy is changing, however. Spurred on by Mitterrand's monetary and budgetary austerity and lured by opportunities in the former East Germany, "Corporate France," as the *Financial Times* recently said, "is launching an unprecedented invasion across the Rhine, attracted by the belated realization that Germany is the key to its success in the European market."[18] German resistance to foreign investment is still a problem, and can be especially so at the grassroots level in the former East Germany. But French business recently has made a record number of takeovers and has largely closed the trade gap.

For example, in 1991 French companies took over 70 West German companies, three times the 1990 total. And in the new eastern laender, France is by far the largest foreign investor since unification. By mid-1992 French companies had bought 78 privatized companies at a value of $1.6 billion, with U.S. businesses, having invested $1 billion, being France's nearest rival in the former East Germany. French activism in the new unified Germany is a bit less impressive than it might be, however, since the German *Treuhandanstalt* government agency in charge of privatizing East German industries has been offering much more than the foreign investors, especially the rich West German cousins, want to absorb. In fact, non-German companies altogether had by the end of 1992 bought up only 5 percent of East German privatizations.

French commercial exports have also done well in the new East German markets. The French share of German imports rose from 11.8 percent in 1990 to 12.2 percent in 1991; consequently the French trade deficit with Germany declined rapidly from Fr 42 billion in 1990 to Fr 7 billion in 1991. French automobiles were the leading export—a 54 percent rise in 1990–1991. Renault is now the best-selling foreign car in unified Germany overall, and in 1991 in the eastern laender the "Renault 19" even outsold the perennial favorite German VW "Golf," because the easterners—in an example of market forces at work—massively bought near-comparable quality (i.e. Renault) at a significantly lower price!

French takeovers have centered in the auto and oil products sector. For example the largest French investment in Germany since World War II (about $4 billion) is an agreement by Elf Aquitaine, the majority state-owned French oil company, to run the monopoly chain of gas stations in eastern Germany.

Partially as a result of low inflation and deficit results, French business is beginning to show more confidence in the German market, perhaps in the face of German competition generally speaking. This is hopeful, because competing in the German market is necessary if French firms are to have a sound European strategy in the next phase of European integration. At the very least the French, to keep a necessary equilibrium, must not let the Germans pull away.

The French Franc and the European Monetary System

Just as French industry has traditionally been outperformed by German industry in the Common Market, so the German mark has been an exceptionally strong currency, and an international reserve currency, whereas the French franc has been a traditionally weak currency.

French monetary policy has therefore had to begin with the fact of long-term German superiority. Before unification, the West German industrial economy was one-third larger than the French, achieved with only a modest population superiority—about 62 million to 55 million—and a smaller natural resource base. Productivity gains over a long period were, with the exception of one five-year period, consistently and signifi-

cantly higher in Germany. So the relative weakness of economic fundamentals kept the French franc a comparatively weak currency, in spite of
several temporarily invigorating political attempts to build a "strong"
franc.

French governments in the postwar decades, faced with industrial
undercompetitiveness, generally opted for a "soft" currency policy of
competitive depreciation, achieved either by official devaluation of the franc
or by letting the markets bid it down. Perennial depreciation is a constant
export stimulus because a declining currency makes exported products
less expensive abroad, partially compensating for lagging productivity. Of
course this policy of capitalizing on weakness made for negative esteem.
France could not shake the reputation of being "not serious" in international trade, of being one of those countries whose government tries to
achieve through currency manipulation the gains its producers fail to
achieve by doing good business. To a certain extent, French business still
drags this old stereotype around.

In terms of deciding national monetary policy—interest rates and
bank requirements—international faith in the German mark leaves the
French finance minister and the French treasury little room to maneuver.
The franc and the mark exchange rates are linked by European monetary
system (EMS) rules within a range of possible fluctuation (2.5 percent on
either side of parity until the 1993 EMS crisis forced an enlargement to
15 percent on either side). The mark has been by far the preferred
currency. The result is that if the Bundesbank raises German interest
rates, buyers will flock to the mark for higher yields unless the Bank of
France follows German policy. French interest rate policy thus has been
in effect set by the Bundesbank. It is not surprising, therefore, that a
series of French governments, both Socialist and conservative, have tried
to create a "strong franc." With the mark weakened somewhat by the
problems of unification, the economic fundamentals existed for a
stronger franc in relation to the mark.[19] However, the currency crisis of
August–September 1992, the so-called First Geldkrieg, showed that, in
spite of the economic fundamentals, speculators continue, after betting
against the weakest currencies (the Italian lira, the Spanish peseta, the
British pound and the Irish punt), to distrust government determination
to defend the French franc. Only continuous joint Bank of France and
Bundesbank interventions in international capital markets during that
crisis avoided a 1992 French devaluation. A "strong franc," by contrast,
should be able comfortably to maintain its parity against the mark, and,
as necessary, match any reevaluation of the German mark.

The goal of a "strong franc" has developed from French government
recognition that a policy of currency depreciation to compensate for
export weaknesses is, whatever its immediate gains, ultimately a loser.

Subsequent inflation always erodes the initial gains from a devaluation, and in the longer term the country whose currency initially appreciates in value captures the greater benefits. French business and political leaders realized that currency depreciation punctuated by regular devaluations

> had also been devaluing the capital stock of the nation's industry. Lower capital values forced business to use rather than replace existing machinery, and then to borrow money when equipment had to be replaced, raising debt levels. All this meant that French industry kept going after soft markets, selling textiles in Africa, and backing away from the competitive edge of high value-added business.
>
> Now, France has learned from the German experience that revaluation (of the currency) obliges industry to cut costs and continually to move its products upscale, where margins and profits are highest. That provides the cash flow to invest more and prepare the ground for further growth. What's more, a unilateral revaluation of the mark would allow Germany to recapture some of the competitiveness it has lost to France due to the faster rise of labor costs. Between 1973 and 1986, unit labor costs in French business rose between two and three times faster than in Germany.[20]

That disadvantageous difference in relative labor costs has been changing since, and especially since German unification.

French industrialists used to think of inflation as something that brought them growth and devaluation as something that gave them competitiveness. In the new France, French business has become a strong-currency convert, despite the painful interest rates involved. Progressively weaned from government's dirigiste reflex, French industry today increasingly, if too slowly, seeks to be competitive.

The European currency debacle of summer 1993 seemed to throw into question not only the European monetary system's survival, but also the very idea of full European monetary union (EMU). The EMS crashed as weaker currencies, including the French franc, couldn't hold their parity against the German mark in the face of sudden cutthroat market speculation. Treaty limits of the exchange rate mechanism (ERM)—holding currencies within 2.5 percent permitted variations on either side of par value, 5 percent total—dissolved as sellers of the weaker currencies forced the British pound, the Italian lira, the Spanish peseta and other currencies beyond the ERM's limits.

Speculators made fantastic profits on the fall of the various currencies. George Soros, the Hungarian-born American manager of a huge investment fund, made $1 billion in a matter of days betting against the British pound. In a sort of public interest gesture, he announced a few months later that he was staying out of renewed speculation against the franc. Nevertheless, the 1993 currency crises made clear that national governments could not face off successfully against the huge amounts of capital speculating in international currency markets. The Bundesbank helped Germany's EC partners selectively—it apparently supported the franc more than the pound, but even the French later questioned how whole-hearted the Bundesbank's aid had been, though the German central bank advertised, unusually, that it had bought EMS partner currencies equivalent to almost $35 billion in July 1993 alone.

Because of the monetary system's collapse, the ERM limits were stretched, in a crisis atmosphere, from 5 percent total to 30 percent total, meaning 15 percent on either side of par value. This very large margin makes it unlikely (for now) that speculators can force central banks (e.g., the Bank of France) to buy up any amount of the national currency put into the market. But it also means that businesses in the EC can no longer rely on stable prices as they have come to do. EC currencies may not weaken toward the now very wide ERM margins, but steady increments of fluctuations will cause substantial uncertainty about production costs.

Is the Maastricht plan for full European monetary union dead? This essay doesn't need to take a definitive position. There are obvious reasons for thinking that after the "Geldkriegs" of 1992–93 a single European currency and a Eurofed are now pipe dreams. But there are also reasons to think that, with the same sort of political will that brought European integration so far in the decade 1985 to 1995, monetary union may be pushed back several years and include fewer rather than more countries, although its benefits are too important ultimately to forego.

France and the Goal of Full European Monetary Union

Professor William H. Buiter of the Yale University Department of Economics, in a letter to *The Financial Times*, correctly put the trick of making monetary union. Its mechanics, he said, "are actually very simple; the principal point is that it should come like a thief in the night. We will wake up and discover that independent central banks have been abolished (after fixing exchange rates forever) and that currency control has been transferred to the European central bank." He forecast that this might occur as early as 2005 to 2010.

Simplistic as it seems, he may be right that reaching EMU should be conceived as cutting a Gordian knot. In any case, the French franc's agonies in relation to the German mark, and, more importantly, the significance of currency difficulties in holding back French economic development, explain why France has shown the strongest commitment to full monetary union with a single currency and a European central bank.

It is striking that French business and industry for one thing has over the past several years become much more clearly European than the rest of French society. French exporters, accepting the risks of competition, see the single market and economic integration as good for business. Much of French business, as in other European countries, in fact already lives and works in a single European market. French bills and coins may be beautiful, but in the fiercely competitive world of international trade and money, French business would not be unhappy to give up the still not fully "strong" franc in exchange for the ECU. Moving to the single European currency in fact entails notable risks and sacrifices for Germany, in at least two ways. First, "foreigners" will be given a voice in German monetary matters—in theory the Germans could even be outvoted in weighted majority Eurofed decisions. Second, a single European currency, based on a group of economies of varying strengths, will embody more inflationary forces and depreciation tendencies than the German mark alone, which not even Bundesbank rigor may keep from having destabilizing consequences.

Full economic and monetary union is to be accomplished in three phases. The first phase, underway with the EMS in 1979, was closed with implementation of the single market, "1992 Project," as of January 1, 1993.

The second phase of EMU is set to begin January 1, 1994, reaffirmed by the EC's European Council in October 1993 even after the severe monetary crisis of summer 1993. It is a transition phase, putting in place the policies and structures that will be finalized in the third EMU stage of a single currency and a European central bank. In this second phase there will be stricter surveillance, by the EC Commission and the Council of Finance Ministers, of five so-called convergence indicators, whose fulfillment will qualify a member country to join the single currency and the Eurofed (see Figure 8.4).

A European Monetary Institute (EMI), located in Frankfurt, will oversee the second phase—an advanced EMS coordinating mechanism and precursor of the Eurofed, which will be set up at the time of the single European currency. To prepare Eurofed's creation, the EMI will increasingly coordinate national monetary policies and augment the role of the ECU in financial markets in the attempt to make it a hard currency.

The third phase of monetary union, which the Maastricht Treaty schedules for 1997 or 1999 (but now is uncertain), will require a decision by each country on whether to join the single currency and the Eurofed. Not all countries will qualify or be permitted to join. The third phase of

1. Inflation:	Must be no more than 1.5 points above the average of the top three EC countries.
2. Long-term interest rates:	Must be within 2 points of the average of the three countries with the lowest rates.
3. Government budget deficit:	Must be less than 3 percent of GDP.
4. Total government public debt:	Must not exceed 60 percent of GDP.
5. Currency stability:	Currency must not have been devalued in the previous two years, and it must have remained in the European Monetary System's "narrow band."

Figure 8 ✦ 4 The five convergence indicators for European monetary union

EMU could well start with five, six or seven countries only, and might, as a response to currency crises, be launched sooner than 1997 by the strongest countries. (The entire third phase could, to the contrary, also be scuppered by crises.) Most important, the Maastricht partners agreed that no country (i.e., Britain or Denmark) could stop the rest from proceeding. This in effect means that the principle of majority voting rather than unanimity has already been accepted for the single currency.

Three possible categories of countries will exist at the moment of creating the single currency and the Eurofed: (1) those that want to join but don't meet the economic and monetary performance standards; (2) those that have the performance but don't want to join (conceivably, the British case); and (3) those that qualify and do join.

Table 8.6 shows the twelve EC countries' convergence indicators (minus currency stability) at the end of 1991, and whether they satisfied the Maastricht Treaty criteria for joining Stage 3. Eight of the twelve EC countries would not have qualified, and a few months later German inflation, because of unification, had risen such that Germany itself would have been disqualified!

Could Paris ever become a true financial center of Europe? The British, by refusing to commit fully to EMU at the Maastricht summit in 1991, gave up any presumptive claim to host the future Eurofed bank. Germany—meaning Frankfurt—is the site for the EMI and the Eurofed.

Nevertheless the French have for several years been building the superstructure of what treasury officials grandly call *la place financière* (the financial plaza). France has conceded Germany's claim and is not bidding to put the Eurofed in Paris, but important steps are being taken to turn

Table 8 ✦ 6 EMU Convergence Indicators: Criteria Satisfied? (Y/N)

Source: The Economist, November 30, 1991, p. 71.

	Inflation Rate, End of 1991	Long-Term Govt. Bonds, End of 1991	Budget Deficit, 1990	1991 Public Debt, %GDP
Germany	3.5 (Y)	8.1 (Y)	–1.9 (Y)	44 (Y)
France	**2.5 (Y)**	**8.7 (Y)**	**–1.6 (Y)**	**47 (Y)**
Italy	6.1 (N)	12.6 (N)	–10.6 (N)	99 (N)
Great Britain	3.7 (Y)	10.0 (Y)	–0.7 (Y)	43 (Y)
Spain	5.5 (N)	11.4 (N)	–4.0 (N)	45 (Y)
Holland	4.4 (Y)	8.6 (Y)	–5.3 (N)	78 (N)
Belgium	2.2 (Y)	8.9 (Y)	–5.6 (N)	127 (N)
Denmark	1.8 (Y)	8.8 (Y)	–1.5 (Y)	66 (N)
Greece	17.9 (N)	20.8 (N)	–19.8 (N)	94 (N)
Portugal	10.2 (N)	14.1 (N)	–5.8 (N)	68 (N)
Ireland	3.5 (Y)	9.3 (Y)	–3.6 (N)	103 (N)
Luxembourg	3.2 (Y)	8.1 (Y)	4.7 (Y)	7 (Y)

Paris into a world financial center. French banks, long government-owned, are Europe's biggest. The stock market, *la Bourse*, now has an advanced, paperless trading system, "CAC," that is open to banks and foreigners. The government bond market is growing in sophistication and is increasingly trading in ECU issues. The MATIF is now a competitor of the British LIFFE as Europe's top futures exchange.

Nevertheless, "financial markets evolve through the leadership of practitioners not governments," and the Paris financial world is still mountains away from the "risk-taking, market-making culture" of London.[21] The French domestic financial base remains weak, with too little private pension-fund money, too many companies still state-owned or state-managed and too much international business kept out because of persisting dirigiste and tutelle-oriented (protection-oriented) government attitudes in finance. Out of a desire to protect France's monetary progress of the last decade there may even be a new mood of state protectionism, "a fortress in French financial services," one manifestation of which is that foreign participation in French franc bond issues has been kept to a minimum.

Conclusion

The value of a country's currency is a measure of how it is considered by others—bankers and industrialists, governments and speculators, allies and adversaries. This judgment about money is not only economic and financial, but also an estimate of the political will of its governments and the lessons of its history. Is a country a trustworthy partner? Can its financial commitment be relied on? Can a government's will be broken?

Nearing the end of a tortured century, the French franc's susceptibility in the markets is, somewhat refreshingly, more political and cultural than economic. Having more than once lost the confidence of its partners and allies, France continues to pay—through its currency—for the dramatic ups and downs, the "glory," of its exceptional history. In de Gaulle's time, the task for France was to regain independence and respect; today the French are looking for international recognition of the country's economic housecleaning. This would certainly be symbolized by a strong franc in the international markets.

Respect comes hard, costs much and is worth the effort. Yet the French today, as before, sometimes seem to lack confidence in themselves. Having changed a great deal, the French economy, at least in certain residual ways, remains a Gaullian, or even a Tocquevillean story.

Endnotes

1. Nico Colchester, *The Economist*, November 23, 1991, special survey of France, "L'état c'est l'Europe" (Europe is the state; cf. Louis XIV, "I am the state"), p. 18.

2. See Suzanne Berger and Michael Piore on the "dual economy": *Dualism and Discontinuity in Industrial Societies* (Cambridge: Cambridge University Press, 1980).

3. See Jean-Claude Casanova, "Les échanges extérieurs: Un équilibre précaire," in Lévy-Leboyer and Casanova, *Entre l'état et le marché: L'économie française des années 1880 à nos jours* (Between the state and the market: French economy from 1880 to the present) (Paris: Editions Gallimard, 1991), pp. 546–549. As Casanova shrewdly observes, France did not "become" the fourth-ranking world exporter, given that in the nineteenth century, until 1871, France already had been the second world exporting power after England. France was surpassed in the 1880s by Germany, around 1900 by the United States, then about 1960 by Japan (which had already surpassed France once before in 1930). Then France itself passed a declining Great Britain in the 1970s. Table 8.1 is taken from Lévy-Leboyer

and Casanova, p. 548, whose source is P. Bairoch, *La position intérnationale de la France* (The international position of France) (Paris: EHESS, 1977).

4. Casanova in Lévy-Leboyer and Casanova, pp. 549–550.

5. See Colchester, p. 8.

6. I am following Lévy-Leboyer and Casanova, using the French term *specificité*.

7. Lévy-Loboyer and Casanova, pp. 10–11.

8. Lévy-Leboyer and Casanova, p. 10. For a detailed exposition of France's economic lag, both in the internal market and in French shares of foreign trade markets, see their Chapter 6.

9. Jean Fourastié, *Les Trente glorieuses. La révolution invisible de 1946 à 1975* (Paris: Editions Fayard, 1979). In English a good study of the French economy is William James Adams, *Restructuring the French Economy* (Washington, D. C.: The Brookings Institution, 1989).

10. Other 1987 figures for percentage of U.S. GNP were Federal Germany, 100.3 percent; United Kingdom, 64 percent; Italy, 60 percent; Norway, 104 percent; Austria, 77 percent; Denmark, 89 percent. For this and several of the following points, see Ehrmann and Schain, pp. 21–23, especially the chart on p. 23. These statistics, done in exchange-rate equivalents, would probably show up less well for France (and other countries) if based on purchasing power parity.

11. See Hall, *Governing the Economy*, op. cit.

12. See Michel Pébéreau in Lévy-Leboyer and Casanova, p. 616.

13. See Colchester, p. 3.

14. See Colchester, p. 9. Only the Swedish and Dutch governments take a larger percentage of GDP as tax revenue than does the French government. Among the G-7 governments, the range extends from Italy's 41 percent to 32 percent in the United States.

15. See Colchester, pp. 9–10.

16. A Socialist deputy, Jean-Michel Belorgey, was an early publicist of this new point of view; see *La Gauche et ses pauvres* (The left and its poor) (Paris: Syros, 1988).

17. Hall in Cerny and Schain, op. cit., p. 83.

18. *The Financial Times*, July 28, 1992, p. 12, from which the following statistics are taken.

19. Even so, the Bérégovoy policy, begun in early 1991, of demonstrating financial strength by disengaging French interest-rate policy

from Bundesbank decisions did not last out the year. As German rates rose to attract capital to finance German unification, French interest rates were twice held to existing levels, despite pressure on the franc as money moved into the DM for higher yields. The result was that the franc in November 1991 was trading at the very bottom of its permitted EMS level. A sudden one-day collapse of 120 points in the New York stock market pushed investors to buy German marks, validating the maxim that "he who predicts a weakening dollar predicts a strengthening mark." Finance Minister Bérégovoy, in a clear defeat for the French policy of interest-rate autonomy, was obliged to raise French interest rates, which he had lowered only a month earlier in order to keep the value of the franc from dropping below its floor. A month later, the Bundesbank thunderously raised interest rates again, whereas the U.S. discount rate was lowered to 3.5 percent to jump start the recession-bound American economy. The frustrated French had again to follow the German lead.

20. See the *International Herald Tribune*, November 25, 1991, pp. 1, 10.

21. See "A Survey of Financial Centers," *The Economist*, June 27, 1992, p. 20.

9
✦

Geopolitics and Foreign Policy

France, the New Germany and European Integration

France is not really herself unless in the front rank. . . . France cannot be France without greatness.

—Charles de Gaulle, *War Memoirs*, p. 3

One must accept things as they are; what use is served by complaining about them? . . . In France, one must be capable of living next door to a dynamic Germany which is a peaceful conqueror. . . . Well, why not? . . . If Germany grows, France will too. . . . Why should France think a priori that it won't be capable of keeping pace, or even taking the lead? Why can't it conquer markets too? . . . Why should France be defeated in advance? . . . France has every chance, and thus the development of Germany is an incentive to do better. . . . That is a good lesson, a great opportunity which France must seize. The greatness of one of the two countries must be accompanied by the greatness of the other. They must proceed together. . . . We are the ones who asked for this [European union project], France and Germany together.

—François Mitterrand at a European Forum, from *European Affairs* 4 (Winter 1990): 37

Introduction

From de Gaulle through François Mitterrand, moving Europe "beyond Yalta" was a historic task for France. The end of divided Europe and unification of the two Germanies was what French policy had long claimed to seek. Success would both free Eastern Europe from the iron corset of communism and make Europe as a whole independent from domination by the superpower rivalry. That historic geopolitical change has now occurred, unexpectedly in the period of only a few years. The healing of Europe's political division has now been sealed off from reversal by the astonishing disappearance of the U.S.S.R. as a state and an empire. The long-term goals of French policy, one could say, have been attained, albeit by forces beyond France's control. In a television interview President Mitterrand, interrupting a journalist's question about whether the Soviet Union's disappearance did not increase instability, said suddenly, "Do you think then we should cry about the U.S.S.R.'s disappearance? Not me."

The questions remain however: What does a Europe beyond Yalta mean for France? What role will France play in the new European equation?

One view has been that, among the Western powers, France is a big loser because of the Cold War's end. A divided Europe and a divided Germany profited France geopolitically. France's main postwar foreign policy stage was Western Europe, and its main power dilemma was how to maintain a political edge over Germany's ever-growing economic influence. As 1970s German Chancellor Helmut Schmidt pointed out with regret, as a "political dwarf" postwar Federal Germany's "economic policy was, and had to be its foreign policy." The conclusion, explicit or implied, was that France had a genuine geopolitical interest in avoiding German unification and the end of superpower spheres of influence in Europe. In a divided Europe, built on a divided Germany, French influence was maximized because West German influence, though ever stronger over the Cold War decades, was minimized. West Germany was limited in its power for two reasons. First, a divided Europe meant that the memory of Nazism and the content and consequences of World War II were still alive and substantive; thus the Germans were still bent to the wheel of atonement. Second, Federal Germany was the border country in

This chapter initially was written while the author was a visiting fellow at the Centre d'Etudes des Relations Internationales (CERI), Paris, fall 1991. It first appeared in the spring 1992 issue of *Foreign Affairs*, which has kindly granted permission to use a much revised and updated version here.

the Western alliance's face-off with the military alliance of communist states. In this situation, any politically vanguard policies by West Germany, any *Sonderweg* or independent German policy outside of NATO's agreed limits, threatened political isolation, German "singularization," and perhaps even literal security dangers, beginning with the possibility of German Finlandization if independent deals were launched with the Soviets. This explains the controversy over Willy Brandt's Ostpolitik beginning in 1969.

Thus, for France, in addition to benefits, the end of a geopolitically divided Europe threatened a new German ascension. The unification of the two Germanies and the liberation of German geopolitical and economic influence conspire toward German preeminence both inside the EC and in managing Western influence in Eastern Europe and the former Soviet Union. The consequence for the French is, at least logically, a rapid evaporation of France's erstwhile ability in the EC to be the political and diplomatic engineer of the German economic locomotive in a Franco–German tandem. Or worse, with the likely expansion of the EC to a larger European Union including EFTA states and former communist states, and centered geographically further east and north, the very concept of the "Franco–German couple," the perennial core of European integration, will be put under stress if not completely thrown into question. Has German unification put into danger the Franco–German compatibility, and thus European integration as a whole? Has it changed the geopolitics of French foreign policy?

France and the European Revolution, 1989–91

France and German Unification

Despite French denials, President Mitterrand in 1989 clearly was reluctant about German unification—not about the principle of national self-determination, which he regarded as right and inevitable, but about the headlong pace at which unification was coming, and about the various risks West German leaders created by moving so quickly. And, furthermore, what exactly would be the nature of the resulting new country? One had to trust in the process.

To French reluctance had to be added that of other governments: the even deeper British reservations on the part of Prime Minister Margaret Thatcher and the total initial opposition of Gorbachev and Schevardnadze to German unification. For all three governments, despite the growing anti–German Democratic Republic (GDR) demonstrations, German unification was simply not on the agenda.

Contrasted with this was early and broad Bush administration confidence in Chancellor Kohl's political instincts and strong American support for German unification. This difference created strains within NATO, within the EC, and within the Franco–German partnership in particular. For example, President Mitterrand was reproached by the German government after a closely guarded meeting in Kiev with Gorbachev in early December 1989, from which rumors filtered that Mitterrand was hoping to cooperate with the Soviets in slowing the pace of unification. Against West German signals, Mitterrand then went ahead with a state visit to an apparently collapsing East German regime on December 20–21, 1989. The West Germans could only think that Mitterrand, received in East Berlin with pomp as the "first Western-allied head of state to visit the GDR," was trying to prop up the East German regime. Mitterrand's trip was politely termed "anachronistic" by the West German leaders, a delicate hint at the stakes involved. If, on the other hand, President Mitterrand was merely miscalculating the speed of German unification, he might have been hoping to achieve a position of protector for the East German opposition, as, several years earlier, he had done when he visited communist Czechoslovakia (receiving a then-dissident writer, later president of the republic, named Vaclav Havel). This, moreover, fits with Mitterrand's 1990 policy to act as Poland's advocate with unifying Germany, pressuring German Chancellor Helmut Kohl to guarantee that unified Germany would not question the existing Oder–Neisse border and would sign a treaty to that effect with Poland as a *pre*condition of unification. This was a useful intervention by Mitterrand, because although the German government had no intention of making territorial claims on Poland, Chancellor Kohl's procrastination in saying so publicly, for domestic electoral reasons involving an appeal to nationalist voters, caused international resentment.

Naturally, German leaders, for their part, did not appreciate Mitterrand's complicating their own strategies.[1] Yet France, as any Gaullist leader would have said, has a right to its own policy. Nevertheless, Kohl and Foreign Minister Hans-Dietrich Genscher were in the more delicate position, and Mitterrand's behavior risked some of the trust that had been built up in Franco–German relations.

It goes without saying that President Mitterrand, along with Prime Minister Thatcher and other EC leaders, was genuinely preoccupied by the geopolitical consequences of German unification in the European equation. In addition to the power result of unification, Mitterrand wanted to keep the process—the timing and the content—of German unification under control, both because of the explosive character of the situation itself, and because, while insisting repeatedly that France was "not afraid" of German unification, and that the Germans had the right, according to the Helsinki Final Act, to decide their future themselves, it would be beneficial for future European relations if Germany's leaders carried forward the unification process in a spirit of close consultation and even some deference to the allies. But Kohl and Genscher achieved a strict separation between the "external" and "internal" aspects of unification, and a strict limitation (which the United States, France and Britain accepted) of what would be decided by the Four Powers, including rejection of a Soviet suggestion that certain Four Power rights carry over for a transition period after unification.

Once President Mitterrand had to accept the German timetable, which presaged the most rapid possible unification of the two Germanies, one overriding goal emerged: to imbed German unification firmly in the Atlantic Alliance and in the European integration process. German unification, European unification and a strong Atlantic Alliance were—all the Western powers agreed, including the newly unified Germany—three integral parts of a whole. Thus French policy determinedly supported unified Germany's full membership in NATO. Mitterrand several times rebuffed suggestions by Soviet leaders Gorbachev and Schevardnadze that unified Germany should have a "French status" in NATO—that is, separate from NATO's integrated military command, though a full political member of the alliance. From the German side, to assuage French concern that unification might lead German policy eastward, away from plans for EC monetary and political union, Helmut Kohl joined Mitterrand's proposal that German unification and renewed EC "deepening" must go together. The Germans well understood that legitimacy for German unification required deeper EC integration. ,German unification and the unification of Europe, or at least of Community Europe, were two sides of the same coin.

As proof that French and Germans were again on the same wavelength after a period of political static, in April 1990 Mitterrand and Kohl proposed jointly to relaunch the movement toward EC political union. There were two purposes: first, to balance progress toward economic union, meaning the Single European Act's "1992 Project," completing the EC's integrated market and the basis for monetary union; and second, to give overall assurances that German unification would not derail European integration. It was this proposal, stimulated at the time by the tension over German unification, that turned into the political union treaty initialed at Maastricht in December 1991.

France and the New Germany

In any case, this kind of linkage between European integration and German unification was already German policy. Kohl and Genscher consistently emphasized that German unification had, in their view, to be "embedded" in European unification, and that NATO, including a unified German membership and continued U.S. military presence in Europe, was "vital" not only for U.S. policy but also for German policy. Kohl, for example, several times emphasized in the course of 1990 that neutrality, as Gorbachev and Schevardnadze were then suggesting, was not a price he would pay for German unification. Genscher explained to Germany's EC partners that if one was worried about growing German power, the best strategy was not to isolate Germany into some independent policy that the Germans didn't want anyway, but rather to tie Germany into a deepened, thickened, and more federalized EC—which the Germans would happily accept because, knowing very well the dangers and temptations for a dominant Germany, to be so tied up had been their proposal all along. Unification would, in other words, not change Germany's EC and western policies. Germany's interests as a democratic country were clear. The powerful slogan was often repeated that Germans wanted a "European Germany," not a "German Europe." Kohl's outlook, summarized by his political advisor Horst Teltschik, was that in German unification "the security of all sides should be increased, and that German unification should become the cornerstone of a stable European peace order."

> All thoughts of neutrality, demilitarization, and alliance or bloc disaffiliation he described as "old thinking." Kohl founded his position in the experience of German history, that peace, stability and security in Europe had always been guaranteed when Germany—the country in the middle of Europe—had lived with all its neighbors in firm ties, with contractual equality and mutually beneficial exchanges.[2]

Thus, as against French worries that unified Germany would resist deepening the EC—preferring to admit the eastern countries into a looser Community in order to shift the internal EC balance eastward and create a special German sphere of influence inside the EC itself—the Germans themselves adopted a cautious policy like the French about new memberships. The EC's commitment to deepening—to EMU and EPU—took priority. Eastern European countries were second, with associate member status as a sort of EC waiting room for Czechoslovakia, Poland and Hungary. "Association" could last a decade or more while their economies struggle to meet EC qualifications. The next enlargement of the EC will be several of the European Free Trade Association (EFTA) countries (Austria, Sweden, Finland etc.), with negotiations to begin in 1993–94.

As early as January 1988, Chancellor Kohl, observing the cracks in Eastern Europe, had proposed a joint Franco–German Ostpolitik, an "eastern policy," to the French. Mitterrand at the time held back. The Germans would doubtless be the leading force in it, and any vigorous Franco–German Ostpolitik might cost the French excessively. Mitterrand preferred to keep France's freedom of maneuver, even for a merely second-level, mainly diplomatic presence in Eastern Europe. One instance of Mitterrand's attempt to play a grand diplomatic role without the economic means was the disastrous Prague Conference on the "European Confederation," over which Czech president Havel and Mitterrand apparently quarrelled bitterly. Havel resented Mitterrand's seeming rich man's reluctance to admit the former communist Central European countries quickly into the EC. The offer of associate membership, ill-defined and for an indefinite term (Mitterrand shocked the Eastern Europeans by talking, a few weeks later, of "decades"), seemed to Havel and other Eastern European renaissance leaders a kind of brush-off. And this approach of caution and reluctance reminded observers of Mitterrand's earlier go-slow recommendation on German unification, suggesting why many commentators, rightly according to the evidence, thought France lagged during this period while others forced the pace of healing Europe's division. Did the French want to "overcome Yalta" or not?

Elsewhere in Central and Eastern Europe and the ex–Soviet Union a similar French policy was followed. The French supported all the revolutions, of course, but worried about destabilizing, overly rapid changes, meaning first of all no change of borders by violence and a geopolitical policy of maintaining the sovereignty of larger states.

Mitterrand's policy, though moving case-by-case, started by preferring the maintenance of existing states over self-determination for secession movements. In the most important case, this meant support right up to the end for Mikhail Gorbachev and for the retention of some kind of Soviet "center" against the final breakup of the U.S.S.R. During the August 1991 coup against Gorbachev, Mitterrand's preference for state continuity even led to a huge diplomatic blunder, an uncharacteristic error of precipitous reaction. Mitterrand assumed right away that the long-dreaded coup against Gorbachev had been successful. In a television interview Mitterrand called the perpetrators "the new leaders" of the Soviet Union, and read, with tired hopefulness, from a quick letter he had received from their spokesman, Gennadi Yaneyev, to the effect that "Soviet reform would continue." It was as if Mitterrand wanted to reassure French opinion that the worst had not happened and that France had a special diplomatic status, since the coup leaders were explaining themselves to Mitterrand. This was surely misjudgment masquerading as serenity.[3]

With the outbreak of war in Yugoslavia, French policy again preferred integrity of the state and negotiations for republic autonomy to the German policy of immediate recognition for self-declared Slovenian and Croatian independence. Some argued the French were just stuck to "history," including a traditional French bias toward "centralism." Another opinion was that French policy was being guided by an old quai d'Orsay foreign ministry bias toward Serbia and anti-German coalition, dating from World Wars I and II. In fact, French policy was not so anachronistic. It was rather a calculation that the principle of national self-determination, while fundamental, must be given limits lest it become self-destructive. It doesn't make sense, in terms of peace and development, to encourage the emergence of a host of economically unviable, politically and militarily threatened states; this is an especial danger in the Balkans. Geopolitical prudence, in realistic balance with the moral imperative of self-determination, requires limiting civil wars and propping up stability inside the Eastern European powder keg. The French approach to collapsing ex-Yugoslavia, which in retrospect may have been better than the German, was at the least forward-looking to the new dangers of the post–Cold War era.

Following the Maastricht EC summit meeting in December 1991 two events suddenly signalled what was called a "new German assertiveness." First, the Bundesbank, sensing inflation, unexpectedly raised German interest rates to their highest level in thirty years. Constitutionally independent of Bonn's political influence, the German central bank also could be hard-nosed about foreign interests. All of Germany's partners in the European monetary system (EMS) were immediately and sharply affected. The "German mark zone" governments, both inside the EMS and outside (e.g., Austria), felt obliged to follow the German lead. The Bank of France resentfully raised interest rates for the second time in a few months, whereas French policy under Finance Minister Pierre Bérégovoy had been trying for a year to break its chain to Bundesbank decisions. The French wanted to create a "strong franc" that would no longer in effect be a DM zone currency. The French and other governments criticized German "nationalist unilateralism." Bundesbank defenders argued that outsiders failed to appreciate how inflation-prone the German situation had become with the inflationary financial burdens of unification and with German trade-union wage demands at twice the inflation level.

In short, governments planning to ease monetary policy to fight recession were put under irresistible pressure by Bundesbank policy. They were whipsawed between the German interest rate hike and the U.S.

Federal Reserve Bank's lowering of the U.S. discount rate to 3.5 percent, the lowest in decades.

Second, Helmut Kohl took a controversial lead in dealing with civil war and disintegration in Yugoslavia. German Foreign Minister Hans-Dietrich Genscher, in a very hard EC debate, forced through diplomatic recognition of Croatia and Slovenia over the objections of several countries, in particular the French partner. The assertive German-led policy of immediate diplomatic recognition also contradicted U.S. and United Nations policies. These were to continue peace negotiations and preserve Yugoslavia's territorial integrity rather than to legitimate the secessions. Germany's unilateralism was, for the erstwhile political "dwarf," an unprecedented postwar foreign policy sortie.[4] Germany thereupon short-circuited the Council of Ministers' compromise resolution, which had a January 15 date, by announcing recognition by Christmas, just as Chancellor Kohl had earlier promised the Croats and Slovenes. True enough, some commentators, including some Americans who had been critical of German reticence in the past, commended Germany's decisiveness and new leadership role.

Is unified Germany, as some fear, a "Fourth Reich" in the making? Not likely, if one is talking literally about some sort of authoritarian-minded German zone in Europe, run from Berlin with an array of imperialistic ambitions. On the other hand, if one means a Germany for which time is working and in whose hands strength is accumulating, then, as one German official sympathetic to foreign worries said, "the Fourth Reich is coming unless others, first of all France and the United States, do something about it." The right strategy for this new version of containment, suggested by the Germans themselves, is to thrice bind German strength: into the EC, Atlantic–NATO, and pan-European (CSCE) frameworks. Unified Germany will be strong, and should be, but it needn't be hegemonic. The French–German partnership has, with certain exceptions, been remarkably coherent. It has originated most important undertakings in moving the EC forward.[5]

Nevertheless, concern about German power remains legitimate, because power in its nature expands unless balanced. And France in particular must balance Germany.

France's European Strategy

Because France is normally a presidential system, especially so in foreign affairs, the president's policy is, uniquely, France's policy. Other heads of government must consult; the French president, except in periods of cohabitation, can decide.

Has President Mitterrand had, since 1981, a statesman's view of international relations? Or has his policy been narrowly nationalist, in the interest of France alone? An interesting sketch of Mitterrand's broad view was given in his 1990 Bastille Day interview on French television:

> I will tell you what my plan, my *grand projet* is. It is to turn the whole of Europe into one space. Now the barriers and the walls have collapsed. The storm is not over . . . but we are getting there. One space, a single and vast market, and, at the same time, constant and structural links established among all the European countries. This is why I have talked about a Confederation. Within that Europe, I would like the Community of the 12 to strive for its own economic, monetary and political entity. In other words, within the single European space, I would like to see a strong nucleus capable of making political decisions collectively. This is the Community. Within the Community and Europe, I would like to see France—we are working at it, and it is not easy—become a model of economic development and social cohesion. That is my plan. Why complicate the issue?

This is genuine Mitterrand—a long-term view, vague yet plausible, historical with a capital H, of the concentric circles of French policy for Europe.

The problem is that this conception remains the French frame of reference even though conditions in Europe have changed radically in the meantime, even though it is clear to everyone, including the French, that new EC members are coming fairly quickly. The Germans, by contrast, while guarding relations with the French partner, already are reasoning in terms of a larger community in which the Franco–German couple will still be fundamental but whose axis of concerns and mix of peoples and national characteristics will be shifted more to the north and east. This does not mean the Eastern European countries first of all, but the present EFTA countries, beginning with Austria and Sweden, which will become members in the next few years, then Norway, perhaps Finland. (In December 1992 the Swiss, otherwise good candidates, voted in a referendum against joining the Community.) In reply to the argument that this will sharply change the Community's character, the Germans ask how this extension of the EC can be refused after they agreed to the "southern" enlargement—Spain, Portugal, Greece—in the 1980s, with all its costs and problems.

Was negotiation of the EC's Maastricht Treaty in December 1991 a success for French policy? Did it confirm France's large role in EC affairs?

In general the answer is certainly yes. Like everyone except the Germans, the French won their specific rounds while the Germans made concessions all around. But although it may not have won any single big point at Maastricht, Germany emerged strengthened overall because of its importance everywhere in the European process. German unification and the eastern laenders' shift to the West were wrapped up in EC integration, while Germany's increased diplomatic and political strength was paradoxically legitimized by Germany's solicitude to one and all.

From the French point of view, the two major Maastricht advances were (1) agreement on full monetary union, including a single currency, and (2) the beginnings of a common European security and defense policy. By accepting the goal of a single European currency, in principle by 1999 at the latest, the new "European Germany" would sacrifice its national treasure, the German mark, on the altar of Europeanism. On the other hand, in agreeing to an integrated military command for a Franco–German-centered European military entity in the Western European Union (WEU), France's Gaullist obsession with maintaining a strictly national defense was also sacrificed. This seemed to concern conventional forces only, but in January 1992 President Mitterrand, in an obviously premeditated declaration, said that the French nuclear force, the *force de frappe*, would inevitably, and rightly so, become part of the debates about a European defense.

Metaphorically, at the Maastricht negotiation French abandonment of military sovereignty was traded for German abandonment of monetary sovereignty. And Franco–German understanding proved itself the keystone of the global Maastricht set of compromises.

The Maastricht monetary union treaty, which outlines the second and third phases of monetary union, entails two major projects, both stunning when considered in historical perspective. The first is to create a single European currency, the ECU, by the end of the century. The second is to establish a European central bank, the Eurofed. A transition institution, a so-called European Monetary Institute, will pave the way for the Eurofed during the second phase of monetary union to begin in 1994.

The French have regarded European monetary union, paradoxical as it seems at first, as a way to regain some control over their own monetary policy. In the EMS, the system in place since 1979, French interest rates, as shown earlier, usually must follow Bundesbank decisions on German interest rates. It has been almost as if France were a secondary economy in a German mark zone. With a single currency, on the other hand, the French will have a voice in "pooled sovereignty" Eurofed decisions on interest rates. How much this will actually increase French government control over French monetary policy is uncertain. In any case, while France's national monetary autonomy is in principle being signed away in the Maastricht Treaty, in practice it was already gone. The goal of monetary union, despite its skeptics, points toward a substantial, real transformation of national sovereignty in a key area of government policy. And the supposedly archnationalist French wanted this so much that in the final negotiating session President Mitterrand proposed, and won, making the start of the single European currency automatic in 1999 if it is not launched in 1997.

The number of countries able to join will result from meeting certain "convergence criteria" set out in the treaty: low inflation rates, low interest rates, and low budget deficit and public debt levels. Ironically, when Maastricht was signed, with Germany suffering the financial burdens of unification, France was the only big EC country that would have met these criteria, a point of pride for the French Socialist government and especially so given memories of 1981–85.

The French and other economically efficient states also won adoption of a beginning of EC social policy legislation. This included health and safety standards, maximum working hours, and so on. It will be good for workers, but will also raise production costs in the less efficient economies. A controversial British veto prevented putting social policy in the treaty itself, which would have made it a legal obligation for each of the twelve members. This forced the other eleven EC governments to make a special protocol on social policy, creating another instance of a "variable speed" Europe "à la carte."

French commitment to an EC social policy is inspired by social democratic thinking but also by political pragmatism: If European integration is to have democratic legitimacy in the different countries, workers must feel it benefits them directly. Economic and political union will not succeed unless Europe has a social face as well as a corporate profile.

The British government, on the other hand, gave two arguments for refusing a legally binding EC social policy. First, treaty-defined social policy would amount to "reinvigorating socialism by the Brussels back door," creating new bureaucracies and re-creating the excessive power of British unions that Margaret Thatcher's government had reduced in the 1980s. Second, Prime Minister John Major argued, without much proof, that Britain's opt-out on social policy would dampen British production costs, making the United Kingdom a special haven for foreign investment.

The French also succeeded at Maastricht in two instances when they directly opposed German proposals. First, the German desire for a more powerful European Parliament, with "co-decision," veto authority in EC legislation, was deflected by the French. Mitterrand's negotiating instructions on the Parliament's powers, his delegate said, had been simple and brief: "the least possible." The Germans wanted, by strengthening the EP, to begin the process of balancing and decentralizing the EC political system.[6] Second, the Germans asked for eighteen additional EP seats, in order to represent the former east German laender. The French again led the counteraction, insisting that the rule of parity among the four biggest countries—Germany, France, Britain and Italy—should not be violated.

Innovations in foreign policy and security policy produced remarkable decisions, even if far off or just improbable in implementation. The goal of a Common Foreign and Security Policy (CFSP) was agreed upon, to go much beyond the merely consultative European Political Cooperation (EPC) that has existed for over a decade. However, again at British insistence, qualified majority decision making—the mechanism of a joint foreign and security policy—is to be limited to *implementation* of decisions, not the decisions themselves.[7] An additional proviso specified that the EC Council will decide, by unanimous vote, what sorts of actions will have majority voting—in other words, the Council will decide by unanimous vote what to decide by majority vote!

What is clear from all this, besides lack of clarity, is that majority voting in EC foreign and security policy, thus a genuinely "common" EC policy, will be difficult and perhaps ultimately impossible to achieve. But merely agreeing on the goal is a beginning. As General de Gaulle once wrote, "the future lasts a long time," and the worst, of course, is never certain.

On defense policy, the Maastricht summit of December followed on the November 1991 NATO summit meeting. There the Americans had agreed with fingers crossed that so long as the leading role in European security remained with NATO, the United States would not object to elevating the WEU, made up of nine European nations without the United States, into a formal connection with the European Community.[8] The Maastricht political union treaty was then able to say that the future "European Union" will have a common defense policy based in the WEU, and that the WEU will have a formal connection to NATO, which for the French implied some form of equality between the two. U.S. policy makers worried that the WEU could become a permanent separate European caucus within NATO, which would complicate decision making and create ill will by making the United States odd man out. Despite European assurances, American concern continues that the Europeans, or at least the French and some others, are tacitly trying to squeeze U.S. influence in Atlantic Alliance policy making.

The Maastricht decision about an eventual common defense policy did not in itself provide for any specifically European military force, but the option is clear. France and Germany in 1987 began putting together a Franco–German 5,000-man brigade. Despite its small size and the fact that the problems of mixing nationalities were being tackled at the lowest level, the French–German operation was derided as "a language school with rifles." Yet the project has continued and been expanded, with Belgians and others set to participate, to establish a "Eurocorps" of 35,000 troop strength. In truth, genuinely mixed fighting forces, binational or multinational, are political crowd pleasers more than effective fighting units. On the other hand, a multinational integrated WEU command, plus standardization policies—as in NATO and in coordination with NATO—could have real military value. But all this is five to ten years away at best, as indicated by the awful NATO and EC problems reacting to the civil wars in former Yugoslavia. From the French point of view the Eurocorps operation has an extra meaning, a dimension of what could be called post-Gaullism. If, as planned, the Eurocorps is eventually given to the multinational WEU as its military arm, French forces would, for the first time, be permanently placed under a non-national command. The French are thus promising to do for a European force what they have refused, since de Gaulle's withdrawal in 1966, to do for NATO. To put it another way, the French have signalled that they are willing to pool military sovereignty with a European force, whereas they refuse to rejoin the integrated NATO military command because, in their view, American influence will always be dominant in NATO. Of course, with the Soviet Union's disappearance the issue of France's rejoining NATO's integrated command is not a priority on anybody's list. And, in spite of all signs to the contrary, all European governments—even the French—want the United States to remain militarily engaged in Europe. It is just politically convenient, especially for the French, to be able to play both sides of the street so long as the essential is not put into question.

A European force does not yet exist, and NATO, even if it remains the overall background European guarantee, is not yet an answer to the real post–Cold War security problems in Europe, no longer because of the out-of-area problem but because U.S. administrations shy from involvement in land wars on the European continent, as the conflict in Bosnia shows. The mission of a separate WEU force would be to implement any European Union military decisions and, in particular, to have a force that could act in Europe outside the NATO area, although European refusal to act militarily in Bosnia indicates the theory is not yet ready to be practiced. If this changes, WEU troops would be "double-hatted," meaning available to NATO also, and NATO–WEU coordination would be tight.

Are the French still Gaullist about the United States? Part of the French mind still believes de Gaulle's assumption that one day American isolationist tendencies will lead to a unilateral military disengagement from Europe. However, a more plausible view, gaining ground in French foreign policy circles, is that de Gaulle's assumption no longer holds in a world of such intense interdependence, and that Atlantic relationships of all kinds are so thick that the American security commitment to Europe, at some level, is virtually permanent. French policy, therefore, is to keep the United States committed to a *rebalanced* NATO, while simultaneously preparing for the contingency of possible withdrawal—thus the WEU. At the same time, the goal is continuously to squeeze American capacity to limit French and European freedom of action.

So recent French–American diplomatic conflicts—about NATO–WEU security "architecture" and about farm subsidies in the GATT Uruguay Round—should be understood as the latest episodes in a long-run love–hate relationship. Secretary of State James Baker exasperatedly queried French Foreign Minister Roland Dumas in their May 1992 meeting: "Well, finally, are you [the French] for us or against us?" Had Dumas replied honestly, the answer would have been "Yes," the old ambiguity, trying to have it both ways, one of the weapons of the weaker power in a geopolitical relationship. Underneath the French game playing is a quite well understood recognition that France's interest is to keep the United States in Europe and to safeguard the American alliance. To the French the diplomatic games over influence and prestige that so infuriate American officials are absolutely normal in an international system based on power factors that relegate France to a permanent second-class position. The French, of course, understand full well why "playing the game" so exasperates France's allies and partners. But what else is there to do, if France is to "exist" diplomatically?

French security policy in the 1990s still wants to have it both ways, with two new caveats. First, security threats to Western Europe have been radically reduced. Second, there is now no *necessary* contradiction between NATO and the WEU, except, obviously, the potential for a political one if the United States decides that the WEU states are unfairly having it both ways. In 1992 French Defense Minister Pierre Joxe, in a quid pro quo for U.S. acceptance of the WEU's attachment to the EC, said that France would increase its participation in NATO military affairs by attending the military committee and the defense planning committee, yet without rejoining the integrated command structure. Thus whether France is still "Gaullist" is today a largely moot issue. If we take de Gaulle's positions of three decades ago as a measuring rod, very much has changed. On the other hand, a certain Gaullist "attitude" remains. In security matters, the issue of a European military force leads sooner or later to the future of the French nuclear force de frappe. Will European integration meet even the sacrosanct independent French nuclear force?

On January 10, 1992, at a national forum on the results of the Maastricht summit negotiations, President Mitterrand surprised everyone by raising the issue publicly for the first time of modifying the doctrine and strategy of the force de frappe. "The beginnings of a common defense," he said, "raise problems that have not yet been resolved and which will have to be resolved. I am thinking in particular of nuclear weapons." The British and French forces "have a clear doctrine for their national defense. Is it possible to imagine a European doctrine? That question will very quickly become one of the major issues in the construction of a European defense."

Indeed it had long been argued that a purely national French nuclear force is in the long run hard to square with the idea of a common European defense. Mitterrand, asking rhetorically whether a complementary European doctrine was conceivable for national nuclear forces was putting a question to which he evidently already had his own answer. A French or Franco–British nuclear umbrella could indeed be raised over the entire Community, a kind of "European extended deterrence" that would keep national control of decision making. Surprising to all those who thought the French could never Europeanize the force de frappe, the confrontation of old Gaullist defense doctrines with new European realities has been placed on the French agenda by the president himself. The great debate to reexamine the Gaullist defense consensus will apparently take place. At the same national meeting, Jacques Delors, president of the EC Commission and a potential presidential candidate, went even further than Mitterrand: "If one day the European Community has a very strong Political Union," he said, "then why not transfer nuclear weapons to that political authority?"[9] A daring view, but would Delors keep it were he to sit, not in the EC's Brussels headquarters, but in the French president's Elysée Palace? And what would happen to the idea of extended EC deterrence if the Community expands east and north to sixteen, twenty, or twenty-four members? Hard questions about exactly whom to protect, against whom and in what situations. Answers would require many years to evolve.

European Citizenship and National Identity

The Maastricht Treaty, finally, also creates a new legal "European citizenship" of the "European Union" (as the treaty renames the Community). EC country passports several years ago already added "European Community" at the top of national covers; but the new European citizenship is an actual legal concept with rights and responsibilities. One aspect, for example, will be a right of EU citizens residing in another EU country to vote in the "foreign" country's local elections and in European parliament elections. This European-wide voting right means that, in addition to revising national sovereignty concepts, European integration is broaching a parallel revision of the meaning of citizenship. Not by idealism but by practice, European integration is pushing the evolution of basic domestic and international political boundaries.

In a study of the French immigration question in relation to problems of defining citizenship and nationality, Patrick Weil says that "One who has the right to vote is French and a citizen."[10] The operative factor is the right to vote, and the voting right expresses both nationality and citizenship. But then what will happen, Weil asks, if, as the Socialists and Mitterrand have proposed, non-EC *foreign workers* resident in France are given the right to vote in municipal elections? Or, if the EPU treaty is implemented on this point, what will happen to citizenship and national identity if Europeans resident in another country than their own are given the right to vote in local and European Parliament elections? Would such people become *citizens* of France? French nationals? Whatever is decided, the future seems to hold a blurring of old distinctions of citizenship and nationality in France and in the other Community countries.

And what about the French peoples' attachment to national identity? Is French national feeling a dying sentiment? The map of the September 20, 1992 referendum result on the Maastricht Treaty (see p. 131) partly reflects an anti-Socialist, anti-Mitterrand, antiforeigner, antirecession vote. But to some extent it also indicates the division between Gaullist and Europeanist sentiments in French political culture, or at least how widely skeptical sentiments about the EC exist. But this is not the same thing as a decline of national feeling. De Gaulle had once written that, "given its history, what will become of the French nation—which founded itself on an exalted idea of its grandeur and its singularity—if it no longer harbors either ambition or political debates?"[11] Does European integration mark the "end of History" in France? No. But the nature of the national debate must and will change.

One needs to imagine, if and when a common European currency is actually in peoples' wallets; if and when European Union citizens living in a second country can vote in local elections and European elections, while voting in national elections at home; if and when the European Court of Justice is accessible to individuals: There is no end of history in sight yet, for old France and for old Europe.

As for erstwhile enemies, France and Germany: Riven with rivalry, is the "Franco–German couple" likely to survive? No doubt. Geopolitically and in the abstract, the demise of communism would seem to make possible the pre–World War I French *alliance de revers* (counteralliance) strategy of using Russia as a counterweight to Germany.[12] But the foundations even of geopolitics change over time. The Franco–German reconciliation and all the various bonds of European integration area are, despite immense obstacles and all shortcomings, becoming new geopolitical facts of life.

It is not surprising that there have been conflicts and misunderstandings in the "Franco–German couple," especially in the suddenness of German unification. It *is* surprising that French–German cooperation is holding up so well, not that there are difficulties. The fact remains that each country is the other's most important partner. Even if the United States remains the only complete superpower and Germany's key security ally, and even if the geopolitical center of the EC moves eastward, building the French–German relationship is, as one high German official put it, the most important task for each country's diplomacy in the next period. Broadly speaking, the two countries together embody all of the major contrasting characteristics of the other EC countries: North–South, industrial–agricultural, Protestant–Catholic, and so on. So what France and Germany can agree, others can usually accept. France—*le fait français*—has been a point of reference and political compass in the Community for Spain, Italy, Portugal, Greece and, to some extent, even Belgium. In an enlarged Community, countries such as Sweden and Norway, and especially Poland, would see France as a natural partner in dealings with Germany, for historical reasons not yet out of mind. French leadership, given German unification and the new German assertiveness, is not likely to be stronger in the next few years than it had been until 1993, with a politically strong and canny President Mitterrand at the helm. The question is rather whether French influence, given the domestic leadership succession underway in 1993–95, can be as strong as before.

The conservative Balladur government, with Alain Juppé (RPR) as foreign minister and François Léotard (UDF) as defense minister, in its first months in office in 1993 clearly wanted basic continuity with President Mitterrand's foreign policies. Foreign policy, it seemed, was going to be the smoothest part of the cohabitation relationship. Security policy in particular is likely to see changes only at the margins for the next few years. The burning European security issue is of course what to do from the outside about the wars in Bosnia. Balladur is not likely to be an interventionist. He agrees with Mitterrand—and France's EC partners and the United States—on minimal involvement.

On the level of organizing European security as a whole in the wake of Maastricht, at the EC's Copenhagen summit of June 22, 1993, Prime Minister Balladur proposed a "European Stability Agreement" to supersede Mitterrand's idea for a European "Confederation." Mitterrand's idea was the more Gaullist, since it was specifically designed without U.S. membership, whereas Balladur's European stability pact invites American and Canadian participation because, the text reads, these countries "have a large interest in European stability and security." If Eduoard Balladur seems to be more congenial than Mitterrand to the United States in geopolitical matters, it may be in part to give himself more room to bargain hard with the United States on trade matters. On these hotly contested foreign trade issues, including the GATT Uruguay Round, EC–U.S. issues and bilateral problems, Eduoard Balladur seemed likely to be as forceful as Mitterrand in fighting for France's and the EC's interests in commercial and monetary negotiations.

After the Cold War

Is France for all that a "loser" in the end of the Cold War? Anton DePorte asked in 1990 the heretical question whether the overcoming of the Yalta system really would "have pleased de Gaulle."

> Do the long-term benefits *to France* of a process which he advocated and promoted so eloquently seem likely to be as great as he thought they would be? Would France's interests really be better served, as de Gaulle believed, by the overcoming of the division of Europe? Would France's independence and rank, its security and influence, for which de Gaulle fought, really be better affirmed in the kind of post-Yalta Europe he envisaged than in the two-bloc system of which it was so long—and not only in de Gaulle's time—the least contented Western member?"[13]

This sort of realist evaluation is not so much wrong as incomplete in what it considers basic. France is not so much a loser but a state that pays a price in Europe's evolution "beyond Yalta."[14] There are also important gains for France—domestic, international, short-term, long-term, economic, psychological, direct, indirect. An exclusively geopolitical and national—in a word, classical—definition of gains and losses cannot account for the attractions of European integration for the European peoples and nations, if not for states qua states. Pure classical concepts intrinsically undervalue the benefits of European integration, as earlier they underestimated the chances for getting beyond Yalta.

What has already been built in the EC, plus the Maastricht plans for a single currency, a Eurofed, a European citizenship, and a common foreign and security policy, amount to a partial transformation—at least in Europe—of national sovereignty and of the nation-state itself. It demands of our thinking (see the concluding chapter) a capacity to break up and reassemble the classical geopolitical unit of national power, according to new facts.

And even in pure power terms the French national dilemma is not zero-sum but rather to find the best, or the least bad alternative in partnership with other states. For geopolitical reasons—relative industrial might, relative population weight and dynamism—the strength of *la France seule* (France alone) was fragile and declining even in the former divided Europe. The French search for grandeur and rank was increasingly perceived as an obvious mismatch of a goal and inadequate means. Furthermore the personal or leadership factor as such can be far from irrelevant: De Gaulle himself was French rank and grandeur. But de Gaulle was of a rare, classical breed, charismatic in the true Weberian sense. With time it becomes less and less meaningful to measure French presidents against one's own "certain idea" of Charles de Gaulle.[15]

Conclusion

France in the new Europe may well continue to be "only" the second-ranking power, and of course that is not certain itself. But France will surely be stronger and more prosperous than it would have been over the long term in the old Europe. Moreover, "the French," as one senior French diplomat asserts, "are less menaced than they imagine. The Germans don't want hegemony. That isn't their policy. What they want is the possibility of a policy of independence when something is very important to them." Geopolitically, it might be better to put the question another way: Can Germany, with its advantages, avoid hegemony?

Endnotes

1. On all these events a good source is the memoir–diary by Kohl's foreign policy advisor Horst Teltschik, *329 Tage* (Berlin: Siedler, 1991).

2. Teltschik, op. cit., pp. 244–245. For a good overview of the Franco–German couple over the long postwar term, see Julius W. Friend, *The Linchpin: French–German relations, 1950–1990* (New York: Praeger, 1991).

3. Yaneyev's letter was in fact sent to several foreign leaders. Later, when Gorbachev's memoir *The Coup* appeared, there was a new flap. In an undercorrected foreign edition, Gorbachev spoke of "disappointment"—still a "painful memory" he said—that Mitterrand did not telephone him as soon as possible after his liberation, as opposed to George Bush's quick reaction. In other language editions, the pertinent sentence did not appear. Gorbachev unconvincingly

denied, in a fence-mending meeting with Mitterrand, that he had ever written the sentence. Mitterrand of course pretended to believe him. It was small potatoes, but a large question, for both, of saving political face.

4. French Foreign Minister Roland Dumas emphasized that unilateral German recognition would be damaging for EC *internal* relations, and others stressed the irony of Germany's adopting at Maastricht the goal of a common foreign policy, then taking such a unilateral attitude in the first post-Maastricht crisis.

5. See, for example, Axel Krause, *Inside the New Europe* (New York: HarperCollins, 1991).

6. Here France and Britain agreed, for different reasons, on keeping the European Council at the center of EC decision making. The British resisted any move toward "federalism" and even got this "F word" excised from the treaty preamble. British tradition understands federalism to mean centralization, as in the submission of Scotland to England, whereas to the Germans federalism means precisely the opposite, decentralization as in the Second Reich.

   One French argument against giving the EP major new powers is that the European Council—the heads of state and government—is the most legitimate EC instance, because the most directly elected. This of course applies to the French president more than to any prime minister. In fact, no French government could accept a powerful EC Parliament without simultaneously legitimizing substantial new powers for the *French* Parliament (see Chapter 3). Each EC government, it seems, tends to propose its own political system as the model for the Community's institutions!

7. "Qualified" majority voting means a majority of "constitutional" weight, set somewhere between simple majority and unanimity. In Council decisions the "qualified" majority is set at around 70 percent. In the current total of 74 total votes, at least 54 votes, cast by at least 8 countries, are needed to prevail. The four major countries—Germany, France, the UK and Italy—have 10 votes each; Spain has 8 votes; Belgium, the Netherlands and Greece have 5 votes; Portugal, Ireland and Denmark have 3 votes; Luxembourg has 2 votes. Thus, no single state can have a veto (in principle this revokes the Luxembourg Compromise made with de Gaulle in 1966). A "blocking minority" requires either two large and two small states, or one large and three small states, or various combinations of small states. Voting shares are revised whenever the EC expands: The total number of votes and member states' voting shares increase.

8. A competing U.S.-inspired British–Italian proposal, that the WEU should exist "equidistant" between the EC and NATO—meaning that it would not become the military arm of the EC and thus not be a future competitor of NATO—was set aside.

9. *Le Monde*, January 12–13, 1992, p. 1, for both the Mitterrand and Delors remarks.

10. Weil, *La France et ses étrangers*, p. 300.

11. Schnapper, op. cit., p. 363.

12. This is a *maurrasien* idea, found in Charles Maurras's *Kiel et Tanger: La république française devant l'Europe* (The republic of France faces Europe) (1895, 1st ed.), brilliantly reanalyzed and critiqued in Pierre Hassner, "The View from Paris," in Lincoln Gordon et al., *Eroding Empire: Western Relations with Eastern Europe* (Washington, D. C.: Brookings Institution, 1987), pp. 190–191.

13. Anton DePorte, "De Gaulle's Europe: Playing the Russian Card," *French Politics and Society*, 8 no. 4 (Fall 1990): 39.

14. In the same sense, Lech Walesa feared that Poland "would pay the price" for the disappearance of the Berlin Wall, because West German policy and economic aid would naturally concentrate on the former East Germany. Horst Teltschik, Kohl's advisor, writes in his recent memoir that the German reply to Walesa sounded thin, "because at bottom I knew that he was right." *329 Tage*, op. cit., p. 16.

15. See Tiersky, "Mitterrand, France, and Europe," *French Politics and Society*, 9 no. 1 (Winter 1991): 9–25.

Conclusion

France and the Future of the European Nation-State

> The *malaise* about identity re-
> sults more from domestic
> politics [than from France's inter-
> national position]. . . . Over time,
> the French search for distinctive-
> ness and autonomy may transfer
> its focus from France to a
> Europe in which France will con-
> tinue to play an important role.
> Thus, at last, France would be-
> come an "ordinary" European na-
> tion, encased in a highly original
> Community. An unromantic
> prospect, but a likely fate.
>
> —Stanley Hoffmann, "French
> Dilemmas and Strategies in
> the New Europe," Harvard
> Center for European Studies,
> Working Paper No. 38, 1992,
> pp. 34–35

French Nationalism: Martyr or Forerunner?

Contemporary France is an
example, a most intense one,
of the internationalization of
the most developed nation-
states in the late twentieth
century. French develop-
ment is affected by several
factors at once: by the evolution of technology, by
France's geography and key
role in the European Com-
munity, and by unavoidable
processes of economic, cultural and political cross-
penetration in an open, liberal and competitive world
system. In conclusion to this

study of France's "enlistment in the ranks" of the highly developed democratic nation-states, as François Furet calls it, I want to point to two issues regarding which France and the EC nation-states are nothing less than a vanguard of world political development. The first is the transformation of national sovereignty, meaning the long-forecast movement, at least in Community Europe, "beyond the nation-state." The second is a few remarks about the effect of international integration on domestic society.

"The critical issue for every student of world order," Stanley Hoffmann wrote three decades ago, "is the fate of the nation-state."[1] Considered from the vantage point of the nuclear balance of terror, the preeminence of national sovereignty in the international order was, he asserted, "dangerous for peace" and "illogical for welfare." On the one hand, nuclear war threatened to emerge, probably accidentally, from some crisis of the permanently dangerous superpower rivalry. On the other hand, the "illogic" of the nation-state for welfare was its economic nationalism and protectionism, which limited the benefits of integration already evident in the EEC's first decade.

In the post–Cold War era, the nation-state as a geopolitical entity is no longer so "dangerous for peace," at least in the important sense that, with Soviet communism and the superpower nuclear rivalry gone, the dangers of nuclear holocaust and world war have been dramatically diminished. To be sure, a sudden proliferation of smaller wars is the new fear in its place. But, in spite of the Gulf War, Somalia, and the wars in the former Soviet Union and former Yugoslavia, the prediction of unlimited small wars remains an open question.

On the other hand, in an increasingly interdependent international order the nation-state is not only illogical for welfare, but also increasingly so, at least in all those ways in which trade and human and cultural contacts, including international human rights—such as rights of immigration, asylum, and the right to rescue—are essential to welfare.

On this score, the French, in spite of allegedly Cartesian thinking, and despite the fact that other European states may be even more protectionist, are generally still perceived by foreigners as less "logical" than others, with less permeable frontiers and cultural mores. History here turns out to be a novel kind of scarlet letter, branding the French with a "G," meaning that France's Gaullist reputation for nationalist pretentiousness and stubbornness lives on so strongly, and somewhat unjustly, because it is part of a much more ancient nationalism. From "the forty kings who made France," through the armies of the Revolution and the Empire, the French infatuation with their own history produced a national narcissism, in addition to a lot of trouble for other peoples. The French, as a nation, have carried unusually heavy national baggage, a particularly sticky national cult of the past, which, in Marx's image, can weigh "like a nightmare on the brains of the living."

French nationalism today is both a martyr and a forerunner. The fading of French exceptionalism is a martyrdom to the cause of preserving national differences; France's bowing to the inevitable is an adumbration of the admixing of national and international elements in a complex, layered local and world culture. The passing of "exceptionalism" feels to the older generations of French people like a burying of part of one's identity. To the middle-aged commentator on French politics, it feels something of the same. It is as if "the Madonna in the frescoes" were put into motion to do the daily tasks of living, becoming less exotic, less mysterious and even less captivating.

France and the Future of the State

In using our analysis of French development to make a few concluding remarks on the future of the national state in Europe, two concepts are crucial: the European Community as a pooling of sovereignty, and qualified majority voting as the outstanding mechanism of "pooled" sovereignty.

National Sovereignty and Pooled Sovereignty

From European integration is emerging, in gradual and limited doses, a series of transformations of national sovereignty. The result over decades will no doubt be, not the disappearance of national sovereignty, but its evolution. Likewise, the "future of the nation-state" will be, not its disappearance, but its transformation. In fact, both aspects of the nation-state—the state and the nation—are evolving. The European national state, the supreme authority in a national territory in modern times, increasingly shares or pools elements of its supreme power of decision. Modern ideas of the nation are also being put into question, as we have seen earlier in our discussions of immigration, nationality and growing multiculturalism. The same issue is raised in the Maastricht Treaty's creation of a European citizenship, not to replace but to complement national citizenship. What is planned today for tomorrow is far from what even some of the 1960s enthusiasts of European integration predicted, that getting beyond the nation-state would not involve a new kind of political community, but probably merely "an obscuring of the boundaries between the system of international organizations and the environment provided by member states."[2]

The single integrated market, with its common external frontier for goods, services and tariffs, is the example of already achieved pooled sovereignty in the EC. In commercial terms, each state's external borders have become the external borders for every other state in the Community. Each government relies on every other government to uphold the Community's pooled sovereign standards in trade and economic matters. The exception to this rule, as was noted earlier, is that there is not yet entirely free movement of people. Implementing the Schengen Agreement, if this occurs fully, will mean that each state will act as a sovereign filter of people coming into the EC for all the other states, and that borders between the EC states will be totally abolished for people as well as goods, services and capital. Even if one or more EC states, such as Britain or Denmark stays out of the network, the principle of pooled sovereignty will have become a reality.

Sovereignty and "Qualified Majority" Voting

National sovereignty can be transformed, in one sense, merely by avoiding it, meaning that in certain cases national sovereignty doesn't need to be either lost or kept: It can be circumvented or, more easily, abolished. Sovereignty may simply "disappear" when functions that sovereignty used to control become regulated by mechanisms other than states or political entities. A good example is the operation of international monetary markets, in which the free flow of capital and the aggressiveness of international speculators have to a considerable extent taken away monetary policy sovereignty from control by national state governments.[3] In another sense, as we have just seen, national sovereignty can be transformed, but not lost, by pooling it. States cede individual sovereignty, not to another state but to an international organism or network of which they are members. The European Community, soon to be the European Union, is the premier example in the world today. In certain policy areas nation-states retain sovereign authority, while in other areas sovereignty will be pooled and vested in the new collective entity. The EC as an institution is developing sovereignty with regard to tariffs and monetary affairs, while the individual states retain sovereignty in foreign policy and defense.

But unwise is any analyst who presumes that today's tendency is fated to continue on to a "natural" conclusion. In the two years since the signature of the Maastricht Treaty, Europe has seen a falloff of the momentum for integration, and a certain "renationalization" of national policies. It is certainly possible to disbelieve that the transfer of sovereignty beyond the European national state will move very far at all in foreign policy and security matters. And eminent commentators predict that not even the single European currency and Central Bank will be achieved. Perhaps so, perhaps not. This book is not a forecast.

The growth of "pooled" national sovereignty in the EC is, in a practical sense, equivalent to the growth of "qualified majority" voting, as opposed to the original requirement of unanimity, in the Council of Ministers. The extent to which European decisions become qualified majority decisions will be a decisive measure of the transformation of sovereignty.

This is not to say that the best solutions are European solutions. There is no *telos* in European political development, no necessary endpoint to which contemporary evolution is tending. Integration may halt at a certain point, and it may even unravel. (Pessimistic observers have been predicting this for decades.) Or it may actually go ahead toward pooled sovereignty in foreign policy, security and defense matters, as the Maastricht Treaty would have it. In any case the time frame is almost certainly much longer than Maastricht's unreasonably optimistic calendar.

France and the Future of the Nation

In considering the nation in the matter of moving beyond the nation-state, Hoffmann aptly cited Comte's maxim *On ne détruit que ce qu'on remplace*, that is, "Nothing is truly destroyed until it is replaced." Any new "formula" for getting beyond the nation-state "would," he wrote, "have to provide world order, of course, but also the kind of social organization in which leaders, elites, and citizens feel at home."[4]

For almost every other people, "home" is the nation and "house" is the state. But France is different. It has been a characteristic of the people, as we quoted Charles Pasqua earlier, that in France the nation and the state have been so tightly entwined. Some French, it is true, hate European integration precisely because they believe that to give up the traditional French state is somehow to give up national identity at the same time. Is European integration thus insidiously rendering the French people in some new sense of the term "homeless"? Are the French a people and a nation—more than just a "sack of potatoes" manipulated by a centralized and sometimes heroic state?[5]

It will be important to get beyond positing issues of European integration only as dichotomies: national sovereignty or its abolition, nationalism or cosmopolitanism. Today, it has become clear that there are intermediate solutions and, practically speaking, the *only* possible solutions are intermediate. Neither national sovereignty nor international integration will collapse, for both are useful to the nation-state and to the welfare of peoples. European integration will not destroy national identities, but modify and intensify them. The French will not disappear but evolve. France, *la belle France*, will be both less and more than in the past.

Raymond Aron, in *Steadfast and Changing*, began with Montesquieu's famous response to the query, "How is it possible to be French?" "Neither more nor less difficult than to be Persian," said Montesquieu. In other words, the Frenchman and the Persian are, or were, equally mystifying beasts—as are all peoples for all other peoples. And Aron added, "But the lesson is never learned and perhaps it should not be. When the 'other' ceases to surprise us will probably be the day man will have lost faith in himself."[6]

Hélas!, the French are less "fantastic" than they once were. To the especial surprise of cultural historians, the French can now even be held to high standards of economic performance and financial discipline, as did the eminent French economist Jean Fourastié, in *Les Trentes glorieuses* (1979). Fourastie's book pointed out that during the "thirty glorious years" of 1945 to 1973, only Federal Germany, Switzerland and Japan increased production and prosperity more rapidly than did France. This was quite an achievement, and Fourastié's documentation of it sparkled with national satisfaction.

But not often remembered from the book is Fourastié's "Afterword," a searing indictment of French shortcomings and missed opportunities during those same years:

> If I have been able to call the thirty years separating the 1945 and 1974 censuses "glorious," this was because I was considering them from the point of view of raising the standard and quality of life of the French people. I must add that they do not seem so to me—far from it—in any other domain. Not regarding philosophical thinking, nor in the arts or letters, nor regarding spiritual life, nor regarding demography, national vitality or virtue. . . . We have not even, with our economic prosperity, reconstituted the personality and social consensus of our people. An attack from outside would leave us even more cowards than that of 1940. . . . As for foreign policy, in spite of the brilliant work of Monnet, we haven't been able to assume, or to keep, the place in Europe, thus in the world, that until 1954 our partners *wanted to make for us*, and that our renewal allowed us to occupy.[7]

Even if pointing to real problems, Fourastié was without a doubt extremely harsh on his compatriots. Since de Gaulle relaunched the trajectory of French politics in 1958, much has been accomplished even if, as always, more remains to be done. France has deep problems, but a comparative perspective must lead to the conclusion that the French have done worse than some peoples in some respects, and better than others in other respects. No fair-minded analysis should conclude from any one of France's problems that its condition is infernal.

The process of European integration offers one last, paradoxical meaning for the French. European integration is a harness that, despite being onerous, also reduces the freedom of action of any single nation to backslide or decline. It is a goad to success, or at least a drag on the temptation to slack off. Even if they were tempted, the French do not have the freedom for national decline of an earlier era. And this must be an invisible source of confidence over the long run.

The quality of French development will depend, naturally, on the French themselves, who are a changing people, always capable of renewal, yet steadfast (for better and worse) in basic ways.

Endnotes

1. See Hoffmann, *Decline or Renewal? France since the 1930s,* p. 363.

2. See *Decline or Renewal?*, p. 397, here quoting Ernst Haas, *Beyond the Nation-State* (Stanford, Calif.: Stanford University Press, 1964), p. 29.

3. See John Goodman, *Monetary Sovereignty: The Politics of Central Banking in Western Europe* (Ithaca, N.Y.: Cornell University Press, 1992), and Peter Kenen, *EMU After Maastricht* (Washington, D. C.: Group of Thirty, 1992).

4. Op. cit., p. 364.

5. To coin a French specialist's dictum: Tell me what you think of May '68, and I'll tell you who you are!

6. Raymond Aron, *Immuable et changeante*, p. 23.

7. Op. cit., p. 277.

Suggested Readings

Adams, William James. *Restructuring the French Economy*. Washington, D. C.: The Brookings Institution, 1989.

Albert, Michel. *Capitalisme contre capitalisme* (Capitalism against capitalism). Paris: Editions du Seuil, 1991.

Aron, Raymond. *Immuable et changeante. De la IVe à la Ve république*. Paris: Calmann-Levy, 1959. Published in English as *France Steadfast and Changing: The Fourth to the Fifth Republic*. Cambridge, Mass.: Harvard University Press, 1960.

———. *The Elusive Revolution*. New York: Praeger, 1969.

———. *Mémoires. 50 années de réflexion politique* (Memoirs: Fifty years of political reflection). Paris: Julliard, 1983.

———. *The Opium of the Intellectuals*. New York: W. W. Norton, 1957.

———. *Progress and Disillusion: The Dialectics of Modern Society*. New York: Mentor Books, 1969.

Attali, Jacques. *Verbatim*. Paris: Fayard, 1993.

Bell, D. S., and Byron Criddle. *The French Socialist Party: Resurgence and Victory*, 2nd ed. New York: Oxford University Press, 1988.

Belorgey, Jean-Michel. *La Gauche et ses pauvres* (The left and its poor). Paris: Syros, 1988.

———. *Le Parlement à refaire*. Paris: Gallimard, 1991.

Berger, Suzanne (ed.). *Organizing Interests in Western Europe*. Cambridge, Mass.: Harvard University Press, 1981.

———, and Michael Piore. *Dualism and Discontinuity in Industrial Societies*. Cambridge, U.K.: Cambridge University Press, 1980.

Bernstein, Richard. *Fragile Glory: A Portrait of France and the French*. New York: Alfred A. Knopf, 1990.

Birnbaum, Pierre. *The Heights of Power*. Chicago: University of Chicago Press, 1982.

Bozo, Frederic. *La France et l'OTAN. De la guerre froide au nouvel ordre européen* (France and NATO: From the Cold War to the New European Order). Paris: Masson, 1991.

Braudel, Fernand. *L'identité française* (2 vols.). Paris: Flammarion, 1986. Published in English as *The Identity of France* (2 vols.). New York: HarperCollins, 1990 and 1992.

Brown, Bernard E. *Protest in Paris: Anatomy of a Revolt*. Morristown, N.J.: General Learning Press, 1974.

————. *Eurocommunism and Eurosocialism: The Left Confronts Modernity.* New York: Cyrco Press, 1978.

Brubaker, Rogers. *Citizenship and Nationhood in France and Germany,* Cambridge, Mass.: Harvard University Press, 1992.

Cameron, David. "The Colors of a Rose: On the Ambiguous Record of French Socialism." Harvard Center for European Studies Paper (Cambridge, Mass.), 1989.

Chapman, Herrick. *State Capitalism and Working-Class Radicalism in the French Aircraft Industry.* Berkeley: University of California Press, 1991.

Club Jean Moulin. *L'État et le citoyen* (The state and the citizen). Paris: Editions du Seuil, 1961.

Cobban, Alfred. *A History of Modern France,* 3 vols. London: Penguin, 1963.

Cohen-Tanugi, Laurent. *Le Droit sans l'état: Sur la démocratie en France et en Amérique* (Law without the state: On democracy in France and in America). Paris: PUF, 1985.

Converse, Philip E., and Roy Pierce. *Political Representation in France.* Cambridge, Mass.: Harvard University Press, 1986.

Crozier, Michel. *The Bureaucratic Phenomenon.* Chicago: University of Chicago Press, 1964.

————. *The Stalled Society.* New York: Viking, 1974.

Czerny, Philip G., and Martin A. Schain (eds.). *Socialism, the State and Public Policy in France.* New York: Methuen, 1985.

Daniel, Jean. *Les Religions d'un president. Regards sur les aventures du Mitterrandism* (A president's religions. On the adventures of Mitterandism). Paris: Grasset, 1988.

DePorte, Anton. *Europe Between the Superpowers,* 2nd ed. New Haven: Yale University Press, 1986.

Duhamel, Alain. *Les Peurs françaises* (French fears). Paris: Flammarion, 1993.

Duhamel, Olivier. *La Gauche et la Ve république* (The left and the Fifth Republic). Paris: PUF, 1980.

Ehrmann, Henry W., and Martin A. Schain. *Politics in France,* 5th ed. New York: HarperCollins, 1992. Earlier editions are by Ehrmann alone.

Favier, Pierre, and Michel Martin-Roland. *La décennie Mitterrand* (The Mitterrand decade), 2 vols. Vol. 1: *Les ruptures, 1981–84* (The innovations, 1981–84); Vol. 2: *Les epreuves, 1984–88* (The challenges, 1984–88). Paris: Seuil, 1990 and 1991.

Feigenbaum, Harvey. *The Politics of Public Enterprise: Oil and the French State.* Princeton, N.J.: Princeton University Press, 1985.

Fourastié, Jean. *Les Trente glorieuses. La révolution invisible de 1946 à 1975* (The thirty glorious years: The invisible revolution from 1946 to 1975). Paris: Editions Fayard, 1979.

Friend, Julius W. *The Linchpin: French–German Relations, 1950–1990.* New York: Praeger, 1991.

Furet, François, Jacques Julliard, and Pierre Rosanvallon. *La République du centre. La Fin de l'exception française* (The centrist republic: The end of French uniqueness). Paris: Calmann-Levy, 1988.

Gaudino, Antoine. *L'Enquête impossible* (The impossible investigation). Paris: Albin Michel, 1990.

de Gaulle, Charles. *The Complete War Memoirs of Charles de Gaulle,* 3 vols. New York: Simon & Schuster, 1967.

———. *The Edge of the Sword.* New York: Greenwood Press, 1975.

———. *Memoirs of Hope,* Vol. 1: *Renewal, 1958–1962.* [Note: This was the first of three scheduled volumes; a partially written second volume, *The Effort, 1962. . . ,* was left incomplete at General de Gaulle's death.]

Giesbert, Franz-Olivier. *Le Président.* Paris: Seuil, 1990.

Giscard d'Estaing, Valéry. *Deux français sur trois* (Two of every three Frenchmen). Paris: Flammarion, 1984; 2nd expanded ed., 1985.

———. *Démocratie française.* Paris: Fayard, 1976. Published in English as *French Democracy.* Garden City, N.Y.: Doubleday, 1977.

Godt, Paul (ed.). *Policy Making in France.* London: Pinter Publishers, 1989.

Goodman, John. *Monetary Sovereignty: The Politics of Central Banking in Western Europe.* Ithaca, N.Y.: Cornell University Press, 1992.

Gordon, Lincoln, et al. *Eroding Empire: Western Relations with Eastern Europe.* Washington, D. C.: Brookings Institution, 1987.

Graubard, Stephen R. (ed.). *A New Europe?* Boston: Beacon Press, 1964.

Grosser, Alfred. *Affaires extérieures: La politique de la France 1944–1984* (Foreign affairs: France's policy 1944–1984). Paris: Flammarion, 1984.

Haas, Ernst. *Beyond the Nation-State.* Stanford, Calif.: Stanford University Press, 1964.

Hall, Peter. *Governing the Economy: The Politics of State Intervention in Britain and France*. New York: Oxford University Press, 1986.

———, Jack Hayward, and Howard A. Machin (eds.). *Developments in French Politics*. London: Macmillan, 1990.

Hayward, Jack. *Governing France: The One and Indivisible Republic*, 2nd ed. London: Weidenfeld and Nicolson, 1983.

———. *The State and the Market Economy: Industrial Patriotism and State Intervention in France*. New York: New York University Press, 1986.

Hoffmann, Stanley. *Decline or Renewal? France since the 1930s*. New York: Viking Press, 1974.

———, et al. *In Search of France*. New York: Harper Torchbooks, 1965.

Hollifield, James F. *Immigrants, Markets and States: The Political Economy of Postwar Europe*. Cambridge, Mass.: Harvard University Press, 1992.

———, and George Ross (eds.). *Searching for the New France*. New York: Routledge, 1991.

Howorth, Jolyon, and George Ross (eds.). *Contemporary France*, Vol. 3. London: Pinter, 1989.

Hurwitz, Leon, and Christian Lequesne (eds.). *The State of the European Community. Policies, Institutions and Debates in the Transition Years*. Boulder, Colo.: Lynne Rienner, 1991.

Jenson, Jane, and George Ross. *The View from the Inside: A French Communist Cell in Crisis*. Berkeley: University of California Press, 1984.

Judt, Tony. *Marxism and the French Left: Studies on Labour and Politics in France, 1830–1981*. New York: Oxford University Press, 1989.

———. *Past Imperfect: French Intellectuals, 1944–1956*. Berkeley: University of California Press, 1992.

Julliard, Jacques. *La Quatrième république, 1947–1958* (The Fourth Republic, 1947–1958). Paris: Calmann-Levy, 1968.

Keeler, John T. S. *The Politics of Neocorporatism in France: Farmers, the State and Agricultural Policy Making in the Fifth Republic*. New York: Oxford University Press, 1987.

Kenen, Peter B. *EMU After Maastricht*. Washington, D. C.: Group of Thirty, 1992.

Keohane, Robert O., and Stanley Hoffmann (eds.). *The New European Community: Decision Making and Institutional Change*. Boulder, Colo.: Westeview Press, 1991.

Kepel, Gilles. *Les Banlieues de l'Islam: Naissance d'une religion en*

France (The suburbs of Islam: Birth of a religion in France). Paris: Seuil, 1987.

Kesselman, Mark, and Guy Groux (eds.). *The French Workers' Movement*. London: Allen & Unwin, 1984.

————, et al. *European Politics in Transition*. New York: Heath, 1992.

Krause, Axel. *Inside the New Europe*. New York: HarperCollins, 1991.

Kriegel, Annie. *The French Communists: Profile of a People*. Chicago: University of Chicago Press, 1972.

Kuisel, Richard. *Capitalism and the State in Modern France*. Cambridge, U.K.: Cambridge University Press, 1981.

Lavau, Georges. *À Quoi sert le parti communiste français?* (What use is the French Communist party?). Paris: Fayard, 1981.

Lévy-Leboyer, Maurice, and Jean-Claude Casanova (eds.). *Entre l'état et le marché: L'économie française des années 1880 à nos jours* (Between the state and the market: The French economy from 1880 to the present). Paris: Editions Gallimard, 1991.

Lichtheim, George. *The New Europe, Today—and Tomorrow*, 2nd ed. New York: Praeger, 1964.

Long, Marceau (ed.). *Être Français aujourd'hui et demain* (To be French today and tomorrow) (2 vols.). Paris: La Documentation Française, 1988.

Luethy, Herbert. *France Against Herself*. New York: Praeger, 1955.

McCarthy, Patrick (ed.). *The French Socialists in Power, 1981–1986*. New York: Greenwood Press, 1987.

Marrus, Michael, and Robert O. Paxton. *Vichy France and the Jews*. New York: Shocken, 1983.

Mitterrand, François. *Le Coup d'état permanent* (The permanent state coup). Paris: Plon, 1964; republished by Julliard, 1984.

————. *Ma part de verité* (My share of truth). Paris: Fayard, 1969.

————. *L'Abeille et l'architecte. Chronique* (The bee and the architect: Chronicle). Paris: Flammarion, 1978.

————. *Réflexions sur la politique extérieure de la France* (Reflections on French foreign policy). Paris: Fayard, 1986.

————. *Lettre à tous les français* (Letter to all the French people). Paris: Parti Socialiste, 1988.

Moisi, Dominique, and Jacques Rupnik. *Le Nouveau continent. Plaidoyer pour une Europe renaissante* (The new continent: Plea for a revitalized Europe). Paris: Calmann-Levy, 1991.

Mossuz-Lavau, Janine, and Mariette Sineau. *Enquête sur les femmes et la politique en France* (Inquiry on women and politics in France). Paris: PUF, 1983.

Nay, Catherine. *The Red and the Black: François Mitterrand and the Story of an Ambition* (trans. Alan Sheridan). New York: Harcourt Brace Jovanovich, 1987.

Nicolet, Claude. *L'Idée républicaine en France, 1789–1924* (Republican thought in France, 1789–1924). Paris: Gallimard, 1982.

Northcutt, Wayne. *Mitterrand: A Political Biography*. New York: Holmes & Meier, 1992.

d'Ormesson, Jean. *Au plaisir de Dieu* (At God's pleasure). Paris: Gallimard, 1974.

Paxton, Robert O. *Vichy France: Old Guard and New Order, 1940–1944*. New York: Columbia University Press, 1972.

Pfister, Thierry. *La vie quotidienne à Matignon au temps de l'union de la gauche* (Daily life at Matignon during the "union of the left" government). Paris: Hachette, 1985.

———. *Dans les coulisses du pouvoir: La comédie de la cohabitation* (Behind the curtains of power: The comedy of cohabitation). Paris: Albin Michel, 1986.

———. *La république des fonctionnaires* (The civil servants' republic). Paris: Albin Michel, 1988.

Posner, Charles (ed.). *Reflections on the Revolution in France: 1968*. London: Penguin, 1970.

Pouvoirs, no. 58, special issue, "La France en guerre" (France at war); see especially Raphaël Hadas-Lebel, "La Ve République et la guerre" (The Fifth Republic and war), pp. 5–24, and Samy Cohen, "Le Président. Chef des armées" (The president: Commander-in-chief of the armed forces), pp. 33–40.

Price, Roger. *A Concise History of France*. New York: Cambridge University Press, 1993.

Quermonne, Jean-Louis. *Le Gouvernement de la France sous la Ve république* (French government in the Fifth Republic). Paris: Dalloz, 1980.

Ross, George, Stanley Hoffmann, and Sylvia Malzacher (eds.). *The Mitterrand Experiment: Continuity and Change in Modern France*. New York: Oxford University Press, 1987.

Sa'adah, Anne. *The Shaping of Liberal Politics in Revolutionary France*. Princeton, N.J.: Princeton University Press, 1990.

Safran, William. *The French Polity*, 2nd ed. White Plains, N.Y.: Longman, 1985.

Sbragia, Alberta (ed.). *Euro-Politics: Institutions and Policy Making in the "New" European Community*. Washington, D. C.: The Brookings Institution, 1992.

Schain, Martin A. *French Communism and Local Power*. New York: St. Martin's Press, 1985.

Schmidt, Vivien A. *Democratizing France: The Political and Administrative History of Decentralization*. New York: Cambridge University Press, 1991.

Schnapper, Dominique. *La France et l'intégration: Sociologie de la nation en 1990* (France and integration: The nation's sociology in 1990). Paris: Gallimard, 1991.

Serre, Françoise de la, Jacques Leruez, and Helen Wallace (eds.). *Les Politiques étrangeres de la France et de la Grande-Bretage depuis 1945* (The foreign policies of France and Great Britain since 1945). Paris: PUF, 1990.

Signoret, Simone. *Nostalgia Isn't What It Used to Be*. New York: Harper & Row, 1978.

Singer, Daniel. *Is Socialism Doomed? The Meaning of Mitterrand*. London: Oxford University Press, 1988.

Smith, Gordon. *Politics in Western Europe*, 5th ed. New York: Holmes & Meier, 1989.

Stoléru, Lionel. *La France à deux vitesses* (Two Frances). Paris: Flammarion, 1982.

Stone, Alec. *The Birth of Judicial Politics in France: The Constitutional Council in Comparative Perspective*. New York: Oxford University Press, 1992.

Suleiman, Ezra, *Politics, Power and Bureaucracy in France: The Administrative Elite*. Princeton, N.J.: Princeton University Press, 1974.

———. *Elites in French Society: The Politics of Survival*. Princeton, N.J.: Princeton University Press, 1978.

Tarrow, Sidney. *Between Center and Periphery: Grassroots Politicians in Italy and France*. New Haven, Conn.: Yale University Press, 1977.

Teltschik, Horst. *329 Tage* (329 Days). Berlin: Siedler, 1991.

Thomson, David. *Democracy in France since 1870*. New York: Oxford University Press.

Tiersky, Ronald. "Declining Fortunes of the French Communist Party," *Problems of Communism* (September–October 1988): 1–22.

———. "France in the New Europe," *Foreign Affairs*, 71 no. 2 (Spring 1992): 131–146.

———. *French Communism, 1920–1972*. New York: Columbia University Press, 1974.

———. "French Foreign Policy Stumbles," *French Politics and Society*, 11 no. 1 (Winter 1993): 89–103.

———. "Mitterrand, France and Europe." *French Politics and Society*, 9 no. 1 (Winter 1991): 9–25.

———. *Ordinary Stalinism: Democratic Centralism and the Question of Communist Political Development*. Winchester, Mass.: Allen & Unwin, 1985.

Tilly, Charles. *The Contentious French: Four Centuries of Popular Struggle*. Cambridge, Mass.: Harvard University Press, 1986.

de Tocqueville, Alexis. *The Old Regime and the Revolution*. New York: Doubleday Anchor, 1955. Originally published 1865.

Todd, Emmanuel. *The Making of Modern France: Ideology, Politics and Culture*. London: Basil Blackwell, 1991.

Todorov, Tzvetan. *On Human Diversity: Nationalism, Racism, and Exoticism in French Thought*. Cambridge, Mass.: Harvard University Press, 1993.

Touraine, Alain. *La Société post-industrielle: Naissance d'une société* (The postindustrial society: Birth of a society). Paris: Editions Denoel, 1969.

Vedel, Georges (ed.). *La Dépolitisation: Mythe ou réalité?* (Depoliticization: Myth or reality?). Paris: Librairie Armand Colin, 1962.

Weil, Patrick. *La France et ses étrangers. L'aventure d'une politique d'immigration 1938–1991* (France and its foreigners: The story of an immigration policy, 1938–1991). Paris: Calmann-Levy, 1991.

Wilson, Frank L. *Interest-Group Politics in France*. New York: Cambridge University Press, 1987.

Winock, Michel. *La fièvre hexagonale. Les grandes crises politiques, 1871–1968* (Hexagonal fever: The great political crises, 1871–1968). Paris: Calmann-Levy, 1986.

Wright, Vincent. *The Government and Politics of France*, 3rd ed. London: Unwin Hyman, 1989.

Zeldin, Theodore. *France 1848–1945* (2 vols.). Vol. 1: *Ambition and Love*; Vol. 2: *Anxiety and Hypocrisy*. New York: Oxford University Press, 1979 and 1981.

Index

✦

Abortion, 103, 199–200
Abstention, voting, 121, 128–132, 137
Adelbert de Perigord, 21
Affaire des foulards. See Chador affair
AIDS, 114, 202–205
    and Health Ministry scandal, 24, 202–205
Albert, Michel, 153–154
Alcoholism, 8
Amendment
    of Fifth Republic Constitution, 62, 76–80
    and Maastricht, 82–83
American model of industrial organization, 153, 157, 158
Anti-Semitism, 36, 110
Apprenticeships. *See* Social treatment of unemployment
Arabs, 34, 148, 186, 188, 189–191
    See also Immigration; Muslims
Aron, Raymond, 6, 14, 16, 20, 23, 24, 25, 42 n10, 167, 254
Article 16 (Fifth Republic Constitution).
    See President, emergency powers of
Article 34. *See* Domain of law
Article 37. *See* Rule making
Article 38, 64
Article 40, 65
Article 44. *See* Blocked vote
Article 48, 64
Article 49.3, 61, 63, 66–67, 78, 106, 109, 124
    and proposal to abolish, 80
Article 89 (of Constitution), 62, 76–80
Attali, Jacques, 124, 136

Bad Godesberg congress, 150
Badinter, Elisabeth, 198
Badinter, Robert, 73, 79
Baker, Josephine, 192
Baldwin, James, 192
Balladur, Edouard, 43 n21, 47, 54, 55, 103, 141, 173
    and 1993 cohabitation, 59–61, 86 n17
    and immigration, 187
Barre, Raymond, 65, 80, 105, 106
Barrot, Jacques, 68
de Beauvoir, Simone, 197–198

Bérégovoy, Pierre, 30, 68, 43 n21, 151, 173, 176–177
Bergeron, Andre, 152
Beurs, 163
    See also Arabs; Muslims; Immigration
Billancourt, Renault factory, 184–185
Birth control, 199
Blocked vote, 61, 65–66, 67, 77–78
Blondel, Marc, 148
Bokassa, Jean-Bédel, 38
Bolsheviks, 17
Bork, Robert, 69
bourgeoisie, 147, 149, 216
    See also Business and businessmen
Braudel, Fernand, 193
Bretton Woods system, 53
Buiter, William H., on monetary union, 232
Bundesbank, 213, 228–231, 233, 237 n19
Buchanan, Patrick, 115
Burke, Edmund, 41 n2
Business and businessmen, 147, 148–154
    competitiveness of, 149, 211–212, 216, 219–221
    and European integration, 148, 152–153, 232
    investment of in Germany, 228–229
    and new partnership with unions, 179
    and traditional fear of unions, 174

Campagnie Financière de Suez, 183
CAP. *See* Common Agricultural Policy
Capet, Hugues, 21
Casanova, Jean-Claude, 219–220, 236–n3
Catholicism, 31–33, 166, 199
CDS. *See* Social Democratic Center
Centralization. *See* Decentralization
Centrism. *See* Recentered republic
Ceyrac, François, 152
CFE–CGC, 148
CFTC. *See* French Confederation of Catholic Workers
CGPME, 151–152
CGT. *See* General Confederation of Labor
Chaban-Delmas, Jacques, 53, 54–55, 100
Chador affair, 194, 200–201
Chevènement, Jean-Pierre, 172

Chirac, Jacques, 65, 74, 86 n18, 100, 102, 104, 161, 183
  and cohabitation of 1986–88, 55, 56–59, 85, 86 n14
  and deployment of land-based nuclear missiles, 56
  and electoral laws, 123–124
  free market policies of, 101
  and Maastricht referendum, 171
  on nationalizations, 1981–82, 181
  and privatization, 30, 182
  and restructuring of RPR, 100
  and rivalry with Giscard d'Estaing, 123
  on unemployment, 179
Citizenship
  criteria for, 44 n27, 187
  European, 243–244
  in Germany, 44 n27, 243–244
Civil society, 145, 158
Class consciousness, 27–30
  and "class in itself," 27–28
  and "class for itself," 27–28
Class and class struggle
  ideology and political culture of, 16–17
  decline of, 27–30, 173
Club of Rome, 115
CNN, 24, 127
CNPF. See National Confederation of French Business
Codetermination, of business policy by unions, 157
Cohabitation, 47, 55, 56–61, 85, 86 n14, 86 n17, 101, 122, 139–142
Colbertism. See Dirigisme
Cohn-Bendit, Daniel, 93
Commission on Nationality and Citizenship, 87 n23, 191, 194
Committees, parliamentary, 68–70
Common Agricultural Policy (CAP), 68, 159–163, 210–211
Common Foreign and Security Policy, 239–243
Communist party. See French Communist party (PCF)
Competitiveness, French. See Business and businessmen
Comte, Auguste, 254
Confederation of Industries (Patronat), 148
Constitutional Council, 23, 48, 71, 72–74, 83
Consultative Committee on Constitutional Reform, 77

Council of State, 48, 71, 74, 88 n30
Couve de Murville, Maurice, 52, 100
Cresson, Edith, 38, 54, 106, 150 , 160, 177, 183–184, 198–199
Crozier, Michel, 18, 23, 145

Debré, Michel, 52, 63, 84 n7, 100
Decentralization, 74–76, 88 n28
Defense policy, 135
Deferre, Gaston, 75, 94
Delors, Jacques, 96, 182, 243
Depoliticization, 166
  See also Partisanship, decline of
Deregulation, 57, 153
Désir, Harlem, 163, 164–165
DGSE (secret service), 116
Dirigisme (French economic statism), 149, 150, 151, 153, 183–184, 211, 214, 218, 224–225, 228
Doctors Without Borders, 163, 165
Domain of law, 64
Dray, Julien, 163, 164–165
Dreyfus Affair, 24, 110
Droit de regard, 52
Dualism, of French economy, 211, 217
Dufoix, Georgina, 203
Duke, David, 115

Ecological Generation, 90, 116, 125, 141
Ecologist parties, 92, 102, 107, 115–117, 121, 124–125
Economic development, French, 215–218
  See also Dirigisme; Exceptionalism; Fiscal policy; Inflation; Monetary Policy
Economic and Social Council, 87 n19, 164
Ehrmann, Henry, 32, 49, 77, 97, 105
Electoral laws, 58, 61, 111–112, 133–134, 135–137, 139–140
  as partisan weapon, 79, 123–124
Elf-Aquitane, 183
Emmanuelli, Henri, 143 n9
ENA. See National School of Administration
Engels, Friedrich, 10, 13, 16, 17, 38
European Community. See European integration
European Court of Justice, 83
European Economic Area, 146
European Free Trade Association, 146
European integration, 3–4, 167
  and cohabitation, 61
  and collective bargaining, 158–159
  and European Parliament, 71

and French business, 152–153, 211–213
and French economic particularism, 210
and French economy, 227–229
and French interest groups, 145–148
and Maastricht convergence criteria, 214–215
and monetary union, 231–235
prospects of in France, 130
European Monetary Institute, 233, 235
European Monetary System, 231, 233
European Monetary Union, 231–235
European Parliament, 70–71, 82, 128, 129, 132–133
European Trade Union Confederation (ETUC), 158
Exchange controls, 214
Exchange Rate Mechanism, 231–232
Exceptionalism, French
  and class conflict, 27–30
  contrasts with economic particularism, 215
  and European integration, 24, 146
  and labor relations, 148
  and "ordinariness" of public policy, 170–173
  and personalization of politicians, 127
  and political economy, 210–216
  and protest, 38–40
  and religion, 31–33
  and sexual harassment, 202
  and structure of industry, 147, 148–149, 151
  and youth, 30–31
Exports, French, 211–213, 218–221, 227, 229–230, 236 n3
  See also Business and businessmen, competitiveness of
External accounts, French, 218–221

Fabius, Laurent, 54, 96, 98, 108, 109, 182, 198, 203, 204
Family, weakening of nuclear, 166, 169 n15
Family reunification rights of immigrants, 186–187, 188
Fanon, Frantz, 110
Farmers. See Peasants and rural life
Fauvet, Jacques, 92
Feminism, 197–199, 200
FEN. See National Education Federation
Ferry, Jules, 194
Finances, of parties and political campaigns, 69–70, 117, 138
"First Geldkrieg," 230

Fiscal policy, 135, 175–177, 213–215
Fiterman, Charles, 108, 119 n15
Floating voters. See Independent voters
FO. See Workers' Force
Force de frappe (nuclear force), 237, 241
Fourastié, Jean, 217, 255
Franco–German relations, 4, 7, 213, 228–231
Franc, 229–232
  See also European Monetary Union; Monetary policy
Franco–Prussian War, 15
Franklin, Benjamin, 2
Free collective bargaining versus codetermination, 157
French Communist party (PCF), 3, 10, 25–26, 75, 90, 92–93, 98, 106, 107–109, 119 n15, 123, 124, 125, 157, 166, 174
  and decentralization, 88 n28
  and displacement by National Front, 110–113
  and events of May 1968, 23, 155
  financing by USSR, 138–139
  and internal factions, 108
  and leverage over Socialist government, 67–68
  and nationalizations of 1981–82, 180–181
  in 1993 election, 141
  and opposition to Maastricht Treaty, 148
  and prejudice in, 36, 111
  and problem of legitimacy, 22–23
  and protest, 40
  and union of the left, 94, 95
  and women, 197, 199
French Confederation of Catholic Workers (CFTC), 148, 157
French Democratic Confederation of Labor (CFDT), 148, 152, 157–158, 164
Furet, Francois, 1, 19, 42 n9, 142, 170

"Gallic Disease," 16
Gallo, Robert, 202
"Gang of Four" (four major parties), 107
Garretta, Michel, 203–204
GATT. See General Agreement on Tariffs and Trade
Gattaz, Yvon, 152
de Gaulle, Charles, 2, 5, 6, 8, 11, 14, 15, 21, 37, 46, 60, 61, 80, 83, 98–99, 114, 125, 142, 162, 167, 235
  and class conflict, 16
  and creation of Fifth Republic, 47–50

on economic renewal, 151
and electoral laws, 61, 122, 123
and emergency powers of presidency, 64
and end of French colonialism, 4–5
and European integration, 171–172
and events of May 1968, 155
on progress in France, 209
and Senate, 63, 87 n19
and strong presidency, 50–51, 52–53,
83–84
use of referendum by, 80–81, 87 n19,
129, 130
Gaullism, 2, 89, 99–100, 121, 135
decline of, 100–101
and European integration, 4
and legitimacy, 21–22
Geismar, Alain, 93
General Agreement on Tariffs and Trade
(GATT), 9–10, 68, 106, 159–163,
210–211
General Confederation of Labor (CGT),
29, 39, 93, 166
and Communist dominance of, 2, 93,
147, 157, 174
and control of Renault unions, 184
decline of, 107
and May 1968, 23, 156
and refusal to sign collective-bargaining
agreements, 147
"Generation Mitterrand," 164
German model of industrial organization,
148, 153–154, 157, 158, 159
German unification, 230
Giscard d'Estaing, Valéry, 51, 65, 81, 94,
100, 104, 125, 144, 154, 161, 222
and accusations of illegitimate campaign
financing, 138
and appointment of women to political
posts, 199
centrist electoral strategy of, 105, 106,
172
and extension of access to Constitutional
Council, 73
on immigration, 36–38
and 1979–80 recession, 105
and rivalry with Chirac, 123
and Senate, 63
and strong presidency, 53
and support of legal abortion, 200
on "threshold of socialism," 224
victory of in 1974 presidential election,
100

Glucksman, André, 34
Gorbachev, Mikhail, 230–231
Gordon, Dexter, 192
Green Party, 90, 115, 116–117, 119 n21,
125, 141, 172
See also Ecologist parties
Greenpeace, 69, 115–116, 163
Grenelle Accords, 22–23, 155–156
Groulte, Benoîte, 198
Guichard, Olivier, 100
Gulf War, 165

Halimi, Giselle, 198
Hall, Peter, 227
Hassner, Pierre, 26
Hernu, Charles, 116
Hervé, Edmond, 203
Herzog, Phillipe, 108
"Hexagon," France as the, 7
Hill, Anita, 201
Hoffman, Stanley, 4, 5, 6, 18, 23, 24, 145,
251, 254
Holliday, Billy, 192
Homelessness, 8, 254
Homosexuals, 202
Hughes, Langston, 192
Hugo, Victor, 39
Huguenots. See Protestants
"Hunting" Party, 115

Immigration, 3, 33–38, 87 n23, 109–110,
114–115, 119 n17, 141, 164–165, 174,
186–197
current policy options for limiting,
196–197
and national identity, 33–35
near abolition of, 186–187
and random identity checks, 187–188
Income inequality, 223
Independent voters, 121, 134
Industrial policy. See Dirigisme
Industry. See Business and businessmen
Inflation, 154, 175–177, 213, 216, 221–222
Intégration, 193
See also Multiculturalism
Interest groups. See Business and
businessmen; Peasants and rural life;
Unions
Interest rates, 213, 230, 237 n19
Intermarriage between French natives and
immigrants, 195–196
International Channel, 24
Iragaray, Luce, 198

Italian Communist party (PCI), 25, 70

Jaurès, Jean, 97
Jews, 31, 33
Job training programs. *See* Social treatment of unemployment
Jospin, Lionel, 96, 200
Judicial review, 71–74, 86 n18
Julliard, Jacques, 91
Junkers, 28
Juppé, Alain, 103

Khrushchev, Nikita, 26
Kohl, Helmut, 60
Krasuki, Henri, 152
Kristéva, Julia, 198
Krivine, Alain, 93

Lajoinie, André, 68, 108
Lalonde, Brice, 90, 95, 116, 125
Le Pen, Jean-Marie, 35, 36, 69, 90, 107, 110, 111, 113–114, 115, 135, 136, 138, 172
Le Pors, Anicet, 108
League for Human Rights, 164
Lebrun, Albert, 50
Legitimacy, political, 21–24
    and events of May, 22–23
    and French Communists, 22–23
    and Gaullists, 21–22
Léotard, Francois, 37, 76, 106, 118, 119 n14
Léotard, Phillipe, 118 n14
Levy–Leboyer, Maurice, 209
Liberalism and liberal view of France, 17–19
Long, Marceau, 87 n23
Louis XIV, 21, 74, 211
Louvre museum, 6
Lustiger, Cardinal Jean-Marie, 33

Maastricht Treaty (Dec. 1991), 5, 77, 92
    and European Parliament, 71, 82
    and French political institutions, 82–83
    and social charter of, 148, 158
    and convergence criteria for Stage 3 of monetary union, 214–215, 233–234
    See also Referendum
Machiavelli, Niccolo, 97
Maire, Edmond, 152
Majority voting (within electoral districts). *See* Electoral laws
Malraux, André, 151
Manifestation, la. See Protest
Marchais, Georges, 107–108, 119 n15, 181
Marx, Karl, 10, 16, 17, 27–28, 38

Marxism, 10, 146
    and class conflict in France, 27–29
    decline of in France, 25–26, 147
    and unions, 154–155
Mauroy, Pierre, 75, 85 n12, 108, 118 n3, 181–182, 198
May 1968, events of, 19–21, 41, 152, 155–156
Media, political influence of, 91
Mégret, Bruno, 114
Mendès-France, Pierre, 22
Messmer, Pierre, 53
Michels, Robert, 113
Michelat, Guy, 32
Michelet, Jules, 13–14, 74
Minimum Income for Reintegration, 226
Ministry of International Trade and Industry (MITI) (Japan), 150
Minority government, 66–67
Missiles, land-based nuclear, 56, 86 n16
Mitterrand, Danielle, 198
Mitterrand, François, 2, 6, 16, 23, 26, 46, 61, 67, 71, 81, 90, 91, 104, 106, 123, 125, 133, 134, 139, 154, 172, 222
    appointment of women to high positions by, 198–199
    and Cohabitation I (1986–88), 56–59, 85–86 n14, 101
    and Cohabitation II (1993–), 59–61, 86 n17, 139–142
    and Constitutional Council, 73–74
    and constitutional reform, 76–80
    and decentralization, 75–76
    and decline of traditional Socialist ideology, 96–97
    and electoral strategy of splitting the right, 137
    and establishment of Socialist party, 94
    and Euromissile issue, 198
    on failure to reduce income inequality, 223
    and farmers, 160
    on Franco–German relations, 7
    on Giscard d'Estaing, 53
    and immigration, 164–165
    and industrial policy, 149, 150
    Keynesian fiscal policy of, 175–176, 217–218
    as last "really French" president, 127–128
    and legal birth control, 199
    and Maastricht referendum, 171
    and nationalizations of 1981–82, 180–182

on 1973 referendum on EC membership, 121–122
and opposition to Soviet Union, 198
and "personal power" of president, 22, 50, 51, 53–54
and privatization, 30, 102–103, 183, 184
and proposal to shorten presidential term, 79–80
and proposals to strengthen Parliament, 77
and *Rainbow Warrior* Affair, 116
and referendum on Maastricht Treaty, 129–130
and reform of electoral laws, 79, 112, 123–124, 127, 135–137
and resolution of chador affair, 200–201
selection of prime ministers by, 198–199
and SOS–Racism, 163–164
and state subsidization of parochial schools, 32, 85 n12
and unemployment, 179
and union of the left, 94, 108, 175
visit to Israel by, 198
Mixed electoral system, 124, 127
Monnet, Jean, 227
Monetary policy, 135, 175–177, 213–215, 222–223, 229–235
See also Fiscal policy; Inflation
Monnerville, Gaston, 62, 72
Montanier, Luc, 202
Montesquieu, 254
Movement of Left Radicals (MRG), 90, 94, 105
MTV, 31
Multiculturalism, 190, 193–194, 200
Muslims, 31, 33, 109–111, 186, 193–194, 200–201
See also Arabs; Immigration

Napoleon I, 75–76
Napoleon III, 39
National Assembly, 63–70, 135
National Association of Manufacturers, 148
National Blood Transfusion Center, 203–204
National character, 14
National Confederation of French Business (CNPF), 148, 151–152
National Education Federation (FEN), 164, 168 n7
National Front, 3, 69, 78, 90, 102, 107, 109–115, 121, 123, 124–125, 135, 165
and illegitimate campaign finances, 138

and immigration, 34–37, 95, 109–110, 114–115, 193
in 1993 election, 141
and opposition to Maastricht Treaty, 172
and profile of supporters, 111–112
as protest party, 138
National identity
and immigration, 33–35, 193–194, 243–245
question of, 3
and religion, 33
National School of Administration (ENA), 88 n30, 173
Nationalization of industry, 180–185
See also Privatization
Nation-state, fate of, 4–6
Néiertz, Veronica, 201
New poor, 10
New Socialist School (PS faction), 164
North Atlantic Treaty Organization (NATO), 93, 155, 198, 239–243

Ouvriers, les. See Working class

Pantouflage, 151–152
Paris Commune, 39
Parliament, 61–70;
Mitterand's proposals to increase role of, 77
and party balance in Fifth Republic, 125–126
Parliamentary democracy, 49, 84 n4
Parochial schools, state subsidization of, 31–32, 103, 85 n12
Parténaires sociaux, 145–148
Particularism, economic. *See* Exceptionalism
Parties, political
"electoralization" of, 117
major, 89–91
minor, 89–90
nonpresidential, 107–117
presidential, 95–107
Partisanship
decline of, 91–92, 121, 132, 137–138, 142, 171
French political tradition of, 92–94
Party of the Democratic Left. *See* Italian Communist party
Pasqua, Charles, 6, 102, 172, 254
Passeron, André, 49
Pasteur Institute, 202, 204
Paxton, Robert, 15, 41 n3

Pei, I. M., 6
PCF. *See* French Communist party
PCI. *See* Italian Communist party
Peasants and rural life, 9, 159–163
    decline of, 160–163, 210–211
    and GATT negotiations, 9–10, 145–146,
        159–163, 210–211
    See also Common Agricultural Policy;
        General Agreement on Tariffs and
        Trade
Pérébeau, Michel, 218
Périgot, François, 148
Pétain, Marshal Phillipe, 15, 99
Peyrefitte, Alain, 18
Pfister, Thierry, 118 n3
Pinay, Antoine, 43 n21
Plissonier, Gaston, 139
Political economy. *See* Exceptionalism;
    Fiscal policy; Inflation; Monetary
    policy
Pompidou, Georges, 51, 52–53, 54–55, 59,
    79, 81, 99–100, 104, 121, 125, 129
Poniatowski, Michel, 105, 138
Pons, Bernard, 66–67
Pooling of sovereignty, 4, 210
Population growth and policy, 34, 37,
    44 n27, 109–110, 194–195
PR. *See* Republican party
Presidency
    before Fifth Republic, 51
    and cohabitation, 56–61
    emergency powers of, 50–51, 64, 80
    length of tenure, 79–80
    powers of, 50–56, 76–77
    and role of prime minister, 51–56
Presidentialism, of top party leaders,
    122–123
Prime minister
    and cohabitation, 56–61
    and presidency, 51–56
Privatization, 30, 58, 102–103, 151,
    182–185
Proportional representation. *See* Electoral
    laws
Protest, 38–40
    and National Front, 110–111
    See also May 1968; Revolution
Protestants, 31, 33

Qaddafi, Muammar, 56
Qualified majority voting, 248 n7

Racism and ethnic prejudice, 8, 195

    and immigration, 110, 190–192
    and SOS–Racism, 163–167
    See also Immigration; SOS–Racism
Radical Party, 103, 105, 107
Radical-Socialist Party, 26, 105
Raimond, Jean-Bernard, 57
Rainbow Coalition, 163
Rainbow Warrior Affair, 115–116
Ralite, Jack, 108
Rally for the Republic (RPR), 65, 78, 89,
    98–103, 111, 136, 139
    and immigration, 36, 115, 187–188
    and internal split on Maastricht
        referendum, 102, 171–172
    and relations with Ecologist parties, 117
    support of by farmers, 161
Reagan, Ronald, 56, 101
Recentered republic, 123, 127, 132,
    133–134, 172
Referendum
    on British EC membership, 81, 129
    on French participation in EC, 121–122
    as institution, 62, 80–82, 129
    on Maastricht Treaty, 5, 92, 102,
        129–131, 171–172
    on power sharing in New Caledonia, 81,
        128, 129
religion, 31–33
    and immigration, 190
Renault, 184–185, 228–229
Republican party (PR), 103, 105
Reserved domain of presidential powers,
    54–55
Resistance (in World War II), 15,
Revolution, 38–39
    and European integration, 24
Rhône–Poulenc, 181
Robespierre, Maximilien, 28
Rocard, Michel, 54, 78, 96, 98, 164–165,
    198
Rosanvallon, Pierre, 92
RPR. *See* Rally for the Republic
Rule making, 64–65

Safran, William, 27, 63
Saint-Gobain, 149–150
Savary, Alain, 85 n12
Sartre, Jean-Paul, 110, 184–185
Schain, Martin, 32, 77, 97, 105
Schengen Agreement, 35, 44 n26, 114, 146,
    195, 196–197
Schnapper, Dominique, 194
SCOLA, 24

Séguin, Phillipe, 6, 102, 172
Séguy, Georges, 152
Senate, 62–63, 86–87 n19
Servan-Schreiber, Jean-Jacques, 147
Sexual harassment, 201–202
SFIO (PS predecessor), 93–94
Shakespeare, William, 210
Shevardnadze, Edouard, 230
Siemens, 150
Signoret, Simone, 23, 43 n13
Simon, Michel, 32
Single European Market, 145–148, 210,
    227–229
Smith, Gordon, 49
Soboul, Albert, 38
Social Democratic Center (CDS), 90, 103,
    105, 106
Social Democratic Party (SPD), of
    Germany, 150
Social security, 225–226
Social treatment of unemployment,
    178–179, 183
Socialist Party (PS), 25, 29, 40, 68, 78, 89,
    95–98, 102, 106, 111, 164
  and accusations over campaign finances
    of, 138, 143 n9
  and chador affair, 200–201
  changed and improved economic policies
    of, 213–214, 218
  collapse of in 1993 elections, 139–140
  and decentralization, 75–76, 88 n28
  and decline of traditional Socialist
    ideology, 95–96, 150, 158
  founding of, 94
  and immigration, 38, 188
  and multiculturalism, 193–194;
  and 1973 referendum on EC, 121–122
  and relations with Communists, 108–109
  and relations with Ecologist parties, 117
  and shift to right, 135
  and unemployment, 154, 221–222
Soisson, Jean-Pierre, 106
Solidarity, 22, 164
Solzhenitsyn, Alexander, 26
Soros, George, 231
SOS–Racism, 163–167
Sovereignty, national, and European
    integration, 4
SPD. See Social Democratic Party
Specificity, French economic, 3
Stalin, Joseph, 26, 65, 76
Stalemate society, 18, 39

Statism, French economic. See Dirigisme
Sullerot, Evelyne, 198
Superior Council of the Judiciary, 79

Tailhook scandal, 201
Taxes, 225–226
  See also Fiscal policy
TF1, 101
Thatcher, Margaret, 101, 102, 182
Thiers, Adolphe,
Thomas, Clarence, 69, 201
Thomas, Isabel, 164
Thomson CEA Industries (TCI), 150
Tilly, Charles, 38
Tocqueville, Alexis de, 1, 2, 14, 23, 27,
    74–75, 144, 145
Toshiba, 150
Trente Glorieuses, 9, 217
Trade deficit, French. See External
    accounts; Exports
Trevi Conference, 35

UDF. See Union for French Democracy
UDR. See Union for the Defense of the
    Republic
Underclass—See New poor
Unemployment, 135, 154, 173–179,
    221–226
  and French left, 10
  and immigration, 35, 110, 191
  and 1993 election, 141, 173
UNICE, 152–153
Union for the Defense of the Republic
    (UDR), 99
Union for France (UPF), 139–140
Union for French Democracy (UDF), 68,
    78, 89, 103–107, 111, 136, 139–140,
    161
  and Ecologist parties, 117
  founding of, 105
  and immigration, 36, 115
Union of the left, 54, 85 n12, 94, 108–109,
    157, 170, 180–181, 217–218
Union for the New Republic (UNR), 23, 99
Unions, 138, 152
  attitude of toward business, 179
  decline of, 154–159
  and unemployment, 173–175
  See also French Democratic
    Confederation of Labor; General
    Confederation of Labor; Workers'
    Force
UNR. See Union for the New Republic

UPF. *See* Union for France
Urbanization, 166
Uruguay Round. *See* General Agreement
    on Tariffs and Trade

Védel, Georges, 77
Vercingétorix, 16
Vichy regime, 15, 39, 99

Waechter, Antoine, 116–117, 119 n21, 125
Weber, Eugene, 193
Weil, Patrick, 243
Weil, Simone, 37, 76, 106, 133
Western European Union (WEU), 237,
    240–242
Wilde, Oscar, 25
Women, political role and status of,
    197–202
Workers' Force (FO), 29, 148, 152, 157
Working class, 28–30, 145, 154–155
Wylie, Laurence, 41–42 n6

Yalta, 229
Yamgnane, Kofi, 37–38, 45 n29, 193–194
Youth and young people, 30–31
  and unemployment, 178
Yugoslavia crisis, 34

Zeldin, Theodore, 193
Zola, Emile, 24–25